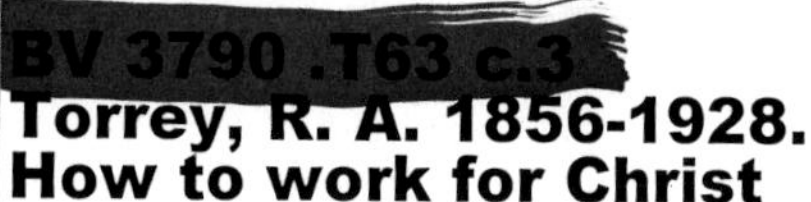

How to Work for Christ

A Compendium of Effective Methods

"Go work to-day in my vineyard."—*Matt. 21: 28.*

By R. A. TORREY

AUTHOR OF "WHAT THE BIBLE TEACHES," "HOW TO BRING MEN TO CHRIST," ETC

NEW YORK

Fleming H. Revell Company

LONDON AND EDINBURGH

Eighteenth Printing

NEW YORK: 158 FIFTH AVENUE
LONDON: 16 ANERLEY HILL

PREFACE

This book is intended for both ministers and laymen. It will be of help to the minister in suggesting to him how to make full proof of his own ministry and how to get his people to work. It will be of help to laymen in pointing out to them many fields of fruitful labor for Christ.

The Church of Christ is full of people who wish to work for their Master but do not know how. This book is intended to tell them how. It contains no untried theories, but describes many methods of work that have been put to the test of actual experiment and have succeeded. As far as known there is no other book that covers the same field. For years it has been upon my heart to write this book, and I have been asked again and again to do so. But I have never found time until now. May it be used of God to the conversion of thousands to Christ.

R. A. TORREY.

TABLE OF CONTENTS

BOOK ONE—PERSONAL WORK.

BOOK TWO—METHODS OF CHRISTIAN WORK.

BOOK I

PERSONAL WORK

CHAPTER I

THE IMPORTANCE AND ADVANTAGES OF PERSONAL WORK

In our study of the various forms of Christian activity, we begin with "Personal Work"; that is hand-to-hand dealing with men, women and children. We begin with it because it is the simplest form of Christian work, and one that every one can do. It is also the most effective method of winning lost souls. The Apostle Peter was brought to Jesus by the hand-to-hand work of his brother Andrew. Andrew first found Christ himself, then he went to Peter quietly and told him of his great find, and thus he led Peter to the Saviour he himself had found. I do not know that Andrew ever preached a sermon; if he did it is not recorded; but he did a great day's work when he led his brother Peter to Jesus. Peter preached a sermon that led to the conversion of 3,000 people, but where would Peter's great sermon have been if Andrew had not first led him to Christ by quiet personal work? Mr. Edward Kimball, a Boston business man, led D. L. Moody, the young Boston shoe clerk, to the Saviour. Where would all Mr. Moody's wonderful work for Christ have been if he himself had not been led to the Saviour by the faithful personal work of his Sunday school teacher? I believe in preaching. It is a great privilege to preach the Gospel, but this world can be reached and evangelized far more quickly and thoroughly by personal work than by public preaching. Indeed, it can only be reached and evangelized by personal work. When the whole church of Jesus Christ shall rouse to its responsibility and privilege in this matter, and every individual Christian become a personal worker, the evangelization of the world will be close at hand. When the membership of any local church shall rouse to its responsibility and privilege in this matter, and each member become a personal worker in the power of the Holy Spirit, a great revival will be close at hand for the community in which that church is located. Personal work is a work that wins but little applause from men, but it accomplishes great things for God.

There are many who think personal work beneath their dignity and their gifts. A blind woman once came to me and said, "Do you think that my blindness will hinder me from working for the Master?" "Not at all; it may be a great help to you, for others seeing your blindness will come and speak to you, and then you will have an opportunity of giving your testimony for Christ, and of leading them to the Saviour." "Oh, that is not what I want," she replied. "It seems to me a waste of time when one might be speaking to five or six hundred at once, just to be speaking to an individual." I answered that our Lord and Saviour Jesus Christ was able to speak to more than five thousand at once, and yet He never thought personal work beneath His dignity or His gifts. Indeed, it was the work the Saviour loved to do. We have more instances of our Saviour's personal work recorded in the Gospels than of His preaching. The one who is above personal work is above his Master.

I. Its Advantages.

Let us look at the advantages of personal work.

1. *All can do it.* In an average congregation there are not more than four or five who can preach to edification. It would be a great pity, too, should all attempt to become preachers; it would be a great blessing if all would become personal workers. Any child of God can do personal work, and all can learn to do effective personal work. The mother who is confined at home by multiplicity of home duties can still do personal work, first of all with her own children, and then with the servants in the home, with the butcher, the grocer, the tramp who calls at the door, in fact, with everybody who comes within reach. I once knew a mother very gifted in the matter of bringing her own children up in the nurture and admonition of the Lord, who lamented that she could not do some work for Christ. I watched this woman

carefully, and found that almost every one who came to the house in any capacity was spoken to about the Saviour, and she was, in point of fact, doing more for Christ in the way of direct evangelistic work than most pastors.

Even the one shut up at home by sickness can do personal work. As friends come to the sick bed, a word of testimony can be given for Christ, or even an extended conversation can be held. A little girl of twelve, the child of very poor parents, lay dying in the city of Minneapolis. She let her light shine for the Master, and spoke among others to a godless physician, to whom, perhaps, no one else had ever spoken about Christ. A poor girl in New York City, who was rescued from the slums and died a year or two afterwards, was used of God to lead about one hundred men and women to Christ, while lying upon her dying bed.

Even the servant girl can do effective personal work. Lord Shaftsbury, the great English philanthropist, was won to Christ in a godless home by the effective work of a nurse girl.

Traveling men have unusually good opportunities for doing personal work, as they travel on the trains from town to town, as they stop in one hotel after another and go from store to store. A professional nurse once came into my Bible class in Chicago, and at the close of the meeting approached me and said: "I was led to Christ by Mr. ——— [a traveling man connected with a large wholesale house]. I was in a hotel parlor, and this gentleman saw me and walked across the parlor and asked me if I was a Christian, and when I told him I was not, he proceeded at once to show me the way of life. I was so startled and impressed to find a traveling man leading others to Christ that I accepted Him as my Saviour then and there. He told me if I ever came to Chicago to come to your Bible class." I have watched this woman for years since, and she herself is a most devoted Christian and effective worker.

How enormous and wonderful and glorious would be the results if all Christians should begin to be active personal workers to the extent of their ability! Nothing else would do so much to promote a revival in any community, and in the land at large. Every pastor should urge this duty upon his people, train them for it, and see that they do it.

2. *It can be done anywhere.* There are but few places where one can preach. There is no place where one cannot do personal work. How often, as we pass factories, engine houses, lodging houses and other places where crowds are gathered, do we wish that we might get into them and preach the Gospel, but generally this is impossible, but it is altogether possible to go in and do personal work. Furthermore, we can do personal work on the street, whether street meetings are allowed or not. We can do personal work in the homes of the poor and in the homes of the rich, in hospitals, workhouses, jails, station houses, and all sorts of institutions—in a word, everywhere.

3. *It can be done at any time.* The times when we can have preaching services and Sunday schools are quite limited. As a rule, in most communities, we cannot have services more than two or three days in the week, and only three or four hours in the day, but personal work can be done seven days in the week, and any time of day or night. Some of the best personal work done in this country in the last twenty years has been done on the streets at midnight and after midnight. Those who love souls have walked the streets looking for wanderers, and have gone into dens of vice seeking the lost sheep, and hundreds upon hundreds of them have thus been found.

4. *It reaches all classes.* There are large classes of men that no other method will reach. There are the shut-ins who cannot get out to church, the street-car men, the policemen, railroad conductors, sleeping-car men, firemen, the very poor and the very rich. Some cannot and others will not attend church or cottage meeting or mission meeting, but personal work can reach them all.

5. *It hits the mark.* Preaching is necessarily general; personal work is direct and personal. There is no mistaking who is meant, there is no dodging the arrow, there is no possibility of giving what is said away to some one else. Many whom even so expert a Gospel preacher as Mr. Moody has missed have been afterwards reached by personal work.

6. *It meets the definite need, and every need of the person dealt with.* Even when men are aroused and convicted, and perhaps converted, by a sermon, personal work is ncessary to bring out into clear light and into a satisfactory experience one whom the sermon has thus aroused, convicted and converted.

7. *It avails where other methods fail.* One of my best workers told me a few weeks ago that she had attended church for years, and had wanted to become a Christian. She had listened to some of the best-known preachers, and still was unsaved, but the very first inquiry meeting she went into she was saved because some one came and dealt with her personally.

8. *It produces very large results.* There is no comparison whatever between what will be effected by good preaching and what will be effected by constant personal work. Take a church of one hundred members; such a church under an excellent pastor would be considered as doing an exceptionally good work if on an average fifty were added annually to this membership. But suppose that that church was trained to do personal work, and that fifty of the one hundred members actually went at it. Certainly one a month won to Christ by each one would not be a large average. That would be six hundred a year instead of the fifty mentioned above. A church of many members, with the most powerful preaching possible, that depends upon the minister alone to win men to Christ by his preaching, would not accomplish anything like what would be accomplished by a church with a comparatively poor preacher, where the membership generally were personal workers.

CHAPTER II

THE CONDITIONS OF SUCCESS

I. The first condition of success in personal work, and in all soul-saving work, is **a personal experimental knowledge of Jesus Christ as a Saviour.** It was because the Apostle Paul could say:

> "This is a faithful saying, and worthy of all acceptation, that Christ Jesus came into the world to save sinners; *of whom I am chief.*" 1 Tim. 1:15

that he had power in bringing other men to that Saviour. It is the man who knows Jesus as his own Saviour, who will have a longing to bring others to this wonderful Saviour whom he has himself found; and it is the man who knows Jesus as his Saviour who will understand how to bring others to the Saviour whom he has found. There are many to-day who are trying to save others, who are not saved themselves. There are others, who, while they are probably saved men, have such a vague knowledge of Christ as their own Saviour, that they cannot hope to make the way of salvation clear to others.

A personal, experimental knowledge of Jesus Christ as a Saviour includes three things:

1. A knowledge that our own sins have been forgiven because Jesus bore them in His own body on the Cross:

2. A knowledge that the risen Christ is delivering us daily from the power of sin;

3. An absolute surrender of our wills to Jesus Christ as our Lord and Master.

II. The second condition of success in personal work is really involved in the first, and is **a life clean within and without.**

In 2 Tim. 2:21 we read.

"If a man therefore purge himself from these, he shall be a vessel unto honour, sanctified, and meet for the master's use, and prepared unto every good work."

If a man is to be used of God, his life must be clean—not only his outward life as the world sees it, but his inward secret life as it is known only to God and to himself. One who holds on to any sin of act or thought or affection cannot expect to have power with a holy God, and consequently cannot expect to have power for God. Many a man and woman of great natural gifts, and unusual knowledge of the Bible, are trying to do work for God and meet with little or no success. People wonder why it is that their work is so devoid of results, but if we knew their secret life as God knows it, we would understand their failure; there is sin before God. It has been often said, and well said, that "God does not demand a beautiful vessel for His work, but He does demand a clean one." Many are working on in disappointment and failure, working hard but accomplishing nothing, because God sees sin in their inner life which they will not give up.

III. The third condition of success in personal work is **a surrendered life, a life wholly given up to God.** Paul was mighty as a worker for Christ because he could say,

"For to me to live is Christ."

The miracle of the five loaves and two fishes, (Matt. 14: 17-20) is deeply significant. The disciples said unto Jesus, "We have here but five loaves, and two fishes." "He said, Bring them hither to me." We are told with a good deal of emphasis upon the definite article, He "took *the* five loaves and *the* two fishes," that is, He took all that they had. It was not much, but they brought it all. Then He blessed it and broke it and there was an abundance for all. But if one of these insignificant barley loaves had been kept back, or one of these little fishes, there would not have been enough to go around. We too, may not have much, it may be only five barley crackers and two little fishes, but if we will bring them all, absolutely all to Christ, He will take them, bless them and multiply them; but if we hold back one cracker or one fish, He will not bless and multiply. **Here lies the secret of failure in many a** one who would work for Christ; there is one cracker kept back, or one little fish. We talk very lightly of absolute surrender to God, but it means more than most people who profess it seem to realize. I would ask each reader of these pages, have you brought all to Christ—absolutely all—absolutely ALL?

IV. The one who would have success in personal work must have **a deep realization that men out of Christ are lost.** Jesus had this. He said,

> "For the Son of man is come to seek and to save that which was LOST." Luke 19: 10.

When He looked upon men living in sin, He knew and realized the utter ruin of their condition. The same thing was true of Paul. We read in Acts 20: 31 that he "ceased not to warn every one night and day *with tears.*" He knew that if one had not a saving knowledge of Jesus Christ he was eternally lost. This overwhelming conviction that men and women out of Christ are eternally lost, seems to be very rare in our day, and this is one great reason why so few have real power in soul-winning. How can we get this realization?

1. First of all, by studying what the Bible has to say about the present standing and condition and future destiny of those who are out of Christ.

2. By believing what the Bible says upon these points without trying to tone it down, and make it fit in with the popular notions of the day.

3. By dwelling upon these truths about the lost condition of men out of Christ until they take hold upon our hearts and we realize their meaning. These things are not pleasant to think about, but they are true, and we ought to think about them until our souls are on fire to save men from the awful condition of utter ruin in which they now are, and from the destiny of eternal shame and despair to which they are hurrying.

V. The fifth condition of success in personal work is **love.** Nothing wins like love. In the first place it leads to untiring effort for the salvation of others. If I really love men, I cannot bear the thought that they should be lost forever, and I will be willing to work day and night to save them from such an awful destiny. In the second place, love attracts others to us. There is nothing so irresistible as love. It is Jesus Christ lifted up on the Cross, a revelation of God's love and of His own love to man, that draws all men unto Him. (Jno. 12: 32.) Men will not put you off if they really believe that you love them, but they will never believe that you love them unless you really do. We need not only love to men, but love to Christ. It was the love of Christ that constrained Paul to his untiring efforts to bring men to a knowledge of Christ. The great men and women of Christian history have been the men and women who have had a great love to Christ, men and women whose hearts were all aglow with love to the glorious Son of God.

But how can we get love? First of all, by dwelling upon Christ's love to us.

"We love Him, because He first loved us." 1 Jno. 4: 19.

We shall never appreciate Christ's love to us until we see it against the black background of our own sin. It is the one who is forgiven much who loves much. (Luke 7: 47.) The one who has never been brought to a deep realization of his own sinfulness before God, will have no warmth of love to that Saviour who, by His own atoning death on the Cross, redeemed him from the awful depth to which he had sunken. The Apostle Paul realized that he was the chief of sinners, and that Jesus loved him and gave Himself for him, so he was full of love to Jesus Christ.

This is a faithful saying, and worthy of all acceptation, that Christ Jesus came into the world to save sinners, *of whom I am chief.*" 1 Tim. 1: 15.

"I am crucified with Christ: nevertheless I live; yet not I, but Christ liveth in me; and the life which I now live in the flesh I live by the faith of the Son of God, who *loved me, and gave himself for me.*" Gal. 2: 20.

If we are to have love to Christ and love to men, the Holy Ghost must impart it. The first fruit of the Spirit is love:

"But the fruit of the Spirit is *love*, joy, peace, longsuffering, gentleness, goodness, faith." Gal. 5: 22.

If we will look to the Holy Spirit to do His whole work in our hearts, He will soon fill them with love to Christ and love to our fellow-men.

VI. The sixth condition of success in personal work is **perseverance.** No work requires so much patience and perseverance as soul-winning. Men are not usually won to Christ in a day. You must hold on to men day after day, week after week, month after month, and if need be, year after year. You must not give them up even though you seem to make absolutely no headway at first, and even though you seem to do more harm than good. When you start out to lead a man to Christ, keep after that man until he is saved, no matter how long it takes. Study how to get at men who are unreachable. Men who cannot be reached in one way can in another. There are very few men in the world to whose hearts there is not an open door somewhere, if we will only search diligently until we find it. If we cannot get in at the door, perhaps we can break up the roof and get in that way. Any one who wishes to win souls at the rate of one every fifteen minutes better go into some other business. Take time; never give up; and do thorough work. I waited and watched fifteen long years to get my chance with one man. Never a day passed for all those fifteen years that I did not speak to God about that man. At last my chance came, and it was my privilege to lead him to Christ. He afterwards became a preacher of the Gospel, and is now in heaven. I was with him the day before he died, and shall never forget that day as long as I live. When you undertake to bring a man to Christ, never give up.

VII. The seventh condition of success in personal work is a **practical knowledge of the Bible.**

"Every Scripture inspired of God is also profitable for teaching, for reproof, for correction, for instruction which is in righteousness: that the man of God may be complete, *furnished completely unto every good work.*" 2 Tim. 3: 16, 17, R. V.

In the Bible is all the truth we need in dealing with men. The Word of God is the only instrument that God has appointed for the salvation of men, and the only instrument He honors is the Word. It is the Word that produces conviction of sin. It is the Word that regenerates. It is the Word that produces faith:

"Now when they heard this, they were *pricked in their heart*, and said unto Peter and to the rest of the apostles, Men and brethren, what shall we do?" Acts 2:37.

"Being *born again*, not of corruptible seed but of incorruptible, by *the Word of God*, which liveth and abideth for ever." 1 Pet. 1:23.

"So then faith cometh by hearing, and hearing by *the Word of God.*" Rom. 10:17.

If then we are to be used in soul-winning, we must know the Bible. There are five texts that ought to sink deep into the heart of every personal worker. They are:

1. "So then faith cometh by hearing, and hearing by *the Word of God.*" Rom. 10:17.
2. "The seed is *the Word of God.*" Luke 8:11, last clause.
3. "Being born again, not of corruptible seed, but of incorruptible, by *the Word of God*, which liveth and abideth for ever." 1 Pet. 1:23.
4. "And take the helmet of salvation, and the sword of the Spirit, *which is the Word of God.*" Eph. 6:17.
5. "Is not *my Word like as a fire?* saith the Lord; and *like a hammer* that breaketh the rock in pieces?" Jer. 23:29.

The personal worker who depends upon any other instrument than the Word of God is doomed to failure. But we must have a practical knowledge of the Bible, that is we must know how to use it for definite results. A great many men have a large theoretical knowledge of the Bible, but no practical knowledge. They do not know how to use the Bible so as to accomplish anything definite by its use. In an inquiry meeting one evening, I asked one of the best Bible scholars in America to speak to an inquirer and show her the way of life, and he whispered in my ear, "I don't know how to do that." A small practical knowledge of the Bible is better in personal work than a large theoretical knowledge. A practical knowledge of the Bible involves four things:

1. A knowledge how to so use the Bible as to show men, and make men realize, their need of a Saviour.

2. A knowledge of how to use the Bible so as to show men Jesus as just the Saviour who meets their need.

3. A knowledge of how to use the Bible so as to show men how to make Jesus their own Saviour.

4. A knowledge of how to use the Bible so as to meet the difficulties that stand in the way of their accepting Christ.

A large part of the following pages will be devoted to imparting this particular kind of Bible knowledge.

VIII. The eighth condition of success in personal work is prayer. God honors prayer. In nothing does He honor it more than in the matter of soul-winning. The one who is to be much used of God in soul-winning, must spend much time in prayer. There are four things for which we must especially pray:

1. We must ask God to bring to us, or us to, the right persons. We cannot speak with every one. If we attempt it, we will spend much time in speaking where we can do no good, that we might have used in speaking where we could have accomplished something for Christ. God alone knows the one to whom He intends us to speak, and we must ask Him to point him out to us, and expect Him to do it.

"Then *the Spirit said unto Philip*, Go near, and join thyself to *this* chariot." Acts 8: 29.

2. We should ask God to give us the right message in each case where we do speak with any one. We can learn much by studying what is the right message for any given class of men, but after all our study, we must look directly to God for the right message in each individual case. Many cases will baffle us, but no case will baffle God. We need and must have the direct guidance of the Holy Spirit in each individual case. Every experienced worker could testify to many instances in which God has led him to use some text of Scripture that he would not otherwise have used, but which proved to be just the one needed.

3. We must pray God to give power to that which He has given us to say. We need not only a message from God, but power from God to send the message home. Most workers have to learn this lesson by humiliating experiences. They sit down beside an unsaved person and reason, and plead, and bring forth texts from the Word of God, but the man does not accept Christ. At last it dawns upon them that they are trying to convert the man in their own strength, and they lift a short but humble prayer to God for His strength, and in a very little while this "very difficult case" has settled the matter and is rejoicing in Christ.

4. We must pray to God to carry on the work after we have done everything in our power, and our work has come to

an end. After having done that which seems to have been our whole duty in any given instance, whatever may have been the apparent result of our work, whether successful or unsuccessful, we should definitely commit the case to God in prayer. If there is anything the average worker in this hurrying age needs to have impressed upon him, it is the necessity of much prayer. By praying more, we will not work any less, and we will accomplish vastly more.

IX. The ninth condition of success in personal work is **the baptism with the Holy Ghost.** In Acts 1:8 we read,

> "But ye *shall receive power*, after that the Holy Ghost is come upon you."

The supreme condition of power in the apostolic church was the definite baptism with the Holy Ghost. The supreme condition of success in soul-winning is the same to-day. Many in these days are trying to prove that there is no such thing as a special baptism with the Holy Spirit, but a candid and careful study of the Acts of the Apostles will show that there is. Very many in our day also know by blessed experience that the baptism with the Holy Spirit is a present day reality. One ounce of believing experience along this line is worth whole tons of unbelieving exegesis, no matter how subtle and learned it may be. There are thousands of men and women in this and other lands who have been brought out of a place of powerlessness into a place of power in the Lord's service, through meeting the conditions plainly laid down in the Bible for receiving the Holy Ghost. This baptism with the Holy Spirit is for every child of God, and the one who would be largely used of God in personal work, must get it at any cost

CHAPTER III

WHERE TO DO PERSONAL WORK

I. Perhaps the easiest and most natural place to do personal work is **after a Gospel meeting.** Whenever you attend a meeting, watch for some one to deal with after the meeting is over. Do not trust to chance in the matter, but as the minister preaches the sermon keep your eyes on the audience and watch who it is that is hit and what hits them, then you can follow up the work that the minister has already done by his sermon. You will soon acquire good judgment in deciding with whom it is wisest to speak. Of course one must be on his guard against being obtrusive in watching others. Before you go to the meeting pray definitely to God to give you some one at the meeting, and then watch for an answer to your prayer. When you have found your man, go for him, and do not let him slip away under any consideration. It is often well to go as quickly as possible to one of the doors of the meeting-house, and without making oneself too prominent, watch people as they come out, and then gently and courteously approach some one, and deal with him about his soul.

There is a great difference in Christian workers. Some seem to never get any one at the close of a meeting unless some one else takes them to them. They wait around with their Bible under their arm for some one to come to them and take them to an inquirer; others keep their eyes open for themselves, and almost always manage to get hold of some one.

In many of the more active churches, the church is divided into sections with an overseer over each division of the church, and individual workers under the overseer. This is an excellent plan. When it is well carried out it prevents any hopeful cases from getting out without being dealt with personally.

II. In homes. The Apostle Paul tells us that he preached the Gospel not only publicly, but "from house to house." (Acts 20: 20.) There is far too little Christian work done in the home. The best home to begin with is your own. Jesus bade the demoniac of Gadara when he was healed to return to his own house and show how great things God had done unto him. (Luke 8: 39.) Every man who is converted should begin to tell the saving power of Christ first in his own home, to his own relatives and friends. Many a mother with her family of children regrets that she has not a wider field of labor for Christ, but she will find one of the grandest of all fields in her own home.

But we should not limit our personal work to our own homes, we should do it in the homes where we visit. In this way those who make us partakers of their hospitality, will entertain angels unawares. (Heb. 13: 2.) A godly man who once visited in the home of Spurgeon's parents, by a few words to the little boy, made an impression upon that boy that went far toward making him the mighty minister of the Gospel that he became in after years.

Then we should do personal work in the houses that we enter in our house-to-house visitation. That man or woman is a poor church visitor who simply makes a pleasant call or talks upon religious generalities. The true visitor will find frequent opportunities for doing effective personal work with some of the inhabitants of the home, or with strangers they may find calling upon them.

III. On the streets. Here again we have the Apostle Paul for an example. Not only did he reason "in the synagogue with the Jews and the devout persons," but also "in the market place every day with them that met with him." (Acts 17: 17, R.V.) As you walk the streets, be listening for the voice of God to say "Go and speak to that man." Very often as one walks the street of a crowded city or the lonely roads of the country, if he is walking with God, the leading will come to speak to some one that he meets by the way, and countless are the souls that have been led out of darkness into light in this way. As you look upon the surging crowd, ask

God if there is some one in this crowd with whom He desires you to speak. Sometimes it is well to stand to one side and watch the people as they pass. Soon there will come a face that interests you, a face it may be that tells a story of sin, or sorrow and need. You can quietly follow this person and watch for an opportunity to engage them in conversation, and then point them to the one who says, "Come unto me all ye that labor and are heavy laden, and I will give you rest."

IV. In the parks and other resorts. The parks are often full of people who have plenty of leisure and are willing to talk upon almost any subject. Go through the park and find your man, engage him in a conversation, and as quickly as you can, lead him up to the great subject that is burning in your own heart. Oftentimes it is well to begin to talk about matters of passing interest, the burning questions of the day, then lead by the shortest possible route to the great question. Sometimes show the one with whom you are talking a tract, and ask his opinion of it, and this will lead easily to the matter uppermost in your mind. Not infrequently if you sit down in a park some one will come and sit down beside you and begin to talk to you, then of course it is very easy to lead them into a conversation about their own soul's need.

V. On a walk or ride. In this we have our Saviour's own example. He made the hearts of the two disciples burn within them while He spoke to them in the way, and opened to them the Scriptures. (Luke 24: 32.) We also have the example of Philip the evangelist. The Spirit bade him go and join himself to the chariot of Queen Candace's treasurer. The treasurer invited him up into the chariot to ride with him, and the memorable conversation and personal dealing that followed led to the conversion and baptism of the treasurer, and the carrying of the Gospel into Ethiopia. (Acts 8: 29-38) There are few more favorable places to do personal work than on a walk or ride with a friend or even with a stranger.

VI. At the place of business. Here again we have the Saviour's example. "As He passed by, He saw Levi the son of Alphaeus sitting at the receipt of custom, and said unto him,

Follow me. And he arose and followed Him." (Mark 2:14.) Of course we ought not to interrupt men and hinder their proper performance of their business duties. Many a workman has rare opportunities to speak with his fellow workmen, sometimes during work hours, sometimes during the noon rest. One of the most earnest Christian ministers I ever knew had been a godless employé in a factory, but the man who worked next to him was a Christian, took an interest in his fellow employé's soul, and was instrumental under God in leading him to Christ. I have met a good many from one of the largest business institutions in our city who have been led to Christ by one consecrated young man in the establishment. This young man has since gone as a foreign missionary, but he was used of God to lead many of his fellow employés to Christ before he went. It is well wherever possible, to go into stores and factories and other places of business for the deliberate purpose of leading those who work there to Christ. Of course, as already said, it will not do to interrupt a man at his business, neither will it do generally to deal with him when others are around and listening, nor should he be taken at an hour when he is in a bad temper; but one who has that discretion that God is so ready to give (James 1:5) will find many opportunities for doing the Master's work. It is quite possible oftentimes to drop a word, or even to have a little talk, when there is not a great pressure of business, with the clerk who sells us goods, or with the barber who shaves us, or with the boy who blacks our shoes. There are five marks of a good opportunity; when one is alone, unoccupied, in good humor, communicative and in a serious mood.

VII. On cars and boats. Traveling on the steam cars affords a very rare opportunity for personal work. Travelers usually have much time that hangs heavily upon their hands, and are glad to get into conversation with any one, but if one is a real Christian, there is one subject always uppermost in his mind, one subject that he would rather talk about than any other, and that is Jesus Christ. When you get into a train, get as good a seat for yourself as you can, put your coat and grip out of the way, move away over to the farther side of the seat, and make the vacant space beside you look as inviting as possible. If the car is at all crowded, you will soon have a fellow-passenger, and the desired opportunity for personal work. Sometimes it is well to keep your coat and grip in the seat beside you until you see the man or woman that you want coming, and then remove them and move along in a way of silent invitation.

It is well to talk with the trainmen and porters. They are usually willing to talk, and many of them have been led to Christ by Spirit-filled workers who were traveling with them.

Many Christian workers go through trains and give tracts to every one on the train. I am not sure that this is the wisest thing to do, but I know that great blessing has come from it in many cases. Certainly it is well to carry a good supply of religious literature with you when you travel. Some of the books of the Bible Institute Colportage Association are excellent for this purpose, such, e.g., as "Probable Sons." People are willing to read almost anything on a train, and these books without any comment oftentimes will lead the reader to Christ, and when they do not do this, they pave the way for a conversation.

Street cars are not as favorable a place for personal work as steam cars. One does not have the time or opportunity that he does on a train, and yet good work can be done on a street car, both with the passengers and with the motorman and conductor. A minister once said to me, "I was greatly ashamed last night going down on the street car. I was sitting inside the car talking on unimportant matters with friends, and as I looked to the front end of the car, I saw one member of my church talking with the driver about his soul, and when I looked to the other end of the car I saw another member of my church talking to the conductor, and there I, the pastor of the church, was doing nothing but wasting my time."

VIII. Prisons, hospitals, and other public institutions. A fine place to do personal work is in public institutions, such as prisons and hospitals, where many people are gathered together and are at leisure from morning till night. Every

Sunday, all over this land, devoted men and women are going into prisons, jails and hospitals, carrying the glad tidings of salvation, and thousands are being converted to God through their faithful personal work. Many of the best Christians that I know to-day were brought to Christ in prison, not so much through the public preaching, as through the personal work of some devoted child of God who went from cell to cell and talked to the men about Christ. But while so much is being done already in this direction, there are many prisons and jails and hospitals where little or nothing is done.

Nurses in hospitals have a rare opportunity of doing personal work in the institutions where they are employed. Fortunately a very large proportion of trained nurses are devoted Christian women, and yet many of them do not realize the opportunities that God has put within their reach. A very unusual opportunity is also open to the Christian physician. Indeed a true Christian physician will oftentimes find opportunities for doing personal work that even the minister of the Gospel cannot find. Sometimes it will be with the patient whom he is treating, sometimes with the relatives and friends of the patient who are in deep anxiety as to the outcome of the sickness.

What has been said does not of course cover all the places where personal work can be done, but it will suggest rich fields of opportunity. To put it in a word, personal work should be done everywhere. We read of the early disciples that "they that were scattered abroad went *everywhere* preaching the Word" (Acts 8:4), that is talking to individuals about Jesus, showing them the word of truth as it is found in the Bible, and leading them to accept it. Every child of God should be at all times on the lookout for opportunities to speak personally to some other man or woman about Christ.

CHAPTER IV

HOW TO BEGIN

One of the most difficult points in personal work is beginning. It is comparatively easy to go on after one has got an opening.

I. The first thing is to **find the one to deal with.** As has already been said, we should pray God to lead us to some one, or some one to us. When we go to church, or when we walk the street, when we are in the park, or on the train, or calling, in a word, whenever we have time that is not demanded by other duties, we should look up to God and definitely ask Him to lead us to the one with whom we are to speak, if it is His will that we employ that time in work for Him. Further than this, we should be on the lookout for opportunities. A fisherman cultivates a keen eye for opportunities to catch fish; and a soul-winner should cultivate a keen eye for opportunities for soul-winning. Whenever we are thrown into the company of a man or woman, the great probability is that it is a providential opening, and we should be ready to meet it as such. It is said of one of the most distinguished Sunday school workers in this country, that he makes it a point whenever he is alone with any individual to speak to him about his soul. The story is told of Uncle John Vassar, that being left alone in a hotel parlor with a strange lady, he at once approached her and began to speak to her about her soul. After he had gone, the woman's husband returned, and she told him what had happened. The husband was in a great rage, and said, "If I had been here, I would have sent him about his business." His wife replied, "If you had been here, you would have thought he was about his business." We ought to make soul winning our business, and improve every possible opportunity.

II. Having found your man, **begin a conversation.** How shall that be done? In the inquiry room, by asking at once a few leading questions to find out just where the man stands, for example: "Are you a Christian?" "Are you saved?" "Have you been born again?" "Upon what do you base your hope of eternal life?" "Are you confessing Christ openly before the world?" "Have you surrendered all you have and are to Christ?" Sometimes it is well to begin in this direct way even when you meet some one casually. The question "Are you saved?" is as a general rule a better one to ask than "Are you a Christian?" It is more likely to set one to thinking. It is more definite and pointed. Many will take the asking of such a question as an impertinence, but that will not prove that the question has not done good. Not a few people who have become angry at a stranger putting a question like this to them have afterward been converted in consequence of it. There are many other questions that one may ask that will set men to thinking and open the way for further conversation. For example you can ask a man, "Do you think that life is worth living?" and after you have engaged him in conversation on this point you can lead him on and tell of the life that really is worth living. Or you can ask an utter stranger, "How do you think a man can get the most real satisfaction out of life, that is, of course, by accepting Jesus Christ as a Saviour. Or you can say to a man, "I have learned the great secret of happiness," and when he asks you what it is, you can tell him. Of course these are only offered as suggestions of ways in which to begin a conversation.

A good way to begin is by handing the person with whom you wish to deal, a well-chosen tract to read. When he has finished the tract, you can ask him what he thinks about it, and thus the way is opened to a conversation on the great subject. It is often well to begin by engaging the person in a general conversation, perhaps on subjects quite remote from religion, and gradually working around to the point. It was thus that Christ engaged the woman of Samaria, making a very simple request of her, that she would give Him a drink,

(Jno. 4: 7.) but before long, he was telling her of the living water. If the person with whom you wish to deal is older than yourself, you might begin by saying, "There is a subject in which I am deeply interested, and I am trying to get all the light upon it that I can; you are much older than I, and perhaps you can help me; the subject is 'How to Be Saved.'"

Showing people little kindnesses very often opens the way for a conversation on the great subject. For example, in a crowded car one can move along and invite some one who is standing to a seat by your side. It is the most natural thing in the world then to get into conversation, and the favor of the person who has been standing is gained, and it will be very easy to lead on to the great subject. When one is riding, and sees some one else walking, an invitation to the walker to ride will afford a splendid opportunity for approaching him on the subject of his soul's salvation. Mr. Moody made a constant practice of inviting those with whom he wished to deal out riding with him. As he drew near to some quiet spot, he would speak to them of what was upon his heart, and then stop the horse and have a season of prayer. No one can tell how many were thus led to Christ. Sometimes it is well to show the people that you would lead to Christ, kindnesses for days and weeks, and even years, waiting for your opportunity to say a word. A devoted Chinese missionary who had made great sacrifices to go to that land, was received by the people with bitterest hatred, but he simply gave himself up to live among them and live for them. One by one opportunities came of showing them kindnesses, and after years of self-sacrificing living, he had so won their confidence that it was an easy matter for him to lead them to Christ, but he had to begin by showing them the most ordinary, every-day kindnesses, far away, apparently, from the subject that was closest to his heart.

Sometimes a person's face will tell the story of discontent, unhappiness or unrest. In such a case it is easy to ask the person if he is happy, and when he says no, tell him you can tell him of One who can make him happy if he will only take Him.

Tact in beginning will come with experience, but it is better to begin awkwardly than not to begin at all. I do not think that any one could begin more awkwardly in this work than I did with the first person whom I led to Christ. I felt that God wanted me to speak to this young man, and I called on him for that purpose, but when I met him I had not the slightest idea what to say. I talked on and on waiting for an opportunity, and at last blundered out awkwardly what I had come for. God blessed the awkward but honest effort, and the young man was saved, and has become a very active and efficient worker for Christ.

The best way to learn how to do personal work is by doing it, gaining wisdom from your mistakes.

III. Having begun the conversation, **find out as soon as possible where the person with whom you are dealing stands.** In order to treat a case intelligently, you need just as much as a physician to know just where the man is at present. But how can we find out to what class any person belongs?

1. First of all *by asking him questions*, such questions as "Are you saved?" "Have you eternal life?" "Have you been born again?" "Do you know that you are a great sinner before God?" "Do you know that your sins are forgiven?" Or you can ask a person directly, "Where do you stand, what do you believe?" He may answer these questions untruthfully, either from ignorance or a desire to mislead you, nevertheless the answers and his manner of giving them will show you a great deal about his real state.

2. *By watching the inquirer's face.* A man's face will often reveal that which his words try to conceal. Any one who cultivates a study of the faces of those with whom he deals, will soon be able to tell in many instances their exact state irrespective of anything they may say.

3. *By observing his tone and manner.* A man's tone or his manner often tells more than his words. A man who is not saved will very likely tell you that he is, but his tone and manner will reveal plainly that he is not. If one gets angry at you for asking these questions, that of itself reveals an uneasy conscience.

4. *By the Holy Spirit.* The Holy Spirit, if we look to

Him to do it, will often flash into our minds a view of the man's position, and just the Scripture that He needs.

IV. When we have learned where the person with whom we are dealing stands, the next thing to do is to **lead him as directly as we can to accept Jesus Christ as a personal Saviour, and to surrender to Him as his Lord and Master.** We must always bear in mind that the primary purpose of our work is not to get people to join the church, or to give up their bad habits, or to do anything else than this, to accept Jesus Christ as their Saviour, the one who bore their sins in His own body on the tree, and the one through whom they can have immediate and entire forgiveness, and as their Master to whom they surrender absolutely the guidance of their thoughts, purposes, feelings and actions.

V. Having led any one to thus accept Christ, the next step will be to **show him from God's Word that he has forgiveness of sins and eternal life.** Acts 10: 43; 13: 39; John 3: 36; 5: 24 will answer for this purpose.

VI. The next step will be to **show him how to make a success of the Christian life upon which he has entered.**

CHAPTER V

HOW TO DEAL WITH THOSE WHO REALIZE THEIR NEED OF A SAVIOUR AND REALLY DESIRE TO BE SAVED

We come now to the question of how to deal with individual cases. We begin with those who realize their need of a Savior, and really desire to be saved. We begin with these because they are the easiest class to deal with.

I. Show them Jesus as a sin-bearer.

The first thing to show one who realizes his need of a Saviour is that Jesus has borne his sins in His own body on the cross. A good verse for this purpose is Is. 53:6:

> "All we like sheep have gone astray; we have turned every one to his own way; and the Lord hath laid on him the iniquity of us all."

Get the inquirer to read the verse himself, then say to him, "The first half of this verse shows you your need of salvation, the second half shows you the provision that God has made for your salvation. Read again the first half of the verse. Is this true of you? Have you gone astray like a sheep? Have you turned to your own way?" "Yes." "Then what are you?" Get the inquirer to say, "I am lost." "We will now look at the provision God has made for your salvation, read the last half of the verse. Who is the one in this verse upon whom our iniquity has been laid?" "Christ." "What then has God done with your sin?" Laid it on Christ." "Is it then on you any longer?" Go over it again and again until he sees that his sin is not on him, but that it is on Christ, and has been settled forever. I often use a simple illustration in making the meaning of the verse plain. I let my right hand represent the inquirer, my left hand represent Christ, and my Bible represent the inquirer's sin. I first lay the Bible on my right hand and say, "Now where is your sin?" The inquirer replies of course, "On me." I then repeat the last half of the verse, "the Lord hath *laid on him* the iniquity of us all," and transfer the Bible from my right hand to my left, and ask, "Where is your sin now?" The inquirer replies, "On Him, of course." I then ask, "Is it on you any longer?" and he says, "No, on Christ." Very many people have been led out into light and joy by this simple illustration.

I sometimes put it in this way, in using this verse, "There are two things which a man needs to know, and one thing he needs to do in order to be saved. What he needs to know is, first, that he is a lost sinner, and this verse tells him that, and second, that Christ is an all-sufficient Saviour, and this verse tells him that. What he needs to do is to accept this all-sufficient Saviour whom God has provided. Now will you accept Him right here and now?"

Another excellent verse to show Jesus as a sin-bearer, is Gal. 3:13:

> "Christ hath redeemed us from the curse of the law, *being made a curse for us:* for it is written, Cursed is every one that hangeth on a tree."

The inquirer should be given the verse to read for himself. When he has read it, you may question him something like this: "What does this verse tell us that Christ has redeemed us from?" "Whom has He redeemed?" "How has He redeemed us from the curse of the law?" "Do you believe that Christ has redeemed you from the curse of the law by being made a curse in your place?" "Will you read it then in the singular instead of in the plural?" Make it clear what you mean, until the inquirer reads the verse in this way: "Christ has redeemed me from the curse of the law, being made a curse for me; for it is written, cursed is every one that hangeth on a tree."

Another good verse for this purpose is 2 Cor. 5:21:

> "For he hath made him to be sin for us, who knew no sin; that we might be made the righteousness of God in him."

Have him read the verse, and then ask questions somewhat as follows: "Who is it that hath been made sin for us?" "For whom has Christ been made sin?" "For what purpose is it that Christ has been made sin for us?" "Can you put this verse in the singular and read it this way: 'For he hath made Him to be sin for me, who knew no sin; that I might be made the righteousness of God in Him'?"

Sometimes it will be well to use all three of these passages, but as a rule the first is sufficient; as far as my own experience goes, it is more effective than either of the other passages—in fact, I deal with very few men with whom I do not use Is. 53: 6 sooner or later.

II. Show them Jesus as a risen Saviour, able to save to the uttermost.

It is not enough to show them Jesus as a sin-bearer, for through believing in Jesus as a sin-bearer one merely gets pardon from sin, but there is something else that the sinner needs, that is deliverance from sin's power. In order to get this, they need to see Jesus as a risen Saviour, able to save to the uttermost. By believing in Christ crucified, we get pardon, but by believing in Christ risen, we get deliverance from sin's power. One of the best verses to use for this purpose is Heb. 7: 25:

> 'Wherefore he is able also to save them to the uttermost that come unto God by him, seeing he ever liveth to make intercession for them."

When the inquirer has read the passage, ask him who it is that is able to save, and to what extent He is able to save. Explain to the inquirer what "to the uttermost" means. Many read this passage as though it taught that Jesus was able to save from the uttermost. This is true, but it is not the truth of this text, it is save *to* the uttermost. Then ask the inquirer why it is that Jesus is able to save to the uttermost. Dwell upon this thought, that *Jesus ever liveth*, that He is not only a Saviour who once died and made atonement for sin, but that He is a Saviour who lives to-day, and is able to keep from sin's power. Then ask the inquirer if he is willing to trust Jesus as a living Saviour, one to whom he can look day by day for victory over sin.

Another good verse to use for this purpose is Jude 24:

> "Now unto him that is *able to keep you from falling*, and to present you faultless before the presence of his glory with exceeding joy."

When the inquirer has read the verse, ask him what this verse says Jesus is able to do, emphasize "to keep you from falling." Explain why it is that Jesus is able to keep from falling; because He is a risen, living Saviour to-day, and get the inquirer to see plainly that he is to look to the risen Christ to keep him from falling.

Matt. 28: 18 is a good verse to use to bring out the extent of Christ's power:

> "And Jesus came and spake unto them, saying, All power is given unto me in heaven and in earth."

A young convert needs to realize that he is to stand, not in his own strength, but in the strength of Christ, and it is a great help for him to see that the one in whom he is to trust has all power in heaven and in earth.

One can also use to advantage 1 Peter 1: 5:

> "Who are kept by the power of God through faith unto salvation ready to be revealed in the last time"

and 1 Cor. 15: 1-4. The latter passage brings out clearly the thought that the doctrine that Christ died for our sins, as blessed as it is, is not the whole Gospel, but only half of it; that the rest of the Gospel is that He was buried and that He rose again. Always get an inquirer to believe not only in Christ crucified, but in Christ risen as well. A man once came to me in deep distress of soul. He was a perfect stranger to me, but told me that he had come quite a distance to tell me his story. He said, "When I was a boy seven years of age, I started to read the Bible through. I had not gotten through Deuteronomy before I found that if one kept the whole law of God for one hundred years, and then broke it at one point, he was under the curse of a broken law. Was that right?" "Yes," I replied, "that is substantially the teaching of the law." He then continued, that he was in deep distress of soul for about a year, but as a boy of eight, he read John 3: 16 and saw how Jesus Christ had died in his place, and borne the curse of the broken law for him, and he added, "My burden rolled away, and I had great joy. Was I converted?" I replied that that sounded very much like an evangelical conversion. "Well," he said, "let me tell you the rest of my story. Years passed by; I came to Chicago to live; I worked in the stockyards and lived in the stockyards region among many godless men; I fell into drink and I cannot break away; every little while this sin gets the mastery of me, and what I have come to ask you is, is there any way in which I can get the victory over sin?" I replied, "There is, I am glad you have come to me; let me show you the way." I opened my Bible to 1 Cor. 15: 1-4, and had him read:

> "Moreover, brethren, I declare unto you the gospel which I preached unto you, which also ye have received, and wherein ye stand; by which also ye are saved, if ye keep in memory what I preached unto you, unless ye have believed in vain. For I delivered unto you first of all that which I also received, how that *Christ died for our sins* according to the Scriptures; and that he was buried, *and that he rose again* the third day according to the Scriptures."

Then I said to him, "What is the Gospel that Paul preached?" He answered, "That Christ died for our sins according to the Scriptures, was buried, and rose again." "That is right," I said. Then I said, "Now you have believed the first part of this Gospel, that Christ died for your sins." "Yes." "Through believing that you have found peace." "Yes." "Well," I continued, "this is only half the Gospel. If you will really believe the other half from your heart, you will get victory over your sin. Do you believe that Jesus rose again?" "Yes, I believe everything in the Bible." "Do you believe that Jesus is to-day in the place of power at the right hand of God?" "I do." "Do you believe that He has all power in heaven and on earth?" "I do." "Do you believe that this risen Christ with all power in heaven and on earth, has power to set you free from the power of your sin?" "Yes," he said slowly, "I do." "Will you ask Him to do it, and trust Him to do it right now?" "I will." We knelt in prayer. I prayed and then he followed. He asked the risen Christ to set him free from the power of sin. I asked him if he really believed He had power to do it. "Yes." "Do you believe He will do it?" "Yes, I do." We rose and parted. Some time after I received a very joyous letter from him, telling me how glad he was that he had come to see me, and how the message he had heard was just the one that he needed. There are thousands of professing Christians to-day who know Jesus as a crucified Saviour, and have found pardon and peace through believing in Him, but they have never been brought to a definite, clear faith in Jesus as a risen Saviour who can save from the power of sin.

III. Show them Jesus as Lord.

It is not enough to know Jesus as a Saviour, we must know Him as Lord also. A good verse for this purpose is Acts 2:36:

> "Therefore let all the house of Israel know assuredly, that *God hath made that same Jesus*, whom ye have crucified, *both Lord and Christ.*"

When the inquirer has read the verse, ask him what God hath made Jesus, and hold him to it until he replies, "Both Lord and Christ." Then say to him, "Are you willing to accept Him as your Divine Lord, the one to whom you will surrender your heart, your every thought, and word, and act?"

Another good verse for this purpose is Rom. 10:9:

> "That if thou shalt confess with thy mouth *the Lord* Jesus, and shalt believe in thine heart that God hath raised him from the dead, thou shalt be saved."

When the inquirer has read the verse, ask him what we are to confess Jesus as. He should reply, "Lord." If he does not so reply, ask him other questions until he does answer in this way. Then ask him, "Do you really believe that Jesus is Lord, that He is Lord of all, that He is rightfully the absolute Lord and Master of your life and person?" Perhaps it will be well to use Acts 10:36 as throwing additional light upon this point:

> "The word which God sent unto the children of Israel, preaching peace by Jesus Christ: (*he is Lord of all*)."

IV. Show them how to make Jesus their own.

It is not enough to see that Jesus is a sin-bearer, and that Jesus is a risen Saviour, and that Jesus is Lord; one must also see how to make this Jesus their own sin-bearer, their own risen Saviour, and their own Lord. There is perhaps no better verse to use for this purpose than John 1:12:

> "But *as many as received him*, to them gave he power to become the sons of God, even to them that believe on his name."

When one has read the verse, you can ask to whom it is Jesus gave power to become the sons of God. "As many as received Him." "Received Him as what?" Then make it clear from what you have already said under the preceding points, that it is to receive Him as sin-bearer, to receive Him as a risen Saviour, to receive Him as our Lord and Master. "Will you just take Him as your sin-bearer now, as your risen Saviour, as your Lord and Master? Will you take Him to be whatever He offers Himself to you to be?" "I will." "Then what does this verse show you that you have a right to call yourself?" "A son of God." "Are you a son of God?" Oftentimes the inquirer will hesitate, but go over it again and again until it is as clear as day to him.

Another excellent passage to use for this purpose is John 3: 16:

> "For God so loved the world, that he gave his only begotten Son, that *whosoever believeth in him* should not perish, but have everlasting life."

Ask the inquirer who it is that receives eternal life. "Whosoever believes in Him." "Do you believe in Him as your sin-bearer?" "Do you believe in Him as your risen Saviour?" "Do you believe in Him as your Lord?" "Well, then, what have you?"

Another good passage to use is Acts 10: 43:

> "To him give all the prophets witness, that through his name *whosoever believeth in him* shall receive remission of sins."

still another, Acts 13: 39:

> "And by him *all that believe* are justified from all things, from which ye could not be justified by the law of Moses."

V. Show the need of confessing Christ with the mouth.

No conversion is clear and satisfactory until one has been led to confess Christ with the mouth before men. Perhaps the best passage to show the need of such open confession with the mouth is Rom. 10: 9, 10:

> "That if thou shalt confess with thy mouth the Lord Jesus, and shalt believe in thine heart that God hath raised him from the dead, thou shalt be saved. For with the heart man believeth unto righteousness; and with the mouth confession is made unto salvation."

When the inquirer has read it, ask him what is the first thing this verse tells us that we must do if we are to be saved. "Confess with thy mouth the Lord Jesus." "Well, will you confess Jesus as your Lord with the mouth now?" Wherever possible, it is good to get the person dealt with to make a public confession of Jesus just as soon as possible. If you are dealing with them in an after-meeting, have them make this confession right then and there, if somewhere else, bring them to a prayer-meeting, or some other service where they can make the confession, as soon as possible.

VI. Lead into assurance.

It is not enough that one should be saved, one ought to have the assurance that he is saved. He ought to be brought to a place where he can say confidently and joyously, "*I know* I am saved, *I know* I have everlasting life." After an inquirer has been led to the acceptance and confession of Christ, an excellent passage to use for this purpose is John 3:36:

> "He that believeth on the Son *hath everlasting life*, and he that believeth not the Son shall not see life, but the wrath of God abideth on him."

When the inquirer has read the passage you can say, "Now this passage tells us that there is some one who has everlasting life; who is it?" "He that believeth on the Son." "What does God say in this passage that every one who believes on the Son has?" "Everlasting life." "Is it absolutely sure that every one who believes on the Son has everlasting life?" "It is, God says so." "Well, do you believe on the Son?" "Yes." "What have you then?" "Everlasting life." "Are you absolutely sure that you have everlasting life?" "Yes." "Why are you sure?" "Because God says so here." In many cases, probably in the majority of cases, it will be necessary to go over this again, and again, before the inquirer says that he is absolutely sure that he has everlasting life because he believes on the Son, but do not let him go until he is thus absolutely sure.

VII. Give directions as to how to live the Christian life.

It is not enough that a person be led to accept Christ, that is only the beginning of the Christian life, and if one is not shown how to lead the Christian life which he has thus begun, his life is likely to be largely one of failure. The reason so many Christian lives are comparative failures is because of a lack of definite and full instruction to the young convert as to how to lead the life which he has begun. The following instructions should be given to every one who has been dealt with as described above; and not only to them, but to every other class of inquirers that may be led to the acceptance of Christ by the methods described in the following pages or in any other way. You will speak to the inquirer somewhat as follows: "You have just begun the Christian life, now you wish to make a success of it. There are six very simple things to do, and it is absolutely sure that any one who does these six things will make a success of the Christian life."

1. "You will find the first of these in Matt. 10: 32. Please read it very carefully:

> "Whosoever therefore shall *confess me before men*, him will I confess also before my Father which is in heaven."

This verse tells us that Christ confesses before the Father those who confess Him before men. You will make a success of the Christian life only if Christ confesses you before the Father, so if you wish to succeed in this life that you have begun, *you must make a constant practice of confessing Christ before men.* Improve every opportunity that you get of showing your colors, and stating that you are upon Christ's side, and of telling what the Lord hath done for your soul."

2. "*Study the Word of God regularly, and hide it in your heart.*" To make this point clear, use the following passages:

> "*Thy word have I hid in mine heart,* that I might not sin against thee." Ps. 119: 11.
>
> "As newborn babes, desire the sincere milk of the word, that ye may grow thereby." 1 Pet. 2: 2.

One of the most frequent causes of failure in the Christian life is neglect of the Word of God. One can no more thrive spiritually without regular spiritual food, than they can thrive physically without regular and proper physical nourishment

3. "*Pray without ceasing.*" To make this point clear, use

"Pray without ceasing." 1 Thess. 5: 17.

"But they that wait upon the Lord shall renew their strength; they shall mount up with wings as eagles; they shall run, and not be weary; and they shall walk, and not faint." Isa. 40: 31.

Have the young convert read these verses again and again and mark them in his Bible.

4. "*Surrender your will absolutely to God, and obey Him in all things.*" To make this plain use Acts 5: 32:

"And we are his witnesses of these things; and so is also the Holy Ghost, whom God hath given *to them that obey him.*"

Show that obedience is a matter of the will more than of the outward life, and that God gives His Holy Spirit to them that obey Him, or surrender their will absolutely to Him. Insist upon the need of this absolute surrender of the will to God.

5. "*Be a constant and generous giver.*" To make the necessity of this plain to the convert, use 2 Cor. 9: 6-8:

"But this I say, He which soweth sparingly shall reap also sparingly, and he which soweth bountifully shall reap also bountifully. Every man according as he purposeth in his heart. so let him give; not grudgingly, or of necessity: for God loveth a cheerful giver. And God is able to make all grace abound toward you, that ye, always having all sufficiency in all things, may abound to every good work."

It is well sometimes to use Mal. 3: 10 as a side light:

"Bring ye all the tithes into the storehouse, that there may be meat in mine house, and prove me now herewith, saith the Lord of hosts, if I will not open you the windows of heaven, and pour you out a blessing, that there shall not be room enough to receive it."

Go over and over it again and again until it is fixed in the young convert's mind that if he is to enjoy the fullness of God's blessing, if God is to make all grace abound toward him, he must give to the Lord's work as the Lord prospers him, that he must be a constant and generous giver. Many young Christians make little headway in the Christian life because they are not plainly instructed on the necessity of regular, systematic and generous giving to the Lord.

6. "*Go to work for Christ and keep working for Christ.*" To show the necessity of this, use Matt. 25: 14-30, explaining the teaching of the parable, that it is the one who uses what

he has who gets more, but the one who neglects to use what he has, loses even that.

Go over these six points again and again; write them down with the texts, and give them to the young convert to take with him. The directions given above may seem to be very full, and it may occur to the reader that it will take a long time to follow them out. This is true, and oftentimes it will not be necessary to use all the texts, but at the same time it is best to be sure that you do thorough work. There is a great deal of superficial and shoddy work done in soul-winning to-day, and this kind of work does not stand. It is better to spend an hour, or two hours, on one person, and get him really rooted and grounded in the truth, than it is to get a dozen or more to say that they accept Christ, when they do not really understand what they are doing. One of the most common and greatest of faults in Christian work to-day is superficial dealing with souls.

CHAPTER VI

HOW TO DEAL WITH THOSE WHO HAVE LITTLE OR NO CONCERN ABOUT THEIR SOULS

The largest class of men and women are those who have little or no concern about their salvation. There are some who contend that there is no use dealing with such, but there is. It is our business when a man has no concern about his salvation to go to work to produce that concern. How shall we do it?

I. Show him that he is a great sinner before God.

There is no better verse for this purpose than Matt. 22: 37, 38:

> "Jesus said unto him, Thou shalt love the Lord thy God with all thy heart, and with all thy soul, and with all thy mind. *This is the first and great commandment.*"

Before the one with whom you are dealing reads these verses, you can say to him, "Do you know that you are a great sinner before God?" Very likely he will reply, "I suppose I am a sinner, but I do not know that I am such a great sinner." "Do you know that you have committed the greatest sin that a man can possibly commit?" "No, I certainly have not." "What do you think is the greatest sin that a man can commit?" Probably he will answer, "Murder." "You are greatly mistaken, let us see what God says about it." Then have him read the passage. When he has read it, ask him, "What is the first and great commandment?" "Thou shalt love the Lord thy God with all thy heart, and with all thy soul, and with all thy mind." "Which commandment is this?" "The first and great commandment." "If this is the first and great commandment, what is the first and great sin?" "Not to keep this commandment." "Have you kept it? Have you put God first in everything; first in your affections, first in your thoughts, first in your pleasures, first in your business, first in everything?" "No, I have not." "What commandment, then, have you broken?" "The first and great commandment."

Some time ago a young man came into our inquiry meeting. I asked him if he was a Christian, and he replied that he was not. I asked him if he would like to be, and he said that he would. I said, "Why, then, do you not become a Christian to-night?" He replied, "I have no special interest in the matter." I said, "Do you mean that you have no conviction of sin?" "Yes," he said, "I have no conviction of sin, and am not much concerned about the whole matter." I said, "I hold in my hand a book which God has given us for the purpose of producing conviction of sin; would you like to have me use it upon you?" Half laughing, he replied, "Yes." When he had taken a seat, I had him read Matt. 22: 37, 38. When he had read the passage I said to him, "What is the first and great commandment?" He read it from the Bible. I said, "If this is the first and great commandment, what is the first and great sin?" He replied, "Not to keep this commandment." I asked, "Have you kept it?" "I have not." "What have you done then?" Said he, "I have broken the first and greatest of God's commandments," and broken down with a sense of sin, then and there he went down before God and asked Him for mercy, and accepted Christ as his Savior.

Another excellent passage to use to produce conviction of sin is Rom. 14: 12.

"So then every one of us shall give account of himself to God."

The great object in using this passage is to bring the careless man face to face with God, and make him realize that he must give account to God. When he has read it, ask him, "Who has to give account?" "Every one of us." "Who does that take in?" "Me." "Who then is to give account?" "I am." "To whom are you to give account?" "To God." "Of what are you to give account?" "Of myself." "Read it that way." "I shall give account of myself to God." "Now just let that thought sink into your heart. Say it over to yourself again and again, 'I am to give account of myself to God.' 'I am to give account of myself to God.' Are you ready to do it?"

Amos 4: 12 can be used in much the same way:

"Therefore thus will I do unto thee, O Israel: and because I will do this unto thee, *prepare to meet thy God*, O Israel."

Another very effective passage with many a careless man is Rom. 2: 16:

"In the day when *God shall judge the secrets* of men by Jesus Christ according to my Gospel."

When the one with whom you are dealing has read the verse, say "What is God going to do in some coming day?" "Judge the secrets of men." "Judge what?" "The secrets of men." "Who is it that is going to judge the secrets of men?" "It is God." "Are your ready to have the secret hidden things of your life judged by a holy God?"

II. Show him the awful consequences of sin.

A very effective passage for this purpose is Rom. 6: 23,

"For the wages of sin is death; but the gift of God is eternal life through Jesus Christ our Lord."

When he has read the passage, ask him, "What is the wages of sin?" "Death." Explain to him the meaning of death, literal death, spiritual death, eternal death. Now say, "This is the wages of sin, have you earned these wages?" "Are you willing to take them?" "No." "Well, there is one alternative, read the remainder of the verse." "The gift of God is eternal life through Jesus Christ our Lord." "Now you have your choice between the two, the wages that you have earned by sin, and the gift of God; which will you choose?"

Another very useful passage along this line is Is. 57: 21:

"There is no peace, saith my God, to the wicked."

Another verse declaring the fearful consequences of sin, is Jno. 8: 34:

'Jesus answered them, Verily, verily, I say unto you, Whosoever committeth sin is the servant of sin."

Have the one with whom you are dealing read the passage, then ask him what every one who commits sin is. "The servant of sin." "What kind of a service is that?" Bring it out that it is very degrading. Ask the inquirer if he appreciates that this is true of him, that he is the servant of sin, and then ask him if he does not want to be set free from this awful bondage.

There is another passage that one can use in much the same way, Rom. 6:16:

> "Know ye not, that to whom ye yield yourselves servants to obey, his servants ye are whom ye obey; whether of sin unto death, or of obedience unto righteousness?"

III. Show him the awfulness of unbelief in Jesus Christ.

Very few out of Christ realize that unbelief in Jesus Christ is anything very bad. Of course they know it is not just right, but that it is something awful and appalling, they do not dream for a moment. They should be shown that there is nothing more appalling than unbelief in Jesus Christ. A good passage for this purpose is Jno. 3:18, 19:

> "He that believeth on him is not condemned: but he that believeth not is condemned already, because he hath not believed in the name of the only begotten Son of God. And this is the condemnation, that light is come into the world, and men loved darkness rather than light, because their deeds were evil."

When the passage has been read, say, "Now this verse tells us of some one who is condemned already; who is it?" "He that believeth not." "Believeth not on whom?" "On Jesus." "How many that believe not on Jesus are condemned already?" "Every one." "Why is every one that believeth not on Jesus condemned already?" "Because he has not believed on the name of the only begotten Son of God." "Why is this such an awful thing in the sight of God?" "Because light is come into the world, and men loved darkness rather than light because their deeds are evil." "In whom did the light come into the world?" "In Jesus." "Jesus then, is the incarnation of light, God's fullest revelation to man: to reject Jesus then, is the deliberate rejection of what?" "Light." "The choice of what?" "Darkness." "In rejecting Jesus, what are you rejecting?" "Light." "And what are you choosing?" "Darkness rather than light." Ask all the questions that are necessary to impress this truth upon the mind of the unbeliever, that he is deliberately rejecting the light of God, and choosing darkness rather than light.

Another very useful passage for the same purpose is Acts 2:36, 37:

"Therefore let all the house of Israel know assuredly, that God hath made that same Jesus, whom ye have crucified, both Lord and Christ. Now when they heard this, they were pricked in their heart, and said unto Peter and to the rest of the apostles, Men and brethren, what shall we do?"

When the passage is read, say, "Now here were certain men under deep conviction of sin, crying out, 'Men and brethren, what shall we do?' What was the sin that they committed that produced such deep conviction?" "They had crucified Jesus." "What had God done with Jesus?" "He had made Him both Lord and Christ." "These men had rejected One whom God hath made both Lord and Christ. Is that a serious sin?" "Yes." "And are you not guilty of that very sin to-day? You are rejecting Jesus, and this Jesus whom you are rejecting, is the very one whom God hath made both Lord and Christ. Is it not an awful sin to deliberately reject one whom God hath thus exalted?"

Another good passage to use is John 16: 8, 9:

"And when he is come, he will reprove the world of sin, and of righteousness, and of judgment: of sin, because they believe not on me."

When the passage has been read, ask the one with whom you are dealing, "Of what sin is it, that the Holy Ghost who knows the mind of God, especially convicts men?" "Of the sin of unbelief." "What then, is the crowning sin in God's sight?" "Unbelief in Jesus Christ." "Why is unbelief in Jesus Christ the crowning sin in God's sight?" Then bring out that it is because it reveals most clearly the heart's deliberate choice of sin rather than righteousness, of darkness rather than light, of hatred to God rather than love to God.

In some cases it is well to use Heb. 10: 28, 29:

"He that despised Moses' law died without mercy under two or three witnesses: of how much sorer punishment, suppose ye, shall he be thought worthy, who hath trodden under foot the Son of God, and hath counted the blood of the covenant, wherewith he was sanctified, an unholy thing, and hath done despite unto the Spirit of grace?"

When the passage has been read, ask the inquirer, "How serious an offence was it in God's sight to despise Moses' law?" "The one who did it died without mercy." "Is there any offense more serious in God's sight than despising the law of Moses?" "Yes, treading under foot the Son of God."

"Does not every one who rejects Jesus Christ, practically tread under foot the Son of God, and count the blood of the covenant wherewith he was sanctified an unholy thing?" "Yes, I suppose he does." "Are you not committing this very sin?"

IV. Show him the awful consequences of unbelief.

For this purpose begin by using Heb 11:6, the first of the verse:

> "But without faith it is impossible to please him."

"Now this verse tells you that there is one thing that God absolutely requires if we are to please him: what is it?" "Faith." "And no matter what else we do, if we have not faith, what is impossible for us?" "To please him."

Follow this up by John 8:24:

> "I said therefore unto you, that ye shall die in your sins: for if ye believe not that I am he, ye shall die in your sins."

"What does this verse tell us will happen to you if you do not believe in Jesus?" "I shall die in my sins." Then have the inquirer read verse 21,

> "Then said Jesus again unto them, I go my way, and ye shall seek me, and shall die in your sins: whither I go, ye cannot come."

That will show the result of once dying in his sins.

Further follow this up by 2 Thess. 1:7-9:

> "And to you who are troubled rest with us, when the Lord Jesus shall be revealed from heaven with his mighty angels, in flaming fire taking vengeance on them that know not God, and that obey not the Gospel of our Lord Jesus Christ; who shall be punished with everlasting destruction from the presence of the Lord, and from the glory of his power."

Say to the inquirer, "This verse tells us of a coming day in which Jesus is to take vengeance upon a certain class of people, and they are to be punished with everlasting destruction from the presence of the Lord and the glory of His power. Who is it that are to be thus punished?" "They that know not God, and that obey not the Gospel of our Lord Jesus Christ." "Are you obeying the Gospel of the Lord Jesus Christ." "No." "If then, Christ should come now, what would be your destiny?" "I should be punished with everlasting destruction from the presence of the Lord, and the glory of His power."

Then turn to Rev. 21: 8. This verse needs no comment, it tells its own story:

"But the fearful, and unbelieving, and the abominable, and murderers, and whoremongers, and sorcerers, and idolaters, and all liars, shall have their part in the lake which burneth with fire and brimstone: which is the second death."

Rev. 20: 15 may also be used:

"And whosoever was not found written in the book of life was cast into the lake of fire."

V. Show him that all one has to do to be lost, is simply to neglect the salvation that is offered in Christ.

A verse which will serve for this purpose is Heb. 2: 3:

"How shall we escape, if we neglect so great salvation; which at the first began to be spoken by the Lord, and was confirmed unto us by them that heard him."

When the verse has been read, ask, "What does this verse tell us is all that is necessary to be done in order to be lost?" "Simply neglect the great salvation." "That is the very thing that you are doing to-day; you are already lost. God has provided salvation for you at great cost: all you need to do to be saved, is to accept the salvation, but you cannot be saved any other way; and all you need to do to be lost, is simply to neglect it. You do not need to plunge into desperate vices, you do not need to be an open and avowed infidel, you do not need to refuse even to accept salvation, if you simply neglect it, you will be lost forever. Will you not let the question of the text sink deep into your heart? 'How shall we escape if we neglect so great salvation?' "

Another passage to use for this purpose is Acts 3: 22, 23:

"For Moses truly said unto the fathers, A Prophet shall the Lord your God raise up unto you of your brethren, like unto me; him shall ye hear in all things whatsoever he shall say unto you. And it shall come to pass, that every soul, which will not hear that Prophet, shall be destroyed from among the people."

"This passage tells us about a Prophet that Moses said the Lord would raise up. Who was that Prophet?" "Jesus."

"What does God tell us to do with that Prophet?" "Hear him 'in all things whatsoever he shall say unto you.'" "What shall happen unto him who does not hearken unto the words of that Prophet?" "He shall be destroyed from among the people." "Are you hearkening unto the words of that Prophet?"

Still another passage to use is Acts 13: 38-41:

> "Be it known unto you therefore, men and brethren, that through this man is preached unto you the forgiveness of sins: and by him all that believe are justified from all things, from which ye could not be justified by the law of Moses.
>
> "Beware therefore, lest that come upon you, which is spoken of in the prophets; Behold, ye despisers, and wonder, and perish: for I work a work in your days, a work which ye shall in no wise believe, though a man declare it unto you."

"These verses tell us about Jesus. They tell us of something that is preached to us through Him. What is it?" "Forgiveness of sins." "They tell us what it is that a man has to do to obtain this forgiveness of sins, what is it?" "Believe on Him." "What blessing comes to all that believe?" "They are justified from all things." "On the other hand, what comes to us if we neglect to believe?" "We shall perish."

Still another passage to use for this purpose is Jno. 3: 36:

> "He that believeth on the Son hath everlasting life: and he that believeth not the Son shall shall not see life; but the wrath of God abideth on him."

When the passage has been read, ask, "What does everyone who believes on the Son get?" "Everlasting life." "But on the other hand, if one simply neglects to believe what will be the result?" "He shall not sec life, but the wrath of God abideth upon him."

VI. Show him the wonderful love of God to him.

Oftentimes when every other method of dealing with the careless fails, a realization of the love of God breaks the heart, and leads to an acceptance of Christ. There is no better passage to show the love of God than Jno. 3: 16:

> "For God so loved the world, that he gave his only begotten Son, that whosoever believeth in him should not perish, but have everlasting life."

Generally it will need no comment. I was once dealing with one of the most careless and vile women I ever met. She moved in good society, but in her secret life was vile as a woman of the street. She told me the story of her life in a most shameless and unblushing way, half-laughing as she did it. I made no further reply than to ask her to read Jno. 3:16 to which I had opened my Bible. Before she had read the passage through, she burst into tears, her heart broken by the love of God to her.

Another excellent passage to use in the same way is Is. 53:5:

> "But he was wounded for our transgressions, he was bruised for our iniquities; the chastisement of our peace was upon him; and with his stripes we are healed."

God used this passage one night to bring to tears and penitence one of the most stubborn and wayward young women with whom I ever dealt. I made almost no comment, simply read the passage to her. The Spirit of God seemed to hold up before her, her Saviour, wounded for her transgressions, and bruised for her iniquities. Her stubborn will gave way, and before many days she was rejoicing in Christ.

Two other passages which can be used in the same way, are, Gal. 3:13 and 1 Pet. 2:24:

> "Christ hath redeemed us from the curse of the law, being made a curse for us: for it is written, Cursed is every one that hangeth on a tree;"
>
> "Who his own self bare our sins in his own body on the tree, that we, being dead to sins, should live unto righteousness: by whose stripes ye were healed."

After showing the love of God through the use of such passages as these mentioned, it is oftentimes well to clinch this truth by using Rom. 2:4, 5:

> "Or despisest thou the riches of his goodness and forbearance and long suffering; not knowing that the goodness of God leadeth thee to repentance? But after thy hardness and impenitent heart treasurest up unto thyself wrath against the day of wrath and revelation of the righteous judgment of God."

Before having the passage read, say, "Now we have been looking at the love of God to you, let us see what God tells us is the purpose of that love, and what will be the result of our despising it." Then have the passage, Rom. 2:4, 5 read by the one with whom you are dealing. When he has read it, ask him what is the purpose of God's goodness. "To lead to repentance." "If it does not lead us to repentance, what does it show us about our hearts?" "That they are very hard and impenitent." "And if we refuse to let the goodness of God lead us to repentance, what will be the result?" "We treasure up wrath unto ourselves against the day of wrath and revelation of the righteous judgment of God."

Of course it will not always be possible to get a person who has little or no concern about his salvation to talk with you long enough to go over all these passages, but not infrequently they will become so interested after the use of the first or second passage, that they will be glad to go through. Oftentimes it is not at all necessary to use all these passages. Not infrequently I find that the first passage, Matt. 22:37, 38, does the desired work, but it is well to be thorough, and to use all the passages necessary.

Sometimes one will not talk with you for any length of time at all. In such a case, the best thing to do is to select a very pointed and searching passage and give it to them, repeating it again and again, and then as they go, say to them something like this, "I am going to ask God to burn that passage into your heart;" and then do not forget to do what you said you were going to do. Good passages for this purpose are Rom. 6:23; Mark 16:16; Jno. 3:36; Is. 57:21.

When the inquirer has been led by the use of any or all of these passages to realize his need of a Saviour, and really desires to be saved, of course he comes under the class treated in the preceding chapter, and should be dealt with accordingly. It is not intended that the worker shall follow the precise method laid down here, it is given rather by way of suggestion, but the general plan here outlined, has been honored of God to the salvation of very many. But let us be sure, whether we use this method or some other, to do thorough-going and lasting work.

Of course it is not supposed that the inquirer will always answer you exactly as stated above. If he does not, make use of the answers that he does give, or if necessary ask the same question another way until he does answer you correctly. The answers given to the questions are found in the text, but people have a great habit of not seeing what is plainly stated in a Scripture text. Oftentimes when they do not answer right, it is well to ask them to look at the verse again, and repeat the question, and keep asking questions until they do give the right answer. Perhaps the inquirer will try to switch you off on to some side-track. Do not permit him to do this, but hold right to the matter in hand.

CHAPTER VII

HOW TO DEAL WITH THOSE WHO HAVE DIFFICULTIES

We will find that a very large number of the persons whom we try to lead to Christ are really anxious to be saved, and know how, but are confronted with difficulties which they deem important or even insurmountable. Whenever it is possible, it is well to show such persons their need of Christ before taking up a specific difficulty. In this way many of the supposed difficulties are dissipated. Oftentimes even when people really are anxious to be saved, there is not that deep, clear, and intelligent knowledge of their need of Christ that is desirable. It is usually a waste of time to take up specific difficulties until there is this clear and definite sense of need.

I. "I am too great a sinner."

This is a difficulty that is very real, and very often met, but fortunately it is also one with which it is very easy to deal. The method of treatment is as follows:

1. *General treatment:*

There is no better passage to use to meet this difficulty than 1 Tim. 1: 15:

> "This is a faithful saying, and worthy of all acceptation, that Christ Jesus came into the world *to save sinners; of whom I am chief.*"

This verse so exactly fits the case, that there is little need for comment. At the close of a Sunday morning service, I spoke to a man of intelligence and ability, but who had gone down into the deepest depth of sin. When asked why he was not a Christian, he replied, "I am too great a sinner to be saved." I turned him at once to 1 Tim. 1: 15. No sooner had I read the verse than he replied, "Well, I am the chief of sinners." "That verse means you, then." He replied, "It is a precious promise." I said, "Will you accept it now?" "I will." Then I said, "Let us kneel down and tell God so." We knelt down and he confessed to God his sins, and asked God for Christ's sake to forgive him. When he had finished his prayer, I asked him if he really had accepted Christ, and he said that he had. I asked him if he really believed that he was accepted, and he said he did. He took the first opportunity afforded him of confessing Christ, and became an active Christian. His broken home was restored, and every day he was found witnessing for his Master.

Another useful passage in dealing with this class is Matt. 9: 12, 13:

> "But when Jesus heard that, he said unto them, They that be whole need not a physician, but they that are sick. But go ye and learn what that meaneth, I will have mercy, and not sacrifice: for I am not come to call the righteous, but sinners to repentance."

This shows the inquirer at once that his sin, instead of being an obstacle in the way of his coming to Christ, really fits him for coming to Christ, as He has not come to call the righteous, but sinners to repentance.

I have frequently used Rom. 5: 6-8:

> "For when we were yet without strength, in due time Christ died for the ungodly. For scarcely for a righteous man will one die: yet peradventure for a good man some would even dare to die. But God commendeth his love towards us, in that, while we were yet sinners, Christ died for us."

At the close of an evening service in Minneapolis, a man who had raised his hand for prayer, hurried away as soon as the benediction was pronounced. I hastened after him, laid my hand upon his shoulder, and said, "Did you not hold your hand up to-night for prayer?" "Yes." "Why then are you hurrying away?" He replied, "There is no use talking to me." I said, "God loves you." He replied, "You do not know whom you are talking to." "I do not care whom I am talking to, but I know God loves you." He said, "I am the meanest thief in Minneapolis." "Then I know God loves you;" and I opened my Bible to Rom. 5: 6-8 and read the passage through. "Now," I said, "if you are the meanest thief in Minneapolis, you are a sinner, and this verse tells us that God loves sinners." The Spirit of God carried the message of love home to his heart, he broke down, and going with me into another room, he told me the story of his life. He had been released from confinement that day, and had started out that night to commit what he said would have been one of the most daring burglaries ever committed in Minneapolis. With his two companions in crime, he was passing a corner where we were holding an open-air meeting. He stopped a few moments to hear what was going on, and in spite of the oaths and protests of his companions, stayed through the meeting, and went with us into the mission. It so happened that a few days before he had dreamed in confinement of his mother, and the hearing of the Gospel added to this, and the few words that had been spoken to him personally, had completed the work. After he had told me his story, we knelt in prayer. Utterly overcome with emotion, through falling tears he looked to God for pardon, and left the room rejoicing in the assurance that his sins had all been forgiven.

It is often well to say to the man who thinks that he is too great a sinner, "Your sins are great, greater far than you think, but they are all settled." In order to show him how they are settled, and to make it clear that they are settled turn to Is. 53:6:

2. *Special cases:*

Among those who regard themselves as too great sinners to be saved, there are special cases:

(1) *The man who says, "I am lost."*

If the difficulty is stated in this way, it is well to use Luke 19:10, as that fits so exactly the inquirer's statement of the case; for the verse says:

"For the Son of man is come to seek and to save *that which was lost.*"

I was once speaking to a young man who was the complete slave of drink and other sins, and urging him to accept the Saviour. He turned to me in a despairing way and said, "Mr. Torrey go talk to those other men, there is no use talking to me, I am lost." I replied, "If you are lost, I have a message from God's Word addressed directly to you." I turned to Luke 19:10 and read, "For the Son of man is come to seek and to save that which was lost." The text fitted the case so exactly, that there was no need of comment or explanation on my part.

(2) *Murderers.*

Among those who think that they are too great sinners to be saved, murderers form an especial class. I find that not a few who have stained their hands with the blood of a fellow-man have a deep-seated impression that there is no hope for a man who has committed this sin. Is. 1: 18 is very useful in such a case. One night I was dealing with a man who was sure that he was beyond all hope. I asked him why he thought so, and he replied, because he had taken the life of a fellow-man. I said, "Let me read you something from God's Word, and I read:

> "Come now, and let us reason together, saith the Lord: though your sins be as scarlet, they shall be as white as snow; though they be red like crimson, they shall be as wool."

I said, "If you have taken the life of a fellow-man, your sins are as scarlet." "Oh," he cried, "the bullet was scarlet, I can see it now." Then I asked him to listen again to the promise, "Though your sins be as scarlet, they shall be as white as snow; though they be red like crimson, they shall be as wool." He saw how the promise exactly covered his case, and it brought hope into a heart that had been filled with despair.

Another useful passage is Ps. 51: 14:

> "Deliver me from bloodguiltiness, O God, thou God of my salvation."

In using this passage, I always call the inquirer's attention to the fact that it is the prayer of a man who had himself stained his hands with the blood of a fellow-man. Then I tell him how God heard the prayer, and delivered him from blood guiltiness, and then turn to Ps. 32: 5 containing the Psalmist's own statement as to how his sin of bloodguiltiness was forgiven.

> "I acknowledged my sin unto thee, and mine iniquity have I not hid. I said, I will confess my transgressions unto the Lord; and thou forgavest the iniquity of my sin."

3. *General Remarks:*

(1) *Never give false comfort by telling the inquirer, "You are not a very great sinner."* This mistake is often made.

Tender hearted people are greatly disturbed over the deep conviction of sin that the Spirit of God produces in the hearts of men, and try to give comfort by telling the inquirer that he is not so great a sinner after all. This is false comfort. There is no man but who is a greater sinner than he ever thinks or realizes.

(2) After meeting the specific difficulty, show the inquirer how to be saved. The method of doing this is explained in Chapter V. This remark applies not only to this difficulty, but to all the difficulties that follow. It is not enough to remove difficulties, we must bring inquirers to a saving knowledge of Christ.

II. "My heart is too hard."

One of the passages given under the former difficulty will also be useful here, Luke 19: 10. Before using it, it may be well to say, "Well then, if your heart is so hard and wicked, you must be lost." "Yes, I am lost." "Very well, I have a promise for you." Turn to Luke 19: 10 and let them read. "You said that your heart was so hard and wicked that you were lost." "Yes." "And this verse tells us that Jesus Christ is come to seek and to save, whom?" "The lost." "And that means you, will you let Him save you now?"

Another useful passage is John 6: 37, the last half of the verse,

"Him that cometh to me I will in no wise cast out."

You can say, "You think your heart is so hard and wicked that you cannot be saved, but would you be willing to come to Christ if He would accept you?" "Yes." "Well, let us listen to what He says." Then read the passage, "Him that cometh to me I will in no wise cast out." "Whom does Jesus say here that He will receive?" "Any one who comes." "Does He say He will receive any one who comes provided their heart is not too hard and wicked?" "No." "What does He say?" "That He will receive any one who comes." "Then He will receive any one who comes no matter how hard and wicked their heart?" "Yes." "Will you come now?"

Ez. 36: 26, 27 is helpful in many cases. You can say to the inquirer, "Yes, your heart is too hard and wicked, but let us see what God promises to do." Then have them read the passage:

"A new heart also will I give you, and a new spirit will I put within you: and I will take away the stony heart out of your flesh, and I will give you an heart of flesh. And I will put my Spirit within you, and cause you to walk in my statutes, and ye shall keep my judgments, and do them."

"What does God here promise to give?" "A new heart." "Are you willing that He should give you a new heart in place of that hard and wicked heart that you have?"

Another passage which is helpful in much the same way is 2 Cor. 5: 17:

"Therefore if any man be in Christ, he is a new creature: old things are passed away; behold, all things are become new."

"Yes," you can say to the one in trouble, "your heart is too hard and wicked, what you need is to be made all over new; there is a way to be made all over, to get a new heart and to be a new man. Let me show you what that way is." Then let them read the passage. When they have read it, ask them, "What does the one who accepts Christ become?" "A new creature." "What becomes of the old things?" "They are passed away." "Do you want to be a new creature, and have old things pass away?" "Yes." "What then is all that you have to do?" "Accept Christ." "Will you do it?"

III. "I must become better before I become a Christian."

This is a very real difficulty with many people. They sincerely believe that they cannot come to Christ just as they are in their sins, that they must do something to make themselves better before they can come to Him. You can show them that they are utterly mistaken in this by having them read Matt. 9: 12, 13:

"But when Jesus heard that, he said unto them, They that be whole need not a physician, but they that are sick. But go ye and learn what that meaneth, I will have mercy and not sacrifice: for I am not come to call the righteous, but sinners to repentance."

When they have read it, if they do not see the point for themselves, you can ask, "To what does Jesus compare Himself in this verse?" "To a physician." "Who is it need a physician, well people or sick people?" "Sick people." "Ought a person who is sick to wait until he gets well before he gets to the doctor?" "No, of course, not." "Ought a person who is spiritually sick to wait until he is better before he comes to Jesus?" "No." "Who is it Jesus invites to come to Himself, good people or bad people?" "Bad people." "Is then the fact that you are not good a reason for waiting or a reason for coming to Jesus at once?"

Luke 15:18-24 also fits the case exactly. Show the inquirer that we have in this story a picture of God's relation to the sinner, and God wishes us to understand that He would have the sinner come in all his rags, and that He will give him a hearty welcome, a robe, a ring and a feast if he comes just as he is.

Luke 18:10-14 also applies. You can say, "Here are two men who came to God. One came on the ground that he was a sinner, the other came on the ground that he was righteous. Which of the two did God accept?" "The one who came on the ground that he was a sinner." "Well, God would have you come just the same way."

IV. "I cannot hold out," (or "I am afraid I shall fail if I try").

1. *General treatment.*

First see if the inquirer is in dead earnest, and if there is not some other difficulty lying back of this. Many a man gives this as a difficulty, when perhaps it is not the real one.

There is perhaps no better verse in the Bible for this difficulty than Jude 24:

> "Now unto him that is *able to keep you from falling*, and to present you faultless before the presence of his glory with exceeding joy."

Its application is so plain as to need no comment.

Another useful passage is 1 Pet. 1:5:

> "Who are *kept by the power of God* through faith unto salvation ready to be revealed in the last time."

When the inquirer has read it, ask him by whose power it is that we are kept. Then you can say, "It is not then a question of our strength at all, but of God's strength. Do you think that God is able to keep you?"

Other passages which are helpful along the same line are:

"For the which cause I also suffer these things: nevertheless I am not ashamed: for I know whom I have believed, and am persuaded that *he is able to keep* that which I have committed unto him against that day." 2 Tim. 1: 12.

"Fear thou not; for I am with thee: be not dismayed; for I am thy God: I will strengthen thee; yea, I will help thee; yea, I will uphold thee with the right hand of my righteousness." Is. 41: 10.

"For I the Lord thy God will hold thy right hand, saying unto thee, Fear not; I will help thee." Is. 41: 13.

A passage which will help by showing the absolute security of Christ's sheep, is Jno. 10: 28, 29:

"And I give unto them eternal life; and they shall never perish, neither shall any man pluck them out of my hand. My Father, which gave them me, is greater than all; and no man is able to pluck them out of my Father's hand."

In many cases a good passage to use is Heb. 7: 25:

"Wherefore he is able also to save them to the uttermost that come unto God by him, seeing he ever liveth to make intercession for them."

2. *Special cases.*

(1) *Those afraid of some temptation that will prove too strong.*

The best passage to use in such a case is 1 Cor. 10: 13:

"There hath no temptation taken you but such as is common to man; but God is faithful, who will not suffer you to be tempted above that ye are able; but will with the temptation also make a way to escape, that ye may be able to bear it."

(2) *Those who dwell upon their own weakness.*

"And he said unto me, My grace is sufficient for thee; for *my strength is made perfect in weakness.* Most gladly therefore will I rather glory in my infirmities, that the power of Christ may rest upon me." 2 Cor. 12: 9, 10.

"He giveth power to the faint; and to them that have no might he increaseth strength. Even the youths shall faint and be weary, and the young men shall utterly fall: but they that wait upon the Lord shall renew their strength; they shall mount up with wings as eagles; they shall run, and not be weary; and they shall walk, and not faint." Is. 40: 29-31.

One evening a lady called me to a man whom she was trying to lead to Christ and asked me if I could help him. I said to him, "What is your difficulty?" He replied, "I have no strength." "Ah," I said, "I have a message that exactly fits your case," and read Is. 40: 29, "He giveth power to the faint, and to them that have no might he increaseth strength." "You say you have no strength, that is no might; now this verse tells us that to those who have no might, that is to people just like you, God increaseth strength." The Holy Spirit took the word of comfort home to his heart at once, and he put his trust in Jesus Christ then and there.

V. "I cannot give up my evil ways."

1. *You must or perish.*

In order to prove this statement, use:

"For the wages of sin is death; but the gift of God is eternal life through Jesus Christ our Lord." Rom. 6: 23.

"Be not deceived; God is not mocked: for whatsoever a man soweth, that shall he also reap. For he that soweth to his flesh shall of the flesh reap corruption; but he that soweth to the Spirit shall of the Spirit reap life everlasting." Gal. 6: 7, 8.

"But the fearful, and unbelieving, and the abominable, and murderers, and whoremongers, and sorcerers, and idolaters, and all liars, shall have their part in the lake which burneth with fire and brimstone: which is the second death." Rev. 21: 8.

Drive this thought home. Show the inquirer no quarter, but keep ringing the changes on the thought, "You must give up your evil ways or perish." Emphasize it by Scripture. When the inquirer sees and realizes this, then you can pass on to the next thought.

2. *You can in the strength of Jesus Christ.*

To prove this, have the inquirer read Phil. 4: 13, and Jno. 8: 36:

"I can do all things through Christ which strengtheneth me."

"If the Son therefore shall make you free, ye shall be free indeed."

3. *Show the risen Christ with all power in heaven and on earth.*

It is in the power of the risen Christ, and through union with Him, that we are enabled to give up our evil ways, so the one who has this difficulty should have the fact that Christ is risen made clear to him. The following passages will serve well for this purpose.

"Moreover, brethren, I declare unto you the Gospel which I preached unto you, which also ye have received, and wherein ye stand; by which also ye are saved, if ye keep in memory what I preached unto you, unless ye have believed in vain. For I delivered unto you first of all that which I also received, how that Christ died for our sins according to the Scriptures; and that he was buried, and that he rose again the third day according to the Scriptures." 1 Cor. 15: 1-4.

"And Jesus came and spake unto them, saying, All power is given unto me in heaven and in earth." Matt. 28: 18.

"Wherefore he is able also to save them to the uttermost that come unto God by him, seeing he ever liveth to make intercession for them." Heb. 7: 25.

4. *Show how to get victory over sin.*

There is perhaps nothing in the Bible that makes the way of victory over sin more plain and simple than Rom. 6: 12-14:

"Let not sin therefore reign in your mortal body, that ye should obey it in the lusts thereof. Neither yield ye your members as instruments of unrighteousness unto sin: but *yield yourselves unto God*, as those that are alive from the dead, and your members as instruments of righteousness unto God. For sin shall not have dominion over you: for ye are not under the law, but under grace."

You can say to the inquirer, "In this verse we are told how to get victory over sin: we are told what not to do, and what to do. What is it we are told not to do?" "Not to let sin reign in our mortal body; not to yield our members as instruments of unrighteousness unto sin." "What are we told to do?" "To yield ourselves unto God as those that are alive from the dead; and to yield our members as instruments of righteousness unto God." "Now do you believe that through union with the risen Christ your Saviour, you are alive from the dead? Will you yield or present yourself unto God as one alive from the dead? Will you now and here present your members as instruments of righteousness unto God?" After the inquirer has been led to do this, show him that whatever we yield to God, God accepts, and that he can now TRUST God for victory over sin, and have deliverance from his evil ways.

VI. "I have tried before and failed."

Those who have tried to be Christians and have failed in the attempt, very naturally hesitate about trying again, and such a case needs to be dealt with, with great care, wisdom and thoroughness.

1. The first thing to do is to say to such a one, "*I can show you how to try and not fail.*" Then point him to 2 Cor. 4: 8:

"And God is able to make all grace abound toward you; that ye, always having all sufficiency in all things, may abound to every good work."

When the person has read the verse, to be sure that he gets its meaning you can say, "This verse tells us that God is able to make all grace abound toward us, that we, 'always having all sufficiency in all things, may abound to every good work.' It is clear then, that there is a way to try and not fail."

2. *Find out the cause of failure.*

In finding out the cause of failure, there are seven points to be looked into:

(1) *Did you put all your trust for pardon in the finished work of Christ?* This is a very frequent cause of failure in the attempt to be a Christian, the person has never been led to see clearly the ground of his salvation, and to trust wholly in the finished work of Christ for pardon. Is. 53:6 is a useful passage at this point:

"All we like sheep have gone astray; we have turned every one to his own way; and the Lord hath laid on him the iniquity of us all."

(2) *Did you surrender absolutely to God?* Many are led to make a profession of faith in Christ without having been led to absolute surrender and the Christian life thus begun, is very likely to prove a failure. The passage to use at this point is Acts 5:32:

"And we are his witnesses of these things; and so is also the Holy Ghost, whom God hath given to them that obey him."

(3) *Did you confess Christ openly before men?* This is one of the most frequent causes of failure. I have talked with very many who have said that they have tried to be Christians and failed, and a very large proportion of them I have found failed at this very point, the lack of a constant, open confession of Christ. Good passages to use at this point are Matt. 10:32, 33 and Rom. 10:10:

"Whosoever therefore shall confess me before men, him will I confess also before my Father which is in heaven. But whosoever shall deny me before men, him will I also deny before my Father which is in heaven."

"For with the heart man believeth unto righteousness; and with the mouth confession is made unto salvation."

(4) *Did you study the Word of God daily?* Here is another frequent cause of failure, neglect of the Bible. Very few of those who have really begun the Christian life, and who have made a practice of daily study of the Word, fail in their attempt to be Christians Good passages to use at this point are 1 Pet. 2: 2 and Ps. 119: 11:

"As newborn babes, desire the sincere milk of the Word, that ye may grow thereby."

"Thy Word have I hid in mine heart that I might not sin against thee."

(5) *Did you look each day to God alone, and not to self at all, for strength and victory?* To emphasize this question, use:

"He giveth power to the faint; and to them that have no might he increaseth strength." Is. 40: 29.

"And he said unto me, My grace is sufficient for thee; for my strength is made perfect in weakness. Most gladly therefore will I rather glory in my infirmities, that the power of Christ may rest upon me." 2 Cor. 12: 9.

"Likewise, ye younger, submit yourselves unto the elder. Yea, all of you be subject one to another, and be clothed with humility: for God resisteth the proud, and giveth grace to the humble." 1 Pet. 5: 5.

(6) *Did you pray constantly?* Use at this point:

"Pray without ceasing." 1 Thess. 5: 17.

"He giveth power to the faint; and, to them that have no might he increaseth strength. Even the youths shall faint and be weary, and the young men shall utterly fall: but *they that wait upon the Lord* shall renew their strength; they shall mount up with wings as eagles; they shall run, and not be weary; and they shall walk, and not faint." Is. 40: 29-31.

"Let us therefore come boldly unto the throne of grace, that we may obtain mercy, and find grace to help in time of need." Heb. 4:16.

(7) *Did you go to work for Christ?* Here use Matt. 25: 14-29.

VII. "The Christian life is too hard."

1. If a person states this as his difficulty, first show him that *the Christian life is not hard.* In Matt. 11: 30 Christ tells us His yoke is easy:

"For my yoke is easy, and my burden is light."

Prov. 3: 17 shows us that wisdom's ways are ways of pleasantness,

"Her ways are ways of pleasantness, and all her paths are peace."

1 Jno. 5: 3, that God's commandments are not grievous:

"For this is the love of God, that we keep his commandments: and his commandments are not grievous."

1 Pet. 1: 8 pictures the Christian life as a life of joy unspeakable and full of glory:

"Whom having not seen, ye love; in whom, though now ye see him not, yet believing, ye rejoice with joy unspeakable and full of glory."

In using the latter passage you might say, "We have a picture of the Christian life in 1 Pet. 1: 8, let us see if it is a hard life." Have the inquirer read the verse, and then ask, "What kind of a life according to this passage, is the Christian life?" 'A life of joy unspeakable and full of glory." "Do you think that is hard?"

2. Show him that *the way of sin is hard.*

Show the inquirer that it is not the Christian life, but the life without Christ that is the hard life. For this purpose use the last half of Prov. 13: 15, and Is. 57: 21:

"But the way of transgressors is hard."

"There is no peace, saith my God, to the wicked."

VIII. "There is too much to give up."

This is often the difficulty even when not stated.

1. First show the inquirer, that *no matter how much there may be to give up, it is better to give up anything than to lose one's soul.*

For this purpose use Mark 8: 36:

"For what shall it profit a man, if he shall gain the whole world, and lose his own soul?"

2. Show the inquirer that *the only things we have to give up are the things which will harm us.*

This is made clear by Ps. 84: 11:

"For the Lord God is a sun and shield; the Lord will give grace and glory; *no good thing will he withhold* from them that walk uprightly."

When the inquirer has read the verse, ask him, "What does this verse tell us that God will not withhold from us?" "Any good thing." "The things then that God asks you to give up, are what kind of things?" "Evil things." "Then all God asks you to give up are the things which are harmful to you. Do you wish to keep them?"

I have found Rom. 8:32 very effective, for it emphasizes the thought that if God loved us enough to give His Son to die for us on the Cross, He will freely give us all things:

> "He that spared not his own Son, but delivered him up for us all, how shall he not with him also freely give us all things?"

I once had a long conversation with a young woman who was having a great struggle about accepting Christ. She was very fond of the world and certain forms of amusement, which she felt she would have to give up if she became a Christian. Finally I said to her, "Do you think God loves you?" "Yes, I know He does." "How much does God love you?" "Enough to give His Son to die for me," she replied. "Do you think if God loved you enough to give His Son to die for you, He will ask you to give up anything that is for your good to keep?" "No, certainly He will not." "Do you wish to keep anything not for your good to keep?" "No." "Then do you not think you had better accept Jesus Christ right here and now?" "Yes," and she did.

Another verse which is useful as showing the inquirer that the things which he has to give up are the things which are passing away, is 1 Jno. 2:15-17:

> "Love not the world, neither the things that are in the world. If any man love the world, the love of the Father is not in him. For all that is in the world, the lust of the flesh, and the lust of the eyes, and the pride of life, is not of the Father, but is of the world. And *the world passeth away*, and the lust thereof: but he that doeth the will of God abideth for ever."

3. **Show the inquirer that *what we give up is nothing to what we get.***

For this purpose use Phil. 3:7, 8:

> "But what things were gain to me, those I counted loss for Christ. Yea doubtless, and I count all things but loss for the excellency of the knowledge of Christ Jesus my Lord; for whom I have suffered the loss of all things, and do count them but dung, that I may win Christ."

You can call the inquirer's attention to the fact that it was Paul who spoke these words, that perhaps no one ever gave up more for Christ than he did, and yet he here tells us that what he gave up was to what he got only as the refuse of the street.

4. Show the inquirer that *if he rejects Christ for fear of what he will have to give up if he accepts Him, he will make a terrible mistake.*

Then you can say to him, "The Bible pictures to us a man who made this very mistake. Will you read the story of his folly and its consequences?" Then turn to Luke 12: 16-21 and let the inquirer read it. When he has read it, ask him if he is willing to follow in the footsteps of the man in the passage.

IX. **"I cannot be a Christian in my business."** (or "It will hurt my business," or "I will lose my position.")

This is a very real difficulty with many, and must be met honestly and squarely.

1. It is well to bear in mind that even when a man really thinks this is true, it is not always so. Many people have an idea that it is impossible to be a Christian in any line of business except Christian work. They must be shown that this is a mistake. When a man makes this excuse, it is often well to ask him what his business is, and why he cannot be a Christian in it. Sometimes you will find that it is a business in which there are many Christians, and you can tell him that there are many Christians in the same business.

2. But oftentimes it is true that the man with whom you are dealing is in a business in which it is impossible to be a Christian, for example, the man may be a bartender or a theatrical manager or something of that sort. In that case say to the man, "You had better lose your business (or position) than to lose your soul." To drive this statement home, use Mark 8: 36:

> "For what shall it profit a man, if he shall gain the whole world, and lose his own soul?"

Do not pass on to the next point until the man sees this and realizes it. Make the man feel that he better lose every dollar that he has in the world than to lose his soul. When the man sees this, and is ready to give up his business at any cost, you can use Matt. 6: 33:

"But seek ye first the kingdom of God, and his righteousness; and all these things shall be added unto you."

This verse will show him that if he puts God and His kingdom first, all needful things will be supplied to him. It is better to starve than to reject Christ, but no man who accepts Christ will be left to starve.

Another very useful passage is Mark 10: 29, 30:

"And Jesus answered and said, Verily I say unto you, There is no man that hath left house, or brethren, or sisters, or father, or mother, or wife, or children, or lands, for my sake, and the Gospel's, but he shall receive an hundred fold now in this time, houses, and brethren, and sisters, and mothers, and children, and lands, with persecutions; and in the world to come eternal life."

X. "I will lose my friends."

Many a person who contemplates beginning the Christian life has none but ungodly companions, and he sees very clearly that if he becomes a Christian he will lose these friends, the only ones that he has; so this difficulty is a very real one.

1. First show the inquirer that he is better off without these friends, for they are enemies of God. Use for this purpose James 4: 4:

"Ye adulterers and adulteresses, know ye not that the friendship of the world is enmity with God? whosoever therefore will be a friend of the world is the enemy of God."

Before giving it to the inquirer to read, say, "Yes, it may be that you will lose your friends, but if your friends are godless, you are better off without them, see what God's Word says about it." Then show them the passage. If this verse does not prove sufficiently effective, follow it up with Prov. 13: 20:

"He that walketh with wise men shall be wise: but a companion of fools shall be destroyed."

Follow this up with Ps. 1: 1, 2:

"Blessed is the man that walketh not in the counsel of the ungodly, nor standeth in the way of sinners, nor sitteth in the seat of the scornful. But his delight is in the law of the Lord; and in his law doth he meditate day and night."

Call the inquirer's attention to the fact that God has promised an especial blessing to those who turn their backs upon godless friendships in order to obey Him.

2. Having made this first point clear, you can say, "You may lose your godless friends, but you will get better friends," and turn them to 1 John 1:3:

"That which we have seen and heard declare we unto you, that ye also may have fellowship with us; and truly our fellowship is with the Father, and with his Son Jesus Christ."

When they have read it you can say, "If you do lose your godless friends by coming to Christ, what two new friends do you get?" "The Father and His Son Jesus Christ." "Which would you rather have for friends, your godless worldly companions, or God the Father and His Son Jesus Christ?" All this may be followed up again by Mark 10: 29, 30.

XI. "I am afraid of ridicule."

1. Show the awful peril in being governed by the fear of man. Use Prov. 29: 25:

"The fear of man bringeth a snare; but whoso putteth his trust in the Lord shall be safe."

You might explain that this snare into which the one who is afraid of ridicule and rejects Christ falls, often results in the eternal ruin of the soul.

Next use Mark 8: 38:

"Whosoever therefore shall be ashamed of me and of my words in this adulterous and sinful generation, of him also shall the Son of man be ashamed, when he cometh in the glory of his Father with the holy angels."

2. Show that it is a glorious privilege to be ridiculed for Christ. Use for this purpose Matt. 5: 11, 12:

"Blessed are ye, when men shall revile you, and persecute you, and shall say all manner of evil against you falsely, for my sake. Rejoice, and be exceeding glad; for great is your reward in heaven: for so persecuted they the prophets which were before you."

XII. "I will be persecuted if I become a Christian."

Never tell any one that he will not be persecuted. On the contrary say, "Yes, I presume you will be persecuted, for God tells us in His Word, that all who live godly in Christ Jesus shall suffer persecution." To prove it show him 2 Tim. 3: 12.

"Yea, and all that will live godly in Christ Jesus shall suffer persecution."

But then tell him that it is a great privilege to be persecuted for Christ's sake, and brings an abundant reward. Have him read Matt. 5: 10-12, and drive home the thought that we ought to rejoice at the privilege of being persecuted rather than to shrink from being a Christian on that account.

Then show him the result of suffering with Christ. Turn to 2 Tim. 2: 12:

"If we suffer, we shall also reign with him; if we deny him, he also will deny us."

Use Rom, 8: 18 to show him how small are the sufferings of this present time in comparison with the glory that we shall obtain through them:

"For I reckon that the sufferings of this present time are not worthy to be compared with the glory which shall be revealed in us." (Comp. 2 Cor. 4: 17.)

Acts 5: 40, 41 is useful as showing how the early church regarded persecution, rejoicing in it rather than shrinking from it:

"And to him they agreed: and when they had called the apostles, and beaten them, they commanded that they should not speak in the name of Jesus, and let them go. And they departed from the presence of the council, rejoicing that they were counted worthy to suffer shame for his name."

Another passage which is also useful in such a case is 1 Pet. 2: 20, 21:

"For what glory is it, if, when ye be buffeted for your faults, ye shall take it patiently? but if, when ye do well, and suffer for it, ye take it patiently, this is acceptable with God. For even hereunto were ye called; because Christ also suffered for us, leaving us an example, that ye should follow his steps."

XIII. "I have no feeling."

This is a very common difficulty. There are many who wish to come to Christ, but do not think they can come because they have not the proper feeling. The first thing to do in such a case, it to find out what feeling the inquirer thinks it is necessary to have in order to become a Christian.

1. "*The joy and peace that Christians tell about.*

The feeling that many inquirers are waiting for is the joy and peace that Christians speak of. Of course the thing to do in such a case, is to show the inquirer that this joy and peace is the result of coming to Christ, and that we cannot expect the result before we come. The first passage to use to show this is Gal. 5:22:

"But the fruit of the Spirit is love, joy, peace, long suffering, gentleness, goodness, faith."

This shows that joy and peace are the fruit of the Spirit, and we cannot expect to have the fruit of the Spirit until we have received the Spirit, and we cannot receive the Spirit until we have accepted Christ. This is brought out very clearly in Eph. 1:13:

"In whom ye also trusted, after that ye heard the word of truth, the gospel of your salvation: in whom also, *after that ye believed*, ye were sealed with that Holy Spirit of promise."

Emphasize the point that it is *after* we believe that we are sealed with the Holy Spirit of promise.

Use also Acts 5:32:

"And we are his witnesses of these things; and so is also the Holy Ghost, whom God hath given *to them that obey him.*"

This will show that the Holy Spirit is given to those who obey Christ, and we cannot expect to receive the Holy Spirit until we have obeyed God by putting our trust in Jesus Christ and confessing Him openly before the world. A verse which will be useful in this connection as showing that it is after we confess Christ that He confesses us before the Father, is Matt. 10:32:

"Whosoever therefore shall confess me before men, him will I confess also before my Father which is in heaven."

And so we have no right to expect the sealing of the Holy Spirit until we have confessed Christ before men.

It is after we have believed that we rejoice with joy unspeakable and full of glory, 1 Pet. 1:8:

"Whom having not seen, ye love; in whom, though now ye see him not, yet believing, ye rejoice with joy unspeakable and full of glory."

Our duty is believing with the heart and confessing with the mouth, leaving the matter of feeling to God; Rom. 10:10:

"For with the heart man believeth unto righteousness; and with the mouth confession is made unto salvation."

2. "*Sorrow for sin.*"

The feeling that many are waiting for, is a feeling of sorrow for sin. If you find this to be the case with any individual with whom you are dealing, proceed as follows:

(1) Use the passages already given to produce conviction of sin. (See Chapter VI, Section I.)

(2) Show that it is not sorrow for sin, but turning away from sin and accepting Christ that God demands. For this purpose use the following passages:

"Let the wicked forsake his way, and the unrighteous man his thoughts: and let him return unto the Lord, and he will have mercy upon him; and to our God, for he will abundantly pardon." Is. 55:7.

"But as many as received him, to them gave he power to become the sons of God, even to them that believe on his name." John 1:12.

"And they said, Believe on the Lord Jesus Christ, and thou shalt be saved, and thy house." Acts 16:31.

"Then Peter said unto them, Repent, and be baptized every one of you in the name of Jesus Christ for the remission of sins, and ye shall receive the gift of the Holy Ghost." Acts 2:38.

XIX. "I have been seeking Christ but cannot find Him."

1. It is well oftentimes to say to one who raises this difficulty "I can tell you just when you will find Christ." This will probably awaken surprise, but insist, "Yes, I can tell you just when you will find Christ. If you will turn to Jeremiah 29:13, you will find the exact time when you will find Christ." Then let him read:

"And ye shall seek me, and find me, *when ye shall search for me with all your heart.*"

"Now this verse tells the time when you will find Christ, when is it?" "When ye shall search for me with all your heart." "The fact is, up to this time, you have not been seeking for Him with all your heart. Are you ready to let go of everything else and seek Him to-day with all your heart?" This passage has been used in a great many cases to lead out one who has been seeking Christ for years, into a real acceptance of Him.

2. It is well sometimes to say to one who raises **this**

difficulty, "Then you are seeking Christ? Well, did you know that Christ also is seeking you?" Then turn to Luke 19: 10 (or Luke 15: 3-10) and read. "Now you say you are seeking Christ, and Christ says He is seeking you, how long ought it to take for you to find one another? Will you just come to Christ and trust Him here and now?"

3. Sometimes the best thing to do is to say, "Well, if you are earnestly seeking Christ, let me show you how to find Him." Then deal with the inquirer in the way described in Chapter V

XV. "Christians are so inconsistent."

This is one of the most common difficulties that we meet. Probably the best passage to use is Rom. 14: 12:

> "So then every one of us shall give account of himself to God."

When a person raises this difficulty, you can say, "So you are troubled about the sins of Christians; let me show you from God's own Word what He says about that." Then have him read the passage. When he has read the passage, ask, "Who does God say you will have to give an account of?" "Myself." "Not of inconsistent Christians then?" "No." "Are you ready to give an account of yourself to God?" The mere reading of this verse without comment, has led many who have been dwelling upon the inconsistency of others, to see themselves lost and undone before God, and to turn and accept Christ right there.

Another useful passage is Rom. 2: 1-5. Hand it to the inquirer and ask him to read it carefully. When he has read it, ask him if this passage does not describe him, if he is not judging others for doing the very things he does himself. Then ask him what God says about those who judge others for what they are doing themselves. Ask him further what God says in the third verse that such a person will not escape. Ask him what the fourth verse tells him that he is really doing; and then ask him what the fifth verse tells him he is treasuring up for himself.

In many cases Matt. 7: 1-5 will be found useful

XVI. "There is some one I cannot forgive."

This is often the difficulty even when it is not stated. I have frequently found that when people told me they could not accept Christ and did not know why, the real difficulty was here, there was some one who had wronged them, or who they thought had wronged them, and they would not forgive them.

1. The first thing to do with such a one is to say, "*You must forgive or perish.*" To prove this, use Matt. 6: 15:

> "But if ye forgive not men their trespasses, neither will your Father forgive your trespasses."

Follow this up with Matt. 18: 21-35:

2. Say to the person, "*The wrong they have done you is nothing to the wrong you have done Jesus Christ.*" Here use Eph. 4: 32:

> "And be ye kind one to another, tender-hearted, forgiving one another, even as God for Christ's sake hath forgiven you."

You might also use Matt. 18: 23-35:

3. Next show the inquirer that he can forgive the other in Christ's strength. Use for this purpose Phil. 4: 13, and Gal. 5: 22, 23:

> "I can do all things through Christ which strengtheneth me."
>
> "But the fruit of the Spirit is love, joy, peace, long-suffering, gentleness, goodness, faith, meekness, temperance: against such there is no law."

XVII. "A professed Christian has done me a great wrong."

1. First you can reply by saying, "*That is no reason why you should wrong Christ; has He wronged you?*" Use Jer. 2: 5:

> "Thus saith the Lord, What iniquity have your fathers found *in me*, that they are gone far from me, and have walked after vanity, and are become vain?"

Ask the inquirer if he has found any evil in Christ, that that is what God is asking Him. One night I turned to an aged man and asked him if he was a Christian. He replied no, that he was a backslider. I asked him why he had backslidden, and he said Christian people had treated him badly. I opened my Bible and read Jer. 2: 5 to him, and asked him, "Did you find any iniquity in God; did God not treat you well?" With a good deal of feeling the man admitted that God had not treated him badly. I held him right to this point of God's treatment of him and not man's, and his treatment of God. It is well to follow this passage up with Is. 53: 5 as bringing out very vividly just what Christ's treatment of us has been.

2. In the next place you can say to the one who raises this difficulty, "*The fact that a professed Christian has done you a great injury is no reason why you should do yourself a greater injury by refusing Christ and losing eternal life and being lost forever.*" Then you can say, "Let me show you what injury you are doing yourself by rejecting Christ." Use for this purpose Jno. 3: 36, and 2 Thess. 1: 7-9:

> "He that believeth on the Son hath everlasting life; and he that believeth not the Son shall not see life; but the wrath of God abideth on him."
>
> "And to you who are troubled rest with us, when the Lord Jesus shall be revealed from heaven with his mighty angels, in flaming fire taking vengeance on them that know not God, and that obey not the gospel of our Lord Jesus Christ."

XVIII. "I have done a great wrong and will have to make it right and cannot."

1. *Tell the inquirer to take Christ first, and leave the matter of settling the wrong with Him*, that he cannot settle the matter as it ought to be settled until he has first taken Christ. Make it very plain that the only thing God requires of a sinner is to accept Christ, and all other questions must be left until that point has been settled. Use John 3: 36 for this purpose, and Acts 10: 43.

2. Show him further that *if there is any wrong to be made right, Christ will give him strength to make it right*, and use for this purpose Phil. 4: 13.

XIX. "I have sinned away the day of grace."

This is a very serious difficulty. It often arises from a poor state of health and a morbid condition of mind, but I have never found a case that would not yield to prayerful and judicious treatment. The best passage to use, and one that generally proves sufficient, is Jno. 6: 37, the last clause:

> "Him that cometh to me I will in no wise cast out."

It is oftentimes necessary to read it over and over and over again, sometimes for days and days. Hold the inquirer to the one thought that God says He is ready to receive any one who will come, urging him to come now.

Another useful passage is Rom. 10: 13:

> "For *whosoever* shall call upon the name of the Lord shall be saved."

Dwell upon the "whosoever."

The case of Manasseh as recorded in 2 Chron. 33: 1-13 is useful as showing the extent to which one can go and yet how God will receive them to Himself, if they only humble themselves before him.

Luke 23: 39-43 is oftentimes useful as showing how one was saved even in the hour of death.

XX. "It is too late."

This difficulty is very much like the preceding one, and the same passage, Jno. 6: 37 is also useful in this case. Oftentimes, however, Deut. 4: 30, 31 will prove more helpful:

> "When thou art in tribulation, and all these things are come upon thee, *even in the latter days*, if thou turn to the Lord thy God, and shalt be obedient unto his voice; (for the Lord thy God is a merciful God;) he will not forsake thee, neither destroy thee, nor forget the covenant of thy fathers which he sware unto them."

In using the passage, emphasize the thought, "even in the latter days."

Still another passage is 2 Pet, 3: 9:

> "The Lord is not slack concerning his promise, as some men count slackness; but is long suffering to us-ward, *not willing that any should perish*, but that all should come to repentance."

It shows that God is not willing that any should perish, and that the reason why He delays His judgment is that men may be brought to repentance.

Luke 23: 39-43 is useful as showing that one was saved even as late as his dying hour, and Rev. 22: 17 tells us that *whosoever will* may take of the water of life freely.

XXI. "I have committed the unpardonable sin."

1. The first thing to do in this case is to *show just what the unpardonable sin is*. For this purpose use Matt. 12: 31, 32,

noting the context. This passage taken in its context makes it plain that the unpardonable sin is blasphemy against the Holy Ghost, and that blasphemy against the Holy Ghost consists in deliberately attributing to the devil, the work which is known to have been wrought by the Holy Spirit. Having shown just what the unpardonable sin is, ask the inquirer, "Have you done this? Have you deliberately attributed the work which you knew to be done by the Holy Spirit to the devil?" In almost every case, if not in every case, it will be found that the inquirer has not done this.

2. Having shown what the unpardonable sin is, and that the inquirer has not committed it, *use John 6: 37* as in the preceding case. Even if the inquirer thinks that he has committed the blasphemy against the Holy Ghost, use John 6: 37. Ask the inquirer what Jesus Christ says about those who come to Him, and then ask him if he will come to Christ right now. If he says, "I have committed the unpardonable sin," reply that it does not say, "Him that has not committed the unpardonable sin that comes to me I will in no wise cast out," but, "Him that cometh to me, I will in no wise cast out," and put the question again, "Will you come?" To every new excuse that arises, simply repeat the promise, "Him that cometh to me I will in no wise cast out," and repeat the question, "Will you come ?" If he raises some new difficulty as probably he will, simply say, "Jesus says, 'Him that cometh to me, I will in no wise cast out,' will you come?" Repeat and repeat and repeat, over and over again, until this promise is fairly burned into the heart praying all the time for the Holy Spirit to carry it home. A man was once sent to me who was in the depths of despair. He had attempted suicide some five times. He felt that he had sinned away the day of grace, and committed the unpardonable sin, and that the devil had entered into him as he did into Judas Iscariot. Day after day I dealt with him, always using Jno. 6: 37. To every excuse and difficulty he would bring up I would simply say, "Jesus says, 'Him that cometh to me I will in no wise cast out," I met him at last one day for a final conflict. I said to him, "Do you believe what Jesus says?" He replied, "Yes, I believe everything in the Bible." "Well," I said, "Did not

Jesus say, 'Him that cometh to me I will in no wise cast out'?" "Yes," he replied. I said, "Will you come?" He replied, "I have committed the unpardonable sin." I said, "Jesus did not say, 'If any man has not committed the unpardonable sin, and comes to me I will in no wise cast him out'; He said, 'Him that cometh to me I will in no wise cast out'; Will you come?" He said, "I am possessed of the devil." I replied, "Jesus did not say, 'If a man is not possessed of the devil and comes to me I will in no wise cast him out'; He said, 'Him that cometh to me, I will in no wise cast out'; Will you come?" He said, "The devil has actually entered into me." I replied, "Jesus did not say, 'If the devil has not entered into a man and he comes to me I will in no wise cast him out'; He said, 'Him that cometh to me, I will in no wise cast out; Will you come?" He said, "My heart is too hard to come." I replied, "Jesus did not say, 'If a man's heart is not too hard and he comes to me, I will in no wise cast him out'; He said, 'Him that cometh to me, I will in no wise cast out'; Will you come?" He said, "I don't feel like coming." I replied, "Jesus did not say, 'If any man feels like coming, and comes to me, I will in no wise cast him out'; He said, 'Him that cometh to me, I will in no wise cast out'; Will you come?" He said, "I don't know as I can come in the right way." I replied, "Jesus did not say, 'If any man cometh unto me in the right way, I will in no wise cast him out'; He said, 'Him that cometh to me, I will in no wise cast out'; Will you come?" He said, "I do not know as I want to come." I replied, "Jesus did not say, 'He that wants to come, and comes to me I will in no wise cast out'; He said, 'Him that cometh to me, I will in no wise cast out'; Will you come?" He said, "I don't know as I know how to come." I replied, "Jesus did not say, 'He that knows how to come, and comes to me I will in no wise cast out'; He said, 'Him that cometh to me, I will in no wise cast out'; Will you come? Will you get down here now and come just the best you know how?" Hesitatingly the man knelt down. I asked him to follow me in prayer. I prayed about as follows: "Lord Jesus, thou hast said 'Him that cometh to me, I will in no wise cast out'; now the best I know how, I just come." The man repeated the words after me.

I said, "Did you really come?" "Yes," he said, "I did." Then I said, "What has Jesus done? Never mind what you feel, but what does Jesus say He has done? 'Him that cometh to me I will in no wise cast out.' What has Jesus done, what does He say He has done?" He replied, "He has received me." I said, "Are you willing to stand there on the naked Word of God?" He replied, "I will." "Now," I said, "You are going to your room. I have no doubt that the devil will give you an awful fight, but will you stand right there on the word of Jesus, 'Him that cometh to me, I will in no wise cast out.'" He replied, "I will." He went to his room. The devil did come and assail him, and try to get him to look at his own heart, his own feelings, and his doubts, but he kept looking to the promise of Jesus, "Him that cometh to me, I will in no wise cast out"; he believed that naked promise, he came out of his struggle a victor. This was eight or nine years ago. To-day he is one of the most useful men in America.

XXII. Heb. 6: 4-6.

"For it is impossible for those who were once enlightened, and have tasted of the heavenly gift, and were made partakers of the Holy Ghost, and have tasted the good word of God, and the powers of the world to come, *if they shall fall away, to renew them again unto repentance;* seeing they crucify to themselves the Son of God afresh, and put him to an open shame."

Very many men and women are in deep distress of soul over this passage. They fear that it describes them, and that there is no hope of their salvation. The way to deal with such a person is to explain to him the exact meaning of the passage.

1. Show him first of all, that it is addressed to Hebrew Christians who were in danger of *apostatizing*, *renouncing Christ* and going back to Judaism. Then ask him if this describes his case. Of course he will say that it does not. Furthermore show him that it does not describe a person who has merely fallen in sin, but one who has *fallen away*, that is apostatized, and deliberately renounced Christ. Ask him if this describes his case. In most cases, of course, it will be found that it does not.

2. In the next place show him that the difficulty is not, that God is not willing to receive such a one back, but that it is impossible "to renew them again unto repentance." that is, that their hearts are utterly hardened, and they have no desire to come to Christ. Then show him that this does not describe his case, the very fact of his being in anxiety and burden of heart proving that it does not.

3. Sometimes all of this fails, if so, simply go over the fourth verse, and ask him if that has really been his experience, if he has actually been made a partaker of the Holy Ghost.

4. Show him by the case of Peter that one who has been a follower of Christ may fall into deep sin, and yet be restored and become more useful than ever. Use for this purpose, Luke 22: 31, 34, Mark 14: 66-72, Jno. 21: 15-19.

5. Finally use Jno. 6: 37, as described above.

XXIII. Heb. 10: 26, 27.

"For *if we sin wilfully after that we have received the knowledge of the truth, there remaineth no more sacrifice for sins*, but a certain fearful looking for of judgment and fiery indignation, which shall devour the adversaries."

Many are troubled by this passage just as others are troubled by Heb. 6: 4-6. I have met many in deepest anguish because they thought that this described their experience. The way to deal with such a one is to show him exactly the meaning of the verse. Explain to him that the word "wilfully" means deliberately, and of stubborn choice. It is the same word that is translated willingly in 1 Pet. 5: 2. It does not describe a man who in weakness falls into sin, but a man who, with his whole heart, rejects obedience to God and the service of Christ, and throws himself with all his soul into sin. Ask him if this describes his case. Finally use Jno. 6: 37.

XXIV. "God seems to me unjust and cruel."

1. The shortest way of dealing with many who say this, is to take them at once to Rom. 9: 20:

"Nay but, O man, *who art thou that repliest against God?* Shall the thing formed say to him that formed it, Why hast thou made me thus?"

Apply the verse directly to the inquirer's case. Ask him if

he realizes who God is, and who he himself is, and say, "You are replying against God. You are accusing God of sin. Now this is God's message to you, 'Nay but, O man, who art thou that repliest against God?'" This verse has been used of the Holy Spirit to break down in repentance and tears many a man who has complained against God.

This may be followed up by Rom. 11:33:

"O the depth of the riches both of the wisdom and knowledge of God! *how unsearchable* are his judgments, and his ways past finding out!"

Show the inquirer that the reason God seems to him to be unjust and cruel is because such is the depth of the riches both of the wisdom and knowledge of God, and so unsearchable are His judgments, that he cannot find them out.

This can be followed up still further by Is. 55:8, 9:

"For my thoughts are not your thoughts, neither are your ways my ways, saith the Lord. For as the heavens are higher than the earth, so are my ways higher than your ways, and my thoughts than your thoughts."

Another excellent passage to use is Job 40:2:

"Shall he that *contendeth with the Almighty* instruct him? *he that reproveth God*, let him answer it."

When the complainer has read the verse, ask him if he wishes to contend with the Almighty. Show him further that he is reproving God, and God says he must answer for it; ask him if he is ready to answer for it.

2. *If the inquirer is complaining of God's cruelty because of some sorrow or anguish in his own life*, it is well to use Heb. 12:5-7, 10-12:

"And ye have forgotten the exhortation which speaketh unto you as unto children, My son, despise not thou the chastening of the Lord, nor faint when thou art rebuked of him; for whom the Lord loveth he chasteneth, and scourgeth every son whom he receiveth.

"If ye endure chastening, God dealeth with you as with sons; for what son is he whom the father chasteneth not?"

"For they verily for a few days chastened us after their own pleasure; but he for our profit, that we might be partakers of his holiness.

"Now no chastening for the present seemeth to be joyous, but grievous; nevertheless afterward it yieldeth the peaceable fruit of righteousness unto them which are exercised thereby.

"Wherefore lift up the hands which hang down, and the feeble knees."

One should deal very tenderly with a case like this, yet at the same time faithfully. Show the inquirer that the sorrows and disappointments and afflictions that he has suffered are God's loving dealings with him, to bring him into a life of holiness and higher joy, that God does not willingly afflict.

One can follow the above passage with Is. 63:9:

"In all their affliction he was afflicted, and the angel of his presence saved them; in his love and in his pity he redeemed them; and he bare them, and carried them all the days of old."

In order to lead the sorrow-stricken soul to see that the sufferings of this present time are not worthy to be compared with the glory which shall be revealed in us, use Rom. 8:18:

"For I reckon that the sufferings of this present time are not worthy to be compared with the glory which shall be revealed in us."

Another useful passage is 2 Cor. 4:17, 18:

"For our light affliction, which is *but for a moment*, worketh for us a far more exceeding and eternal weight of glory; while we look not at the things which are seen, but at the things which are not seen: for the things which are seen are temporal; but the things which are not seen are eternal."

3. Sometimes it is well to say in such a case, "You would not think that God was unjust and cruel if you only realized the depth of your own sin against Him," and use Matt. 22:37, 38 to show him the greatness of his sin, in the way described in Chapter VI.

4. It is a wise plan to follow up all the preceding methods by showing the complainer the wonderful love of God. Jno. 3:16 and Is. 53:5 will serve well for this purpose.

XXV. "I cannot see why it was necessary that Christ should die in order that men be saved."

There are very many who will tell you this. Of course those who say this are frequently mere triflers, and trying to find a hiding place from God's truth and their own duty, but some say this with a good deal of sincerity of purpose. I have found one of the most effective passages to use in such a case to be Rom. 9:20. It is well to follow this up by showing the doubter the greatness and depth of his own sin in the way described in Chapter VI. No man after he has been led by the Word of God and His Spirit to see himself as God sees him, will any longer have any difficulty with God's way of salvation, but will be only too glad to find that a sin-bearer has been provided for him.

XXVI. "There are so many things in the Bible that I can not understand."

1. The first step in such a case is to show the objector why he cannot understand. A good passage to use for this purpose is 1 Cor. 2: 14:

> "But the natural man receiveth not the things of the Spirit of God for they are foolishness unto him: neither can he know them, because they are spiritually discerned."

It can be used in this way: when the man has said, "There are so many things in the Bible that I cannot understand," reply, "Yes, that is just what the Bible says." Then show the man the passage, and say to him, "This verse tells you just why you cannot understand what is in the Bible, because the natural man receiveth not the things of the Spirit of God: for they are foolishness *unto him*,' and I suppose that many of them appear like foolishness to you." "Yes." "This verse tells you why it is, 'because they are spiritually discerned.' The truth is, you are spiritually blind. If you will turn from sin and accept Christ, you will get spiritual sight, and then many things which you cannot understand now will become as plain as day."

Is. 55: 8, 9 can also be used:

> "For my thoughts are not your thoughts, neither are your ways my ways, saith the Lord. For as the heavens are higher than the earth, so are my ways higher than your ways, and my thoughts than your thoughts."

You can say to the one with whom you are dealing, "This tells why you cannot understand God's truth. Why is it?" "Because His thoughts are higher than my thoughts."

Dan. 12: 10 is also useful:

> "Many shall be purified, and made white, and tried; but the wicked shall do wickedly: and *none of the wicked shall understand;* but the wise shall understand."

Before the man reads it, you can say to him, "I can show you a passage in the Bible that tells you just exactly why you cannot understand, and also how you can understand. When he has read it, ask him who it is that does not understand. "The wicked." "And who shall understand?" "The wise."

A passage which can also be used to good effect is 2 Pet. 3:16-18:

"As also in all his epistles, speaking in them of these things; in which are some things hard to be understood, which they that are unlearned and unstable wrest, as they do also the other scriptures, unto their own destruction. Ye therefore, beloved, seeing ye know these things before, beware lest ye also, being led away with the error of the wicked, fall from your own steadfastness."

1 Cor. 13:11, 12 and Rom. 11:33 can also be used.

2. The second step is to show how to understand. Jno. 7:17 makes this as plain as day:

"*If any man will do his will,* he shall know of the doctrine, whether it be of God, or whether I speak of myself."

Follow this up with Ps. 119:18, and James 1:5:

"Open thou mine eyes, that I may behold wondrous things out of thy law."

"If any of you lack wisdom, let him ask of God, that giveth to all men liberally, and upbraideth not; and it shall be given him."

XXVII. "I cannot believe."

We will take up skeptics more at length in Chapter XI. At this point we take up the matter merely as an honest difficulty that some find in the way of accepting Christ.

1. When one states this as a difficulty, it is often well to ask him what he cannot believe. A man once said to Mr. Moody, "I cannot believe." Mr. Moody said, "Who can't you believe?" "He replied "I cannot believe." "Who can't you believe, can't you believe God?" "Yes," the man replied, "I can believe God, but I cannot believe myself." Mr. Moody said, "I don't want you to believe yourself, I want you to believe God." Oftentimes the difficulty is with some doctrine that has nothing directly to do with salvation; for example, a man will say, "I cannot believe the account of creation given in the first chapter of Genesis, and I cannot believe the story about Jonah and the whale." Now of course a man ought to believe the Bible account of creation given in

the first chapter of Genesis, and he ought to believe the story about Jonah, but these are not questions to discuss with an unsaved man. When a man states some such difficulty as this, the best thing to do is to say, "Can you believe in Jesus Christ?" "Yes, I can believe in Jesus Christ." "But will you believe in Him, will you accept Him as your Saviour, your sin-bearer, and your Lord and Master?" Show the man that it does not say, believe this doctrine or that doctrine and thou shalt be saved, or this incident or that incident in the Bible, but "believe on the Lord Jesus Christ and thou shalt be saved." For this purpose use Acts 16: 31, and Jno. 3: 16:

> "And they said, *Believe on the Lord Jesus Christ,* and thou shalt be saved, and thy house."
>
> "For God so loved the world, that he gave his only begotten Son, that whosoever *believeth in him* should not perish, but have everlasting life."

After the man has really believed on Christ and been saved, and grown somewhat in Christian knowledge, he will be in a position to take up secondary questions. Many a well-meaning worker makes a great mistake in discussing secondary questions with an unsaved man, when he is in no position to understand them at all, but should be held to the vital point of the acceptance of Jesus Christ as a Saviour and Lord and Master.

2. In many cases, perhaps in most cases, when one says, "I cannot believe," the real difficulty that lies back of their inability to believe, is unwillingness to forsake sin, and it is well to say to such a person, "Is your unbelief the real difficulty, is there not some sin in your life that you are unwilling to give up?" I was once called to deal with a man, and was told that he was a skeptic, and needed help along that line. I said to him, "Are you a skeptic?" He replied, "Yes." I asked him what made him a skeptic, and he said because he could not see where Cain got his wife. I said to him, "Is that your real difficulty?" "Yes." I replied, "Then if I remove that difficulty, and show you where Cain got his wife, will you become a Christian?" He said, "Oh, no, I cannot promise that." "But," I said, "you said that was your difficulty, the thing that kept you from accepting Christ; now if I remove that difficulty, and you are honest, of course you will accept

Christ." The man laughed and saw that he was cornered. "Now," I said, "Let me ask you a question; is not the real difficulty some sin in your life?" The man broke down and confessed that it was, and he told me what the sin was, and professed to give it up and accept Christ then and there. when you are convinced that the real difficulty in the case is sin, a good passage to use is Jno. 5:44:

> "How can ye believe, which receive honor one of another, and seek not the honor that cometh from God only."

Say to the man before he reads it, "Yes, I suppose you cannot believe, but Jesus Christ tells us just why it is that men cannot believe," and then have him read the passage. Then you can say to him, "The reason why you cannot believe according to this verse, is because you are seeking the honor that comes from man and not the honor that comes from God alone Is this not so?" Be courteous, but do not let the inquirer dodge that point

Is. 55.7 is also a good passage to use:

> "Let the wicked forsake his way, and the unrighteous man his thoughts: and let him return unto the Lord, and he will have mercy upon him; and to our God, for he will abundantly pardon."

This will show the man that he not only needs to forsake his way, but his thoughts as well, and that if he will, and return to the Lord, He will have mercy upon him and abundantly pardon.

3. Finally in dealing with this difficulty, it is well to show a man how to believe. You can say to him after you have dealt with him along the lines already mentioned, "I can show you how to believe." Then give him Jno. 7:17:

> "If any man *will do his will*, he shall know of the doctrine, whether it be of God, or whether I speak of myself."

Ask him if he will will to do the will of God, if he will surrender his will to God. Then show him James 1:5-7:

> "If any of you lack wisdom, *let him ask of God*, that giveth to all men liberally, and upbraideth not; and it shall be given him. But let him ask in faith, nothing wavering. For he that wavereth is like a wave of the sea driven with the wind and tossed. For let not that man think that he shall receive any thing of the Lord."

Follow this up with John 20:31:

> "But *these are written*, that ye might believe that Jesus is the Christ, the Son of God; and that believing ye might have life through his name."

Then give him the Gospel of John to study prayerfully. We will go into this more at length in Chapter XI.

CHAPTER VIII

HOW TO DEAL WITH THOSE WHO ENTERTAIN FALSE HOPES

I. The hope of being saved by a righteous life.

This is the most common of false hopes. Even among those who profess to be Christians, there are many who are really depending upon their lives as Christians for their acceptance before God. Those who are depending upon their righteous lives for salvation, are readily known by their saying such things as this: "I am doing the best I can." "I do more good than evil." "I am not a great sinner." "I have never done anything very bad." This mistake can be directly met by Gal. 2: 16:

> "Knowing that a man is not justified by the works of the law, but by the faith of Jesus Christ, even we have believed in Jesus Christ, that we might be justified by the faith of Christ, and not by the works of the law: for *by the works of the law shall no flesh be justified.*"

After the passage has been read, you can say to the one with whom you are dealing, "Now you are expecting to be justified and accepted before God by what you are doing, by your own life and character; but God tells you in this passage, that 'by the works of the law shall no flesh be justified.'" Follow this up by Rom. 3: 19, 20:

> "Now we know that what things soever the law saith, it saith to them who are under the law: that every mouth may be stopped, and all the world may become guilty before God. Therefore *by the deeds of the law there shall no flesh be justified in his sight:* for by the law is the knowledge of sin."

Call attention to the fact that here again we are told that, "by the deeds of the law there shall no flesh be justified in his sight," and furthermore, that the purpose of the law is to stop the mouths of men. Then take him to Gal. 3: 10:

> "For *as many as are of the works of the law are under the curse*: for it is written, Cursed is every one that continueth not in all things which are written in the book of the law to do them."

Before he reads it, say to him, "I want you to read a verse from the Word of God that tells you just how God regards one who is trying to be saved by his righteous life, as you are." Then let him read the passage. When he has read the passage, ask him where God says that he is, and hold him to the point until he sees that in depending upon his good deeds for salvation, he is under the curse.

James 2: 10 will also be found useful:

"For whosoever shall keep the whole law, and yet *offend in one point*, he is guilty of all."

Before the man reads the verse you can say, "Well, if you are going to be saved by your righteous life, let us see what God requires in order that a man may be saved on that ground." After he has read the verse, show him that if he is going to be saved by the law, he must keep the whole law, for if he offends in one point he is guilty of all.

A verse which is useful in showing the kind of righteousness that God demands, is Matt. 5: 20:

"For I say unto you, That except your righteousness shall exceed the righteousness of the scribes and Pharisees, ye shall in no case enter into the kingdom of heaven."

This verse shows that no man's righteousness comes up to God's standard, and if a man wishes to be saved, he must find some other way of salvation than by his own deeds. It is sometimes well in using this passage, to say to the inquirer, "You do not understand the kind of righteousness God demands, or you would not talk as you do. Now let us turn to God's own Word and see what kind of righteousness it is that God demands."

2. There is another way of dealing with this class, by using such passages as these:

"And he said unto them, Ye are they which justify yourselves before men; but God *knoweth your hearts:* for that which is highly esteemed among men is abomination in the sight of God." Luke 16: 15.

"In the day when *God shall judge the secrets of men* by Jesus Christ according to my gospel." Rom. 2: 16.

"But the Lord said unto Samuel, Look not on his countenance, or on the height of his stature; because I have refused him: for the Lord seeth not as man seeth; for man looketh on the outward appearance, but *the Lord looketh on the heart.*" 1 Sam. 16: 7.

These passages show that God looks at the heart. Hold the inquirer right to that point. Every man, when brought face to face with that, must tremble, for he knows that whatever his outward life may be, his heart will not stand the scrutiny of God's all-seeing and holy eye. No matter how self-righteous a man may appear, we need not be discouraged, for somewhere in the depths of every man's heart is the consciousness of sin, and all we have to do is to work away until we touch that point. Every man's conscience is on our side.

3. Matt. 22: 37, 38 can also be used with those who expect to be saved by their righteous lives. You can say to the man, "If you expect to be saved by your righteous life, you are greatly deceived, and certainly entertain a false hope. For so far from living a righteous life, you have broken the very first and greatest of God's commandments." Of course he may not believe this at first, but you can turn him to the passage mentioned, and show him what the first and greatest of God's commandments is, and ask him if he has kept it. This passage is especially useful if a man says, "I am doing the best I can," or if he says, "I am doing more good than evil." You can say to him, "You are greatly mistaken about that. So far from doing more good than evil, you have broken the first and greatest of God's laws," and then show him the passage.

4. A fourth method of dealing with this class is to use Heb. 11: 6 and Jno. 6: 29:

> "But *without faith* it is impossible to please him: for he that cometh to God must believe that he is, and that he is a rewarder of them that diligently seek him."
>
> "Jesus answered and said unto them, *This* is the work of God, *that ye believe on him whom he hath sent*."

These passages show that the one thing which God demands is faith, that the work of God is to believe on Him whom He hath sent, and that without faith it is impossible to please God whatever else a man may possess. John 16: 9 can also be used to show that unbelief in Christ is the greatest sin:

> "Of sin, *because they believe not on me*."

5. Still another way of dealing with this class is by the use of Jno. 3: 36:

"He that believeth on the Son hath everlasting life: and he that believeth not the Son shall not see life; but the wrath of God abideth on him."

This shows that the gift of eternal life depends solely upon a man's acceptance of Jesus Christ. That the sin which brings the heaviest punishment is that of treading under foot the Son of God, can be shown by Heb. 10: 28, 29:

"He that despised Moses' law died without mercy under two or three witnesses: of how much sorer punishment, suppose ye, shall he be thought worthy, who hath trodden under foot the Son of God, and hath counted the blood of the covenant, wherewith he was sanctified, an unholy thing, and hath done despite unto the Spirit of grace?"

Before using this passage, it is well to say, "You think you are very good, but do you know that you are committing the most awful sin in God's sight which a man can commit?" If he replies, "I do not think so," then tell him, "Let me show you from God's Word that you are." Then turn to this passage and read it with great solemnity and earnestness.

A very useful passage with many a self-righteous man is Luke 18: 10-14. You can say to the man, "There is a picture in the Bible of a man just like you, who expected to be accepted before God on the ground of his righteousness, and who had, as men go, much righteousness to present to God, but let us see what God says to him." Then have him read the passage.

It is well to bring all those who expect to be saved by a righteous life into the presence of God, for in His holy presence self-righteousness fades away. (See Is. 6: 5 and Job 42: 5, 6.) But how shall we bring any one into the presence of God? By opening to them passages that reveal the holiness of God, and by praying the Holy Spirit to carry these passages home. It is also well whenever possible, to get the inquirer to pray. Many a man who is stoutly maintaining his excellence before God, has given way when he has been brought to get down on his knees in God's very presence.

II. "God is too good to damn any one."

This is what another class of those who entertain false hopes think.

1. When any one says this, you can reply, "We know

nothing about God's goodness, except what we learn from the Bible. If we give up the Bible, we have no conclusive proof that God is love, and can therefore build no hopes upon His goodness. But if we accept the Bible statement that God is love, we must also accept the Bible representations of the goodness of God. Let us then go to the Bible and find out the character of God's goodness." Then turn the inquirer to Rom. 2:4, 5:

> 'Or despisest thou the riches of his goodness and forbearance and long suffering; *not knowing that the goodness of God leadeth thee to repentance?* But after thy hardness and impenitent heart treasurest up unto thyself wrath against the day of wrath and revelation of the righteous judgment of God."

When the man has read the verse, you can say to him, "This verse tells us what the purpose of God's goodness is; what is it?" "To lead us to repentance." "And what does this verse tell us will be the result if we do not permit the goodness of God to lead us to repentance, but trample it under foot and make it an excuse for sin?" He will find the answer to this question in verse five, and hold him to it until he sees it, that if we despise the riches of His goodness, then we are treasuring up unto ourselves "wrath against the day of wrath and revelation of the righteous judgment of God." You can also use Jno. 8:21, 24 and Jno. 3:36 to show the man that however good we may be, if we do not believe in Jesus with a living faith, we shall die in our sins, and not go where Jesus is, and that we shall not see life, but that the wrath of God abideth upon us.

2. Still another way to deal with this man is to show him that it is not so much God who damns men, as men who damn themselves in spite of God's goodness, because they will not repent and come to Christ and accept the life freely offered. For this purpose use 2 Pet. 3:9-11:

> "The Lord is not slack concerning his promise, as some men count slackness; but is long suffering to us-ward, *not willing that any should perish,* but that all should come to repentance. But the day of the Lord will come as a thief in the night; in the which the heavens shall pass away with a great noise, and the elements shall melt with fervent heat, the earth also and the works that are therein shall be burned up. Seeing then that all these things shall be dissolved, what manner of persons ought ye to be in all holy conversation and godliness?"

Another good passage to use in this way is Jno. 5:40:

"*And ye will not come* to me, that ye might have life."

Press the thought of this text home, that if any one does not obtain life, it is because they will not come to Christ, and that men therefore are damned in spite of God's goodness if they will not come to Christ and accept life. In much the same way one can use Ez. 33:11:

"Say unto them, As I live, saith the Lord God, I have no pleasure in the death of the wicked; but that the wicked turn from his way and live: turn ye, turn ye from your evil ways; for why will ye die, O house of Israel?"

It is sometimes well to say, "You are right in thinking that God is not willing to damn any one; furthermore He offers life freely to you, but there is one difficulty in the way. Let us turn to Jno. 5:40 and see what the difficulty is." When he has read it, you can say, "You see now, that the difficulty is not that God wishes to damn you, but that you will not come to Christ that you might have life."

3. If these methods do not succeed, 2 Pet. 2:4-6, 9 may prove effectual:

"For if *God spared not the angels that sinned*, but cast them down to hell, and delivered them into chains of darkness, to be reserved unto judgment; and spared not the old world, but saved Noah the eighth person, a preacher of righteousness, bringing in the flood upon the world of the ungodly; and turning the cities of Sodom and Gomorrha into ashes condemned them with an overthrow, making them an ensample unto those that after should live ungodly;

"The Lord knoweth how to deliver the godly out of temptations, and to reserve the unjust unto the day of judgment to be punished."

Before using the passage you can say, "The best way to judge what God will do is not by speculating about it, but by looking at what He has done in the past." Then turn to these passages and let him read. When he has read it, ask him, "What did God do with the angels that sinned?" "What did He do with the world of the ungodly in the days of Noah?" "What did He do with the wicked in the days of Sodom and Gomorrha? What then may you expect Him to do with you in spite of any theories that you may have about His character and actions." This should all be done not in a controversial way, but with great earnestness, tenderness and solemnity.

You can say still further, "God has not left us to speculate as to what He will do with the persistently impenitent, He has told us plainly in Matt. 25: 41, 46":

> "Then shall he say also unto them on the left hand, Depart from me, ye cursed, into everlasting fire, prepared for the devil and his angels:
>
> "And these shall go away into everlasting punishment: but the righteous into life eternal."

You may say still further, that God does bear long with man, but His dealings with man in the past show that at last His day of waiting will end, and in spite of man's doubt of His word, and doubt of his severity in dealing with the persistently impenitent, He does at last punish. You might use 2 Chron. 36: 11-21 as an illustrative case in point.

4. It is well sometimes to add to all the other passages, Jno. 3: 18, 19:

> "He that believeth on him is not condemned: but he that believeth not is condemned *already*, because he hath not believed in the name of the only begotten Son of God. And this is the condemnation, that light is come into the world, and men loved darkness rather than light, because their deeds were evil."

Before having the inquirer read the verses, you can say, "You say God is too good to damn anyone, but the truth is that you are condemned already. It is not a question of what is going to happen to you in the future, but a question of your present position before God." When he has read the passage, ask him, "When is it that the one who believeth not is condemned?" "Already." "Why is it that he is condemned?" "Because light is come into the world, and he loves darkness rather than light."

5. Luke 13: 3 is very effective in some case, for it shows how the "good" God deals with persons who persist in sin. The passage can be used in this way: "You say God is too good to damn any one, but let us see what God Himself says in His Word." Then turn to the passage and read, "Except ye repent, ye shall all likewise perish." Repeat the passage over and over again until it has been driven home. An earnest missionary in the western part of New York was once holding meetings in a country village. The Universalist minister of the place was very anxious to engage the missionary in

a controversy, but the missionary always said that he was too busy for controversy. One day the Universalist minister came into the house where the missionary was calling; he was delighted to see him, for he thought that his opportunity for a discussion had come at last. He began the customary universalist argument about God being too good to damn any one. After he had gone through the usual volume of words, the missionary simply replied, "I am too busy for argument, but I just want to say to you, that except you repent, you shall likewise perish." The Universalist was somewhat angry, but replied sneeringly, "That is not argument, it is simply a quotation from the Bible," and then ran on with another stream of words. When he had finished his second speech, the missionary simply replied, "I have no time for argument, but I just want to say to you, except you repent, you shall likewise perish." Again the Universalist sneered and poured forth another torrent of what he called argument. When he had finished this time, the missionary again said, "I have no time for controversy, I simply want to say to you that except you repent, you shall likewise perish. Now I must go, but let me say, you will not be able to forget what I have said." The Universalist preacher laughed, and said he guessed he would forget it quick enough, that the missionary had used no argument whatever, but had simply quoted the Bible. The following day there was a knock at the missionary's door, and when it was opened, the Universalist preacher came in. The missionary said, "I have no time for argument." "O sir!" said the other, "I have not come to argue with you. You were right yesterday when you told me there was one thing I would not be able to forget; I feel that it is true, that except I repent I must perish, and I have come to ask you what I must do to be saved." The missionary showed the man the way of life, and the result was, the Universalist became a real believer in Christ, and a preacher of the truth he had previously labored to pull down.

III. "I am trying to be a Christian."

The third class of those who entertain false hopes, are those who say, "I am trying to be a Christian."

1. Show the inquirer that it is trusting and not trying that saves. For this purpose use Is. 12:2:

"Behold, God is my salvation; *I will trust*, and not be afraid: for the Lord Jehovah is my strength and my song; he also is become my salvation."

When he has read it, ask him what it is the prophet says, "I will try?" "No, I will trust." Another verse which can also be used to show that it is not trying to be a Christian, but believing on Christ that saves, is Acts 16:31:

"And they said, Believe on the Lord Jesus Christ, and thou shalt be saved, and thy house."

Jno. 1:12 is very useful. Before using it, you can say, "What God asks of you is not to try to be a Christian, or to try to live a better life, or to try to do anything but simply to receive Jesus Christ who did it all." Then have the passage read and say to the inquirer, "Will you now stop your trying, and simply receive Jesus as a Saviour?" Make it very clear what this means and hold the inquirer to this point.

2. Another way of dealing with this class is to show the inquirer that it is *not trying* what we can do, *but trusting* what Jesus has done that saves from guilt. Use for this purpose Rom. 3:23-26:

"For all have sinned, and come short of the glory of God; being justified freely by his grace through the redemption that is in Christ Jesus: whom God hath set forth to be a propitiation through faith in his blood, to declare his righteousness for the remission of sins that are past, through the forbearance of God; to declare, I say, at this time his righteousness: that he might be just and *the justifier of him which believeth in Jesus.*"

When the inquirer has read the passage, ask him if this teaches us that we are justified by trying to do something. "No." "Then how are we justified?" Hold him to it until he say, "Freely by His grace, through the redemption that is in Christ Jesus," and sees that it is on the simple condition of faith. Another very effective passage to use in the same way is Rom. 4:3-5:

"For what saith the scripture? Abraham believed God, and it was counted unto him for righteousness. Now to him that worketh is the reward not reckoned of grace, but of debt. But *to him that worketh not, but believeth* on him that justifieth the ungodly, *his faith* is counted for righteousness."

This makes it clear as day that it is not our trying, but our believing on Him that justifies us. Acts 10: 43 and 13: 38 can be used in a similar way.

3. It is also well to show the inquirer, that it is not our trying in our own strength, but our trusting in Christ's strength that saves from the power of sin. To make this clear, use the following passages:

> "Now unto him that is able to keep you from falling, and to present you faultless before the presence of his glory with exceeding joy." Jude 24.
>
> "For whatsoever is born of God overcometh the world: and this is the victory that overcometh the world, even our faith. Who is he that overcometh the world, but he that believeth that Jesus is the Son of God?" 1 John 5: 4, 5.
>
> "For the which cause I also suffer these things: nevertheless I am not ashamed: for I know whom I have believed, and am persuaded that he is able to keep that which I have committed unto him against that day." 2 Tim. 1: 12.
>
> "Who are kept by the power of God through faith unto salvation ready to be revealed in the last time." 1 Pet. 1: 5.

Do not let this class of inquirers go until they are perfectly clear that they are saved, and are no longer merely "trying to be Christians."

IV. "I feel saved": or "I feel that I am going to heaven."

There are very many in this class, very many who think that their entrance into heaven is sure because they "feel saved," or feel that they are going to heaven.

1. The first thing to do with this class is to show them the utter unreliability of our feeling as a ground of hope. An excellent passage for this purpose is Jer. 17: 9:

> "The heart is deceitful above all things, and desperately wicked: who can know it?"

Follow this up with Prov. 14: 12:

> "There is a way *which seemeth right* unto a man, but the end thereof are the ways of death."

After reading the latter passage, you can say to the inquirer, "The way you are going seems to be right, it seems to you as if it would lead to heaven, but what does this passage tell us about a way that seemeth to be right unto a man?" "The end thereof are the ways of death." Then drive the thought home that it will not do to rest our hope upon anything less sure than the Word of God. Luke 18: 9-14 may be used in this way. You can say, "We are told in the Bible about a man who felt saved, and felt sure of going to heaven, let us read about him." Then let him read the story of the Pharisee, and show how he was not saved for all his self-confidence. Is. 55: 8 can also be used to enforce the thought that God's thoughts are not our thoughts, and while we may think we are saved, God may clearly see that we are not.

2. Having shown how little confidence is to be put in our feeling, show the true ground of hope, namely God's Word. Use for this purpose Titus 1: 2:

> "In hope of eternal life, which God, that cannot lie, promised before the world began."

You can say, "Paul had a hope of eternal life. Upon what was that hope built?" "The Word of God 'that cannot lie.'" Then say to the person, "Do you want a hope built upon that sure ground?" Take him then to John 3: 36. That verse tells clearly how to get such a hope. One afternoon I was speaking to a woman who, a few weeks before, had lost her only child. At the time of the child's death she had been especially interested, but her serious impressions had largely left her. After a time I put to her the question, "Do you not wish to go where your little one has gone?" She replied, "I expect to." "What makes you think that you will," I asked. She answered, "I feel so: I feel that I will go to heaven when I die." I then asked her if there was anything she could point to in the Word of God which gave her a reason for believing that she was going to heaven when she died. She replied that there was not. She then turned to me and began to question me: "Do you expect to go to heaven when you die?" "Yes, I know I shall." "How do you know it? Have you any word from God for it?" "Yes," I answered, and turned to Jno. 3: 36. She was then led to see the difference between a faith that depended upon her feeling, and a faith that depended upon the Word of God.

V. The hope of being saved by a mere profession of religion, or by a faith that does not save from sin and lead to repentance.

In many communities it is very common to meet men and

women who believe they are saved because they hold to an orthodox creed, or because they have been baptized or made a profession of religion. This is one of the most dangerous of all false hopes, but it can be readily dealt with.

1. A good passage to begin with is Titus 1:16:

> "They profess that they know God; but in works they deny him, being abominable, and disobedient, and unto every good work reprobate."

You can say to the person, "You profess to know God, but God Himself tells us that many who profess to know Him are lost; let me show it to you in His Word." When they have read the verse, you can say, "Now if one professes to know God, but denies Him in his life, what does God Himself say that such a one is?" "Abominable and disobedient, and unto every good work reprobate." Another passage which can be used in very much the same way is Matt. 7:21, 22, 23.

> "*Not every one that saith unto me Lord, Lord,* shall enter into the kingdom of heaven; but he that doeth the will of my Father which is in heaven. Many will say to me in that day, Lord, Lord, have we not prophesied in thy name? and in thy name have cast out devils? and in thy name done many wonderful works? And then will I profess unto them, I never knew you: depart from me, ye that work iniquity."

You might say, "God tells us plainly in His Word that one may make a profession of religion, may be active even in Christian work, and yet be lost after all." Then have him read the verses. When they are read, you can say, "According to these verses, will a mere profession of religion save any one?" "No, doing the will of the Father which is in heaven." "Are you doing His will?"

2. A second way of dealing with this class is to say, "God tells us plainly that in order to be saved we must be born again." Then show them John 3:3-5:

> "Jesus answered and said unto him, Verily, verily, I say unto thee, *Except a man be born again*, he cannot see the kingdom of God. Nicodemus saith unto him, How can a man be born when he is old? can he enter the second time into his mother's womb, and be born? Jesus answered, Verily, verily, I say unto thee, Except a man be born of water and of the Spirit, he cannot enter into the kingdom of God."

When these verses are read, you can say, "Now these verses make it clear, that in order to enter the kingdom of God, one must be born again. Now let us turn to other parts of the Bible and see what it is to be born again." For this purpose use the following:

> "Whosoever is born of God *doth not commit sin*, for his seed remaineth in him: and he cannot sin, because he is born of God." 1 John 3:9.
>
> "If ye know that he is righteous, ye know that *every one that doeth righteousness* is born of him." 1 John 2:29.
>
> "Therefore if any man be in Christ, *he is a new creature:* old things are passed away; behold, all things are become new." 2 Cor. 5:17.

3. A third method of dealing with this class is by saying, "Yes, faith does indeed save, but it is a certain kind of faith that saves." To show what the faith that saves is, turn to Gal. 5:6:

> "For in Jesus Christ neither circumcision availeth any thing, nor uncircumcision; but *faith which worketh by love.*"

This passage says that it is faith which worketh by love. Rom. 10:9, 10 that it is a faith of the heart:

> "That if thou shalt confess with thy mouth the Lord Jesus, and shalt believe *in thine heart* that God hath raised him from the dead, thou shalt be saved. For *with the heart* man believeth unto righteousness; and with the mouth confession is made unto salvation."

while James 2:14 tells us that it is faith which shows itself in works:

> "What doth it profit, my brethren, though a man say he hath faith, but have not works? can that faith save him?" (R. V.)

4. 1 Jno. 5:4, 5 is also very useful as showing that one who really has faith in Jesus as the Son of God, and is born of God, overcomes the world. The passage reads as follows:

> "For whatsoever is born of God *overcometh the world;* and this is the victory that overcometh the world, even our faith. Who is he that overcometh the world, but he that believeth that Jesus is the Son of God?"

The fact that one is living in sin and not overcoming the world, but being overcome by it, is conclusive proof that he really has not faith that Jesus is the Son of God, and that he has not been born of God.

CHAPTER IX

HOW TO DEAL WITH THOSE WHO LACK ASSURANCE

It is not enough that a man be saved: to be of the most use to God he must know that he is saved, and no small part of our work as personal workers will be to lead into assurance of salvation, men and women who do not as yet know that they are saved. There are two classes of those who lack assurance.

I. Those who lack assurance because of ignorance.

1. There are many who lack assurance for the simple reason that they do not know that it is any one's privilege to know that they have eternal life. Oftentimes if you ask people if they know that they are saved, or if they know that their sins are forgiven, they reply, "Why no, no one knows that." You can say, "Yes, the Bible says that all who believe may know it," and then show them 1 Jno. 5:13:

> "These things have I written unto you that believe on the name of the Son of God; *that ye may know* that ye have eternal life, and that ye may believe on the name of the Son of God."

It is well to begin with this passage, and not to leave it until it becomes very clear that it is every believer's privilege to know that he has everlasting life. Follow this up with Jno. 1:12:

> "But as many as received him, to them gave he power to become the sons of God, even to them that believe on his name."

This verse shows that Christ gives to as many as receive Him, power to become the sons of God. A good way to use this verse is to ask the inquirer questions regarding it. "What does every one who receives Him receive power to become?" "A son of God." "Are you sure that every one who receives

Jesus obtains power to become a son of God?" "Yes." "What makes you sure." "God says so here." "Have you received Jesus?" "Yes." "What then have you received power to become?" Just hold the inquirer to the point that it is not what he feels he has power to become, but what God here in His Word says he has power to become. It will usually be necessary to go through it again and again and again.

Jno. 3: 36 can be used in a similar way. "He that believeth on the Son hath everlasting life." Ask the inquirer, "Who does this verse say has everlasting life?" "He that believeth on the Son." "How many that believe on the Son have everlasting life?" "Why, every one." "Are you sure of that?" "Yes." "Why?" "Because God says so here." "What is it God says?" "He that believeth on the Son hath everlasting life." "Does God merely say that he that believeth on the Son 'shall have' everlasting life?" "No, He says he 'hath' it." "Do you believe on the Son?" "I do." "What then does God say you have?" In a little while he will see it and say, "Everlasting life." Then have him say it over and over again, "I have everlasting life, I have everlasting life." Have him stand by it because God says so, and then have him kneel down and thank God for giving him everlasting life. Do not let the inquirer go while he continues to say, "I hope I have everlasting life." Insist upon his resting absolutely upon what God says. One night I found a young man upon his knees in great distress at the close of an evening service. I showed him from the Bible how Jesus Christ had borne his sins, and asked him if he would accept Christ as his Saviour. He said he would, and seemed to do it; but he seemed to get no light, and went out of the meeting in deep distress still. The next night he was there again, professing to accept Christ, but with no assurance that his sins were forgiven. I tried to show him from John 3: 36 what God said of those who believed on the Son, but the light did not come. Finally he rose to leave the room. As he turned to leave me he said, "Will you pray for me?" I said, "Yes." He walked a few steps down the aisle and I called after him, "Do you believe I will pray for you?" He turned toward me with a look of astonishment, and said, "Yes, of course." I said, "Why do you think I will pray for you?" "Because you said so." I said, "Is not God's Word as good as mine?" He saw it at once, that while he was willing to believe my word, he was not willing to believe God's Word. He received assurance on the spot and knew that he had everlasting life.

Another verse which can be used to advantage with this class is Jno. 5:24:

> "Verily, verily, I say unto you, He that heareth my word, and believeth on him that sent me, hath everlasting life, and shall not come into condemnation; but is passed from death unto life."

This verse has been used of God to bring many into assurance of salvation. 1 Jno. 5:12 is also very plain:

> "He that hath the Son hath life; and he that hath not the Son of God hath not life."

Acts 13:39 has been greatly used of God in dealing with this class. "By him all that believe are justified from all things, etc.," Ask the inquirer, "What does this verse say that all who believe are?" "Justified." "Justified from what?" "From all things." "Do you believe?" "I do." "What are you then?" It will probably be necessary to go over it several times before the inquirer answers, "I am justified"; but when he does, tell him to thank God for justifying him, and to confess Christ before the world. See to it that he does it. I was dealing one night with a young woman who was in great distress of soul because she could not see that she had forgiveness of sin. I went carefully over the ground to find if she really had accepted Christ, and it appeared clear that she had. Then I had her read Acts 13:39, "By him all that believe are justfied from all things." "Now," I said, "Who does God say in this verse are justified from all things?" "All that believe." "Believe on whom?" "Believe on Christ." "Do you believe on Christ?" "I do." "Have you really accepted Him as your Saviour and Lord and Master?" "Yes." "Then you are sure you believe on Him?" "Yes." "And what does this verse say that all who believe are?" "Justified." "What then are you?" She would not say, "I am justified," but wept over the thought that her sins were not forgiven. I went over it again and again and again. At last the simple meaning of the words seemed to dawn upon her darkened mind. I asked her as before, "Who does God say are justified?" "All that believe." "From what are they justified?" "From all things." "Who is justified from all things?" "All that believe." "Who says so?" "God says so." "Do you believe?" "I do." "What are you then?" A joyous light spread over her countenance, and she said, "Why I am justified from all things," and immediately she turned toward her friend standing near and said to me, "Now won't you speak to my friend about Christ?"

2. Many inquirers of this class stumble over the fact that they have not the witness of the Holy Spirit. Show them that the witness of the Word to their acceptance is sufficient, from 1 Jno. 5: 10:

> "He that believeth on the Son of God hath the witness in himself: he that believeth not God hath made him a liar; *because he believeth not the record that God gave* of his Son."

This verse tells us that if we believe not the witness of God, in His Word, we make Him a liar. I was once dealing with a very intelligent young man along this line. He professed that he had accepted Jesus Christ, but that he did not know that he had eternal life. I showed him God's testimony that "he that hath the Son hath life." (1 Jno. 5: 12.) "Now," I said, "You have the Son." "Yes." "And God says that he that hath the Son hath what?" "Life." Then I read the tenth verse, "He that believeth not God hath made Him a liar; because he believeth not the record that God gave of His Son." "Now," I said, "God's record concerning His Son is that eternal life is in Him," (verse 11), and that "He that hath the Son hath life," (verse 12). Now this is God's record. If you do not believe it, no matter what your feelings are, what are you doing?" In a little while the man replied, I am making God a liar, but I never saw it before." Then and there he trusted the naked Word of God, and went out with the knowledge that his sins were forgiven, and that God had given him eternal life.

Also show those who are waiting for the witness of the Holy Spirit, that it is after we believe the testimony of the

Word that we are sealed with the Holy Spirit of promise, using Eph. 1: 13 for this purpose:

> "In whom ye also trusted, after that ye heard the word of truth, the gospel of your salvation: in whom also *after that ye believed*, ye were sealed with that holy Spirit of promise."

The natural order in assurance is this: First, assurance of our justification, resting upon the naked Word of God, (such passages as Acts 13: 39); second, public confession of Christ with the mouth, (Rom. 10: 10); and third, the witness of the Holy Spirit, (Eph. 1:13, Rom. 8: 16). The trouble with many is, that they wish to invert this order, and have the witness of the Holy Spirit before they confess Christ with the mouth.

It is very important in using these texts, to make clear what saving faith is, because many say that they believe, when they do not in the sense of these texts, and so get a false assurance, and entertain false hopes, and never get deliverance. There is a good deal of careless dealing with those who lack assurance. Workers are so anxious to have inquirers come out clearly, that they urge them on to assurance when they have no right to assurance because they have not really accepted Christ. It is better for a man not to have assurance that he is saved, than for a man to have assurance that he is saved when in reality he is not. Jno. 1: 12, 2 Tim. 1: 12 and Rom. 10: 10 make very clear what the character of saving faith is.

II. Those who lack assurance because of sin.

Oftentimes the trouble with those who lack assurance is, that there is some sin or questionable practice in their lives which they ought to confess and give up. When this is the case, it will not do to deal with the inquirer along the lines mentioned above. Take him rather to such passages as John 8: 12:

> "Then spake Jesus again unto them, saying, I am the light of the world: he that followeth me shall not walk in darkness, but shall have the light of life."

When the man has read the passage you can tell him that Jesus' promise was that if we follow Him we shall have the light of life. Say to him, "You have not the light of life. so the probability is that you are not following Him. Are you following Him?" Push the inquirer along this line to find if there is not some point in which he is untrue to Christ, or to the leading of the Holy Spirit. One night in an after-meeting, I was passing around here and there asking different ones about their Christian experience. A gentleman and his wife, friends from another church, had come down to the meeting. I noticed the gentleman looked at his wife as much as to say, "Speak to her." In a little while I came around to her, and asked her how she was getting on in her Christian life. She replied that she was all in the dark. I simply quoted Jno. 8:12 and passed on, but the arrow went home. She and her husband stayed after every one else had gone, and I had a private conversation with her. I asked her if she was rebelling against the will of God at any place. She confessed that she was, that her husband had received a great anointing of the Holy Spirit and she had not, and what was more, she was afraid her husband would go into Christian work and she did not want him to, and so she had gotten utterly in the dark. After some conversation and prayer, she surrendered wholly to the will of God, and the next morning received a wonderful baptism with the Holy Spirit.

Is. 55:7 is a good passage to use with those who lack assurance because of sin. Prov. 28:13 and Ps. 32:1-5 are good passages to use with those who have some unconfessed sin that is keeping them out of the enjoyment of fellowship with God. These passages show that when sin is forsaken and confessed we receive pardon and light and assurance.

Oftentimes it is well when one lacks assurance, first, to put the question clearly to him, "Do you know of any sin which you are cherishing, or anything in your life which your conscience troubles you about?"

CHAPTER X

HOW TO DEAL WITH BACKSLIDERS

One of the largest classes found in the inquiry room, and in all personal work in our day, are those who are, or call themselves backsliders. They are not all alike by any means, and they ought not all to have the same treatment. There are two classes of backsliders:

I. Careless backsliders, those who have no great desire to come back to the Saviour.

1. There is perhaps no better passage to use with such than Jer. 2:5:

> "Thus saith the Lord, What iniquity have your fathers found in me, that they are gone far from me, and have walked after vanity, and are become vain?"

Drive God's question contained in the text right home to their hearts, "What iniquity have you found in the Lord?" Dwell upon God's wonderful love to them, and show them the base ingratitude and folly of forsaking such a Saviour and friend. Very likely they have wandered away because of the unkind treatment of some professed Christian, or of some minister, but hold them right to the point of how the Lord treated them, and how they are now treating Him. Use also Jer. 2:13:

> "For my people have committed two evils; they have forsaken me the fountain of living waters, and hewed them out cisterns, broken cisterns, that can hold no water."

Have the inquirer read the verse, and ask, "Is not that verse true; what does the Lord say that you forsook when you forsook Him?" "The fountain of living waters." "And to what does He say you turned?" "Broken cisterns that can hold no water." "Is not that true in your experience; did you not forsake the fountain of living waters, and have you not found the world broken cisterns that can hold no water?" I have yet to find the first backslider of whom this is not true, and I have used it with many. Then illustrate the text by showing how foolish it would be to turn from a fountain of living water to broken cisterns or muddy pools. If this verse does not accomplish the desired result, use Jer. 2:19:

> "Thine own wickedness shall correct thee, and thy backslidings shall reprove thee: know therefore and see that it is an evil thing and bitter, that thou hast forsaken the Lord thy God, and that my fear is not in thee, saith the Lord God of hosts."

When they have read it, ask them if they have not found it an "evil thing and bitter" that they have forsaken the Lord their God. It is well sometimes to go over the misfortunes and troubles that have come since they forsook the Lord, for it is a fact as every experienced worker knows, that when a man who has had a real knowledge of Christ backslides, misfortune after misfortune is likely to overtake him. Prov. 14:14, the first half of the verse, is also a good passage to use:

> "The backslider in heart shall be filled with his own ways."

1 Kings 11:9 can also be used:

> "And the Lord was angry with Solomon, because his heart was turned from the Lord God of Israel, which had appeared unto him twice."

One of the best passages to show the folly and evil results of backsliding is Luke 15:13-17. Go into detail in bringing out the point of the picture here given of the miseries that came to the backslider in the far country.

2. It is well sometimes to use Amos 4:11, 12:

> "I have overthrown some of you, as God overthrew Sodom and Gomorrah, and ye were as a firebrand plucked out of the burning: yet have ye not returned unto me, saith the Lord. Therefore thus will I do unto thee, O Israel: and because I will do this unto thee, prepare to meet thy God, O Israel."

Before the passage is read you can say, "There is a passage in the Old Testament that contains a message from God to backsliding Israel, and I believe it is a message for you also. Then have him read the passage carefully and after he has read it, ask him what the message of God to backsliding Israel was. "Prepare to meet thy God." Then say to him, "It is God's message to you too, as a backslider to-night, 'prepare to meet thy God.'" Go over this again and again until the thought rings in the heart of the man.

II. Backsliders who are sick of their wandering and sin, and desire to come back to the Lord.

These are a very different class from those just mentioned, though of course they are related. They are perhaps as easy a class to deal with as we ever find. There are many who once had a knowledge of the Lord who have wandered into sin, and who are now sick and tired of sin, and are longing to come back, but think that there is no acceptance for them. Point them to Jer. 3: 12, 13, 22:

> "Go and proclaim these words toward the north, and say, Return, thou backsliding Israel, saith the Lord; and I will not cause mine anger to fall upon you: for I am merciful, saith the Lord, and I will not keep anger forever. Only acknowledge thine iniquity, that thou hast transgressed against the Lord thy God, and hast scattered thy ways to the strangers under every green tree, and ye have not obeyed my voice, saith the Lord.
>
> "Return, ye backsliding children, and I will heal your backslidings Behold we come unto thee; for thou art the Lord our God."

This will show them how ready the Lord is to receive them back, and that all He asks of them is that they acknowledge their sin and return to Him.

Hos. 14: 1-4, is full of tender invitation to penitent backsliders, and also shows the way back to God.

> "O Israel, return unto the Lord thy God; for thou hast fallen by thine iniquity. Take with your words, and turn to the Lord: say unto him, Take away all iniquity, and receive us graciously: so will we render the calves of our lips. Asshur shall not save us; we will not ride upon horses: neither will we say any more to the work of our hands, Ye are our gods: for in thee the fatherless findeth mercy. I will heal their backsliding, I will love them freely: for mine anger is turned away from him."

I use this passage more frequently than almost any other with the class of whom we are speaking, especially the first and fourth verses. I show them first of all that God is inviting the backslider to Himself, and second that He promises to heal their basksliding and love them freely, and third, that all that He asks is that they take words of confession and return to Him (verse 2). The following verses all set forth God's unfailing love for the backslider, and His willingness to receive him back.

'But thou hast not called upon me, O Jacob; but thou hast been weary of me, O Israel.

"Thou hast bought me no sweet cane with money, neither hast thou filled me with the fat of thy sacrifices: but thou hast made me to serve with thy sins, thou hast wearied me with thine iniquities. I, even I, am he that blotteth out thy transgressions for mine own sake, and will not remember thy sins." Is. 43: 22, 24, 25.

"He feedeth on ashes: a deceived heart hath turned him aside, that he cannot deliver his soul, nor say, Is there not a lie in my right hand? Remember these, O Jacob and Israel; for thou art my servant: I have formed thee; thou art my servant: O Israel, thou shalt not be forgotten of me. I have blotted out, as a thick cloud, thy transgressions, and, as a cloud, thy sins: *return unto me; for I have redeemed thee.*" Is. 44: 20-22.

"For I know the thoughts that I think toward you, saith the Lord, thoughts of peace, and not of evil, to give you an expected end. Then shall ye call upon me, and ye shall go and pray unto me, and I will hearken unto you. And ye shall seek me, and find me, when ye shall search for me with all your heart." Jer. 29: 11-13.

"And there ye shall serve gods, the work of men's hands, wood and stone, which neither see, nor hear, nor eat, nor smell." Deut. 4: 28.

"(For the Lord thy God, is a merciful God;) he will not forsake thee, neither destroy thee, nor forget the covenant of thy fathers which he sware unto them." Deut. 4: 31.

"If my people, which are called by my name shall humble themselves, and pray, and seek my face, and turn from their wicked ways, then will I hear from heaven, and will forgive their sin, and will heal their land." 2 Chron. 7: 14.

One of the most useful verses in dealing with an intelligent backslider who wishes to return to the Lord is, 1 Jno 1: 9:

"If we confess our sins, he is faithful and just to forgive us our sins and to cleanse us from all unrighteousness."

It is well sometimes to follow this up with 1 Jno. 2: 1, 2.

"My little children, these things write I unto you, that ye sin not. And if any man sin, we have an advocate with the Father, Jesus Christ the righteous, and he is the propitiation for our sins: and not for ours only, but also for the sins of the whole world."

Often it is helpful to give illustrations of great backsliders who returned to the Lord, and how lovingly He received them. For this purpose you can use Mark 16: 7.

"But go your way, tell his disciples *and Peter* that he goeth before you into Galilee: there shall ye see him, as he said unto you."

This tells of Christ's loving message to Peter after he had so grievously sinned, and deliberately denied his Master. 2 Chron. 15: 4 and 33: 1-9, 12, 13 give illustrations of great backsliders who returned to the Lord, and how lovingly He received them.

Luke 15: 11-21 is perhaps the most useful passage of all in dealing with a backslider who wishes to return, for it has both the steps which the backslider must take, and also a picture of the loving reception from God that awaits him.

When a backslider returns to Christ, he should always be given instructions as to how to live so as not to backslide again. These instructions will be found in Chapter V., Sec. II.

CHAPTER XI

HOW TO DEAL WITH PROFESSED SKEPTICS AND INFIDELS

There are various classes of skeptics, and it is not wise to use the same methods in dealing with all

I. Skeptics who are mere triflers.

A very large share of the skeptics of our day belong to this class. Their professed skepticism is only an excuse for sin, and a salve for their own consciences. As a rule it is not wise to spend much time on an individual of this class, but rather give him something that will sting his conscience and arouse him out of his shallowness A good passage for this purpose is 1 Cor. 1: 18:

> "For the preaching of the cross is to *them that perish foolishness;* but unto us which are saved it is the power of God."

Very likely the skeptic will say, "The Gospel and the whole Bible is all foolishness to me." You can reply by saying, "Yes, that is exactly what God says." "But," the man will say, "You don't understand me, the Gospel and the whole Bible is foolishness to me." "Yes," you can reply, "that is exactly what the Bible says." The man's curiosity will be piqued, and his mind opened by his curiosity to receive a word of truth, off his guard. Then have him read 1 Cor. 1: 18. Then you can say, "You said that the Gospel was foolishness to you, and God Himself says that 'the preaching of the cross is to them that perish foolishness,' and it is foolishness to you because you are perishing; 'but unto us which are saved it is the power of God.'" Oftentimes it will be well to leave the man without another word of comment. Be careful not to laugh at him, and not to produce the impression that you are joking; but leave him with the thought that he is indeed perishing.

2 Cor. 4: 3, 4 can be used in much the same way. Before the passage is read you can say to the man, "You are a skeptic because the Gospel is hidden to you, but God Himself has told us in His Word to whom the Gospel is hidden, and why it is hidden to them." Then let him read the passage:

> "But *if our gospel be hid, it is hid to them that are lost:* in whom the god of this world hath blinded the minds of them which believe not, lest the light of the glorious gospel of Christ, who is the image of God, should shine unto them."

When he has read it, you can say, "That verse explains to you the secret of your difficulty. The Gospel is hidden to you because you are lost, and the reason it is hidden is because the god of this world has blinded your mind, lest the light of the glorious Gospel of Christ, who is the image of God, should shine upon you." I have also found 1 Cor. 2: 14 useful:

> "But the natural man receiveth not the things of the Spirit of God: for they are foolishness unto him: neither can he know them, because they are spiritually discerned."

I have used it to show the man that it was no more than was to be expected that the things of the Spirit of God would be foolishness unto him, because they were spiritually discerned. I was dealing one night with a very bright student. He could hardly be called altogether a trifler, for he was a young man of a good deal of intellectual earnestness. He said to me, "This is all foolishness to me." I replied by saying, "That is exactly what the Bible says." He looked very much astonished, and protested that I did not understand him, that he had said it was all foolishness to him. "Yes," I replied, "that is what the Bible says. Let me show it to you." I opened my Bible to the passage and let him read. When he had read it, I said, "That explains why it is foolishness to you; 'the natural man cannot receive the things of the Spirit of God for they are foolishness unto him.' 'Why," he said, "I never thought of that before." The Spirit of God carried it home to his heart, and the man was lead to an honest acceptance of Christ.

2 Thess. 1: 7-9 can be used with good results with a trifling skeptic or agnostic If the man says in an uppish way, "I am an agnostic," you can say, "Well. God has told us

a good deal about agnostics and their destiny; let us see what He has said." Then have him read this passage:

"And to you who are troubled rest with us, when the Lord Jesus shall be revealed from heaven with his mighty angels, in flaming fire *taking vengeance on them that know not God*, and that obey not the gospel of our Lord Jesus Christ; who shall be punished with everlasting destruction from the presence of the Lord, and from the glory of his power."

When it is read you can say, "Now an agnostic is one that knows not God; and this verse tells us exactly what is the destiny of an agnostic and all those who know not God. This is God's own declaration of their destiny." Then have him read it again if he will, and if he will not, quote it to him. He may laugh at you, and if he does, the Word of God often sinks deeply into the heart, even when it is treated with a sneer.

Mark 16:16 has been found very useful in dealing with trifling skeptics; when a man says to you that he is a skeptic or an infidel, it is well sometimes to say to him, "God has said some very plain words about infidels." Then give to him the passage:

"He that believeth and is baptized shall be saved; but he that believeth not shall be damned."

and say, "I simply want to leave that message of God with you," and pass on. Jno. 3:36 can be used in a similar way.

Sometimes it is well to say to the trifling skeptic, "I can tell you the origin of your skepticism, but I can do better, I can tell you what God says of the origin of your skepticism." Then show him Jno. 8:47:

"He that is of God heareth God's words: ye therefore hear them not, *because ye are not of God*."

2 Thess. 2:10-12 can be used in extreme cases.

"And with all deceivableness of unrighteousness in them that perish; *because they received not the love of the truth*, that they might be saved. And for this cause God shall send them strong delusion, that they should believe a lie: *that they all might be damned who believed not the truth, but had pleasure in unrighteousness*."

You can say to the man, "There is a very interesting passage in the Bible regarding skeptics. It tells what is the origin of their skepticism and what is the outcome of it." Then have him read the passage. When he has read it, say, "Now what does this passage say about the origin of skepticism?" Show him it is "because they received not the love of the truth, that they might be saved." "What is the result of their refusal to receive the truth?" "God shall give them over to strong delusion that they shall believe a lie." "And what is the outcome of it all?" "That they all might be damned who believed not in the truth, but had pleasure in unrighteousness."

Ps. 14:1 is useful in some cases, though it needs to be used with discretion and kindness. Before giving it to the man to read, you can say, "I do not wish to say anything unkind to you, but God Himself has said a very plain word about those who say there is no God; let me show it to you." Then let him read:

"The fool hath said in his heart, There is no God."

When he has read it, say, "I am not saying that, but God has said it. Now it is a matter between you and God, but I would advise you not to forget what God has said." Of course this applies especially to one who is skeptical about, or denies the existence of God.

In dealing with a skeptic who is a trifler, and in fact with all skeptics, don't argue, don't get angry, be very gentle but very solemn, and very much in prayer, depending upon the Holy Spirit to give you words to say and to carry them home

II. An earnest-minded skeptic.

Many skeptics are not triflers. There are very many men and women in our day who are really very desirous of knowing the truth, but who are in an utter maze of skepticism. There is no more interesting class of people to deal with than this. In beginning work with them, it is well to ask them the following preliminary questions:

1. "*What can't you believe?*"

Get as full an answer as possible to this question, for many a man thinks he is a skeptic when really he does believe the great fundamental truths. Furthermore, in finding out what a man does believe, no matter how little it is, you have a starting point to lead the man out to further faith

2. "*Why can't you believe?*"

This will oftentimes show the man how utterly without foundation are his grounds for unbelief.

3. "*Do you live up to what you do believe?*"

This will give you an opportunity in many cases to show a man that his trouble is not so much what he does not believe, as his failure to live up to what he does believe. Only the other night I was dealing with a man who told me that his trouble was that he could not believe, but we had not gotten far in the conversation until it became clear to us that his trouble was not so much that he could not believe, but that he did not live up to what he did believe.

4. "*What do you believe?*"

A few important lines along which to carry out this inquiry are, "Do you believe that there is an absolute difference between right and wrong?" "Do you believe that there is a God?" "Do you believe in prayer?" "Do you believe any part of the Bible, if so what part?"

Having asked the man these preliminary questions, proceed at once to show him how to believe. I have found no passage in the Bible equal to John 7:17 in dealing with an honest skeptic:

> "If any man *will do his will*, he shall know of the doctrine, whether it be of God, or whether I speak of myself."

It shows the way out of skepticism to faith, and has been used of God to the salvation of countless skeptics and infidels. You can say to the skeptic, "Now Jesus Christ makes a fair proposition. He does not ask you to believe without evidence, but He asks you to do a thing that your own conscience approves, and promises that if you do it, you will come out of skepticism into knowledge. What Jesus asks in this verse, is that you will to do God's will; that is, that you surrender your will to God. Will you do it?" When this point has been settled, next say to him, "Will you make an honest search to find out what the will of God is, that you may do it?" When this point has been settled, ask the man, "Do you believe that God answers prayer?" Very likely the skeptic will reply that he does not. You can say to him, "Well I know that He does, but of course I don't expect you to accept my opinion, but here is a possible clew to knowledge. Now the method of modern science is to follow out any possible clew to see what there is in it. You have given me a promise to make an honest search to find the will of God, and here is a possible clew, and if your promise was honest, you will follow it. Will you pray this prayer? 'O God, show me whether Jesus is thy Son or not; and if You show me that He is, I promise to accept Him as my Saviour and confess Him as such before the world.'" It is well to have him make his promise definite by putting it down in black and white. After this is done, show him still another step. Take him to John 20:31·

> "But these are written, that ye might believe that Jesus is the Christ, the Son of God; and that believing ye might have life through his name."

Here we are told that the Gospel of John was written that we might believe that Jesus is the Christ, the Son of God. Tell him, "Now this Gospel is given for this purpose, to show that Jesus is the Christ the Son of God. Will you take this Gospel and read it, honestly and carefully?" Very likely he will say, "I have read it often before." You can say, "I want you to read it in a new way. Will you read it this way? Read a few verses at a time, and each time before you read, will you ask God to give you light on the passage that you are about to read, and promise that if He does, you will follow as much as you see to be true. Now when you have read the Gospel through, come back to me and tell me the result." I would again carefully go over all the points as to what he was to do. It would be well also to ask him to especially notice the following verses in the Gospel: 1:32-34; 3:2; 3:3; 3:16; 3:18, 19; 3:32; 3:34; 3:36; 4:10; 4:14; 4:23; 4:34; 4:52, 53; 5:8, 9; 5:22-24; 5:28, 29; 5:40; 5:44; 6:8-14; 6:19; 6:27; 6:29; 6:35; 6:40; 6:66-68; 7:17; 7:37-39; 7:45, 46; 8:12; 8:18; 8:21; 8:24; 8:31, 32; 8:34; 8:36; 8:38; 8:42; 8:47; 9:17; 9:24, 25; 9:35-39; 10:9; 10:11; 10:27-29; 10:30; 11:25, 26; 11:43-45; 12:26; 12:32; 12:35, 36; 12:42, 43; 12:46; 12:48-50; 13:3; 13:13; 14:3; 14:6; 14:9; 14:15, 16; 14:21; 14:24; 14:27; 15:5; 15:7; 15:9-11; 15:18, 19; 15:23-26; 16:3; 16:7-11; 16:13, 14; 16:24; 17:3; 17:5; 17:12; 17:14; 17:22; 17:24; 17:25, 26; 18:37; 19:6; 19:7-8; 20:8; 20:13-19; 20:24, 25; 20:27-29; 20:31; 21:24. This method of treatment if it is honestly followed by the skeptic will never fail.

If the skeptic does not believe even in the existence of God, you will have to begin one step further back. Ask him if he believes there is *an absolute difference between right and wrong.* If he says that he does not, which will be very rarely the case, it is just as well to tell him then and there that he is a mere trifler. If he says that he does, ask him if he will take his stand upon the right and follow it wherever it carries him. He will very likely try to put you off by saying, "What is right?" You can say to him that you do not ask him to take your conception of right, but will he take his stand upon the right and follow it wherever it carries him, and make an honest attempt to find out what the right is. Next say to him, "You do not know whether there is a God and whether He answers prayer or not. I know that there is a God and that He answers prayer; but I do not ask you to accept my opinion, but here is a possible clew to knowledge; will you follow it?" If he refuses, of course you will know at once that he is not an honest skeptic, and you can tell him so. If he is willing to try this clew have him offer this prayer, "O God, if there is any God, show me whether Jesus Christ is Thy Son or not, and if You show me that He is, I promise to accept Him as my Saviour and confess Him as such before the world," then have him proceed by reading the Gospel of John, etc., as in the former case. If the man is not an honest skeptic, this course of treatment will reveal the fact, and you can tell him that the difficulty is not with his skepticism, but with his rebellious and wicked heart. If a man says he does not know whether there is an absolute difference between right and wrong, you can set it down at once that he is bad, and turn to him and say frankly but kindly, "My friend, there is something wrong in your life. No man who is living a right life will doubt that there is an absolute difference between right and wrong. You probably know what the wrong is, and the trouble is not with your skepticism but with your sin.

A man who was a thorough-going agnostic once came to me and stated his difficulties. The man had had a very remarkable experience. He had dabbled in Unitarianism,

Spiritualism, Buddhism, Theosophy, and pretty much every other ism extant. He was in a state of absolute agnosticism. He neither affirmed nor denied the existence of God. He told me that I could not help him, for his case was "very peculiar," as indeed it was, but I had Jno. 7:17 to build my hope upon, and the man seemed honest. I asked him if he believed there was an absolute difference between right and wrong, he said that he did. I asked him if he was willing to take his stand upon the right and follow it wherever it carried him. He said that he was. I called out my stenographer and dictated a pledge somewhat as follows: "I believe that there is an absolute difference between right and wrong, and I hereby take my stand upon the right to follow it wherever it carries me. I promise to make an honest search to find if Jesus Christ is the Son of God, and if I find that He is, I promise to accept Him as my Saviour and confess Him as such before the world." I handed the pledge to the man and asked him if he was willing to sign it. He read it carefully and then signed it. I then said to him, "You don't know there is not a God?" "No," he said, "I don't know that there is no God. Any man is a fool to say that he knows there is not a God. I neither affirm nor deny." "Well," I said, "I know there is a God, but that will do you no good." I said further, "You do not know that God does not answer prayer." "No," he said, "I do not know that God does not answer prayer, but I do not believe that He does." I said, "I know that He does, but that will not do you any good, but here is a possible clew to knowledge. Now you are a graduate of a British university. You know that the method of modern science is to follow out a possible clew to see what there is in it. Will you follow out this clew? Will you pray this prayer: 'O God, if there is any God, show me whether Jesus Christ is Thy Son or not, and if You show me that He is, I promise to accept Him as my Saviour and confess Him as such before the world'?" "Yes," he said, "I am willing to do that, but there is nothing in it; my case is very peculiar." I then turned to John 20:31 and read, "These are written, that ye might believe that Jesus is the Christ, the Son of God; and that believing ye might have life through His name." After reading the verse, I said, "John wrote this Gospel that 'ye might believe that Jesus is the Christ, the Son of God,' will you take this Gospel and read it, not trying to believe it, but simply with a fair mind, willing to believe it if it approves itself to you as true?" He said, "I have read it time and time again, and could quote a good deal of it." I said, "I want you to read it in a new way; read a few verses at a time, ask God for light each time you read, and promise to act upon so much as you see to be true." This the man promised to do, but closed by saying, "There is nothing in it, my case is very peculiar." I went over again the various points and bade the man good-bye. A short time after I met him again. He hurried up to me, and almost the first words he said were, "There is something in that." I replied, "I knew that before." "Why," he said, "ever since I have done what I promised you to do, it is just as if I had been taken up to the Niagara river and was being carried along." Some weeks after I met the man again; his doubts had all gone. The teachings of the men he had formerly listened to with delight, had become utter foolishness to him. He had put himself in a way to find out the truth of God, and God had made it known to him, and he had become a believer in Jesus Christ as God's Son, and the Bible as God's Word.

There is no more interesting class, and no easier class to deal with, than honest skeptics. Many are afraid to tackle them, but there is no need of this. There is a way out of skepticism into faith laid down in the Bible that is absolutely sure if any one will take it. As for skeptics who are triflers, it is not best to spend much time on them, but simply to give them some searching passages of Scripture, and to look to the Spirit of God to carry the Word home.

III. Special classes of skeptics.

1. *Those who doubt the existence of God.*

The passages given under I. and II. may be used with this class, and usually it is wise to use them before the specific passages given under this head.

(1) An excellent passage to use with those who claim to doubt the existence of God is Rom. 1:19-22:

"Because that which may be known of God is manifest in them; for

God hath shewed it unto them. For the invisible things of him from the creation of the world are clearly seen, *being understood by the things that are made*, even his eternal power and Godhead; so that they are without excuse: because that, *when they knew God, they glorified him not as God, neither were thankful;* but became vain in their imaginations, and their foolish heart was darkened. Professing themselves to be wise, they became fools."

Ask the doubter to read this passage carefully. When he has done so, you can say to him, "Of course you never saw God, but this verse tells us how the invisible things of Him whom we have never seen can be known, and how is it?" "By the things that are made." "What does Paul say we can understand by the things that are made?" "His eternal power and Godhead." "Is not this true, do not the facts of nature prove an intelligent creator?" It is well sometimes to illustrate by a watch or something of that sort. Show the inquirer a watch and ask him if he believes it had an intelligent maker, and why he thinks so; then ask him about his eye which shows more marks of intelligence in its construction than a watch, or anything man ever made. Having dealt upon this argument and made it clear, ask him what God says those are who do not believe in God as revealed in His works. Bring out the fact that God says they are "without excuse." Then you can say to him, "The twenty-first verse tells us why men get in the dark about God." Have him read this verse also. "According to this verse, why is it that men get in the dark about God?" "Because that, when they knew God, they glorified Him not as God, neither were thankful." "Is not this true about you? Was there not a time when you knew God, believed that there was a God, but did not glorify Him as God, neither returned thanks to Him? What does God say is the result of this course?" "They became vain in their imaginations, and their foolish heart was darkened." "Now is this not precisely your case? Has not your foolish heart been darkened by not glorifying God when you knew Him? Now the twenty-second verse describes such persons, exactly what does it say about them?" "Professing themselves to be wise, they became fools."

In something the same way you can use Ps. 19: 1, 2:

"The heavens declare the glory of God; and the firmament sheweth his handiwork. Day unto day uttereth speech, and night unto night sheweth knowledge."

"According to this passage, what declares to us the glory of God?" "The heavens." "What shows His handiwork?" "The firmament." "Do you know anything about the stars?" Let the skeptic tell what he knows about the stars. If he knowns nothing, tell him something about their greatness, their magnitude, and their wonderful movements, and then ask him if it does not indicate a wonderful creator. Endeavor to make him see that he is not honest in his denial of God.

(2) Tell him that there is still one verse you wish to give him, and that you hope he will bear in mind that it is not you who says it, but God; and that it applies to his case exactly. Then have him read the first half of Ps. 14:1:

"The fool hath said in his heart, There is no God."

When he has read it, ask him who it is according to this verse, who says "there is no God." "The fool." "Where is it that he says there is no God?" "In his heart." "Why is it then that the fool says there is no God; is it because he cannot believe in God, or because he does not wish to believe in God?" You can add that the folly of saying in one's heart there is no God, is seen in two points, first, because there is a God, and it is folly to say there is not one when there is; and second, because the doctrine that there is not a God always brings misery and wretchedness. Put it right to the man, and ask him if he ever knew a happy atheist. Before leaving him, you can tell him that he is losing the greatest blessing for time and for eternity, by doubting the existence of God. Turn him to Rom. 6:23 and show him that this is so:

"The wages of sin is death; but the gift of God is eternal life through Jesus Christ our Lord."

When he has read the verse, say to him, "This verse tells us that we have our choice between eternal death, which is the wages that we have earned by sin, and eternal life, which is the gift of God, but of course if we do not believe in God, we cannot look to Him for this gift." You can further tell him that in his present state of mind it is impossible for him to do anything that pleases God, and show him Heb. 11:6 and have him read it if he will, and if he will not, read it to him.

2. *Those who doubt that the Bible is the Word of God.*

The method of dealing with honest skeptics described above, is as a rule the best method of dealing with this class, but other plans will be useful with some.

(1) Oftentimes men say, "I do not believe the Bible as a whole is the Word of God, but I accept what Jesus Christ says." If one says this, get him to take his stand clearly and definitely upon this statement, that he accepts the authority of Jesus Christ. Get him to commit himself to this point. When he has done it, say to him, "Well, if you accept the authority of Jesus Christ, you must accept the authority of the whole Old Testament, for Jesus Christ has set the seal of His authority to the entire book." This the man will not believe at first, but turn him to Mark 7:13; show him the context, thereby proving to him that Jesus here calls the law of Moses the Word of God. Then say to him, "If you accept the authority of Jesus, you must accept the authority of at least the first five books of the Bible as being the Word of God. You can follow this up by Matt. 5:18:

> "For verily I say unto you, Till heaven and earth pass, one jot or one tittle shall in no wise pass from the law till all be fulfilled."

Here Jesus sets His authority to the absolute inerrancy of the Old Testament law. Then turn him to John 10:35:

> "If he called them gods unto whom the word of God came, and *the Scripture cannot be broken.*"

Show him how that here Jesus quotes a passage from the Psalms, (Ps. 82:6), and says that the Scripture cannot be broken, and hereby sets the stamp of His authority to the absolute inerrancy of the entire Old Testament Scriptures. Turn him next to Luke 24:27:

> "And beginning at Moses and all the prophets, he expounded unto them in all the scriptures the things concerning himself.'

Show him from this passage how Jesus quoted the entire Old Testament Scriptures, Moses and the prophets, as being of conclusive authority. Then go on to the 44th verse, and call his attention to the fact that Jesus said that "all things must be fulfilled, which were written in the law of Moses, and in the prophets, and in the Psalms." Remind him that the Jew divided his Bible, the present Old Testament Scriptures, into three parts, the Law, the Prophets and the Psalms, and that Jesus took up each one of these parts in detail, and set the stamp of His authority upon the whole. Therefore hold him to the point that if he accepts, the authority of Christ, he must accept the authority of the whole Old Testament, and he has already said that he did accept the authority of Christ.

To prove that Christ set the stamp of His authority to the New Testament, take him to Jno. 14: 26:

> "But the Comforter, which is the Holy Ghost, whom the Father will send in my name, he shall teach you all things, and bring all things to your remembrance, whatsoever I have said unto you."

Here Jesus plainly declares that not only would the teaching of the apostles be true, but that it would contain all the truth, and furthermore, that their recollection of what He Himself said, would not be their own recollection, but the recollection of the Holy Ghost. Follow this up with Jno. 16: 12, 13:

> "I have yet many things to say unto you, but ye cannot bear them now. Howbeit when he, the Spirit of truth, is come, he will guide you into all truth: for he shall not speak of himself; but whatsoever he shall hear, that shall he speak: and he will shew you things to come."

Show him that Jesus Himself, said, 'I have many things to say unto you, but ye cannot bear them now. Howbeit when He, the Spirit of truth, is come, He will guide you into all truth." Therefore, tell him, that Jesus said the apostles would be taught of the Holy Spirit, that the Holy Spirit would guide them *into all the truth*, and that their teaching would be more complete than His own. "Therefore, if you accept the authority of Jesus, you must accept the authority of the entire New Testament."

(2) If the objector says that Paul never claimed that his teachings were the Word of God, turn him to 1 Thess. 2: 13:

> "For this cause also thank we God without ceasing, because, when ye received *the word of God which ye heard of us*, ye received it not as the word of men, *but as it is in truth, the word of God*, which effectually worketh also in you that believe."

(3) A passage which is useful as describing the character of Bible inspiration is 2 Peter 1: 21:

> "For the prophecy came not in old time by the will of man: but holy men of God *spake as they were moved by the Holy Ghost.*"

1 Cor 2:14 is useful as proving verbal inspiration, (see especially Am. R. V.).

(4) Sometimes it is well to say to the doubter, "The Bible itself xplains why it is that you do not believe the Bible is the Word of God." Then show him Jno. 8:47. Follow this up by saying, "That you do not believe the Bible is God's word does not alter the fact," and show him Rom. 3:3, 4:

> "For what if some did not believe? shall their unbelief make the faith of God without effect? God forbid: yea, let God be true, but every man a liar; as it is written, That thou mightest be justified in thy sayings, and mightest overcome when thou art judged."

You can go further yet and say, that God Himself tells us that there is awful guilt attaching to the one who will not believe the record that He has given, and then show him 1 Jno. 5:10:

> "He that believeth on the Son of God hath the witness in himself: *he that believeth not God hath made him a liar;* because he believeth not the record that God gave of his Son."

Ask him when he has read it, "What does God say here of the one who does not believe the record that He has given of His Son?" and make him see that God says he has made God a liar.

(5) Finally you may use Luke 16:30, 31:

> "And he said, Nay, father Abraham: but if one went unto them from the dead, they will repent. And he said unto him, If they hear not Moses and the prophets, neither will they be persuaded, though one rose from the dead."

Before reading it, say, "Well, God says that the case of one who will not listen to the Bible is very desperate. Just read and see what He says upon this point," and then have him read the verse.

3. *Those who doubt the divinity of Christ.*

It is very common in our day to have men say that they believe in God, but they do not believe that Jesus Christ was the Son of God. The best way, as a rule, to deal with such, is along the line described in I. and II., especially under II.; but sometimes there is a man who has real difficulties on this point, and it is well to meet him squarely.

(1) In the first place, show such a one that we find several divine titles applied to Christ, the same titles being applied to Christ in the New Testament that are applied to Jehovah in the Old, Acts 10:36 and 1 Cor. 2:8, compare Ps. 24:8-10;

"The word which God sent unto the children of Israel, preaching peace by Jesus Christ: (he is *Lord of all*)." Acts 10: 36.

"Which none of the princes of this world knew: for had they known it, they would not have crucified *the Lord of glory*." 1 Cor. 2: 8.

"Who is this King of glory? The LORD strong and mighty, the LORD mighty in battle. Lift up your heads, O ye gates; even lift them up, ye everlasting doors; and the King of glory shall come in. *Who is this King of glory? The LORD of hosts, he is the King of glory.* Selah." Ps. 24: 8-10.

Heb. 1: 8; Jno. 20: 28, Rom. 9: 5, Rev. 1: 17, compare Is. 44: 6.

"But unto the Son he saith, Thy throne, O God, is for ever and ever: a sceptre of righteousness is the sceptre of thy kingdom." Heb. 1: 8.

"And Thomas answered and said unto him, My Lord and my God." John 20: 28

"Whose are the fathers, and of whom as concerning the flesh Christ came, who is over all, *God blessed forever*." Rom. 9: 5.

"And when I saw him, I fell at his feet as dead. And he laid his right hand upon me, saying unto me, Fear not; *I am the first and the last*." Rev. 1: 17.

"*Thus saith the LORD* the King of Israel, and his redeemer the LORD of hosts; *I am the first, and I am the last,* and beside me there is no God." Is. 44: 6.

(2) Show him further that offices are ascribed to Christ that only God could fill. For this purpose use Heb. 1: 3, 10:

"Who being the brightness of his glory, and the express image of his person, and *upholding all things by the word of his power*, when he had by himself purged our sins, sat down on the right hand of the Majesty on high."

"And, thou, Lord, in the beginning hast *laid the foundation of the earth;* and *the heavens are the work of thine hands*."

(3) Show him that the Bible expressly declares that Jesus Christ should be worshiped as God. Use for this purpose Heb. 1: 6, Phil. 2: 10, Jno. 5: 22, 23, compare Rev. 5: 13:

"And again, when he bringeth in the first begotten into the world, he saith, *And let all the angels of God worship him*." Heb. 1: 6.

"That *at the name of Jesus* every knee should bow, of things in heaven, and things in earth, and things under the earth." Phil. 2: 10.

"For the Father judgeth no man, but hath committed all judgment unto the Son: that all men should honour the Son, *even as they honour the Father*. He that honoureth not the Son honoureth not the Father which hath sent him." John 5: 22, 23.

"And every creature which is in heaven, and on the earth, and under the earth, and such as are in the sea, and all that are in them, heard I saying, Blessing, and honour, and glory, and power, be unto him that sitteth upon the throne, *and unto the Lamb* for ever and ever." Rev. 5:13.

(4) Show him that Jesus claimed the same honor as His Father, and either He was divine, or the most blasphemous impostor that ever lived. For this purpose use Jno. 5:22, 23. Drive home the truth that the one who denies Christ's divinity puts Him in the place of a blasphemous impostor. Mark 14:61, 62:

"But he held his peace, and answered nothing. Again the high priest asked him, and said unto him, Art thou the Christ, the Son of the blessed? And *Jesus said, I am:* and ye shall see the Son of man sitting on the right hand of power, and coming in the clouds of heaven." (cf. vs. 63, 64.)

(5) In the next place show him that the Bible says the one who denies the divinity of Christ, no matter who he may be, is a liar and an antichrist. For this purpose use 1 Jno. 2:22, 23, compared with 1 Jno. 5:1, 5:

"*Who is a liar but he that denieth that Jesus is the Christ?* He is antichrist, that denieth the Father and the Son. Whosoever denieth the Son, the same hath not the Father: [but] he that acknowledgeth the Son hath the Father also."

"Whosoever believeth that Jesus is the Christ is born of God: and every one that loveth him that begat loveth him also that is begotten of him."

"Who is he that overcometh the world, but he that believeth that Jesus is the Son of God?"

1 Jno. 5:10-12 shows that he who does not believe that Jesus is divine makes God a liar, "because he believeth not the record that God gave of his Son."

(6) Make it clear to the inquirer that God regards it as a matter of awful folly and guilt deserving the worst punishment, to reject Christ as the Son of God. For this purpose use Heb. 10:28, 29:

"He that despised Moses' law died without mercy under two or three witnesses: of how much sorer punishment, suppose ye, shall he be thought worthy, who hath trodden under foot the Son of God, and hath counted the blood of the covenant, wherewith he was sanctified, an unholy thing, and hath done despite unto the Spirit of grace?"

follow this up with Jno. 8:24 which shows beyond a question that one who does not believe in the divinity of Christ cannot be saved, and Jno. 20:31 which shows that we obtain life through believing that Jesus is the Christ the Son of God.

(7) I have found that making clear the fact that Christ rose from the dead, and that this was God's seal to His claim to be divine, is very helpful in dealing with many who have doubts as to His divinity. I have also found Acts 9: 20 very helpful:

"And straightway he preached Christ in the synagogues, *that he is the Son of God.*"

I call attention to who it was in this verse that declared Jesus to be the Son of God, namely Saul of Tarsus. I then bring out what it was that led Paul to say this; that is, his actually seeing Jesus in the glory, and hearing the words that He spoke to him. Then I make it clear that one of three things is true; either Saul actually saw Jesus in the glory, or else he lied about it, or else he was deceived, being in a heated state of imagination or something of that kind. Then I show how he could not have lied about it, for men do not manufacture a lie for the sake of suffering for it thirty or thirty-five years.

Second, I show that the circumstances were such as to preclude the possibility of an optical delusion, or an overheated state of the imagination, for not only did Paul see the light, but those who were with him, and those who were with him also heard the voice speaking, though they did not hear what the voice said. Furthermore, there was a second man, Ananias, who received a commission independently, to go to Saul and lay hands upon him, and his eyes would be opened, and Saul's eyes were opened, which of course could not be the result of imagination. So Saul of Tarsus must actually have seen Christ in the glory, and if he did, in the way described, it settles it beyond question that Jesus is the Son of God; so the divinity of Christ is not a theological speculation, but an established fact.

4. *Those who doubt the doctrine of future punishment, or the conscious, endless suffering of the lost.*

As a rule it is not wise to discuss this difficulty with one who is not an out and out Christian. No one who has not surrendered his will and his mind to Jesus Christ is in a position to discuss the details of future punishment, but if one is skeptical on this point, though a Christian (in that he has accepted Christ as a personal Saviour) it is well to show him the teach ing of God's Word. A great deal is made by those who deny the conscious, endless suffering of the lost, of the words "death" and "destruction," which are said to mean annihilation, or at least non-conscious existence. Say to such a one, "Let us see how the Bible defines its own terms." Rev. 21:8 defines what death means when used in the Scriptures as the punishment of the wicked:

"But the fearful, and unbelieving, and the abominable, and murderers, and whoremongers, and sorcerers, and idolaters, and all liars, shall have their part in the lake which burneth with fire and brimstone: *which is the second death.*"

Rev. 17:8, cf. Rev. 19:20 shows what "perdition" (same Greek word as translated elsewhere "destruction"), means in the Scriptures:

"The beast that thou sawest was, and is not; and shall ascend out of the bottomless pit, and go *into perdition;* and they that dwell on the earth shall wonder, whose names were not written in the book of life from the foundation of the world, when they behold the beast that was, and is not, and yet is." Rev. 17:8.

"And the beast was taken, and with him the false prophet that wrought miracles before him, with which he deceived them that had received the mark of the beast, and them that worshiped his image. These both were cast alive *into a lake of fire burning with brimstone.*" Rev. 19:20.

Rev. 17:8 tells us that the beast was to go into "perdition," (destruction), Rev. 19:20 tells us just where the beast went, "into a lake of fire burning with brimstone." This then is "perdition." But Rev. 20:10 shows us the beast still there at the end of one thousand years, *and being still consciously tormented, and to be tormented day and night forever and ever.* This then is what the Bible means by "perdition" or "destruction," conscious torment forever and ever in a lake of fire. Rev. 20:15 shows that those who are subjected to the terrible retribution here described, are those who are not found written in the book of life:

"And whosoever was not found written in the book of life was cast into the lake of fire."

Matt. 10:28 shows that there is a destruction for the soul apart from the destruction for the body:

"And fear not them which kill the body, but are not able to kill the soul: but rather fear him which is able to destroy both soul and body in hell."

Luke 12:5 shows that *after one is killed*, (and is of course dead), there is still punishment in hell:

"But I will forewarn you whom ye shall fear: fear him, which *after he hath killed* hath power to cast into hell; yea, I say unto you, Fear him."

Mark 3:28, 29, R. V., shows that there is such a thing as an eternal sin:

"Verily I say unto you, All their sins shall be forgiven unto the sons of men, and their blasphemies wherewith soever they shall blaspheme: but whosoever shall blaspheme against the Holy Spirit hath never forgiveness, but is guilty of *an eternal sin.*"

Luke 16:23-26 shows that the condition of the wicked dead is one of conscious torment.

Mark 14:21 shows that the retribution visited upon the wicked is of so terrible a character, that it would be better for him upon whom it is visited if he had never been born:

"The Son of man indeed goeth, as it is written of him: but woe to that man by whom the Son of man is betrayed! good were it for that man if he had never been born."

2 Pet. 2:4 and Jude 6 show that hell is not a place where the inhabitants cease to exist, but where they are reserved alive for the purposes of God:

"For if God spared not the angels that sinned, but cast them down to hell, and delivered them into chains of darkness, *to be reserved unto judgment.*"

"And the angels which kept not their first estate, but left their own habitation, he *hath reserved in everlasting chains* under darkness unto the judgment of the great day."

Heb. 10:28, 29 shows that while the punishment for the transgression of the Mosaic law was death, sorer punishment awaits those who have trodden under foot the Son of God.

Matt. 25:41 shows that the wicked *go* to the place prepared for the devil and his angels, and share the same endless conscious torment:

"Then shall he say also unto them on the left hand, Depart from me, ye cursed, into everlasting fire, prepared for the devil and his angels."

The character of this place and the duration of its punishment is very clearly stated in Rev. 19:20 and 20:10.

CHAPTER XII

HOW TO DEAL WITH THOSE WHO WISH TO PUT OFF A DECISION UNTIL SOME OTHER TIME

Oftentimes when you have swept away every difficulty, and the way of salvation is made as clear as day, still the inquirer is not ready to decide then and there. He wishes to put off a decision until some future time. There are several classes of those who wish to put off a decision:

I. One of the largest classes is composed of those who say, **"I want to wait,"** or **"Not to-night,"** or **"I will think about it,"** or **"I will come to-morrow night,"** or some other such thing.

Give to such a person Is. 55:6:

> "Seek ye the Lord *while he may be found*, call ye upon him while he is near."

When the inquirer has read the passage, ask him when it is that he is to seek the Lord. When he says, "While He may be found," ask him when that is. Make it clear that the only time when he can be absolutely sure of finding the Lord is right now. Ask him if he can be sure of finding the Lord to-morrow if he does not seek Him to-day. Sometimes it is well to give illustrations from life concerning those who put off seeking the Lord, and when the next day came it was too late to find Him.

Prov. 27:1 is also a good verse to use:

> "Boast not thyself of to-morrow; for thou knowest not what a day may bring forth."

When the verse has been carefully and intelligently read, (if it is not read carefully and intelligently at first, ask the one with whom you are dealing to read it again), ask him what it is that God says it is unwise to boast one's self of. "To-morrow." Ask him **why it is unwise to boast** one's self of to-morrow. "Because thou knowest not what a day may bring forth." Ask him if he knows what a single day will bring forth. Suggest to him some of the things that it may bring forth, and then ask him if he does not think he better take Christ then and there.

Prov. 29:1 has often been used of the Holy Spirit to bring men to an immediate decision:

> "He, that being often reproved hardeneth his neck, shall *suddenly* be destroyed, and that without remedy."

It is well after the verse has been read, to ask the one with whom you are dealing, "What becomes of the one who being often reproved hardeneth his neck?" When he answers, "He shall suddenly be destroyed," ask him if he is willing to run the risk. Or you can use Matt. 25:10-12:

> "And while they went to buy, the bridegroom came; and they that were ready went in with him to the marriage: and the door was shut. Afterward came also the other virgins, saying, Lord, Lord, open to us. But he answered and said, Verily I say unto you, I know you not."

Ask him who it was that went in to the marriage, and when he answers, "They that were ready," ask him if he is ready. Then ask him what happened afterward to those who were not ready. Ask him who those who were not ready were. Then put it to him, "Are you willing to be on the outside?"

Another excellent passage to use is Luke 12:19, 20:

> "And I will say to my soul, Soul, thou hast much goods laid up *for many years;* take thine ease, eat, drink, and be merry. *But God said* unto him, Thou fool, *this night* thy soul shall be required of thee: then whose shall those things be, which thou hast provided?"

After the verses have been read, ask, "For how many years did this man think that he had his goods laid up?" "Many years." "But what did God say to him?" "How many years do you think you have before you still? But what may God say to you? When may He say it?"

A passage especially effective in dealing with those who say, "I am not ready," is Matt. 24:44

> "Therefore be ye also ready: for in such an hour as ye think not the Son of man cometh."

Another passage which can also be used with good effect is 1 Kings 18:21:

"And Elijah came unto all the people, and said. How long halt ye between two opinions? if the Lord be God, follow him: but if Baal, then follow him."

An excellent way to use this verse is by asking the person whether he would be willing to wait a year and not have an opportunity under any circumstances, no matter what came up, of accepting Christ. When he answers, No, I might die within a year," ask him if he would be willing to wait a month, a week, a day. Ask him if he would like God, the Holy Spirit, and all Christians to leave him alone for a day, and he not have the opportunity under any circumstances of accepting Christ. Almost any thoughtful person will say "No." Then tell him if that is the case, he better accept Christ at once. Dr. Chalmers was the first one to use this method, and it has been followed by many others with great success.

Other passages which can be used with this class are:

"Go to now, ye that say, To-day or to-morrow we will go into such a city, and continue there a year, and buy and sell, and get gain: whereas ye know not what shall be on the morrow. For what is your life? It is even a vapour, that appeareth for a little time, and then vanisheth away." James 4: 13-14.

"Because there is wrath, beware lest he take thee away with his stroke: then a great ransom cannot deliver thee." Job 36: 18.

Luke 13: 24-28.

"Then said Jesus again unto them, I go my way, and ye shall seek me, and shall die in your sins: whither I go, ye cannot come." John 8: 21.

"Then Jesus said unto them, Yet a little while is the light with you. Walk while ye have the light, lest darkness come upon you: for he that walketh in darkness knoweth not whither he goeth." John 12: 35.

"Then said Jesus unto them, Yet a little while am I with you, and then I go unto him that sent me. Ye shall seek me, and shall not find me: and where I am, thither ye cannot come." John 7: 33, 34.

II. Those who say, **"I must get fixed in business first, and then I will become a Christian."**

With such persons use Matt. 6: 33

"But seek ye first the kingdom of God, and his righteousness; and all these things shall be added unto you."

This verse makes it very clear that we must seek the kingdom of God first, and everything else must be made secondary:

III. Those who say, "**I am waiting for God's time.**"

Quite frequently this is said in all honesty. Many people have an idea that God has a certain time for saving people, and we must wait until this time comes. If any one says this, ask him if he will accept Christ in God's time if you will show him just when God's time is. When he says he will, turn him to 2 Cor. 6: 2.

"(For he saith, I have heard thee in a time accepted, and in the day of salvation have I succoured thee: behold, *now is the accepted time*, behold, now is the day of salvation.)"

This verse shows him that God's time is now. Or turn to Heb. 3: 15

'While it is said, *To-day* if ye will hear his voice, harden not your hearts, as in the provocation."

This shows that God's time is to-day.

IV. Those who say, "**I am too young to be a Christian,**" or "**I want to wait until I am older.**"

With such a person open your Bible to Eccl. 12: 1 and read:

"Remember now thy Creator *in the days of thy youth*, while the evil days come not, nor the years draw nigh, when thou shalt say, I have no pleasure in them."

Matt. 19: 14 and 18: 3 are also good passages to use, as they show that youth is the best time to come to Christ, and that all must become as children, even if they are old, before they can enter into the kingdom of heaven.

It is oftentimes wise in dealing with persons who wish to put off a decision until some time in the future, to use the passages given for dealing with those who have little or no concern about their salvation, (Chapter VI.), until such a deep impression is made of their need of Christ, that they will not be willing to postpone accepting Him. As a rule in dealing with those under I., it is best to use only one passage, and drive that home by constant repetition. One night I was dealing with a man who was quite excited, but kept saying, "I cannot decide to-night." Over and over again I quoted Prov. 29. 1. In reply to every answer he made, I would give this passage. I must have repeated it a great many times in the course of the conversation, until the man was made to feel, not only his need of Christ, but the danger of delay, and the necessity of a prompt decision. He tried to get away from the passage, but I held him to this one point. The passage remained with him, and it was carried home by the providence of God, for he came nearly being destroyed on the street that night; he was assaulted. He came back to the meeting the next night with his head all bandaged, and then and there accepted Christ. The pounding he received from his assailant would probably have done him little good, if the text of the Scripture had not been previously pounded into his head.

CHAPTER XIII

HOW TO DEAL WITH THE DELUDED

I. Roman Catholics.

1. Very few Roman Catholics have assurance of salvation, indeed very few understand that it is our privilege to know that we have forgiveness of sins and eternal life. A good way then to deal with a Roman Catholic is to ask him if he knows that his sins are forgiven. Very likely he will say that he does not, and that no one else knows it either. Then you can show him that it is the believer's privilege to know that he has forgiveness of sins. For this purpose use Acts 13: 39, "By Him all that believe *are justified*, etc." and Eph. 1: 7:

> "In whom *we have* redemption through his blood, *the forgiveness of sins*, according to the riches of his grace." Eph. 1: 7.

In a similar way, you can show him that it is our privilege to know that we have eternal life. For this purpose use 1 Jno. 5: 13. Oftentimes when he is brought to see that it is our privilege to know that we have forgiveness of sins and eternal life, he will desire to know it too, and will begin to see that we have something that he does not possess. There is one point at which we always have the advantage in dealing with a Roman Catholic, namely, there is a peace and power in Christianity as we know it, that there is not in Christianity as he knows it, and he can be made to appreciate the difference.

2. Another good way to deal with a Roman Catholic is to show him the necessity of the new birth, and what the new birth is. When the one with whom you are dealing tells you that he is a Roman Catholic, it is well to ask him if he has been born again. Very likely he will say that he does not know what that means, (though oftentimes Roman Catholics do talk about the new birth). Show him Jno. 3: 3-5, 7, and emphasize what Jesus says, that we must be born again. If he asks what the new birth is, show him the following passages.

"Therefore if any man be in Christ, he is a new creature: old things are passed away; behold, all things are become new." 2 Cor. 5: 17.

"Whereby are given unto us exceeding great and precious promises: that by these ye might be *partakers of the divine nature*, having escaped the corruption that is in the world through lust." 2 Pet. 1: 4.

"Then will I sprinkle clean water upon you, and ye shall be clean: from all your filthiness, and from all your idols, will I cleanse you. *A new heart also will I give you*, and a new spirit will I put within you: and I will take away the stony heart out of your flesh, and I will give you an heart of flesh. And I will put my spirit within you, and cause you to walk in my statutes, and ye shall keep my judgments, and do them." Ez. 36: 25-27.

Many Roman Catholics understand the new birth to mean baptism, and oftentimes if you ask a Roman Catholic if he has been born again, he will say "Yes," and if you ask him when, he will tell you at his baptism. It will then be necessary to show him that baptism is not the new birth. For this purpose use 1 Cor. 4: 15:

"For though ye have ten thousand instructors in Christ, yet have ye not many fathers: for in Christ Jesus I have begotten you through the gospel."

Here Paul tells the believers in Corinth that in Christ Jesus he had begotten them through the Gospel. If the new birth meant baptism, he must have baptized them, but in 1 Cor. 1: 14 he declares he had not baptized them.

Or you can say, "No, baptism is not the new birth, for I can show you a person who we are told was baptized, and yet St. Peter told him he had not been born again. Then turn to Acts 8: 13:

"Then Simon himself believed also: and when he was baptized, he continued with Philip, and wondered, beholding the miracles and signs which were done."

When you have made it clear that Simon had been baptized, turn to Peter's statement in the 21st to the 23d verses, to show that he had not been born again. It is well to go a step further and show the inquirer what the Biblical evidences of the new birth are. For this purpose use the following passages:

"If ye know that he is righteous, ye know that every one that doeth righteousness is born of him." 1 John 2: 29.

"Whosoever is born of God doth not commit sin; for his seed remaineth in him: and he cannot sin, because he is born of God.

"We know that we have passed from death unto life, because we love the brethren. He that loveth not his brother abideth in death.

"But whoso hath this world's good, and seeth his brother have need, and shutteth up his bowels of compassion from him, how dwelleth the love of God in him?" 1 John 3: 9, 14, 17.

If the inquirer is sufficiently interested, he will now want to know how to be born again. This question is answered in:

"But *as many as received him*, to them gave he power to become the sons of God, even to them that believe on his name." John 1: 12.

"Being born again, not of corruptible seed, but of incorruptible, *by the word of God*, which liveth and abideth forever." 1 Pet. 1: 23.

"Of his own will begat he us *with the word of truth*, that we should be a kind of firstfruits of his creatures." Jas. 1: 18.

3. A third way of dealing with a Roman Catholic is to use Acts 3: 19:

"Repent ye therefore, and be converted, that your sins may be blotted out, when the times of refreshing shall come from the presence of the Lord."

This shows the necessity of repentance and conversion in order that our sins may be blotted out. What repentance is will be shown by Is. 55: 7 and Jonah 3: 10:

"Let the wicked forsake his way, and the unrighteous man his thoughts: and let him return unto the Lord, and he will have mercy upon him; and to our God, for he will abundantly pardon."

"And God saw their works, that they turned from their evil way; and God repented of the evil, that he had said that he would do unto them; and he did it not."

In a similar way Acts 16: 31 can be used to show that the way to be saved is by simply believing on the Lord Jesus Christ; then to show what it is to believe on the Lord Jesus Christ, use Jno. 1: 12 and 2 Tim. 1: 12.

4. Another good text to use in dealing with Roman Catholics, and one which comes right at the heart of their difficulties, is 1 Tim. 2: 5:

"For there is one God, and *one mediator between God and men*, the man Christ Jesus."

The Roman Catholic, if he is a true Roman Catholic, is always seeking some mediator beside Jesus Christ, and this verse declares expressly that there is but "one mediator between God and men, the man Christ Jesus," and not the priests or saints or the Virgin Mary or any one else. Sometimes it is well to follow this up with 1 Tim. 4: 1-3, but it is not well as a rule to use this passage until one has made some headway.

It is also well to show the advantage of Bible study, for as a rule the Roman Catholic does not study his Bible at all, and in many cases is practically forbidden by the priest to study it. For this purpose use Jno. 5: 39; 1 Pet. 2: 1, 2; 2 Tim. 3: 13-17; James 1: 21, 22; Ps. 1: 1, 2; Josh. 1: 8; Mark 7: 7, 8, 13; Matt. 22: 29. These texts, except the one in 1 Pet. 2: 1, 2 are all practically the same in the Douay or Roman Catholic Bible as they are in the Protestant Bible.

5. Still another way to deal with a Roman Catholic is to use the same method that you would with any sinner who does not realize his need of a Saviour, and has no real concern about his salvation (See Chapters VI and XII), that is to awaken a sense that he is a sinner and needs Christ. This as a rule is the best way if you can get the Roman Catholic to listen to you.

Many people think there is no use talking with Roman Catholics, that they cannot be brought to Christ. This is a great mistake. Many of them are longing for something they do not find in the Roman Catholic Church, and if you can show them from the Word of God how to find it, they come very easily, and make some of the best Christians. Always be sure of one thing, do not attack the Roman Catholic Church. This only awakens their prejudice and puts them in a bad position to be helped. Simply give them the truth, and the errors in time will take care of themselves. Not infrequently our attacks upon the Roman Catholic Church, only expose our ignorance, for oftentimes they do not believe just what we suppose they do. It is frequently desirable to use a Roman Catholic Bible in dealing with a Roman Catholic. Of course if one is going to do that, he should study up the texts beforehand in that version. Very many of the texts are for all practical purposes the same in the Roman Catholic version of the Bible as in our own. One of the chief differences is that they translate "repent," "do penance."

II. Jews.

A great many Jews to-day are inquiring into the claims of Jesus the Nazarene, and are open to approach upon this subject. The best way to deal with a Jew is to show him that his own Bible points to Jesus as the Christ. Among the most useful passages for this purpose are Is. 53 (the entire chapter).

"And after threescore and two weeks shall Messiah be cut off, but not for himself: and the people of the prince that shall come shall destroy the city and the sanctuary; and the end thereof shall be with a flood, and unto the end of the war desolations are determined." Dan. 9: 26.

"And I will pour upon the house of David, and upon the inhabitants of Jerusalem, the spirit of grace and of supplications: and they shall look upon me whom they have pierced, and they shall mourn for him, as one mourneth for his only Son, and shall be in bitterness for him, as one that is in bitterness for his firstborn." Zech. 12: 10.

"But thou, Bethlehem Ephratah, though thou be little among the thousands of Judah, yet out of thee shall he come forth unto me that is to be ruler in Israel; whose goings forth have been from of old, from everlasting." Micah 5: 2.

If the Jew objects that these passages are different in his Hebrew Bible, do not allow yourself to be put off in this way, for they are not. He may say that Is. 53 does not refer to the Messiah. In that case ask him to whom it does refer. If he is a well-posted Jewish controversialist, very likely he will say, to suffering Israel. If he does say so, go through the chapter and show that it cannot refer to suffering Israel, because the one who suffers is plainly suffering for the sins of another, Is. 53: 4, 5, and 8, and the other for whom he is suffering is God's people Israel, so of course the sufferer cannot himself be Israel.

The whole book of Hebrews is excellent to use with a Jew, especially the ninth and tenth chapters, and the seventh chapter, the 25th to the 28th verses.

The great difficulty in the way of the Jew coming out as a Christian, is the terrific persecution which he must endure if he does. Undoubtedly it costs a great deal to-day for a Jew to become a Christian, but if he brings up this question as he undoubtedly will, show him the passages already given under the head of those who are afraid of persecution, Chapter VII, Sec. XII.

There are a number of good tracts for Jews which can be had from the Mildmay Mission to the Jews, 79 Mildmay Road, London. and also from the publishers of "Our Hope," 80 Second St., New York, N. Y.

III. Spiritualists.

Many people who call themselves Spiritualists, claim to believe in the Bible. Such persons make a great deal of Samuel's appearing to Saul, 1 Sam. 28: 11-20. It is not necessary to deny that Samuel really appeared to Saul, but show the one with whom you are dealing what the result was to Saul, of thus consulting one who had a familiar spirit.

A good passage to use in dealing with all Spiritualists, is 1 Chron. 10: 13, 14:

"So Saul died for his transgression which he committed against the Lord, even against the word of the Lord, which he kept not, and also *for asking counsel of one that had a familiar spirit*, to inquire of it; and inquired not of the Lord: therefore he slew him, and turned the kingdom unto David the son of Jesse."

Another excellent passage is Is. 8: 19, 20:

"And when they shall say unto you, *Seek unto them that have familiar spirits*, and unto wizards that peep, and that mutter: should not a people seek unto their God? for the living to the dead? *To the law and to the testimony:* if they speak not according to this word, it is because *there is no light in them.*"

1 Jno. 4: 1-3 is also a useful passage, as it brings out how not all spirits are to be believed. 2 Thess. 2: 9-12 is also useful. All these passages can be followed up by:

"Regard not them that have familiar spirits, neither seek after wizards, to be defiled by them: I am the Lord your God." Lev. 19: 31.

"And the soul that turneth after such as have familiar spirits, and after wizards, to go a whoring after them, I will even set my face against that soul, and will cut him off from among his people." Lev. 20: 6.

"There shall not be found among you any one that maketh his son or his daughter to pass through the fire, or that useth divination, or an observer of times, or an enchanter, or a witch, or a charmer, *or a consulter with familiar spirits*, or a wizard, or a necromancer. For all that do these things are an abomination unto the Lord: and because of these abominations the Lord thy God doth drive them out from before thee." Deut. 18: 10-12.

"Manasseh was twelve years old when he began to reign, and reigned fifty and five years in Jerusalem. And his mother's name was Hephzibah. And he did that which was evil in the sight of the Lord, after the abominations of the heathen, whom the Lord cast out before the children of Israel.

"And he made his son pass through the fire, and observed times, and used enchantments, *and dealt with familiar spirits and wizards:* he wrought much wickedness in the sight of the Lord, to provoke him to anger." 2 Kings 21: 1, 2, 6.

These passages all show how God regards consulting spiritualists and mediums.

IV. Christian Scientists.

Many people in our day are being led astray into Christian Science, and we need to be ready to help them. Most Christian Scientists claim to believe the Bible. Take them to 1 Jno. 4: 1-3:

"Beloved, believe not every spirit but try the spirits whether they are of God: because many false prophets are gone out into the world. Hereby know ye the Spirit of God: every spirit that *confesseth that Jesus Christ is come in the flesh* is of God: and *every spirit that confesseth not that Jesus Christ is come in the flesh is not of God:* and this is that spirit of antichrist, whereof ye have heard that it should come; and even now already is it in the world."

This passage strikes at the very foundation of Christian Science. Christian Science denies as one of its fundamental postulates, the reality of matter, and the reality of the body, and of necessity the reality of the incarnation. Show them by this passage that the Bible declares that every spirit that confesses not Jesus Christ *come in the flesh*, is not of God, but is the spirit of antichrist. Christian Science also denies the doctrine of substitution. Of course many Christian Scientists are not aware of this fact, for it is the common practice in leading one into Christian Science, not to let him see at once, all that is involved in it. Therefore take the one with whom you are dealing to such passages as the following:

"For he hath made him to be sin for us, who knew no sin; that we might be made the righteousness of God in him." 2 Cor. 5: 21.

"Christ hath redeemed us from the curse of the law, *being made a curse for us:* for it is written, Cursed is every one that hangeth on a tree." Gal. 3: 13.

"Who his own self bare our sins in his own body on the tree, that we, being dead to sins, should live unto righteousness: by whose stripes ye were healed." 1 Pet. 2: 24.

"And almost all things are by the law purged with blood; and *without shedding of blood* is no remission." Heb. 9: 22.

In these passages the doctrine of substitution is clearly brought out.

The average Christian Scientist in defending his position, makes a great deal of the fact that the Christian Scientists have physical cures. Of this there can be no question. Many people are better physically because of Christian Science treatment, so it is neither necessary nor wise to deny the reality of all their cures. Admit the cure, and then show that the fact that one cures sickness proves nothing for the truth of the position he holds, or for his acceptance before God. Use for this purpose the following passages:

"Many will say to me in that day, Lord, Lord, have we not prophesied in thy name? and in thy name have cast out devils? and in thy name done many wonderful works? And then will I profess unto them, I never knew you: depart from me, ye that work iniquity." Matt. 7: 22, 23.

"And then shall that Wicked be revealed, whom the Lord shall consume with the spirit of his mouth, and shall destroy with the brightness of his coming: even him, whose coming is *after the working of Satan with all power and signs and lying wonders.*" 2 Thess. 2: 8, 9.

"And no marvel; for Satan himself is transformed into an angel of light. Therefore it is no great thing if his ministers also be transformed as the ministers of righteousness; whose end shall be according to their works." 2 Cor. 11: 14, 15.

V. Followers of false prophets.

New false prophets are constantly rising, and it is impossible to mention them all by name, furthermore they oftentimes disappear as rapidly as they appear, but practically the same method of treatment will serve to help.

1. First show the deluded one Christ's own warning that false Christs and false prophets would arise. For this purpose use Mark 13: 22, 23:

"For false Christs and false prophets shall rise, and shall shew signs and wonders, to seduce, if it were possible, even the elect. But take ye heed: behold, I have foretold you all things."

Dwell upon the point that the fact that they heal the sick, and perform other wonders is no proof at all that they are not false prophets, that Christ distinctly foretold that the false Christs and the false prophets would do these things.

2. Then give them the following five rules by which they can escape every snare of the false prophet.

(1) The first rule is found in Jno. 7:17, *a will wholly surrendered to God.*

> "If any man will do his will, he shall know of the doctrine, whether it be of God, or whether I speak of myself."

Make this point very clear, for many of these people claim to have wholly surrendered their wills to God, but question them unsparingly on this point, and oftentimes you will find that the will is not surrendered.

(2) The second rule is found in 2 Tim. 3:13-17. This rule is *a careful study of the Word of God, and a thorough comparison of any one's claims to be a prophet, or a Christ, or the Messenger of the Covenant, or John the Baptist, or anything of that sort, with the teachings of the Word of God.* The followers of false prophets generally make a hobby of some few verses in the Bible, and do not study the book as a whole.

(3) The third rule is found in James 1:5-7, *prayer to God for wisdom.*

> "If any of you lack wisdom, let him ask of God, that giveth to all men liberally, and upbraideth not; and it shall be given him. But let him ask in faith, nothing wavering. For he that wavereth is like a wave of the sea driven with the wind and tossed. For let not that man think that he shall receive anything of the Lord."

Of course the prayer must be sincere, with a readiness to follow the leading of God. Many pray for guidance and still go on in delusion, but the prayer is not sincere. They ask for guidance, but do not utterly renounce their own wisdom and wait upon God for His wisdom. Very many have been led out of the error of following various false prophets when they in utter self-distrust have gone to God for light and guidance.

(4) The fourth rule is found in Matt. 23:8-10, *call no man master.*

> "But be not ye called Rabbi: for one is your Master, even Christ; and all ye are brethren. And call no man your father upon the earth: for one is your Father, which is in heaven. Neither be ye called masters: for one is your Master, even Christ."

Call no man Master, acknowledge no man as an absolute and

final authority, accept the authority of no one, and nothing but Christ and the Bible, in matters of faith and religion. It is well to dwell upon this point, for this is the very point at which many are led astray, the swallowing of some man whole, with all his arrant pretensions. The natural, selfish heart of man craves some man to do our thinking for us in matters of religion, and this makes men ready to swallow whole the teachings of some man. It is this that gives power to popery, priestcraft, Christian Science, Mormonism, and all similar delusions.

(5) The fifth rule is found in Prov. 29: 25, *Be afraid of no man.*

> "The fear of man bringeth a snare: but whoso putteth his trust in the Lord shall be safe."

Many a false prophet keeps his power over people through fear. While they do not more than half believe in him, they are afraid if they leave he will in some way bring sickness or some other curse upon them. Very likely the one with whom you are dealing will be in this very position. Show them how clearly they are in a wrong position, the very fact that they are afraid of the man proving this. Show the deluded man that the Holy Spirit is "not a spirit of fear, but of power, and of love, and of a sound mind." If the deluded person insists that the false prophet does his work in the name of Christ and succeeds, and therefore must be accepted of God, turn him to Matt. 7: 22, 23. This shows very clearly that one may even cast out devils in the name of the Lord, and yet be one whom He never knew.

It is well in dealing with those who are under the spell of a false prophet, to be able to show them what the marks of a false prophet are. The first and most common of these is a greed for money. To show this, use Titus 1: 10, 11, and 2 Pet. 2: 3:

> "For there are many unruly and vain talkers and deceivers, specially they of the circumcision: whose mouths must be stopped, who subvert whole houses, teaching things which they ought not, *for filthy lucre's sake.*"
>
> "And *through covetousness* shall they with feigned words make merchandise of you: whose judgment now of a long time lingereth not, and their damnation slumbereth not."

Make it very clear if the pretended prophet is trying to get money from the people (as usually he very clearly is), that that in itself is a mark that he is a false prophet. A second mark of the false prophet is vaunting one's self. To show the deluded one this, use Jude 16 and 1 Cor. 13: 4, R. V.:

> "These are murmurers, complainers, walking after their own lusts; and *their mouth speaketh great swelling words*, having men's persons in admiration because of advantage."
>
> "Love suffereth long, and is kind; love envieth not; love vaunteth not itself, is not puffed up."

A third mark of the false prophet is the claim to an authority that Jesus Christ forbade any man ascribing to himself. To show this to some person who is in the snare of the false prophet, use Matt. 23: 8, 12. A fourth mark of a false prophet, is a false application of Scripture either to himself, or to places with which he is connected. Thus for example, the Mormons take passages which apply to Israel, and apply them to their own Zion. When any place under the false prophet's control is named for some Bible place, and Scriptural promises referring to the literal Bible place are applied to the place under the prophet's control, just show the one who is being deceived by this sort of thing how utterly unwarranted such an application is. Fifth, there is usually an untrue note somewhere in the doctrine taught by the false prophet. He may teach a good deal that is Biblical and true, but somewhere he betrays his Satanic origin. The points at which this false note of doctrine are most likely to be found, are on the doctrine of future punishment, the matter of the use of meats, or upon legalism of some form—the observation of the seventh day, the matter of tithes, or something of that sort. In the matter of future punishment, false prophets generally go off sooner or later into either annihilationism or restorationism or a combination of the two.

After all the most important thing to do in dealing with one who is under a delusion, is to bring forward the fundamental, saving truth of the Gospel, salvation through the atoning work and upon the single condition of faith in Jesus Christ. Oftentimes error, like typhoid fever, has to be left to take its course and work itself out. I know many men to-day who are out in a clear Christian experience, who for a while were completely under the control of some of our modern false prophets, even thinking that all who did not agree with them were utterly wrong, and saying so in the most bitter terms; but in answer to prayer, and the study of the Word of God, God has led them out of the darkness into the light.

CHAPTER XIV

HOW TO DEAL WITH CHRISTIANS WHO NEED COUNSEL, REBUKE, ENCOURAGEMENT OR COMFORT

It is often necessary to do personal work with those who are really Christians, but whose Christian experience for one cause or another is unsatisfactory.

I. Christians who are neglecting the open confession of Christ.

There are many who are professing Christians who are not making an open confession of Christ as they ought. The experience of such is of course always unsatisfactory. No one can make satisfactory progress in the Christian life who is not confessing Christ openly before men. One of the best passages of Scripture to use with this class is Matt. 10: 32, 33:

> "*Whosoever therefore shall confess me before men*, him will I confess also before my Father which is in heaven. But whosoever shall deny me before men, him will I also deny before my Father which is in heaven."

The meaning and application of this verse is so plain as to need no comment.

Another excellent passage to use is Rom. 10: 9, 10:

> "*If thou shalt confess with thy mouth* the Lord Jesus, and shalt believe in thine heart that God hath raised him from the dead, thou shalt be saved. For with the heart man believeth unto righteousness; and *with the mouth confession is made unto salvation*."

According to this passage, our very salvation depends upon the confession of Jesus Christ with the mouth. There are many who say that they are Christians and who believe that they are saved, because in their hearts they believe in Jesus and have accepted Him as a Saviour. They will tell you that they do not regard a public confession of Christ as necessary. The passage just given will show them how utterly unscriptural is their position. A short time ago a man who called himself a Christian, and who entertained the hope that he really was a child of God, but who lacked joy in his experience, approached me with the question, "Do you think it is necessary that a man should publicly confess Christ in order to be saved?" I replied, "It is a matter of very little moment what I think is necessary, the great question is, what does God tell us in His own Word?" Then I gave him Rom. 10: 9, 10 to read. "Now," I said, "that is what God says." The meaning and application of the passage were so plain, that the man had nothing further to say, but promised to make an open confession of Christ before the world.

Another helpful passage to use is John 12: 42, 43:

"Nevertheless among the chief rulers also many believed on him; but because of the Pharisees they did not confess him, lest they should be put out of the synagogue: for they loved the praise of men more than the praise of God."

In many cases I have found that where these other passages did not seem to lead to decisive action, Mark 8: 38 did:

"Whosoever therefore shall be ashamed of me and of my words in this adulterous and sinful generation; of him also shall the Son of man be ashamed, when he cometh in the glory of his Father with the holy angels."

II. Christians who are neglecting the Bible.

There are many to-day who make a profession of faith in Jesus Christ, and of whom doubtless many are saved, who are making little or no progress in the Christian life because of neglect of the Bible. A good passage to use with such is 1 Pet. 2: 2:

"As newborn babes, desire the sincere milk of the word, that ye may grow thereby."

I was once calling upon a member of the church. I put to her the question, "How are you getting along in your Christian life?" She replied, "I am not getting on at all; my Christian life is a disgrace to me, a disgrace to the church, and a disgrace to Jesus Christ." I then asked, "Are you studying the Word of God daily?" She replied that she was not. "No wonder then that your Christian experience is not satisfactory," said I. A little baby was lying in a carriage close at hand. I pointed to the child and said, "Suppose that you fed this baby every two hours to-day, once every six hours to-morrow, not at all the next day, three or four times the next day, and then let her go two or three days without feeding at all, how do you think the baby would thrive?" She replied, "I do not think the baby would thrive at all, I think she would die." "Well," I said, "this is the exact way in which you are treating your soul." This point is emphasized by the passage just given.

Another passage to use with this class is Acts 20: 32:

"And now, brethren, I commend you to God, and to the word of his grace, which is able to build you up, and to give you an inheritance among all them which are sanctified."

Other helpful passages are:

"Wherefore lay apart all filthiness and superfluity of naughtiness, and receive with meekness the engrafted word, which is able to save your souls. But be ye doers of the word, and not hearers only, deceiving your own selves." James 1: 21, 22.

"But evil men and seducers shall wax worse and worse, deceiving, and being deceived. But continue thou in the things which thou hast learned and hast been assured of, knowing of whom thou hast learned them; and that from a child thou hast known *the holy scriptures, which are able to make thee wise unto salvation* through faith which is in Christ Jesus. All scripture is given by inspiration of God, and is profitable for doctrine, for reproof, for correction, for instruction in righteousness: that the man of God may be perfect, thoroughly furnished unto all good works." 2 Tim. 3: 13-17.

"And take the helmet of salvation, and the sword of the Spirit, which is the word of God." Eph. 6: 17.

"Wherewithal shall a young man cleanse his way? By taking heed thereto *according to thy word.*

"*Thy word have I hid in mine heart*, that I might not sin against thee.

"The entrance of thy words giveth light; it giveth understanding unto the simple." Ps. 119: 9, 11, 130.

"Blessed is the man that walketh not in the counsel of the ungodly, nor standeth in the way of sinners, nor sitteth in the seat of the scornful. But his delight is in the law of the LORD; and *in his law doth he meditate day and night.*" Ps. 1: 1, 2.

In the use of the last passage especially emphasize the second verse, "His delight is in the law of the LORD; And in his law doth he *meditate day and night.*" In a similar way you can use Josh. 1: 8:

"This book of the law shall not depart out of thy mouth; but thou shalt *meditate therein day and night*, that thou mayest observe to do according to all that is written therein: for *then* thou shalt make thy way prosperous, and then thou shalt have good success."

A passage which is useful as emphasizing the need of *daily* searching the scriptures is Acts 17: 11:

"These were more noble than those in Thessalonica, in that they received the word with all readiness of mind, and searched the scriptures *daily*, whether those things were so."

In urging upon others the daily study of the Scriptures it is always well to give them a few simple directions as to how to study the Bible.

III. Christians who are neglecting prayer.

One of the commonest causes in our day of an unsatisfactory Christian experience, is neglect of prayer. A personal worker will often find those who complain that they are not making satisfactory progress in the Christian life. In such a case the worker should always inquire whether they make a regular practice of prayer and to what extent. When it is found that prayer is being neglected, the following passages will be found useful:

"Ye lust, and have not: ye kill, and desire to have, and cannot obtain: ye fight and war, yet ye have not, *because ye ask not*." James 4: 2.

In using this passage, emphasize the seven closing words:

"And I say unto you, Ask, and it shall be given you; seek, and ye shall find; knock, and it shall be opened unto you. For every one that asketh receiveth; and he that seeketh findeth; and to him that knocketh it shall be opened. If a son shall ask bread of any of you that is a father, will he give him a stone? or if he ask a fish, will he for a fish give him a serpent? or if he shall ask an egg, will he offer him a scorpion? If ye then, being evil, know how to give good gifts unto your children: how much more shall your heavenly Father give the Holy Spirit *to them that ask him?*" Luke 11: 9-13.

"Is any among you afflicted? *let him pray*. Is any merry? let him sing psalms. Is any sick among you? let him call for the elders of the church; and let them pray over him, anointing him with oil in the name of the Lord: And the prayer of faith shall save the sick, and the Lord shall raise him up; and if he have committed sins, they shall be forgiven him. Confess your faults one to another, and pray one for another, that ye may be healed. *The effectual fervent prayer of a righteous man availeth much.*

"Elias was a man subject to like passions as we are, and he prayed earnestly that it might not rain; and it rained not on the earth by the space of three years and six months. And he prayed again, and the heaven gave rain, and the earth brought forth her fruit." James 5: 13-18.

"And said unto them, Why sleep ye? rise and *pray, lest ye enter into temptation.*" Luke 22: 46.

The last passage is especially helpful as emphasizing one of the most important purposes of prayer. Another exceedingly instructive passage along this line is Is. 40: 31:

"But *they that wait upon the Lord* shall renew their strength; they shall mount up with wings as eagles; they shall run, and not be weary; and they shall walk, and not faint."

A passage which is useful as suggesting the need of regular seasons of prayer is Ps. 55: 17:

"Evening, and morning, and at noon, will I pray, and cry aloud: and he shall hear my voice."

Other passages which are useful in dealing with people of this class are:

"And in the morning, rising up a great while before day, he went out, and departed into a solitary place, and there prayed." Mark 1: 35.

"Now when Daniel knew that the writing was signed, he went into his house; and his windows being open in his chamber toward Jerusalem, he kneeled upon his knees three times a day, and prayed, and gave thanks before his God, as he did aforetime." Dan. 6: 10.

"And when he had sent them away, he departed into a mountain to pray." Mark 6: 46.

"And it came to pass in those days, that he went out into a mountain to pray, and continued all night in prayer to God." Luke 6: 12.

"*Pray without ceasing.*" 1 Thess. 5: 17.

IV. Christians who are leading careless lives.

There are many whom one would hesitate to say are not Christians at all and are not saved, but whose lives are not out and out for Christ as they should be. In dealing with such, the following passages will be found particularly useful: 2 Cor. 6: 14-7: 1; especially emphasize in these verses, the words, "Come ye out from among them, and be ye separate."

"No man can serve two masters: for either he will hate the one, and love the other; or else he will hold to the one, and despise the other. *Ye cannot serve God and mammon.*" Matt. 6: 24.

In the above passage, dwell upon and drive home the closing words, "Ye cannot serve God and mammon."

"*Love not the world*, neither the things that are in the world. If any man love the world, the love of the Father is not in him. For all that is in the world, the lust of the flesh, and the lust of the eyes, and the pride of life, is not of the Father, but is of the world. And the world passeth away, and the lust thereof: but he that doeth the will of God abideth forever." 1 John 2: 15-17.

"Ye adulterers and adulteresses, know ye not that *the friendship of the world is enmity with God?* whosoever therefore shall be a friend of the world is the enemy of God.

"But he giveth more grace. Wherefore he saith, God resisteth the proud, but giveth grace unto the humble. Submit yourselves therefore to God. Resist the devil, and he will flee from you. Draw nigh to God, and he will draw nigh to you. Cleanse your hands, ye sinners; and purify your hearts, ye double minded." James 4: 4, 6-8.

"Follow peace with all men, and holiness, without which no man shall see the Lord." Heb. 12: 14.

"Wherefore gird up the loins of your mind, be sober, and hope to the end for the grace that is to be brought unto you at the revelation of Jesus Christ; as obedient children, not fashioning yourselves according to the former lusts in your ignorance: but as he which hath called you is holy, so be ye holy in all manner of conversation; because it is written, Be ye holy; for I am holy. And if ye call on the Father, who without respect of persons judgeth according to every man's work, pass the time of your sojourning here in fear: forasmuch as ye know that ye were not redeemed with corruptible things, as silver and gold, from your vain conversation received by tradition from your fathers; but with the precious blood of Christ, as of a lamb without blemish and without spot." 1 Peter 1: 13-19.

"For the time is come that judgment must begin at the house of God: and if it first begin at us, what shall the end be of them that obey not the gospel of God? And if the righteous scarcely be saved, where shall the ungodly and the sinner appear?" 1 Peter 4: 17, 18.

"And that which fell among thorns are they, which, when they have heard, go forth, and are *choked with cares and riches and pleasures of this life*, and bring no fruit to perfection." Luke 8: 14.

In using the above passage, dwell upon the thought contained in the words, "choked with cares and riches and pleasures of this life."

"And take heed to yourselves, lest at any time your hearts be overcharged with surfeiting, and drunkenness, and cares of this life, and so that day come upon you unawares. For as a snare shall it come on all them that dwell on the face of the whole earth. Watch ye therefore, and pray always, that ye may be accounted worthy to escape all these things that shall come to pass, and to stand before the Son of man." Luke 21: 34-36.

"Let your loins be girded about, and your lights burning; and ye yourselves like unto men that wait for their lord, when he will return from the wedding; that when he cometh and knocketh, they may open unto him immediately. Blessed are those servants, whom the lord when he cometh shall find watching; verily I say unto you, that he shall gird himself, and make them to sit down to meat, and will come forth and serve them. And if he shall come in the second watch, or come in the third watch, and find them so, blessed are those servants." Luke 12: 35-38.

"I beseech you therefore, brethren, by the mercies of God, that ye present your bodies a living sacrifice, holy, acceptable unto God, which is your reasonable service. And be not conformed to this world: but be ye transformed by the renewing of your mind, that ye may prove what is that good, and acceptable, and perfect, will of God." Rom. 12: 1, 2.

"And he that doubteth is damned if he eat, because he eateth not of faith: for whatsoever is not of faith is sin." Rom. 14: 23.

"I have fought a good fight, I have finished my course, I have kept the faith: henceforth there is laid up for me a crown of righteousness, which the Lord, the righteous judge, shall give me at that day: and not to me only, but unto all them also that love his appearing." 2 Tim. 4: 7, 8.

V. Christians who are not working for Christ.

A large proportion of the professing church to-day is doing little or nothing for the Master. The personal worker who shall succeed in getting other Christians to work will be accomplishing at least as much for Christ as the one who leads the unsaved to Him. The Bible abounds in passages which can be effectively used for this purpose. The following will be found useful: Mark 13: 34-37, emphasize the words "to every man his work;" Matt. 24: 44-51: Matt. 25: 14-30: A verse which is useful in showing idle Christians that every professed follower of Christ ought to be a witness for Him and a soul winner, is Acts 8: 4:

"Therefore they that were scattered abroad went everywhere preaching the word."

Eph 4: 14-16 is also useful:

"That we henceforth be no more children, tossed to and fro, and carried about with every wind of doctrine, by the sleight of men, and cunning craftiness, whereby they lie in wait to deceive; but speaking the truth in love, may grow up into him in all things, which is the head, even Christ: from whom the whole body fitly joined together and compacted *by that which every joint supplieth*, according to the effectual working in the measure of every part, maketh increase of the body unto the edifying of itself in love."

In using this passage, point out the words, "that which every joint supplieth," and explain their meaning. Other verses that will be found useful are Eph. 5: 14-21:

"She hath done what she could." Mark 14: 8.

"Let him know, that he which converteth the sinner from the error of his way shall save a soul from death, and shall hide a multitude of sins." James 5: 20.

"And they that be wise shall shine as the brightness of the firmament; and they that turn many to righteousness as the stars for ever and ever." Dan. 12: 3.

"And, behold, I come quickly; and my reward is with me, *to give every man according as his work shall be*." Rev. 22: 12.

VI. Christians who are undergoing temptation.

There come to all Christians, and especially to all young Christians, times of special temptation and trial. At such times they need and should have, the counsel and encouragement of other Christians. We should bear one another's burdens, and so fulfill the law of Christ. (Gal. 6: 2.) Here is a large field of usefulness for the personal worker. The following passages will be found exceedingly useful in strengthening the brethren when under trial and temptation.

"My brethren, count it all joy when ye fall into divers temptations; knowing this, that the trying of your faith worketh patience. But let patience have her perfect work, that ye may be perfect and entire, wanting nothing." James 1: 2-4.

"Blessed is the man that endureth temptation: for when he is tried, he shall receive the crown of life, which the Lord hath promised to them that love him." James 1: 12.

"Be sober, be vigilant; because your adversary the devil, as a roaring lion, walketh about, seeking whom he may devour: whom resist stedfast in the faith, knowing that the same afflictions are accomplished in your brethren that are in the world. But the God of all grace, who hath called us unto his eternal glory by Christ Jesus, after that ye have suffered a while, make you perfect, stablish, strengthen, settle you." 1 Pet. 5: 8-10.

(It is well when possible to use the R. V. of the last passage.)

"There hath no temptation taken you but such as is common to man: but God is faithful, who will not suffer you to be tempted above that ye are able; but will with the temptation also make a way to escape, that ye may be able to bear it." 1 Cor. 10: 13.

"And he said unto me, My grace is sufficient for thee: for my strength is made perfect in weakness. Most gladly therefore will I rather glory in my infirmities, that the power of Christ may rest upon me. Therefore I take pleasure in infirmities, in reproaches, in necessities, in persecutions, in distresses for Christ's sake: for when I am weak, then am I strong." 2 Cor. 12: 9, 10.

"Pray without ceasing." 1 Thess. 5: 17.

"I can do all things through Christ which strengtheneth me." Phil. 4: 13.

"I have written unto you, fathers, because ye have known him that is from the beginning. I have written unto you, young men, because ye are strong, and the word of God abideth in you, and ye have overcome the wicked one." 1 Jno. 2: 14.

"Wherewithal shall a young man cleanse his way? By taking heed thereto according to thy word." Ps. 119: 9.

"He giveth power to the faint; and to them that have no might he increaseth strength. Even the youths shall faint and be weary, and the young men shall utterly fall: but they that wait upon the LORD shall renew their strength; they shall mount up with wings as eagles; they shall run, and not be weary; and they shall walk, and not faint." Is. 40: 29-31.

VII. Christians who are undergoing persecution.

Many professed Christians fail in the hour of persecution who would have stood if they could have had a few words of counsel from some fellow Christian. The following passages are useful in giving the needed word of counsel and encouragement:

"Blessed are they which are persecuted for righteousness' sake: for theirs is the kingdom of heaven. Blessed are ye, when men shall revile you, and persecute you, and shall say all manner of evil against you falsely, for my sake. Rejoice, and be exceeding glad: for great is your reward in heaven: for so persecuted they the prophets which were before you." Matt. 5: 10-12.

"Beloved, think it not strange concerning the fiery trial which is to try you, as though some strange thing happened unto you: but rejoice, inasmuch as ye are partakers of Christ's sufferings; that, when his glory shall be revealed, ye may be glad also with exceeding joy. If ye be reproached for the name of Christ, happy are ye; for the spirit of glory and of God resteth upon you: on their part he is evil spoken of, but on your part he is glorified." 1 Pet. 4: 12-14.

"Yet if any man suffer as a Christian, let him not be ashamed; but let him glorify God on this behalf." 1 Pet. 4: 16.

"For even hereunto were ye called: because Christ also suffered for us, leaving us an example, that ye should follow his steps: who did no sin, neither was guile found in his mouth: who, when he was reviled, reviled not again; when he suffered, he threatened not; but committed himself to him that judgeth righteously." 1 Pet. 2: 21-23.

"For it is better, if the will of God be so, that ye suffer for well doing, than for evil doing. For Christ also hath once suffered for sins, the just for the unjust, that he might bring us to God, being put to death in the flesh, but quickened by the Spirit." 1 Pet. 3: 17, 18.

"Yea, and all that will live godly in Christ Jesus shall suffer persecution." 2 Tim. 3: 12.

"Confirming the souls of the disciples, and exhorting them to continue in the faith, and that we must through much tribulation enter into the kingdom of God." Acts 14: 22.

"And to him they agreed: and when they had called the apostles, and beaten them, they commanded that they should not speak in the name of Jesus, and let them go. And they departed from the presence of the council, rejoicing that they were counted worthy to suffer shame for his name.

"And daily in the temple, and in every house, they ceased not to teach and preach Jesus Christ." Acts 5: 40-42.

"Wherefore seeing we also are compassed about with so great a cloud of witnesses, let us lay aside every weight, and the sin which doth so easily beset us, and let us run with patience the race that is set before us, looking unto Jesus the author and finisher of our faith; who for the joy that was set before him endured the cross, despising the shame, and is set down at the right hand of the throne of God. For consider him that endured such contradiction of sinners against himself, lest ye be wearied and faint in your minds. Ye have not yet resisted unto blood, striving against sin." Heb. 12: 1-4.

"Fear none of those things which thou shalt suffer: behold, the devil shall cast some of you into prison, that ye may be tried; and ye shall have tribulation ten days: be thou faithful unto death, and I will give thee a crown of life." Rev. 2: 10.

"Fear not, little flock; for it is your Father's good pleasure to give you the kingdom." Luke 12: 32.

VIII. Christians who are passing through affliction.

When times of affliction come to Christians, especially to young Christians, a few words fitly spoken by a fellow Christian are oftentimes of great help. Not infrequently they save the afflicted one from years of darkness and barrenness in their Christian experience. There are many to-day who are of little or no use in the church, who would have been of use if some wise worker had come to them in the hour of affliction and given them good counsel from God's own Word. We should all be constantly on the lookout for opportunities of this kind, and we will find them round about us almost every day of our lives. No thoughts of our own can possibly be of as much help in such an hour as the promises and encouragements of God's Word. The following passages will be found useful and sufficient, if wisely used in the power of the Holy Spirit:

"And ye have forgotten the exhortation which speaketh unto you as unto children, My son, despise not thou the chastening of the Lord, nor faint when thou art rebuked of him: for whom the Lord loveth he chasteneth, and scourgeth every son whom he receiveth. If ye endure chastening, God dealeth with you as with sons; for what son is he whom the father chasteneth not?

"Now no chastening for the present seemeth to be joyous, but grievous: nevertheless afterward it yieldeth the peaceable fruit of righteousness unto them which are exercised thereby." Heb. 12: 5-7, 11.

"To an inheritance incorruptible, and undefiled, and that fadeth not away, reserved in heaven for you, who are kept by the power of God through faith unto salvation ready to be revealed in the last time. Wherein ye greatly rejoice, though now for a season, if need be, ye are in heaviness through manifold temptations: that the trial of your faith, being much more precious than of gold that perisheth, though it be tried with fire, might be found unto praise and honour and glory at the appearing of Jesus Christ." 1 Pet. 1: 4-7.

"Humble yourselves therefore under the mighty hand of God, that he may exalt you in due time: casting all your care upon him; for he careth for you." 1 Pet. 5: 6, 7.

"God is our refuge and strength, *a very present help in trouble.* Therefore will not we fear, though the earth be removed, and though the mountains be carried into the midst of the sea; though the waters thereof roar and be troubled, though the mountains shake with the swelling thereof." Ps. 46: 1-3.

"Yea, though I walk through the valley of the shadow of death, I will fear no evil: for thou art with me; thy rod and thy staff they comfort me." Ps. 23: 4.

"And call upon me in the day of trouble: I will deliver thee, and thou shalt glorify me." Ps. 50: 15.

"The righteous cry, and the LORD heareth, and delivereth them out of all their troubles." Ps. 34: 17

"The LORD is my light and my salvation; Whom shall I fear? the LORD is the strength of my life; of whom shall I be afraid? When the wicked, even mine enemies and my foes, came upon me to eat up my flesh, they stumbled and fell. Though an host should encamp against me, my heart shall not fear: though war should rise against me, in this will I be confident. One thing have I desired of the LORD, tnat will I seek after; that I may dwell in the house of the LORD all the days of my life, to behold the beauty of the LORD, and to enquire in his temple. For *in the time of trouble he shall hide me in his pavilion:* in the secret of his tabernacle shall he hide me; he shall set me up upon a rock. And now shall mine head be lifted up above mine enemies round about me: therefore will I offer in his tabernacle sacrifices of joy; I will sing, yea, I will sing praises unto the Lord.

"I had fainted, unless I had believed to see the goodness of the LORD in the land of the living. Wait on the LORD: be of good courage, and he shall strengthen thine heart: wait, I say, on the LORD." Ps. 27: 1-6, 13, 14.

"Come unto me, all ye that labour and are heavy laden, and I will give you rest. Take my yoke upon you, and learn of me; for I am meek and lowly in heart: and ye shall find rest unto your souls." Matt. 11: 28, 29.

The one who is to use these passages should first read them over and over again with himself alone, and think of their relation to the specific trial of the one whom he proposes to help.

IX. Christians who have lost loved ones.

The ministry of comfort to those whose homes have been invaded by death is one of the most blessed of Christian ministries. It is a ministry that is open to us all, but the attempts of many well-meaning persons in this direction, who try to comfort with their own fancies rather than with the sure Word of God, oftentimes do more harm than good. But the one who knows his Bible, and what it has to say upon the subject of death and of the future, will be able to bind up many a broken heart. Jesus declared in the synagogue at Nazareth, that God had anointed Him to heal the broken hearted, (Luke 4: 18), and every follower of Jesus should seek an anointing for the same blessed work. The Bible abounds in passages which are useful for this purpose, but the following are among those which experience proves to be most effective:

"Let not your heart be troubled: ye believe in God, believe also in me. In my Father's house are many mansions: if it were not so, I would have told you. I go to prepare a place for you. And if I go and prepare a place for you, I will come again, and receive you unto myself; that where I am, there ye may be also.

"Peace I leave with you, my peace I give unto you: not as the world giveth, give I unto you. Let not your heart be troubled, neither let it be afraid." Jno. 14: 1-3, 27.

"Jesus answered and said unto him, What I do thou knowest not now; but thou shalt know hereafter." Jno. 13: 7.

"Be still, and know that I am God: I will be exalted among the heathen, I will be exalted in the earth." Ps. 46: 10.

"And I heard a voice from heaven saying unto me, Write, Blessed are the dead which die in the Lord from henceforth: Yea, saith the Spirit, that they may rest from their labours; and their works do follow them." Rev. 14: 13.

"And he said, While the child was yet alive, I fasted and wept; for I said, Who can tell whether GOD will be gracious to me, that the child may live? But now he is dead, wherefore should I fast? Can I bring him back again? I shall go to him, but he shall not return to me." 2 Sam. 12: 22, 23.

"But I would not have you to be ignorant, brethren, concerning them which are asleep, that ye sorrow not, even as others which have no hope. For if we believe that Jesus died and rose again, even so them also which sleep in Jesus will God bring with him. For this we say unto you by the word of the Lord, that we which are alive and remain unto the coming of the Lord shall not prevent them which are asleep. For the Lord himself shall descend from heaven with a shout, with the voice of the archangel, and with the trump of God: and the dead in Christ shall rise first: then we which are alive and remain shall be caught up together with them in the clouds, to meet the Lord in the air: and so shall we ever be with the Lord. Wherefore comfort one another with these words." 1 Thess. 4: 13-18.

(I have found this the most comforting of any single passage in the Word of God.)

"Therefore we are always confident, knowing that, whilst we are at home in the body, we are absent from the Lord: (for we walk by faith, not by sight:) we are confident, I say, and willing rather to be absent from the body, and to be present with the Lord." 2 Cor. 5: 6-8.

"I am in a strait betwixt two, having a desire to depart, and to be with Christ; which is far better." Phil. 1: 23.

"So also is the resurrection of the dead. It is sown in corruption, it is raised in incorruption: it is sown in dishonour, it is raised in glory: it is sown in weakness, it is raised in power: it is sown a natural body, it is raised a spiritual body. There is a natural body, and there is a spiritual body.

"And as we have borne the image of the earthy, we shall also bear the image of the heavenly.

"For this corruptible must put on incorruption, and this mortal must put on immortality.

"So when this corruptible shall have put on incorruption, and this mortal shall have put on immortality, then shall be brought to pass the saying that is written, Death is swallowed up in victory. O death, where is thy sting? O grave, where is thy victory? The sting of death is sin; and the strength of sin is the law. But thanks be to God, which giveth us the victory through our Lord Jesus Christ. Therefore, my beloved brethren, be ye stedfast, unmoveable, always abounding in the work of the Lord, forasmuch as ye know that your labour is not in vain in the Lord." 1 Cor. 15: 42-44, 49, 53, 54-58.

The worker must make a study of each individual case, and decide which of the passages given above will be most helpful in the specific case. Sometimes it will be found well to use them all. They should not be merely read, but dwelt upon, and their meaning explained and applied, wherever necessary. In all the reading and the explanation and the application, we must depend upon the Holy Spirit for His wisdom and power.

X. Christians who have not received the Holy Spirit.

There are many professing Christians in our day who have not definitely received the Holy Spirit. They have not entered into the fulness of joy and peace and power that there is for us in Christ. They are practically in the same condition that the disciples in Ephesus were in until Paul came and put to them the question, "Have ye received the Holy Ghost?" (Acts 19: 2) and the position that the believers in Samaria were in until Peter and John came down and "prayed for them, that they might receive the Holy Ghost: for as yet He was fallen upon none of them," (Acts 8: 15, 16). There are many to-day who are inquiring what they must do that they may receive the Holy Ghost, and there are others that ought to be asking this question. The personal worker should know how to show any one who has not received the Holy Spirit, just what he must do that he may receive the Holy Spirit. The following are the steps that should be pointed out:

1. *The one who would receive the Holy Ghost must depend for his acceptance before God upon the finished work of Christ alone, and not upon anything he himself has done or can do.*

To make this point clear to the inquirer use Gal. 3: 2:

"This only would I learn of you, *Received ye the Spirit by the works of the law, or by the hearing of faith?*"

This passage is often interpreted to mean that we receive the Holy Spirit by simply believing that we are going to receive Him. This is not at all the meaning of the passage as found in the context. The Christians in Galatia had been told by certain false teachers that came in among them, that in order to be justified it was not enough to simply believe on Jesus Christ and His finished work, but in addition to this they must keep the Mosaic law regarding circumcision. Paul in the passage before us shows them the folly of this position by appealing to their own experience. He calls to mind the fact that they had received the Holy Ghost not by keeping the Mosaic law, but simply by the hearing of faith, that is by believing God's testimony regarding Christ and His atoning work, and resting in that for pardon.

The first step then, toward receiving the Holy Spirit, is to turn our eyes entirely away from ourselves, and anything we ever have done or can do, and fix them upon Jesus Christ, and His atoning work on the Cross, and depend upon that finished work of Christ for our pardon and acceptance before God.

2. *The one who would receive the Holy Ghost must put away all sin.*

To make this clear to the inquirer use Acts 2:38:

> "Then Peter said unto them, *Repent*, and be baptized every one of you in the name of Jesus Christ for the remission of sins, and *ye shall receive the gift of the Holy Ghost.*"

This passage makes it clear that in order to receive the Holy Ghost we must repent. Repentance is a change of mind about Christ and a change of mind about sin. It is a change first of all from a Christ-rejecting attitude of mind, to a Christ-accepting attitude of mind. This is involved in what has been already said regarding the first step, but there must also be a change of mind regarding sin; a change of mind from a sin-loving and sin-indulging attitude of mind, to a sin-rejecting attitude of mind, that is, we must renounce all sin. One of the commonest hindrances to the receiving of the Holy Spirit, is holding on to some sin. The worker should deal very faithfully at this point with the inquirer. Find out whether there is not some sin in the life that is not renounced.

Find if there is not some sin in the past that has not been confessed and straightened out. Instruct the inquirer to go alone with God and ask God to search his heart, and to show him anything in his life that is displeasing to Him. If anything is thus brought to light, insist that it must be renounced. Tell the inquirer that every known sin must be given up. Dwell upon the fact that the Holy Spirit is the *holy* Spirit, and that He will not manifest Himself in His fulness in an unholy heart, that is in a heart which holds on to sin.

3. *The one who would receive the Holy Spirit must surrender his will absolutely to the will of God.*

To show this use Acts 5:32:

> "And we are his witnesses of these things; and so is also the Holy Ghost, whom God hath given *to them that obey him*."

This passage shows that God gives the Holy Spirit to them that obey Him. Show that the essential thing about obedience is the attitude of the will, and that real obedience involves the absolute surrender of the will to God. Hold the inquirer to the necessity of such an absolute surrender to God. This is the point of difficulty in very many lives. Perhaps more people are kept out of the blessing of the conscious receiving of the Holy Spirit by a lack of absolute surrender than by any other one thing. In many an instance the Holy Spirit is given at once in fulness as soon as one is led to an absolute surrender of the will to God. If one will not thus surrender, there is no use of trying to go further, God will accept no compromise at this point.

4. *The one who would receive the Holy Spirit should ask God for this definite gift.*

To show this to the inquirer use Luke 11:13:

> "If ye then, being evil, know how to give good gifts unto your children: how much more shall your heavenly Father give the Holy Spirit *to them that ask him?*"

This tells us plainly that God gives the Holy Spirit to them that ask Him. It can be illustrated by the use of Acts 2:1-4, cf. Acts 1:14; Acts 4:31 and Acts 8:15, 16:

> "And when the day of Pentecost was fully come, they were all with one accord in one place. And suddenly there came a sound from heaven as of a rushing mighty wind, and it filled all the house where

they were sitting. And there appeared unto them cloven tongues like as of fire, and it sat upon each of them. And they were *all filled with the Holy Ghost*, and began to speak with other tongues, as the Spirit gave them utterance." Acts 2: 1-4. (Compare Acts 1: 14. "These all *continued with one accord in prayer* and supplication, with the women, and Mary the mother of Jesus, and with his brethren.")

"And *when they had prayed*, the place was shaken where they were assembled together; and they were *all filled with the Holy Ghost*, and they spake the word of God with boldness." Acts 4: 31.

"Who, when they were come down, *prayed for them*, that they might receive the Holy Ghost: (for as yet he was fallen upon none of them: only they were baptized in the name of the Lord Jesus)." Acts 8: 15, 16.

The inquirer should be led to at once definitely seek the filling with the Holy Spirit. It is well to pray with the inquirer then and there for this definite gift.

5. *The final step in receiving the Holy Ghost is simply faith.*

There are many who take all the steps mentioned thus far, and yet fail of the blessing simply because they do not believe. Mark 11: 24 can be used to make this clear:

"Therefore I say unto you, What things soever ye desire, when ye pray, *believe that ye receive them*, and ye shall have them."

The R. V. of this passage is particularly suggestive.

"All things whatsoever ye pray and ask for, *believe that ye have received them*, and ye shall have them."

The inquirer should be instructed not to look to his feelings, but to the Word of God, and to believe that he has received whether he has any sensation or experience or not, simply because God has promised in His Word. In a very large proportion of cases, people receive the Holy Ghost simply by believing God's Word, and that their prayer is heard, without any feeling; and afterwards what they believe they "have received," they do actually obtain in personal experience as a conscious possession. Great help will be found in showing the inquirer how to receive by faith, in 1 Jno. 5: 14, 15:

"And this is the confidence that we have in him, that, *if we ask anything according to his will, he heareth us:* and if we know that he hear us, whatsoever we ask, *we know that we have the petitions that we desired of him.*"

Make it very clear to the inquirer by the use of this passage that when we ask anything according to the will of God, we know that He heareth us, because the passage says so, and when we know that He heareth us, we know that we have the petitions we have asked of Him, *whether we feel it or not.*

Then show the inquirer that when we pray for the Holy Spirit we pray for something according to the will of God. The following passages make this clear:

"If ye then, being evil, know how to give good gifts unto your children: how much more shall your heavenly Father give the Holy Spirit to them that ask him?" Luke 11: 13.

"Then Peter said unto them, Repent, and be baptized every one of you in the name of Jesus Christ for the remission of sins, and ye shall receive the gift of the Holy Ghost. For the promise is unto you, and to your children, and to all that are afar off, even as many as the Lord our God shall call." Acts 2: 38, 39.

"And be not drunk with wine, wherein is excess, but *be filled with the Spirit.*" Eph. 5: 18.

Then have the inquirer kneel down and definitely pray for the Holy Spirit. When he has offered this prayer, ask him if he has received what he sought. If he is not clear about it, open your Bible to 1 Jno. 5: 14, 15 and lay it before him and have him read it, and then ask him if he has asked for something according to God's will, and when he says he has, ask him, "What then do you know?" and hold him to it until he says, "I know that God has heard me." Then have him read the 15th verse and ask him, "If you know that God has heard you, what further do you know?" Hold him to it until he says, "I know that I have the petition that I asked of Him." Then ask him, "What do you know you have received?" and hold him to it until, resting upon the simple naked promise of God's Word, he can say, "I know I have received the Holy Ghost." Many are waiting for certain estatic experiences of which they have heard others speak. In dealing with an inquirer, do not deny the reality of these experiences, for they doubtless are real in many instances, but show the inquirer that there are no such experiences described in the Bible, that the manifestations of having received the Holy Spirit mentioned in the Bible are a new joy and peace in Christ,

"But the fruit of the Spirit is love, joy, peace, longsuffering, gentleness, goodness, faith, meekness, temperance: against such there is no law." Gal. 5: 22, 23,

a new and clearer knowledge of Christ,

"But when the Comforter is come, whom I will send unto you from the Father, even the Spirit of truth, which proceedeth from the Father, he shall testify of me." Jno. 15: 26.

and especially new power in service for Christ,

"And, being assembled together with them, commanded them that they should not depart from Jerusalem, but wait for the promise of the Father, which, saith he, ye have heard of me. For John truly baptized with water; but ye shall be baptized with the Holy Ghost not many days hence.

"But *ye shall receive power*, after that the Holy Ghost is come upon you: and ye shall be witnesses unto me both in Jerusalem, and in all Judea, and in Samaria, and unto the uttermost part of the earth." Acts 1: 4, 5, 8.

"And when they had prayed, the place was shaken where they were assembled together; and they were all filled with the Holy Ghost, and they spake the word of God with boldness. And the multitude of them that believed were of one heart and of one soul: neither said any of them that ought of the things which he possessed was his own; but they had all things common. And *with great power* gave the apostles witness of the resurrection of the Lord Jesus: and great grace was upon them all." Acts 4: 31-33.

Also make it clear to the inquirer that the manifestations that result from receiving the Holy Spirit, are to be expected not before we believe, but after we believe, after we take by simple faith God's Word. God's way is not first experience and then faith, but first faith resting upon the naked Word of God, and then experience; "Believe *that ye have received*, and ye shall have."

VI. Christians who do not have victory in their Christian life.

There are many professed Christians, and doubtless many who are really saved people, whose lives seem to be lives of constant defeat and discouragement. In dealing with such a person seek to find out what is the cause of defeat. It will be found in one or more of the following points:

1. *Because they have not learned to rest absolutely in the finished work of Christ for pardon and for peace.*

The church is full of people who are looking to something

that they themselves can do to find acceptance before God. No one can have a clear, satisfactory and victorious Christian experience who has not learned to rest entirely in the finished work of Christ for pardon. If this is found to be the cause of failure, use Is. 53:6, Gal. 3:13, 2 Cor. 5:21 and similar passages, to show that our sins are pardoned not on account of anything that we have done or can do, but on the account of what Jesus Christ did when He bore our sins in His own body on the Cross.

Next show the inquirer that the pardon and peace thus purchased by the atoning blood of Christ, becomes ours on the simple condition of our believing on Christ. To show this, use the following passages:

"Therefore *being justified by faith* we have peace with God through our Lord Jesus Christ." Rom. 5:1.

"But to him that worketh not, but believeth on him that justifieth the ungodly, *his faith is counted for righteousness.*" Rom. 4:5.

"But now the righteousness of God without the law is manifested, being witnessed by the law and the prophets; even the righteousness of God which is by faith of Jesus Christ unto all and upon all them that believe: for there is no difference: for all have sinned, and come short of the glory of God; *being justified freely by his grace* through the redemption that is in Christ Jesus: whom God hath set forth to be a propitiation through faith in his blood, to declare his righteousness for the remission of sins that are past, through the forbearance of God; to declare, I say, at this time his righteousness: that he might be just, and *the justifier of him which believeth in Jesus.*" Rom. 3:21-26.

"And be found in him, *not having mine own righteousness*, which is of the law, *but that which is through the faith of Christ*, the righteousness which is of God by faith." Phil. 3:9.

In the last passage the Revised version brings out the thought more clearly than the Authorized.

2. *Because they have not surrendered absolutely to the will of God.*

This is the cause of failure in a very large proportion of cases. If this is found to be the cause of failure in any specific case, use Acts 5:32, and Rom. 6:13, 19:

"Neither yield ye your members as instruments of unrighteousness unto sin: but *yield yourselves unto God*, as those that are alive from the dead, and your members as instruments of righteousness unto God.

"I speak after the manner of men because of the infirmity of your flesh: for as ye have yielded your members servants to uncleanness and to iniquity unto iniquity; even *so now yield your members servants to righteousness* unto holiness." Rom. 6:13, 19.

3. *Because of neglect of the study of the Word.*

If this is the case, use 1 Pet. 2:2, Ps. 119:11 and Eph. 6:17:

"Thy word have I hid in mine heart, that I might not sin against thee." Ps. 119:11

"And take the helmet of salvation, and the sword of the Spirit, which is the word of God:" Eph. 6:17.

4. *Because of neglect of prayer.*

Where this is the case, use 1 Thess. 5:17, Luke 22:40 and Is. 40:29-31:

"And when he was at the place, he said unto them, *Pray that ye enter not into temptation.*" Luke 22:40.

5. *Because of failure to constantly confess Christ before men.*

The one who would lead a victorious Christian life, must be constantly witnessing for Christ. Make this very plain, and for this purpose use Matt. 10:32, 33:

"Whosoever therefore shall confess me before men, him will I confess also before my Father which is in heaven. But whosoever shall deny me before men, him will I also deny before my Father which is in heaven."

6. *Because of neglect to work for Christ.*

One who would lead a victorious life must be constantly at work for the Master. If the cause of failure is at this point, use Matt. 25:29:

"For unto every one that hath shall be given, and he shall have abundance: but from him that hath not shall be taken away even that which he hath."

Explain its meaning by the context. The evident meaning of the passage is, that one who uses the talents that he has in the Master's service will get more, but the one who neglects to use the talents he has will lose even those.

7. *Because they have not received the Holy Spirit.*

There are very many to-day who are leading lives of constant failure where they might be leading lives of constant victory, simply because they do not even so much as know that it is the privilege of the individual believer to be filled with the Holy Spirit. If this is the case, use Eph, 5:18, the last half of the verse, and Gal. 5:16, 22, 23:

> "This I say then, Walk in the Spirit, and ye shall not fulfill the lust of the flesh.
>
> "But the fruit of the Spirit is love, joy, peace, longsuffering, gentleness, goodness. faith, meekness, temperance: against such there is no law."

Then show the inquirer how to receive the Holy Spirit as explained under the former heading.

CHAPTER XV

SOME HINTS AND SUGGESTIONS FOR PERSONAL WORK

A few general suggestions that will be helpful to the personal worker remain to be made.

I. As a rule, choose persons to deal with of your own sex. There are, of course, exceptions to this rule. One should always be looking to the Holy Spirit for His guidance as to whom to approach, and He may lead us to one of the opposite sex, but unless there is clear guidance in the matter, it is quite generally agreed among those who have had much experience in Christian work that, on the whole, women usually do the most satisfactory work with women, and men with men; especially is this true of the young. It is always a bad sign when a young man is always looking for women to deal with, and a young woman looking for young men to deal with. Many exceedingly unfortunate complications have risen in actual life from young men trying to lead young women to Christ, and vice versa. Of course, an elderly, motherly woman will oftentimes do excellent work with a young man or boy, and an elderly, fatherly man will sometimes do good work with a young woman or girl.

II. As a rule, choose persons to deal with of about your own age. A young man as a rule can get hold of young men better than any one else can and a man of mature years can handle a man of his own age better than a young man, or better even than an old man. It is not wise usually for a young and inexperienced person to approach one very much older and maturer and wiser than himself, on such an important subject as this. The older person naturally looks with a good deal of distrust, if not contempt, upon those much younger than himself. There are, of course, exceptions even to this rule. Frequently a man who has gained wisdom by years, and who has the confidence of people, can do excellent work with a young man or boy. As a rule people do the best work with people of their own class, educated men with educated men, business men with business men, workingmen with workingmen, women of position with women of similar position to themselves. There are many exceptions to this. Many a servant girl has been known to lead her mistress to Christ, and many a laboring man his employer.

III. **Whenever it is possible, deal with a person alone.** No one likes to open his heart freely to another on the most personal and sacred of all subjects, when there are others present. Many will from mere pride defend themselves in a false position when others are present, who would freely admit their error or sin or need if they were alone with you. It is far better for a single worker to deal with a single unconverted person, than for several workers to deal with an inquirer, or a single worker to deal with several inquirers. Nothing can be more unfortunate than for a number of workers to swarm around one poor individual who is trying to find the way of life. If such an individual is a person of any independence of character, he is very likely to feel that he is being hectored and bothered, and for that very reason take an attitude of opposition. If you have several to deal with, it is better if possible to take them one by one. Workers often find that they have made no headway while talking to several at once, but by taking the individuals off by themselves they soon succeed in leading them one by one to Christ. Where two unsaved people are being dealt with at once, oftentimes each is afraid of the other, and they bolster one another up in their false position.

IV. **Let your reliance be wholly in the Spirit of God and in the Word of God. Have no confidence in yourself.** One of the greatest hindrances to successful personal work is self-confidence. But while there should be no self-confidence, there should be boldness, boldness that comes from believing in the power of the Holy Ghost, and in the power of the Word of God. No matter with whom you are dealing, or how stubborn he may be, never forget that the Spirit of God and the Word of God have power to break the hardest heart. Be always looking to the Spirit to produce conviction of sin, and expect Him to do it, but let your whole dependence be in Him, and in His Word alone.

V. Do not content yourself with merely reading passages from the Bible, much less with merely quoting them, but **have the one with whom you are dealing read the passages himself.** In this way the truth finds an entrance into the heart through the eye as well as through the ear. It is remarkable how much deeper an impression the Word of God oftentimes makes when it is actually seen with the eyes, than it does when it is merely heard with the ears. Sometimes it is well to have a marked Bible, with the word that you wish especially to impress marked in some striking way so that it will catch the eye, and thus the mind and heart of the reader.

VI. It is oftentimes well to use but a single passage of Scripture. One verse of Scripture iterated and reiterated will be burned into the memory and will haunt the one with whom you are dealing long after you have left them. I have known a passage to haunt a man for weeks and finally result in his conversion. Do everything in your power to drive it home and clinch it so that the one with whom you are dealing cannot forget it, but will hear it ring in his memory long after your voice has ceased.

Dr. Ichabod Spencer tells in his "Pastoral Sketches" of how he dealt with a young man who had many difficulties. Dr. Spencer kept continually quoting the passage, "Now is the accepted time, now is the day of salvation." The young man tried to get Dr. Spencer off onto something else, but over and over again he kept saying the words, "Now is the accepted time, now is the day of salvation." The young man returned the next day rejoicing in the Lord, and thanking Dr. Spencer that he had "hammered" him with that text. The words kept ringing in his ears during the night, and he could not rest until he had settled the matter by accepting Christ.

It is a good thing when a person can point to some definite verse in the Word of God, and say, "I know on the authority of that verse that my sins are forgiven, and that I am a child of God." Indeed it is well never to let a person go until they can point you definitely to the verse in God's Word upon which they rest their hope of salvation. Be sure that they grasp it, so that if Satan comes to them when they are alone, and asks them how they know that they are saved, they can open their Bible to that verse, and put their finger upon it and defy Satan in all his wiles.

There are times, however, when a powerful effect is produced by piling up passages along some line until the mind is convinced and the heart conquered. Especially is this true in showing people their need of a Saviour, and showing them Jesus as the Saviour that they need.

VII. Always hold the person with whom you are dealing to the main point of accepting Christ. If he wishes to discuss outside questions, such as the claims of various denominations, or the mode of baptism, or theories of future punishment, or fine points about the higher criticism, or any other question than the central one of his need of a Saviour, and Christ the Saviour that he needs, tell him these questions are important to take up in their right place and time, but the time to settle them is after he has settled the fundamental question of accepting or rejecting Christ. Many a case has been lost by an inexperienced and foolish worker allowing himself to be involved in a discussion of some side issue which it is utter folly to discuss with an unregenerated person.

VIII. Be courteous. Many well-meaning but indiscreet Christians by their rudeness and impertinence repel those whom they would win to Christ. It is quite possible to be at once perectly frank and perfectly courteous. You can point out to a man his awful sin and his need of a Saviour without insulting him. Your words may be very searching, while your manner is very gentle and winning, indeed the more gentle and winning your manner is, the deeper your words will go, for they will not stir up the opposition of those with whom you are dealing. Some workers approach those with whom they wish to work in such a manner that the latter at once assume the defensive, and clothe themselves with an armor that it is impossible to penetrate.

IX. Avoid unwarranted familiarities with those with whom you deal. I have seen many workers lay their hands upon the shoulders of those with whom they are dealing, or even put their arms around them. Now there are cases in which that is proper and wise. If a man is dealing with an old wrecked and ruined drunkard who thinks he has not a friend in the world, it may be well to place your hand upon his shoulder, or over his shoulder, but one needs to be exceedingly cautious about these matters. A man of fine sensitiveness is repelled when a stranger takes any familiarities with him. This is even more true of a lady of good breeding. I have even seen a male worker so indiscreet as to lay his hand upon a lady's shoulder. There is no place where good breeding counts for more than in personal work.

X. Be dead in earnest. Only the earnest man can make the unsaved man feel the truth of God's Word. It is well to let the psssage we would use with others first sink deep into our own souls. I know of a very successful worker who has for a long time used the one passage, "Prepare to meet thy God," with every one with whom she nas dealt. But that passage has taken such complete possession of her own heart and mind that she uses it with tremendous effect. A few passages that have thoroughly mastered us are much better than many passages that we have mastered from some text book.

One of the great needs of the day is men and women who are thoroughly in earnest, who are completely possessed with the great fundamental truths of God's Word. The reader of this book is advised to ponder upon his knees such of the passages suggested in it as he decides to use, until he himself feels their power. We read of Paul that he "ceased not to warm every one night and day with tears." (Acts 20:31.) Genuine earnestness will go further than any skill learned in a training class or from the study of such a book as this.

XI. Never lose your temper when trying to lead a soul to Christ. How many a case has been lost by the worker losing his temper. Some persons are purposely exasperating, but even such may be won by patient perseverance and gentleness:

they certainly cannot be won if you lose your temper, nothing delights them more, or gives them more comfort in their sin. The more iritating they are in their words and actions, the more impressed they will be if you return their insults with kindness. Oftentimes the one who has been the most insufferable will break down in penitence. One of the most insulting men I ever met afterward became one of the most patient, persistent and effective of workers.

XII. Never have a heated argument with one whom you would lead to Christ. Heated arguments always come from the flesh and not from the Spirit. (Gal. 5: 20, 22, 23.) They arise from pride, and unwillingness to let the other person get the best of you in argument. If you care more about winning him to Christ than you do about winning your case, you will often let the other man think that he has the best of the argument, absolutely refusing to argue. If the one with whom you are talking has mistaken notions that must be removed before he can be led to Christ, show him his error quietly and pleasantly. If the error is not on an essential point, refuse to discuss it at all, and hold the person to the main question.

XIII. Never interrupt any one else who is dealing with a soul. Too much emphasis cannot be laid upon this point. You may not think the other is doing the work in the wisest way, but if you can do any better, bide your time, and you will have the opportunity. Many an unskilled worker has had some one at the very point of decision, when some meddler, who thought he was wiser, has broken in and upset the work. Do not even stand by one who is talking to another and listen to what he is saying. Incalculable mischief may be done in this way. The thought of the one who is being dealt with is distracted, his heart is closed up, and a case that might have been won is lost.

On the other hand, do not let others interrupt you. Of course, sometimes it is not possible to altogether prevent it, but stop the interruption just as soon as possible. Just a little word plainly but courteously spoken will usually prevent it. but at any cost insist upon being left alone.

XIV. Don't be in a hurry. One of the commonest and gravest faults in Christian work to-day is haste. We are too anxious for immediate results, and so we do superficial work. It is very noticeable how many of those with whom Christ dealt came out slowly; Nicodemus, Joseph, Peter, and even Paul (though the final step in his case seems very sudden) were cases in point. It was three days even after the personal appearance of Jesus to Paul on the way to Damascus, before the latter came out clearly into the light and openly confessed Christ. (Acts 22: 16.) One man with whom slow but thorough work has been done, and who at last has been brought out clearly for Christ and who knows just where he stands and what to do, is better than a dozen with whom hasty work has been done, who think they have accepted Christ, when in reality they have not. It is often a wise policy to plant a truth in a man's heart and leave it to work. The seed on rocky ground springs up quickly, but withers as quickly.

XV. Get the person with whom you are dealing on his knees before God. This rule has exceptions. Sometimes it is not possible to get the person to kneel, and sometimes it is not wise; but it is wonderful how many difficulties disappear in prayer, and how readily stubborn people yield when they are brought into the very presence of God Himself. I remember talking with a young woman in an inquiry room for about two hours, and making no apparent headway, but when at last we knelt in prayer, in less than five minutes she was rejoicing in our Saviour. Sometimes it is well to have a few words of prayer before you deal with an individual at all, but of course this is not at all wise in many cases; however, in almost every case it is wise if the person is willing to pray, to have a few words of prayer before you close. If the way of life has been made perfectly clear to the inquirer, have him also lead in prayer. There are those who object to getting an unsaved person to pray, but there is clear Bible warrant for it. Cornelius was not a saved man. This is perfectly clear from Acts 11: 14, nevertheless he was sincerely seeking the light, and God sent him word that his prayers had come up for a memorial before Him. Now, any one who is honestly seeking light even though he has not as yet that knowledge of Jesus that brings salvation, is in practically the same position as Cornelius, and one of the best things to do is to get that one to pray. It is certainly right for a sinner seeking pardon through the atoning blood to pray. (Luke 18: 13, 14.) Some may say, "One who has no faith has no right to pray." But such a one has faith, their prayer is the first evidence of that faith. (Rom. 10: 13, 14.)

XVI. Whenever you seem to fail in any given case, go home and pray over it and study it to see why you failed. Never give up a case because of one failure. If you have been at a loss to know what Scripture to use, study this book to see the different classes we meet and how to deal with them, and find out where this person belongs and how to deal with him, and then go back if you can, and try again. In any case you will be better prepared for the next case of the same kind. The greatest success in this work comes through many apparent defeats. It will be well to frequently study these hints and suggestions, and see if your failure has come through neglect of them. But be sure to take to God in prayer the case in which you yourself have failed.

XVII. Before parting with the one who has accepted Christ, be sure to give him definite instructions as to how to succeed in the Christian life. These instructions will be found at the close of Chapter V. It is well to give these instructions in some permanent form. For this purpose two tracts have been written by the author of this book, one called "The Christian Life Card," and the other "How to Make a Success of the Christian Life." Either of these can be secured from the Bible Institute Colportage Association, Chicago.

XVIII. When you have led any one to Christ, follow him up and help him in the development of his Christian life. There is nothing sadder in Christian work to-day than the number who are led to Christ, and then neglected. Such are almost certain to get on very poorly. No greater mistake could be possible. The work of following up those who are converted is as important as the work of leading them to Christ, and as a rule no one can do it so well as the person who has been used in their conversion.

All the methods of dealing in personal work, given in the foregoing chapters, will suggest texts and lines of thought for helpful sermons.

PRINTED IN THE UNITE̵ STATES OF AMERICA

BOOK II

METHODS OF CHRISTIAN WORK

CHAPTER I

HOUSE TO HOUSE VISITATION

I. Its importance and advantages.

1. *It is apostolic.*

The Apostle Paul was a house to house visitor. In Acts 20: 20 he calls to the minds of the Ephesian elders the fact that he had taught them not only publicly, but also "from house to house." Many of us feel above this work, but the Apostle Paul, the prince of preachers, found a great deal of time to do it. We have also the example of Christ Himself. Not a little of His work was done in the home. One of the most touching scenes of His life was in the home at Bethlehem, with Mary sitting at His feet listening to the words of eternal life (Luke 10: 39).

2. *It brings you near to the people.*

When Mr. Moody was in Glasgow, some one asked him how to reach the masses, and his reply was, "Go for them." There is no better way of going for them, and getting near to them, than by going into their homes. One of the simplest solutions of the problem of how to reach the unchurched in city and country is to go right into their homes.

3. *You can get hold of people that you cannot reach in any other way.*

There are people who never enter a church, who will not attend a theatre service nor a mission meeting, who will not even attend an open-air meeting, but there is nobody who does not live somewhere, therefore you can get hold of everybody by house to house visitation. There are special classes who can be reached in this way and in this way alone, for instance the very poor, who are afraid to enter a church because of their shabby dress, or who may be utterly unable to leave home on account of the multiplicity of home duties. The sick also can be reached only in this way. Then there are in every city many who would not attend church if they could; among these are the infidels, the great majority of Roman Catholics, and still other classes of non-church-going people, who are never seen within the walls of an evangelical church. Some workers pay no attention to Roman Catholics because they think that they are already Christians; others pay no attention to them because they think that they cannot be reached. Doubtless many Catholics are true Christians, but they have a very perverted kind of Christianity. And a very large proportion of them, moreover, are not Christians at all; they have no saving knowledge of Jesus Christ; they are wrapped in superstition and darkness. A large proportion of the Catholic population will not go into a tent meeting, a mission hall, nor even stop at an open-air meeting. Take for example the Poles in some of our large cities. The only way to reach them is to go right into their homes. That the Catholics cannot be reached is a very great mistake. Many a minister can tell of the large number of them that have been converted and come into the church. When converted they make most faithful church members. They have been trained regarding their duty to the church, and when once shown their duty to the Lord Jesus Christ they make splendid Christians. There is no better way to reach them than by house to house visitation. You may not get them the first time, nor the second, nor the third, but they are bound to yield at last, to simple genuine kindness.

4. *It wins people's confidence and attention.*

Many people seem to feel that a great honor has been bestowed upon them when the missionary, minister or Christian worker calls at their home and takes an interest in them. I once called upon a saloon-keeper, but I did not realize what an honor he considered had been conferred upon him, until a neighboring saloon-keeper afterwards upbraided me for not calling upon him, and asked me if he was not just as good as the other man. Few Christian workers realize how much good it does people to go into their homes, and what a short road it is to their confidence and attention. You first go to them, and they will afterwards come to you.

5. *It gives you an opportunity to see how the people live, and thus teaches you how to deal with them.*

It has been well said that "one-half of the world does not know how the other half lives," and we never will know until we go right into their homes. It is a perfect revelation to see some people on Sunday in their Sunday clothes, and then go on Monday and see them at work in the home. You are forced to say, "Does this woman come from a house like this?" or, "Does this child come from a home like this?"

6. *They will open their hearts to you more freely at their homes than elsewhere.*

People feel at home at home. They are always more or less restrained at church, or in an inquiry meeting, or in a mission hall—less probably in a mission hall than in a church, and still less in a cottage meeting than either—but when you get them at home they throw off restraint and talk freely. You never know what is going on in people's hearts until you go to their homes and they open their hearts to you there.

7. *It offers opportunity for close dealing with souls.*

You can get at a man for close personal dealing far better in a quiet house than anywhere else. People do not like to open their hearts in public, and even an inquiry meeting is more or less public.

8. *It affords opportunities for suggestions regarding home life.*

The great majority of people need to be taught how to live in this world. They need to be taught plain truths on plain subjects. The ignorance of many poor people on the little affairs of every-day life is perfectly astonishing. One great trouble with many poor people is that they do not know how to live, they do not know what to eat, or how to cook what they buy; they do not know how to dress, or how to spend their money to the best advantage. They do not know how to train their children. They do not know how to eat properly at the table, nor how to make a bed or air their houses. A family living in Minneapolis were in great poverty and destitution; they were in absolute need of the bare necessities of life. The attention of a friend of mine was called to them, and he sent me $7 with the request that I should go and look them up, investigate the case, and if I found them in real distress, give them this money. I called and found them in very great need. The mother was sick in bed, the father out of work, the glass out of the window and an old garment stuffed in the place. They were without the commonest necessities of life, and I saw at once that it was a case of real distress. Being quite without experience at the time, I gave the family the $7 as requested. Thinking it well to follow up the work, I called again. To my astonishment, I found that they had used the $7 in purchasing a mirror that reached from the floor to the ceiling. It was simple ignorance on their part.

I once gave a man some money to buy groceries for a family in extreme destitution. When he came back I asked him what he had bought. He told me among other things, that he had bought three pounds of cheese and a lot of loaf sugar. I asked him why he bought the loaf sugar, and he said the father said the children liked to have it to eat. A few instructions as to the most economical food to buy and how to prepare it, would save many a family from want, without it being necessary to give them a cent.

9. *It sanctifies the home.*

Let a minister of Jesus Christ, a true man of God, go into a home and talk and read the Bible and pray, and that home is a different place ever afterward. If the minister is a man who in his prayer actually brings God down to the place where he is praying, it will make a change in that household. The same is true of the visit of a godly woman. Oftentimes after that they will be on the point of doing something wrong, when they will think what the messenger of Jesus Christ said in that prayer. They will think hallowed things when they go into that room. Many a home has been changed by the presence of the minister of God. You can set up a family altar for them. When you get people converted who have had religious training, they know what family worship means, but if they have never had family worship, it never occurs to them that they ought to have family worship at home. Tell them to "set up a family altar," and you might as well talk Greek to them, but go into their homes, read the Bible to them and pray, then ask them, "do you enjoy this?" and when they say

"Yes," tell them to keep right on doing it every day, and show them how to keep on.

10. *It results in many conversions.*

It is a question whether any other form of Christian work results in as many satisfactory conversions as house to house visitation. Of course it is a great deal more gratifying to our pride to stand up before a large audience and speak to them; there is an exhilaration in doing that, but when it comes down to definite results, I do not know of any kind of work that brings larger results in souls won for Christ, than patient house to house visitation. I have often thought that a person who would devote his whole life to going from house to house week after week, would have a far more splendid record at the close of life than the minister who preaches to from one hundred to one thousand every Sunday. Take the London Home Missionary Society, they are doing a magnificent work in many directions, but a very large proportion of it is this kind of work. Many women are employed for simple house to house visitation, and they are accomplishing great results. In country work I am sure we have been laying comparatively too much stress on the church as a church, and the gathering at the central meeting house, and too little on the work in the scattered homes.

A great deal of foreign missionary work, and oftentimes the best part of it, is house to house work. Foreign missionaries have been far wiser in their work in this direction than we have at home. Perhaps it is so partly from the necessities of the case.

II. How to do house to house visitation.

1. *Be systematic.*

It pays to be systematic in everything. The man who has a plan for doing things and carries out his plan is the man who reaps the largest results. Many, however, spend their whole time in making plans which they never carry out. Better have a poor plan which you execute, than a perfect plan that you spend your whole time in elaborating.

2. *A thorough house to house visitation should be made by districts.*

What I mean by thorough house to house visitation is that every habitation in the district should be visited. This is the true way to begin a country pastorate. In a town where there are other churches than your own, you can invite the Methodists to the Methodist church, the Congregational people to the Congregational church, etc., but you should not be too sensitive about calling on people that do not belong to your own flock. Better to call upon some one that belongs to some one's else flock, than to leave some one neglected. Surely if your own church is the only one in the vicinity, you should visit every habitation in that part of the country. It will take time; you will have less time for general reading and for study than if you did not do this work, but you are in the ministry to win souls, and not primarily for the glorification of your intellect. You must spend and be spent, you must make full proof of your ministry. Just so in the city, you should yourself visit every family, or else get every family visited. It is not the man who can preach good sermons who succeeds, it is the man who gets hold of the people. In district visitation, it should be borne in mind that people are constantly moving, and need to be visited very frequently.

In an evangelistic campaign, one of the first things that should be done is to have a house to house canvass of every house and habitation anywhere within reach of the church, or churches, where the meetings are to be held. Every family in the town or district where you are working should be visited. That means not merely that some one should go to the door with a dodger in his hand which he hastily gives to the first one who comes to the door, it means that some one should go into every house in the town. Visitors should be sent out two and two to go to every house and deal with the people personally about their salvation. If it is a union meeting it is well that the two should be of different denominations. There should be a thorough house to house canvass of every city at least once a year, covering the entire city. This is easily accomplished when the churches unite in the work.

3. *Select homes for regular visitation.*

In some communities you must visit every home regularly,

and where you cannot do it yourself, you can see that it is done. In other communities it is wise to visit only part of the homes regularly.

How shall we select the homes?

(1) *By a thorough canvass.*

As you go around visiting from house to house you will find some homes that should be visited regularly, and others that it will not do to visit regularly. Do not be too hasty in concluding that it is of no use to visit a certain family. For instance, do not conclude because a family is Roman Catholic it is of no use to visit them regularly. Every one of much experience knows that some of the "hopeless" families are those which turn out best in the long run.

(2) *Select persons who do not attend church.*

Every person who does not attend church should be visited. Not merely the members of your church should be visited regularly and systematically, but those who do not attend at all should be visited.

(3) *The parents of the children who attend the Sunday School.*

You have a good excuse and a wide opening in visiting the parents of children who attend your Sunday School. Of course there may be exceptions. There are sometimes children attending Sunday School whose parents do not know that they are attending, and who would be angry and opposed if they did know. In such cases the parents should not be visited, or if they are visited, nothing should be said to them about the children attending the Sunday School.

(4) *Parents of children you get hold of on the street.*

Talk with the children as you go about the street, and if you find children that do not attend Sunday School anywhere, go and visit their homes, go and deal with their parents, and gather the whole family into the church of God.

When Mr. Moody was engaged in Sunday School work in Chicago, he was constantly picking up children on the street and getting them into the Sunday School, and afterwards getting into their homes. One day on the street he met a little girl with a pail. He asked her if she went to Sunday School. She said she did not. He then gave her a hearty invitation to his school, and she promised to go, but she did not keep her promise. He at once began to watch for that girl. Weeks after he saw her on the street. He started for her, and she broke into a dead run and he ran in pursuit. Down one street and up another she went, the eager missionary running behind her. Finally she shot into a saloon and he followed. On she went up a back flight of stairs and Mr. Moody still in close pursuit. She dashed into a room and under a bed. He followed and pulled her out by the foot and had a talk with her. Her mother was a widow with several children; her father had been a drunkard. Mr. Moody had a talk with the mother and called again and again, until at last the whole family was won for Christ, and became prominent in the work of the Chicago Avenue Church. There are many families that you can get hold of in no other way than by such persistent pursuit.

(5) *Funerals afford a good opportunity to get hold of a family.*

Almost everybody wants a minister to conduct a funeral. When you once get an entrance into a home this way, do not let go of it. I do not know how many families I have gotten hold of by being invited to conduct a funeral in the home. Do not consider your work done when the funeral has been conducted, just consider that an opening for further work.

(6) *Weddings also afford good opportunities for getting into homes.*

When you conduct a wedding do not be satisfied when the $5.00 is safely deposited in your pocket. You have gained an opening into another family, another opportunity of winning a family for Christ, follow it up.

4. *Keep books.*

Be just as systematic and thorough as a man in business. Have your families classified alphabetically and by streets. Keep an accurate record of when you called last and the result of your call. If one has a large parish, the card system of indexing is better than the use of books.

5. *Always remember to pray before starting out.*

If there is any work that requires wisdom, it is house to house visitation, and God alone can give the wisdom that is necessary.

6. *Introduce yourself the best way you can.*

It is impossible to lay down rules about this. It often takes almost infinite tact to get into a home, and quite as much tact to keep there after you get in. Frequently it is necessary not to let it be known in first coming to the home, that you are there on a religious errand. Proceed to win the confidence of the people. Be very courteous. Do not notice any rudeness on the part of the people that you are visiting; leave your pride at home, and no matter what insults are offered you, let them pass unheeded. Remember that you are there not to serve your own interests, nor to spare your own feelings, but as an ambassador of Jesus Christ, and to win souls to Him. If you keep your eyes open, an opportunity will afford itself for doing some kindly thing that will open the hearts of the people to you, and win their confidence. A young lady got into one home by offering to do the washing of an overworked woman. It was hard work, but it won that woman and her husband and child to Christ. The woman, who was thoroughly worldly, became a very active Christian, and the husband, who was a drunkard, is now in heaven. The child has grown up into a fine young man.

Take an interest in the things the people you are visiting are interested in. One minister got an entrance into the home of a surly farmer by proving that he could plow. Be sure and notice the children. Children are worth noticing anyhow, and there is no surer road to the confidence and affection of the parents than by showing attention to the children.

7. *As soon as possible begin to open the Scriptures.*

Very frequently it is not wise to begin this at once. It must be led up to. When the time comes, the Scriptures should be thoroughly applied. Use them to convince of sin, to reveal Christ, to bring to a decision, to lead to entire consecration, and to instruct in the fundamental duties and truths of Christianity. It is astonishing how little the average man or woman really catches of a plain sermon. If there is to be thorough indoctrination in fundamental truths it must be done largely in the homes.

CHAPTER II

COTTAGE MEETINGS

I. Their importance and advantages.

1. *You can reach people who cannot be reached in any other way.*

(1) People who cannot go to church on account of family duties. There are a great many people in every city, and still more in the country, for whom it is absolutely impossible to go to church. A mother may have a large family of children and no servant. Many others are detained at home on account of sickness. Few of us realize how many people there are in every place who cannot go to church either on account of their own physical infirmities, or the infirmities of those with whom they have to stay.

A great many cannot go to church on account of age. Who that has ever seen it will forget the joy that lights up the face of these elderly people when you bring a meeting to them? How often such people have asked me if we could not have a meeting in their home. One of the greatest joys in Christian life and service is to hold a cottage meeting for people who cannot go to church.

(2) People who will not go to church. I recall a family who would not go to church at all through simple indifference. They were an intelligent family, a father and mother, two boys and two girls. As they would not go to church, we took the church just as near them as we could get it. We held a cottage meeting next door to their home. They came to it out of friendship to the family where the meeting was held. They were interested at once, came to church, and the parents and grown-up children were converted.

Some people will not go to church on account of their clothes. It is all very well for us to say, "Never mind about your clothes," but at the same time it is not very pleasant to go to a place where almost everybody else is better dressed than you are yourself. But one can go to a cottage meeting in the poorest of clothes and not be noticed.

Some people will not go to church because of their positive hatred to the Gospel, and yet the same people can often be induced to attend a cottage meeting.

2. *You can hold cottage meetings where you cannot get a large room or rent a hall.*

You can always get cottage room. How many sections of the United States to-day have no church accessible to the population. In the center of the town there will be found two or three churches struggling for supremacy, but three or four miles out in the country there is no church at all. Many churches are trying to maintain possession of "strategic points" where they can glorify the denomination instead of God, while other points are entirely neglected. The only way to reach the people in these far-away and neglected communities is by cottage meetings. I look back upon my early pastorate in the country with great regret. I fancied I was killing myself with preaching three times on Sunday. I kept it up for three years, and people made me believe I would kill myself. I held these three meetings on Sunday, and during the week conducted a class in German, a class in geology, and other things of that sort, instead of attending to my proper business, and now I think with bitter regret of the district I could have worked if I had only known how. There was not another church for miles in any direction. Scores and scores of people could never get to church. There was enough work in that pastorate alone to have kept a man busy if it had been done right. A church which at one time was the largest in that region had almost died because about the only work done was the ordinary preaching. Do not be content with preaching your regular sermons on Sunday, but have services all over your parish for miles in every direction, and work the parish for all it is worth. Search out the destitute places and hold cottage meeting for several nights in the week. Set the other pastors in the district an example of how to work a parish. There is not one parish in fifty to-day that is worked as it should be. The spiritual destitution of the city is nothing compared with the spiritual destitution of the country. Wherever you get a parish, be sure and work it for all there is in it. If there is any part of that neighborhood where nobody is doing anything, go to work there. Do not be afraid of stepping on some one's else toes, but be sure and go to work.

3. *The informality of cottage meetings.*

There should be nothing stiff about a cottage meeting. Of course some people turn a cottage meeting into a stiff church service, but that is not necessary. In these meetings you can get people to talk that you could not get to open their mouths in a church prayer meeting, and you can so train them in a cottage meeting that they will soon be able to take part in the church prayer meeting.

4. *In a cottage meeting, if you have worked it up as it should be, you have to pack people together like sardines in a box*, while in the church there is a gulf between the minister and the pews, and the people usually get in pews as remote from the minister as possible.

5. *Its simplicity—anybody can have a cottage meeting.*

It is the simplest thing in the world to hold a cottage meeting, though it is not always the easiest thing in the world to have a good cottage meeting.

6. *The cottage meeting sanctifies the home.*

It brings religion right into the home. It turns the home into the house of God. The home should be a consecrated place, and the cottage meeting does much to make it so. There is no other place like the place where you have come together for prayer, and where, it may be, you have been brought to the Lord Jesus Christ. The home that has been used for a cottage meeting becomes a hallowed place

7. *Cottage meetings are apostolic.*

The first churches were in the homes (1 Cor. 16: 19). We are going back to apostolic times when we return to the homes to hold religious services. A very large share of Paul's work was holding cottage meetings.

8. *Cottage meetings take the gospel to the people.*

There are two ways of reaching the people. One way is

to invite them to come to you, the other way is to go to them. The latter is God's way, the former is the twentieth century way.

II. How to prepare for a cottage meeting.

1. *Get on your knees before God.*

That does not need any amplification, but it needs a good deal of exemplification.

2. *Select a place to hold the meeting.*

(1) Because of the commodiousness and accessibility of a room. If you can get a large room, get it, unless you are pretty sure you are going to have a small meeting. If you get a large room it will be an incentive to you to work hard to have a large meeting. If possible get a room that is accessible. Of course if you cannot do better, you can get a room where you have to climb two or three flights of stairs, but if a room can be had on the first floor, so much the better. There may be reasons why a room that is quite inaccessible will be better in some special case, for your meeting.

(2) Because of some one you wish to reach. This is an important point in the selection of a room. It may be there is a father you want to get at—the wife and children have been reached, but the father will not come to the meeting. The only way you can get him to a meeting is to have a meeting in his own home. Have the meeting in that case in his house. I prayed for one man for fifteen years. I tried to talk with him, but every time I would talk with him he would be worse than ever. I think he used to swear in my presence more than anywhere else just because he knew I was a Christian. But I got him one time where I had him cornered. He was sick for two weeks in a Christian home. He heard the Bible read and heard prayer every day during these two weeks and heard religious conversation constantly. At the end of these two weeks, the day he got up and got out, he took Christ as his Saviour, and afterwards became a preacher of the gospel. You must be as wise as a serpent in looking for souls.

(3) Select a room because of the popularity of the family Avoid as far as possible selecting a home that is unpopular. Many an inexperienced worker tries to hold a meeting and

gets for that purpose what appears to be a desirable home, but afterwards wonders why the people will not come to it. Probably the reason is that there is something about the family that makes them unpopular. There may sometimes be reasons for holding the meeting in such a home, but as a rule, if you know a family that everybody likes, that is the place to hold your meeting, other things being equal.

3. *Work up the meeting.*

(1) Have a great deal of invitation work done, not by yourself only, but by others as well. Be sure and not do it all yourself. Mr. Moody used to say, "It is a great deal better to get ten men to work than to do the work of ten men." Be careful as to whom you invite. If there is enmity existing between the person at whose house the meeting is to be held and some other person in the vicinity, you would better bring about a reconciliation between the two before inviting the latter person to the meeting. A minister should not cater to the prejudices of the people, but he should know their prejudices, and be governed in his actions by his knowledge of them. You have to deal with people on the practical basis of what they are, and not on the ideal basis of what they ought to be. Oftentimes it is well to leave the whole matter of invitation to the lady of the house. In some homes they are willing that you should invite everybody, while in others they are particular as to whom you invite. Reaching the poor in the alleys is far easier than reaching the wealthy people up on the avenues. You can go into the homes of the poor and invite them to come and hear the Gospel, but for some reason you do not want to go into the homes of the people living in the elegant houses. But it is quite easy for people who are rich themselves, and who are Christians as well, to invite other rich people to gather at their homes, and then have some one there to open up to them the Word of God.

4. *Provide for the singing and playing too, if it is possible.*

Instrumental music, however, is not absolutely necessary. We have fallen into the way of depending too much upon instrumental music. The best singing is oftentimes without any musical instrument. It is well to bear in mind that very poor singing goes a good ways in a poor home. As far as possible, you should have the hymns you are going to use selected beforehand, and selected with care.

5. *Go to the place of holding the meeting, early.*

If when you arrive you find the chairs arranged in a most formal way, looking like a funeral, get things a little disarranged. Do not put the chairs in straight lines, but arrange them as for a social gathering.

Another reason for going to the place early is to be ready to welcome people when they come. When they come do not leave them to take care of themselves; get them to talking, and open the meeting in an informal way before they know it has begun. Make everybody feel as much at home as you can. While people are still talking you can suggest a song, and when that is over, have some one lead in prayer. Oftentimes it is well not to let people know that it is going to be a prayer meeting; call it a social and make it a social, but give it a religious turn.

III. How to conduct the meeting.

1. *Always begin promptly.*

That is if it has been announced as a meeting beginning at a certain time, be sure and begin at that time. In regard to the form of beginning the meeting, it is not necessary to have any particular form.

2. *Be as informal as possible.*

3. *Get every one to sing.*

People like to sing. Oftentimes the people who have the poorest voices and the least knowledge of music are the ones most fond of singing. Encourage them to sing. This will shock the really musical people present, but not one person in a thousand is really musical, and you can afford to shock them. If necessary sing the same verse over and over again until the people learn it; do it with enthusiasm. Comment on the hymns. Use for the most part familiar hymns, though a new hymn with a catchy tune will often take well.

Everything about the meeting should be made cheery and bright. There are hosts of people in the world who have very little brightness in their lives, and if you have a bright cottage meeting, they will find it out and come.

4. *Make everything brief.*

Have no long prayers, no long sermons and no long testimonies. One man went to a cottage meeting and read a chapter with seventy verses and read the whole chapter. I have heard of a man praying fifteen minutes in a cottage meeting. Those were doubtless extreme cases, but not a few cottage meetings have been killed by long-winded leaders.

5. *Take a simple subject to speak upon.*

Some foolish workers take the cottage meeting as an opportunity for displaying their profound knowledge of theology. Such people kill the meeting. Do not preach, but talk in an informal homely way. Do not talk too loud.

6. *Draw the people out.*

One of the advantages of a cottage meeting is that you can draw the people out. Be sure and use this opportunity of getting people to speak in meeting. To you it may be a very simple matter to speak in meeting, yet most of us can remember when it was a very difficult thing to do, but it is far more difficult for those plain people among whom we hold most of our cottage meetings. It is, however, very easy to draw them out by simply saying, "Now, Mrs. Jones, what do you think about this matter?" "Mr. Brown, what have you to say of this?" Before they know it you have got them to talking on the subject of religion just as they would talk about their sewing or washing or everyday work. A young lady used to attend a service that I conducted. She warned me beforehand that I must not call upon her to speak, that she had heart trouble, and if she got excited, it was dangerous; at the same time she was unhappy because she did not take part in meeting. One day when a meeting was going on, quite naturally I turned to her and in an informal way asked her a question upon the subject that was under discussion. Without thinking at all, she got up and expressed her opinion upon it. Afterward I said to her, "You have spoken in meeting, you did not seem to have much trouble about it." She now enjoys speaking in meeting and her heart trouble has disappeared. Perhaps you could not do this in a church or chapel meeting, but it is the easiest thing in the world in a cottage meeting to get everybody talking on the subject of religion just the same as on any other subject. It is a remarkable fact that when you go into a house and approach the subject of religion after having talked about other things, the people immediately begin to talk in another tone of voice, and in a different way. You must break up that sort of thing. Cultivate the habit of gliding into the subject of religion as naturally as into any other subject.

7. *Do not have a stereotyped way of conducting a cottage meeting.*

It is not well to have a stereotyped way of doing anything. Go to some churches and they put into your hands an order of service. Every part of the service has its fixed place. It gets to be an abomination in the church service, but it is far more of an abomination in a cottage meeting. One of the greatest advantages of a cottage meeting is its informality. Some men get into the way of uttering stereotyped prayers. When he gets to the point where he prays for the Jews, you know that his next prayer will be for the sick of the congregation, etc., etc. That sort of thing is unspeakably tiresome even in church, but it is utterly unendurable in a cottage meeting.

8. *Do not let the meeting get away from you.*

We have said to draw the people out and get them to talking, but if you are not very careful they will get to talking, and the meeting will run away from you. Let your ideal be perfect freedom and at the same time perfect control.

9. *Oftentimes have a season of sentence prayers.*

Sentence prayers are one of the best things that our Young People's Society of Christian Endeavor have introduced into our church life. Of course sentence prayers can become formal and stereotyped and meaningless. When I first began to go to prayer meeting there were three or four good old men who monopolized the whole time. To begin with, the minister would give out a hymn, and then make a long prayer, and then sing another hymn, and then read a long chapter, and talk fifteen or twenty minutes, and then throw the meeting open. This meant that brother Brown would grind out a long prayer, and then brother Jones would grind out another long prayer, they would sing a hymn, and then brother Smith would pray anywhere from ten to twenty minutes. Another hymn would be sung and the minister would pronounce the benediction, and the affair was over, and all would go home glad the thing was through. Many people cannot pray five minutes in public, and it is a good thing they cannot, and they fancy that it is impossible for them to pray at all unless they can get off an elaborate address to God. But anybody can ask for what he wants. Make it clear to people that this is real praying, asking God for what we really want. How near God seems to draw during a season of sentence prayers! You can say, "If there is one thing you want to-day more than anything else, just put that in your sentence prayer. Never forget that prayer is simply asking God for what you want, and expecting to get it."

10. *Oftentimes have requests for prayer.*

Do not be mechanical about that. I would not always have the same kind of a meeting. I knew a man who was very successful in cottage meeting work who used to have the people get up and move around and talk with one another, and then sit down and go on with the meeting.

11. *Have periods of silent prayer.*

Oftentimes the most hallowed moments in a meeting are when all the people are silent before God. Before having these periods of silent prayer, you must be careful to warn people to keep their thoughts fixed upon God, and to keep pouring out their souls before God in prayer. You and I may not need that warning, but many Christians do. If not warned, Mrs. Jones is likely to spend the time thinking about Mrs. Brown's hat, and Mrs. Brown about Mrs. Jones' dress. They would not be thinking about God at all.

12. *Do personal work.*

A cottage meeting that does not close with personal work has been mismanaged. The cottage meeting offers a very unusual opportunity for this kind of work. The meetings are small, it is rare indeed that there are more than forty people present. You should find out how many of these people are saved. It does not follow that because a person is saved, we do not need to do personal work with him. Saved people can get help in these meetings that they cannot get in a large meeting. It is the easiest and simplest thing in the world to get a mother to talking, say about her children. Draw her away from the crowd, and then lead her on to the subject of her soul's salvation, or her spiritual condition. People feel more at home in their own house, and you can get into their hearts as you cannot in a more public gathering.

13. *Close promptly.*

Be sure to do that. If nine o'clock is understood to be the hour of closing, close promptly at that time, if possible. It is a good thing to establish a reputation for beginning and closing promptly. In this way you will get many people to go to your meeting who would not otherwise go. They can stay to a certain hour, and if they know you will close promptly at the hour appointed, they will go to the meeting. If the interest is so great that you wish to continue the meeting, close the meeting at the appointed time, giving all those who desire to leave an opportunity to do so, and then have a second meeting. You must never forget that a great many people have to get up early in the morning, and in order to do so, they must go to bed early. It is very embarrassing for timid people to get up and leave a meeting while it is going on. Then again, the woman of the house where you are holding the meeting may be obliged to get up at five o'clock in the morning to prepare breakfast, and so must go to bed early. Furthermore, it is far better to close the meeting while there is good interest, than to wait until the interest dies out. If you close at high tide, people will want to come again. If people desire to stay around and chat at the close of a meeting, be sure and have them chat on the subject of religion. If people are disposed to hang around after the meeting is over and make themselves a nuisance, you can say pleasantly, "It is getting late; and Mrs. B. wants to shut up her house. I guess we must be going."

As to the time of holding the meeting, the evening is the usual time, but sometimes the afternoon is a good time, especially in country districts.

CHAPTER III

PARLOR MEETINGS

Parlor meetings are much the same in thought and in method as cottage meetings, with this difference, that cottage meetings are intended to reach people of the middle classes and the poor, while parlor meetings are intended to reach the rich. There are many who think there is no use trying to reach the rich with the Gospel. This is a great mistake. Some of the most devoted and delightful Christians that I have ever known have been people of much wealth and high position. Indeed, perhaps the dearest Christian friend I ever had, and the one from whom I learned the most by personal contact, was a man who stood very high socially and politically in his country. I think this man more fully realized the meaning of Christ's words, "Except ye be converted and become as little children," than any other man I ever knew. I have known people of much wealth in our own country, and members of the nobility in England, Germany and Russia who were among the most humble Christians that I have ever met.

I. Advantages and importance.

The principal advantage in parlor meetings is that they reach many who can be reached in no other way. It may be admitted that the rich are the hardest class to reach of any. It is much easier to bring the Gospel to people who live in the slums than to the people who live in palaces, but many of these latter have been reached by parlor meetings.

II. How to conduct.

1. *Get some Christians of wealth and position to open their parlors for the meetings.*

Rich Christians should make far larger use of their homes than they do, to reach people of their own class. Many of them do not open their homes simply because their attention has never been called to the fact that this is a way in which they can do good. Many of them show a great readiness to do this when it is suggested to them.

2. *Have the lady of the house invite her intimate friends.*

Many of them will come out of curiosity, others will come out of friendship. Oftentimes it gets to be a fad to attend these meetings and people go scarcely knowing why. It does not matter so much why they go, as long as they go; for if the Gospel is presented in the power of the Holy Spirit after they get there some of them will be converted.

3. *Get an attractive and Spirit-filled speaker.*

Sometimes it is well to have the speaker himself a person of wealth or position, but there are many who have never known what it means to be rich themselves who still have a peculiar faculty for winning the confidence and esteem of wealthy people.

4. *Sometimes take up some line of Bible study.*

Bible study under a wise teacher can be made exceedingly interesting for people of wealth and fashion. Indeed, many of these people hardly know how to use their time, and Bible study presents to them a pleasing novelty. Of course the teacher must be a wise man or a wise woman, and filled with the Holy Spirit. Sometimes it is possible to have a regular class for systematic Bible instruction, extending through many weeks or months.

5 *Sometimes have an address on some living religious topic by a Spirit-filled man or woman.*

6. *It is well oftentimes to interest those who are gathered together for parlor meetings in some missionary work or charity.*

Many of them like to give, and it is a blessing to them to give. They should be educated to know just what the crying needs of the wide world are.

7. *Aim directly at the conversion of those who attend.*

Very little is accomplished after all in parlor meetings, unless the unsaved ones are brought to Christ. The probability is, that they will be brought to Christ at the parlor meeting or else will never be brought to Him. If any man should have a profound sense that it is "now or never," it is the one who is addressing a company of wealthy men or women gathered together for a parlor meeting in a Christian home.

A woman of wealth once asked a Christian man who called at her home, "Are you a missionary?" "Yes," he replied. "Do you ever speak to people about their souls?" "I do." "Well," she replied, "I wish you would speak to me about my soul." He did, and led her to Christ. When the conversation was over, the lady said, "I have often wished I was poor; missionaries come and talk to my servants about Christ, but they never speak to me. My pastor calls upon me, but he never speaks about my own religious needs, and I have often wished that I was poor so that some one might speak to me about my soul."

Preparation for a parlor meeting need not be elaborate. The principal thing is to teach those who gather together the great fundamental truths of the Gospel in the power of the Holy Spirit. If there is music, it should be of the very best, but should be spiritual, rather than classical. The class of people that you are aiming to reach are quite sated with high class music, but simple Gospel singing in the power of the Holy Ghost is a novelty to them, and will touch their hearts and lead to the conversion of many of them. An attractive young woman with a sweet voice, a true knowledge of Christ, a burden for souls, and the power of the Holy Spirit, will be greatly used of God.

CHAPTER IV

THE CHURCH PRAYER MEETING

I. Importance and advantages.

The prayer meeting ought to be the most important meeting in the church. It is the most important meeting if it is rightly conducted. Of course the church prayer meeting in many churches is more a matter of form than a center of power. The thing to do in such a case is not to give up the prayer meeting, but to make it what it ought to be. There are five reasons why the church prayer meeting is of vital importance.

1. *It brings power into all the life and work of the church.*

If there is any real power in the church it is from God, and God has given it in answer to prayer. The prayer meeting is the real expression of the prayer life of the church. Of course all the living members of the church are praying in private, but it is in the prayer meeting that they come together and pray as a church. God delights to honor the prayers of the church as a whole (Acts 12: 5, Acts 1: 14). If the prayer meeting of a church runs down, it is practically certain that all the life of the church will run down, and its work prove a failure as far as accomplishing anything real and lasting for God is concerned.

2. *It develops the membership of the church.*

In the regular services of the church, but few members of the church are developed; the minister plays the leading rôle; but in the prayer meeting there is an opportunity for the exercise of gifts on the part of the whole body. Altogether too little stress is laid in modern church life on the development of the gifts of the church. The whole organization is conducted on the idea of the work being done by one man or by a few men. It was not so in early church gatherings.

Here the people came together for mutual benefit, and every member of the church was allowed to exercise his gifts (1 Cor. 14: 26). About the only place where this is possible in modern church life is in the prayer meeting. A real prayer meeting is one of the most apostolic meetings that we have in our modern churches.

3. *It results in many conversions.*

If a prayer meeting is conducted as it ought to be, many people will be converted in the prayer meeting. In not a few churches the presence of the Holy Spirit is much more manifest in the prayer meeting than in any other gathering of the church, and unconverted men and women and children coming in there feel His presence, and are convicted of sin and oftentimes converted to Christ. Of course there is nothing in many prayer meetings to convert any one, but if a prayer meeting is conducted as it ought to be, conversions may be looked for at every meeting.

4. *It promotes the life and fellowship of the church.*

In a large church it is quite impossible for people to get very close to one another in the Sunday services. Everything conspires to prevent it, but in the prayer meeting not only do people get in closer physical contact, but heart touches heart in a way that is unknown in the more formal service. People warm up toward one another, and come to understand one another in the prayer meeting as in perhaps no other service. Love is increased and multiplied. There has perhaps never been a time in the history of the church when this was more important than to-day. People belong to the same church, and sit under the same minister, and look into one another's faces once a week for years, and scarcely know one another's names, but in the prayer meeting people learn to know and to love one another.

5. *It promotes the home and foreign mission work of the church.*

It is very difficult, and in many cases altogether impossible, to keep up a strong missionary interest without a church prayer meeting. Not only does the prayer meeting afford opportunity for missionary intelligence, but it also affords an opportunity for the many in the church to pour out their heart in prayer for the missionary work. When Jesus wished to promote a missionary interest among His disciples, He set them to praying for missions (Matt. 9: 38; 10: 1). If we wish to promote the foreign missionary interest in any church, we must get the church to praying for missions.

II. How to conduct.

1. *Remember that the prayer meeting is primarily a* PRAYER *meeting.*

Do not transform it into a lecture course or into a Bible class. It would be going too far to say that the prayer meeting should be only a prayer meeting. There are, of course, times when this should be the case, when the whole hour should be given up to prayer, but this is not wise as a universal rule; but at least it ought to be pre-eminently a prayer meeting. Many of our modern prayer meetings are so only in name. There may be a prayer by the minister at the opening of the meeting, and a prayer by some one else in closing, but the meeting is largely given up to talking, and oftentimes very desultory and unprofitable talking at that. Let prayer be the prominent thing in the prayer meeting. It may be that the major part of the time is not taken up by prayer, but see to it that the Bible comment and the testimony has something to do with prayer, and leads naturally to prayer.

2. *Draw out all the membership of the church in the prayer meeting.*

The prayer meeting is the place for the cultivation of the gifts of the membership of the church. In many churches it is only the chosen few who exercise their gifts and get the fullest measure of blessing. It will not do to say that every member should take part in every prayer meeting. In a large church this is impossible, and furthermore it leads to a certain mechanical way of taking part that is unprofitable and vain; but the pastor should see to it that all the membership take part sometime. If there is any attendant at the prayer meeting who never takes part, make a study of that person and find out what his gifts are, and give him an opportunity for their exercise. Assign backward ones something definite to do; it may be nothing more than to read a verse of Scripture. It is not wise, however, to allow people to be content with simply getting up week after week and quoting some passage of Scripture. It is better to give the person some suggestive verse to study during the week, and then let them bring some thought that has come to them in meditating upon that verse.

3. *Assign portions of Scripture to study.*

For example, one of the most helpful series of prayer meetings I ever conducted took up the book of Psalms; about seven Psalms were given out each week, and the people were requested to read these Psalms over and over again, and then to come to the meeting prepared to give some thought that had come to them in the study of these Psalms. When this request was made, one of the most experienced members of the church went to a public library and got down all the leading commentaries on the Psalms and began to study them. He confessed afterwards that he had gotten far greater blessing from the comments made by some of the plainest and most uneducated people in the church than he had gotten from all the commentaries that he had studied. A prominent minister who dropped in during these meetings was so impressed by the interest and power of the meeting, that he afterwards adopted the same plan in his own church. He said that it gave him an entirely new idea of the possibilities of the prayer meeting.

4. *Have a well chosen list of subjects.*

It is not well always to have a list of subjects that is followed week after week in the prayer meeting. It is quite possible to get into a stereotyped and formal way in doing this, but lists of subjects are oftentimes helpful. Usually the best list of subjects is the one you make up for yourself. Get as many lists of subjects as you can for suggestion, and then make your own. Usually it is not wise to have a list of subjects that extends over too long a period. A list of subjects extending over an entire year oftentimes gets to be a great nuisance.

5. *Have definite requests for prayer.*

There is a discouraging vagueness in the prayers at many prayer meetings. When something definite is presented for the meeting, it goes far to give life to the meeting; the prayers no longer wander all over creation, but aim at a definite object. It is well when the requests for prayer are read to have the people bow their heads in silent prayer. Do not read the requests so rapidly as to make it impossible for each one to be remembered definitely. After a few requests have been read, it is well to have some one lead in prayer, then read others and have some one else lead in prayer, and so on through the list. It is well oftentimes to have the requests made verbally from the audience, but there is a great advantage in having them written out. If people are not interested enough to write the request out, it is doubtful if there is much good in asking for the thing desired; furthermore, if the request is written out, it can be read so that everybody in the room hears it.

6. *Have a definite opportunity for thanksgiving and praise.*

Thanksgiving should always go hand in hand with prayer. The Apostle Paul said, "In nothing be anxious; but in everything by prayer and supplication *with thanksgiving* let your requests be made known unto God" (Phil. 4: 6). This is a good rule for the conduct of a prayer meeting. Giving definite thanksgiving and praise for blessings already received, will increase our faith in asking for new and larger blessings. There is nothing that seems to promote the presence of the Spirit more than true thanksgiving; indeed a large share of the testimony and the talk in prayer meeting should be along the line of thanksgiving and praise.

7. *Make much of music in the prayer meeting.*

Of course the prayer meeting ought not to be a song service, but it should be a service in which there is much song. Every one should be encouraged to sing. See to it that all do sing. The singing should be in the Spirit, but should also be with the understanding. Dwell on the meaning of the words. Have verses sung over and over until they are sung from the heart. A prayer meeting should be one of the brightest, cheeriest gatherings ever held on earth. If it is made so, there will be no need of urging people to come out to the meeting, and scolding them for not coming; they will want to come. It will be the brightest spot in the whole life of the week.

8. *Train the people to feel the importance of the prayer meeting.*

To do this it is not necessary to scold people for not attending, but often drop a word that emphasizes the importance of the prayer meeting. Let people know of the good time that you are having. Speak to people personally about coming out. Have people go after them and bring them out, and keep after them until they come. Make the meetings so interesting that when they do come once they will want to come again.

9. *Make people feel at home.*

About the stiffest thing on earth is a stiff prayer meeting, but if the prayer meeting is made a homey place, people will want to come again and again. It is well to stand at the door to welcome people as they come in, having a smile and pleasant word for all who come. It is not at all necessary that the pastor be behind the desk during the opening moments of the meeting; he can oftentimes do more good down by the door than he can in his seat of honor.

10. *Sometimes make the prayer meeting like a social.*

Do not have the people sit down in stiff rows, but have them stand up and move around. Then the meeting can be begun in an informal way, and you are in the midst of the meeting almost before you know it.

11. *Always aim at, and look for, conversions in the prayer meeting.*

If the prayer meeting is conducted as it ought to be, many unconverted people will come, and the whole atmosphere of the place is such as to prepare people for a personal acceptance of Jesus Christ. There is no place where it is so easy to speak to people about their souls as after a good warm prayer meeting. Oftentimes when the opportunity is given for requests for prayer, the question should be put, "Is there not some one here to-night who wishes us to pray that they may be saved to-night," or some question of that character.

12. *Stand at the door and shake hands with people and speak to people as they go out.*

There is oftentimes untold good in a hearty handshake. I stood one night at the door of our prayer meeting shaking hands with people as they went out, and a lady said to me, "I have been in Chicago for a long time; I have gone to church again and again but you are the first Christian that has shaken hands with me." I believe another said that the only reason she went to prayer meeting was to get a good handshake.

13. *Make the prayer meeting a matter of prayer.*

Ask God to teach you how to conduct the prayer meeting and make it what it ought to be. Ask God definitely to bless every prayer meeting that you conduct or attend; do it expectantly. Always go to the prayer meeting expecting that you are going to have a good time. I always do and am never disappointed.

14. *Make the prayer meeting a matter of study.*

Do not make it so much a study as to what you will say, but as to how it can be improved. Avoid getting into ruts. It is not well to keep in a rut even if it is a good rut.

III. Some suggestions.

1. *Don't take up all the time yourself.*

The prayer meeting is not so much your meeting as the meeting of the whole church. You have your opportunity to air your views on the Lord's Day; be fair and give the other people an opportunity on the prayer meeting evening.

2. *Don't let anyone else take up all the time.*

There is liable to be in every community a prayer meeting killer, a man given to making long prayers or long speeches, and as stale as they are long. Everybody looks blue as soon as he gets up to speak. This must not be permitted, but just how can it be stopped? First of all, look to God to give you wisdom, in the second place don't lose your temper, in the third place watch for your opportunity. Sometimes he will say something that will enable you to break in with a remark; then ask somebody else their opinion, and some one else theirs, and then propose a song. Sometimes it will be necessary to say to the member, publicly and plainly, but kindly, that you are glad his heart is so full, but the time is getting very short and there are many who want to speak. Sometimes it will be wisest to go to the man privately and tell him that it is not wise for him to take up so much time in the meeting. If you have tact, you can generally do this without hurting his feelings, but at any cost he must be stopped.

3. *Don't begin late.*

If a prayer meeting is announced to begin at a certain hour, begin at the very tick of the clock. This encourages more people to attend than most people suspect.

4. *Don't run over time.*

If the prayer meeting is announced to close at a certain time, close at that time. It may be wise to have a second prayer meeting, but close the meeting at the time announced.

5. *Don't let the meeting drag.*

If it begins to drag, ask some one a question that will draw them out, or say something yourself that will set other people to thinking and talking. Oftentimes the best thing to do is to propose a season of silent prayer, but do not urge people to "fill up the time." That leads to unprofitable talking. People ought not to speak merely to fill up time; they ought not to speak unless they have something to say that is worth listening to. Far better a season of silent prayer than a season of vain talking.

Sometimes it is well to bring the meeting to a close before the announced hour comes. Some leaders make the mistake of thinking that it is necessary to carry the meeting through to the announced hour, no matter how it drags.

6. *Don't have bad air.*

The air in the room has more to do with the excellence or dullness of the meeting than most people suspect.

7. *Don't be stereotyped.*

The fact that a prayer meeting conducted in a certain way was a good prayer meeting, does not prove that every prayer meeting should be conducted in just that way. It is well to do unexpected things; it wakes people up; but be sure that you do not do foolish things in your desire to do unexpected things.

CHAPTER V

THE USE OF TRACTS

Comparatively few Christians realize the importance of tract work. I had been a Christian a good many years, and a minister of the Gospel several years, before it ever entered my head that tracts were of much value in Christian work. I had somehow grown up with the notion that tracts were all rubbish, and therefore I did not take the trouble to read them, and far less did I take the trouble to circulate them, but I found out that I was entirely wrong. Tract work has some great advantages over other forms of Christian work.

I. Importance and advantages.

1. *Any person can do it.*

We cannot all preach; we cannot all conduct meetings; but we can all select useful tracts and then hand them out to others. Of course some of us can do it better than others. Even a blind man or a dumb man can do tract work. It is a line of work in which every man, woman and child can engage.

2. *A tract always sticks to the point.*

I wish every worker did that, but how often we get to talking to some one and he is smart enough to get us off on to a side track.

3. *A tract never loses its temper.*

Perhaps you sometimes do. I have known Christian workers, even workers of experience, who would sometimes get all stirred up, but you cannot stir up a tract. It always remains as calm as a June morning.

4. *Oftentimes people who are too proud to be talked with, will read a tract when no one is looking.*

There is many a man who would repulse you if you tried to speak to him about his soul, who will read a tract if you leave it on his table, or in some other place where he comes upon it accidentally, and that tract may be used for his salvation.

5. *A tract stays by one.*

You talk to a man and then he goes away, but the tract stays with him. Some years ago a man came into a mission in New York. One of the workers tried to talk with him, but he would not listen. As he was leaving, a card tract was placed in his hands which read, "If I should die to-night I would go to ——. Please fill out and sign." He put it in his pocket, went to his steamer, for he was a sailor, and slipped it into the edge of his bunk. The steamer started for Liverpool. On his voyage he met with an accident, and was laid aside in his bunk. That card stared him in the face, day and night. Finally he said, "If I should die to-night I would go to hell, but I will not go there, I will go to heaven, I will take Christ right here and now." He went to Liverpool, returned to New York, went to the mission, told his story, and had the card still in his pocket, filled out and signed with his name. The conversation he had had in the mission left him, but the card stayed by him.

6. *Tracts lead many to accept Christ.*

The author of one tract ("What is it to believe in the Lord Jesus Christ?") received before his death upwards of sixteen hundred letters from people who had been led to Christ by reading it.

II. Purposes for which to use a tract.

1. *For the conversion of the unsaved.*

A tract will often succeed in winning a man to Christ where a sermon or a personal conversation has failed. There are a great many people who, if you try to talk with them, will put you off; but if you put a tract in their hands and ask God to bless it, after they go away and are alone they will read the tract and God will carry it home to their hearts by the power of the Holy Ghost. One of our students wrote me in great joy, of how he had at last succeeded in winning a whole family for Christ. He had been working for that family for a long time but could not touch them. One day he left a tract with them, and God used that tract for the conversion of four or five members of the family. Another student held a cottage meeting at a home, and by mistake left his Bible there. There was a tract in the Bible. When he had gone, the woman of the house saw the Bible, picked it up, opened it, saw the tract and read it. The Spirit of God carried it home to her heart, and when he went back after the Bible she told him she wanted to find the Lord Jesus Christ. The tract had done what he could not do in personal work. I once received a letter from a man saying, "There is a man in this place whom I tried for a long time to reach but could not. One day I handed him a tract, and I think it was to the salvation of his whole family."

2. *To lead Christians into a deeper and more earnest Christian life.*

It is a great mistake to limit the use of tracts to winning the unsaved to Christ. A little tract on the Second Coming of Christ, once sent me in a letter, made a change in my whole life. I do not think the tract was altogether correct doctrinally, but it had in it an important truth, and it did for me just the work that needed to be done.

There is a special class of people with whom this form of ministry is particularly helpful, those who live where they do not enjoy spiritual advantages. You may know some one who is leading a very unsatisfactory life, and you long to have that person know what the Christian life really means. His pastor may not be a spiritual man, he may not know the deep things of God. It is the simplest thing in the world to slip into a letter a tract that will lead him into an entirely new Christian life.

3. *To correct error.*

This is a very necessary form of work in the day in which we live. The air is full of error. In our personal work we have not always time to lead a man out of his error, but oftentimes we can give him a tract that can do the work better than we can. If you tried to lead him out of his error by peronal work, you might get into a discussion, but the tract cannot. The one in error cannot talk back to the tract.

For example, take people that are in error on the question of of seventh day observance. It might take some time to lead such a one out of the darkness into the light, but a tract on that subject can be secured that has been used of God to lead many out of the bondage of legalism into the glorious liberty of the Gospel of Christ.

4. *To set Christians to work.*

Our churches are full of members who are doing nothing. A well-chosen tract may set such to work. I know of a young man who was working in a factory in Massachusetts. He was a plain, uneducated sort of fellow, but a little tract on peronal work was placed in his hands. He read it and re-read it, and said, "I am not doing what I should for Christ." He went to work among his companions in the factory, inviting them to the church, and to hear his pastor preach. Not satisfied with this, he went to doing personal work. This was not sufficient, so he went to work holding meetings himself. Finally he brought a convention to his city. Just that one plain factory man was the means of getting a great convention and blessing to that place, and all from reading that little tract. He was also instrumental in organizing a society which was greatly blessed of God. It would be possible to fill this country with literature on Christian work that would stir up the dead and sleeping professors of religion throughout the land, and send them out to work for the Lord Jesus Christ.

III. Who should use tracts.

1. *Ministers of the Gospel should use them.*

Many ministers do make constant use of them in their pastoral work, leaving well chosen tracts where they make their pastoral calls, handing out tracts along the line of the sermons that they preach. It is said of Rev. Edward Judson of New York, that he seldom makes a call without having in his pocket a selection of tracts adapted to almost every member of the family, and especially to the children. "At the close of the Sunday evening preaching service, he has often put some good brother in the chair, and while the meeting proceeds he goes down into the audience and gives to each person a choice leaflet, at the same time improving the opportunity to say a timely word. In this way he comes into personal touch with the whole audience, gives each stranger a cordial welcome, and leaves in his hand some message from God. At least once a year he selects some one tract that has in it the very core of the Gospel. On this he prints the notices of the services, and selecting his church as a center, he has this tract put in the hands of every person living within half a mile in each direction, regardless of creed or condition. He sometimes uses 10,000 tracts at one distribution, and finds it very fruitful in results."

2. *Sunday School teachers.*

Every Sunday School teacher should be on the lookout for tracts to give to his scholars. In this way he can do much to supplement his hour's work on the Lord's Day.

3. *Traveling men.*

Traveling men have a rare opportunity for doing tract work. They are constantly coming in contact with different men, and finding out their needs. A Christian "drummer" with a well-assorted selection of tracts can accomplish immeasurable good.

4. *Business men.*

Business men can use tracts to good advantage with the very men with whom they have business engagements. They can also do excellent work with their own employés. Many-a business man slips well chosen tracts into many of the letters which he writes, and thus accomplishes an effective ministry for his Master.

5. *School teachers.*

It is very difficult for school teachers in some cities and towns to talk very much with their pupils in school. Oftentimes the rules of the school board prevent it entirely, but a wise teacher can learn all about her scholars and their home surroundings, and can give them tracts just adapted to their needs.

6. *Housekeepers.*

Every Christian housekeeper should have a collection of well assorted tracts. She can hand these out to the servant girls, the grocery men, the market men, the butcher, to the tramps that come to the door. They can be left upon the table in the parlor and in bedrooms. Only eternity will disclose the good that is accomplished in these ways.

IV. How to use tracts.

1. *To begin a conversation.*

One of the difficulties in Christian work is to begin. You see a person with whom you wish to talk about the Lord Jesus Christ. The great difficulty is in starting. It is easy enough to talk after you have started, but how are you going to start a conversation naturally and easily? One of the simplest and easiest ways is by slipping a tract into the person's hand. After the tract has been read, a conversation naturally follows. I was once riding in a crowded car. I asked God for an opportunity to lead some one to Christ. I was watching for the opportunity for which I had asked, when two young ladies entered. I thought I knew one of them as the daughter of a minister. She went through the car looking for a seat, and then came back. As she came back and sat down in the seat in front of me, she bowed, and of course I knew I was right as to who she was. I took out a little bundle of tracts, and selecting one that seemed best adapted to her case, I handed it to her, having first asked God to bless it. She at once began to read and I began to pray. When she had read the tract, I asked her what she thought about it. She almost burst into tears right there in the car, and in a very few moments that minister's daughter was rejoicing in the Lord Jesus Christ as her personal Saviour. As she afterwards passed out of the car, she said, "I want to thank you for what you have done for me in leading me to Christ."

2. *Use a tract to close a conversation.*

As a rule when you have finished talking with some one, you should not leave him without something definite to take home to read. If the person has accepted Christ, put some tract in his hands that will show him how to succeed in the Christian life. If the person has not accepted Christ, some other tract that is especially adapted to his need should be left with him.

3. *Use tracts where a conversation is impossible.*

For example, one night at the close of a tent meeting in Chicago, as I went down one of the aisles a man beckoned to me, and intimated that his wife was interested. She was in tears, and I tried to talk with her, but she stammered out in a broken way, "We don't talk English." She had not understood a word of the sermon, I suppose, but God had carried something home to her heart. They were Norwegians, and I could not find a Norwegian in the whole tent to act as interpreter, but I could put a Norwegian tract in her hand, and that could do the work. Time and time again I have met with men deeply interested about their soul's salvation, but with whom I could not deal because I did not talk the language that they understood.

One day as I came from dinner, I found a Swede waiting for me, and he said he had a man outside with whom he wished me to talk. I went outside and found an uncouth looking specimen, a Norwegian. The Swede had found him drunk in an alley and dragged him down to the Institute to talk with me. He was still full of whisky, and spit tobacco juice over me as I tried to talk with him. I found he could not talk English, and I talked English to the Swede, and the Swede talked Swedish to the Norwegian, and the Norwegian got a little bit of it. I made it as clear as I could to our Swede interpreter, and he in his turn made it as clear as he could to the Norwegian. Then I put a Norwegian tract in his hands, and that could talk to him so that he understood perfectly.

Oftentimes a conversation is impossible because of the place where you meet people. For example, you may be on the street cars and wish to speak to a man, but in many instances it would not be wise if it were possible, but you can take the man's measure and then give him a tract that will fit him. You may be able to say just a few words to him and then put the tract in his hands and ask God to bless it.

4. *Use tracts to send to people at a distance.*

It does not cost a tract much to travel. You can send them to the ends of the earth for a few cents. Especially use them to send to people who live in out of the way places where there is no preaching. There are thousands of people living in different sections of this country where they do not hear preaching from one year's end to another. It would be impossible to send an evangelical preacher to them, but you can send a tract and it will do the preaching for you.

V. Suggestions as to the use of tracts.

1. *Always read the tracts yourself before giving them to others.*

This is very necessary. Bad tracts abound to-day, tracts that contain absolutely pernicious doctrine. They are being circulated free by the million, and one needs to be on his guard, lest he be doing harm rather than good in distributing tracts. Of course we cannot read all the tracts in foreign languages, but we can have them interpreted to us, and it is wise to do so. Besides positively bad tracts, there are many tracts that are worthless.

2. *Suit your tract to the person to whom you give it.*

What is good for one person may not be good for another.

3. *Carry a selection of tracts with you.*

I do not say a *collection*, but a *selection*. Tracts are countless in number, and a large share of them are worthless. Select the best, and arrange them for the different classes of people with whom you come in contact.

4. *Seek the guidance of God.*

This is of the very highest importance. If there is any place where we need wisdom from above, it is in the selection of tracts, and in their distribution after their selection.

5. *Seek God's blessing upon the tract after you have given it out.*

Do not merely give out the tract and there let the matter rest, but whenever you give out a tract ask God to bless it.

6. *Oftentimes give a man a tract with words and sentences underscored.*

Men are curious, and they will take particular notice of the underscoring. It is oftentimes a good thing to have a tract put up in your office. Men who come in will read it. I know a man who had a few words put upon his paper weight.

A great many who came into his office saw it, and it made a deep impression upon them.

7. *Never be ashamed of distributing tracts.*

Many people hand out tracts to others as if they were ashamed of what they were doing. People are not likely to read tracts if you hand them to them as if you were ashamed to do it; but if you act as though you were conferring a favor upon them, and giving them something worth reading, they will read your tract. It is often well to say to a person, "Here is a little leaflet out of which I have gotten a good deal of good. I would like to have you read it."

CHAPTER VI

OPEN-AIR MEETINGS

I. Their importance and advantages.

1. *They are Scriptural.*

Jesus said, "Go out quickly *into the streets* and lanes of the city, and bring in hither the poor, and the maimed, and the halt, and the blind." Every great preacher of the Bible was an open-air preacher. Peter was an open-air preacher, Paul was an open-air preacher, and so were Elijah, Moses and Ezra. More important than all, Jesus Christ Himself was an open-air preacher, and preached for the most part out of doors. Every great sermon recorded in the Bible was preached in the open air; the sermon on the Day of Pentecost, the Sermon on the Mount, the sermon on Mars Hill, etc. In this country we have an idea that open air preaching is for those who cannot get any other place to speak, but across the water they look at it quite differently. Some of the most eminent preachers of Great Britain preach in the open air.

2. *Open-air meetings are portable, you can carry them around.*

It would be very difficult to carry a church or mission building with you, but there is no difficulty about carrying an open-air meeting with you. You can get an open-air meeting where you could by no possibility get a church, mission hall or even a room. You can have open-air meetings in all parts of the city and all parts of the country.

3. *Open-air meetings are more attractive in the summer than hot, sweltering halls or churches.*

When on my vacations, I used to attend a country church It was one of the hottest, most stifling and sleepy places I ever entered. It was all but impossible to keep awake while the minister attempted to preach. The church was located in a beautiful grove where it was always cool and shady, but it seemed never to enter the minds of the people to go out of the church into the grove. Of course only a few people attended the church services. One day a visiting minister suggested that they have an open-air meeting on the front lawn of a Christian man having a summer residence near at hand. The farmers came to that meeting from miles around, in wagons, on foot and every other way. There was a splendid crowd in attendance. The country churches would do well in the summer to get out of their church building into some attractive grove near at hand.

4. *Open-air meetings will accommodate vast crowds.*

There are few church buildings, especially in the country, that will accommodate more than one thousand people; but people by the thousands can be accommodated by an open-air meeting. It has been my privilege to speak for several summers in a small country town with less than a thousand inhabitants. Of course the largest church building in the town would not accommodate more than five hundred people. The meetings, however, were held in the open air, and people drove to them from forty miles around, and at a single meeting we had an attendance of 15,000 people. Whitfield was driven to the fields by the action of church authorities. It was well that he was. Some of his audiences at Moorfields were said to number 60,000 people.

5. *Open-air meetings are economical.*

You neither have to pay rent nor hire a janitor. They do not cost anything at all. God Himself furnishes the building and takes care of it. I remember that at a Christian Worker's Convention a man was continually complaining that no one would hire for him a mission hall in which to hold meetings. At last I suggested to him that he had all out doors, and could go there and preach until some one hired him a hall. He took the suggestion and was greatly used of God. You do not need to have a cent in your pocket to hold an open-air meeting. The whole out doors is free.

6. *You can reach men in an open-air meeting that you can reach in no other way.*

I can tell of instance after instance where men who have not been at church or a mission hall for years have been reached by open-air meetings. The persons I have known to be reached and converted through open-air meetings have included thieves, drunkards, gamblers, saloon-keepers, abandoned women, murderers, lawyers, doctors, theatrical people, society people, in fact pretty much every class.

7. *You can reach backsliders and people who have drifted away from the church.*

One day when we were holding a meeting on a street corner in a city, a man in the crowd became interested, and one of our workers dealt with him. He said, "I am a backslider, and so is my wife, but I have made up my mind to come back to Christ." He was saved and so was his brother-in-law.

8. *Open-air meetings impress people by their earnestness.*

How often I have heard people say, "There is something in it. See those people talking out there on the street. They do not have any collection, and they come here just because they believe what they are preaching." Remarks like this are made over and over again. Men who are utterly careless about the Gospel and Christianity have been impressed by the earnestness of men and women who go out on to the street and win souls for Christ.

9. *Open-air meetings bring recruits to churches and missions.*

One of the best ways to fill up an empty church is to send your workers out on the street to hold meetings before the church service is held, or better still, go yourself. When the meeting is over, you can invite people to the church (or mission). This is the divinely appointed means for reaching men that cannot be reached in any other way (Luke 14: 21). All Christians should hear the words of Christ constantly ringing in their ears, "Go out quickly into the streets and lanes of the city, and bring in hither the poor," etc.

10. *Open-air meetings enable you to reach* MEN.

One of the great problems of most ministers of the Gospel to-day is how to get hold of the *men*. The average church audience is composed very largely of women and children.

One of the easiest ways to get hold of the men is to go out on the streets, that is where the men are. Open-air meetings are as a rule composed of an overwhelming majority of men.

11. *Open-air meetings are good for the health.*

An English preacher was told that he must die, that he had consumption. He thought he should make the most of the few months he had allotted to live, so he went out on the streets and began preaching. The open-air preaching cured his consumption, and he lived for many years, and was the founder of a great open-air society.

II. Where to hold open-air meetings.

To put it in a single word, hold them where the people are that you wish to reach. But a few suggestions may prove helpful.

1. *Where the crowds pass.*

Find the principal thoroughfare where the crowds throng. You cannot hold your meeting just at that point, as the police will not permit it, but you can hold it just a little to one side of that point, and the crowds as they pass will go to one side and listen to you.

2. *Hold them near crowded tenements.*

In that way you can preach to the people in the tenements as well as on the street. They will throw open their windows and listen. Sometimes the audience that you do not see will be as large as the one you do see. You may be preaching to hundreds of people inside the building that you do not see at all. I knew of a poor sick woman being brought to Christ through the preaching she heard on the street. It was a hot summer night, and her window was open, and the preaching came in through the window and touched her heart and won her to Christ. It is good to have a good strong voice in open-air preaching, for then you can preach to all the tenements within three or four blocks. Mr. Sankey once sang a hymn that was carried over a mile away and converted a man that far off. I have a friend who occasionally uses in his open-air meetings a megaphone that carries his voice to an immense distance.

3. *Hold meetings near circuses, base-ball games, and other places where the people crowd.*

One of the most interesting meetings I ever held was just outside of a base-ball ground on Sunday. The police were trying to break up the game inside by arresting the leaders. We held the meeting outside just back of the grand stand. As there was no game to see inside, the people listened to the singing and preaching of the Gospel outside. On another Sunday we drove down to Sell's circus and had the most motley audience I ever addressed. There were people present from almost every nation under heaven. The circus had advertised a "Congress of Nations," so I had provided a congress of nations for my open-air meeting. On that day I had a Dutchman, a Frenchman, a Scotchman, an Englishman, an Irishman and an American preach. We took care at the open-air meeting to invite the people to evening meeting at the mission. That night a man came who told us that he was one of the employés of the circus, and was touched that afternoon by the preaching of the Gospel, and had come to learn how to be a follower of the Lord Jesus Christ. He accepted the Saviour that night.

4. *Hold meetings in or near parks or other public resorts.*

Almost every city has its resorts where people go on Sunday. As the people will not go to church, the church ought to go out to the people. Sometimes permission can be secured from the authorities to hold the meetings right in the parks. Wherever this is impossible they can be held near at hand. One who is now a deacon of our church spent his Sundays at Lincoln Park before he was converted; an open-air meeting was held close at hand, and here he heard the Gospel and was converted.

5. *Hold meetings in groves.*

It would be well if every country church could be persuaded to try this. Get out of the church into a grove somewhere, and you will be surprised at the number of people who will come who would not go near the church at all.

6. *Hold open-air meetings near your missions.*

If you have a mission, be sure and hold an open-air meeting near it. It is the easiest thing in the world to keep a mission full even during the summer months, if you hold an open-air meeting in connection with it, but it is almost impossible to do so if you do not.

7. *Hold open-air meetings in front of churches.*

A good many of our empty churches could be filled if we would only hold open-air meetings in front of them. Years ago, when in London, I went to hear Newman Hall preach. It looked to me like a very orderly and aristocratic church, but when I left the church after the second service, I was surprised to find an open-air meeting in full blast right in front of the church, and people gathered there in crowds from the thoroughfare.

8. *Be careful about the little details in connection with the location.*

On a hot day, hold the meeting on the shady side of the street. On a cool day, on the sunny side. Make it as comfortable for the audience as possible. Never compel the audience to stand with the sun shining in their eyes. Preach with the wind, and not against it. Take your own position a little above the part of the audience nearest you, upon a curbstone, chair, platform, rise in the ground, or anything that will raise your head above others so that your voice will carry.

III. Things to get.

1. *Get it thoroughly understood between yourself and God that He wants you to do this work, and that by His grace you are going to do it whatever it costs.*

This is one of the most important things in starting out to do open-air work. You are bound to make a failure unless you settle this at the start. Open-air work has its discouragements, its difficulties and its almost insurmountable obstacles, and unless you start out knowing that God has called you to the work, and come what come will, you will go through with it, you are sure to give it up.

2. *Get permission from the powers that be to hold open-air meetings.*

Do not get into conflict with the police if you can possibly avoid it. As a rule it is quite easy to get this permission if you go about it in a courteous and intelligent way. Find out what the laws of the city are in this regard, and then observe them. Go to the captain of the precinct and tell him that you wish to hold an open-air meeting, and let him see that you are not a disturber of the peace or a crank. Many would-be open-air preachers get into trouble from a simple lack of good sense and common decency.

3. *Get a good place to hold the meeting.*

Do not start out at random. Study your ground. You should operate like a general. We are told that the Germans studied France as a battle ground for years before the Franco-Prussian war broke out, and when the war broke out there were officers in the German army that knew more about France than the officers in the French army did. Lay your plan of campaign, study your battle field, pick out the best places to hold the meetings, look over the territory carefully and study it in all its bearings. There are a good many things to be considered. Do not select what would be a good place for some one to throw a big panful of dishwater upon you. These little details may appear trivial, but they need to be taken into consideration. It is unpleasant, and somewhat disconcerting, when a man is right in the midst of an interesting exhortation, to have a panful of dishwater thrown down the back of his neck.

4. *Get as large a number of reliable Christian men and women to go with you as you possibly can.*

Crowds draw crowds. There is great power in numbers. One man can go out on the street alone and hold a meeting; I have done it myself; but if I can get fifteen or twenty reliable men to go with me, I will get them every time. Please note that I have said *reliable* Christian men and women. Do not take anybody along with you to an open-air meeting that you do not know. A man that is in the habit of making a fool of himself, be sure and leave at home. He may upset your whole meeting. Do not take a man or woman with you who has an unsavory reputation. Probably some one in the crowd will know it and shout out the fact. Take only people who are of established reputation, and well balanced. Never pick up a stranger out of the crowd and ask him to speak. Some one will come along who appears to be just your sort, but if you ask him to speak you will wish you had not done so.

5. *Get the best music you can.*

Get a baby organ and a cornet if you can. Be sure and have good singing if it is possible. If you cannot have good singing, have poor singing, for even poor singing goes a good ways in the open air. One of the best open-air meetings I ever attended was where two of us were forced to go out alone. Neither of us was a singer. We started with only one hearer, but a drunken man came along and began to dance to our singing, and a crowd gathered to watch him dance. When the crowd had gathered, I simply put my hand on the drunken man, and said, "Stand still for a few moments." My companion took the drunken man as a text for a temperance sermon, and when he got through I took him for a text. People began to whisper in the crowd, "I would not be in that man's shoes for anything." The man did us good service that night. He first drew the crowd, and then furnished us with a text. The Lord turned the devil's instrument right against him that night. If you can, get a good solo singer, or even a poor solo singer will do splendid work in the open air, if he sings in the power of the Spirit. I remember a man who attempted to sing in the open air, who was really no singer at all, but God in his wonderful mercy gave him that night to sing in the power of the Spirit. People began to break down on the street, tears rolled down their cheeks, one woman was converted right there during the singing of that hymn. Although the hymn was sung in such a miserable way from a musical standpoint, the Spirit of God used it for that woman's conversion.

6. *Get the attention of your hearers as soon as possible.*

When you are preaching in a church, people will oftentimes stay even if they are not interested, but unless you get the attention of your audience at once in the open air, one of two things will happen, either your crowd will leave you or else they will begin to guy you. In the first half dozen sentences you must get the attention of your hearers. I was once holding a meeting in one of the hardest places of a city. There were saloons on three of the four corners, three breweries, and four or five Roman Catholic churches were close at hand. There was scarcely a Protestant in that part of the city. The first words I spoke were these, "You will notice the cross on the spire of yonder church." By this means I secured their attention at once, and then I talked to them about the meaning of that cross. On holding a meeting one labor day, I started out on the subject of labor. I spoke only a few moments on that subject, to lead them around to the subject of the Lord Jesus Christ. Holding a meeting one night in the midst of a hot election, near where an election parade was forming, I started out with the question, "Whom shall we elect?" The people expected a political address, but before long I got them interested in the question whether or not we should elect the Lord Jesus Christ to be the ruler over our lives.

7. *Get some good tracts.*

Always have tracts when you hold an open-air meeting. They assist in making permanent the impressions and fixing the truth. Have the workers pass around through the crowd handing out the tracts at the proper time.

8. *Get workers around in the crowd to do personal work.*

Returning from an open-air meeting years ago in the city of Detroit, I said to a minister who was stopping at the same hotel that we had had several conversions in the meeting. He replied by asking me if a certain man from Cleveland was not in the crowd. I replied that he was. He told me that he thought if I looked into it I would find that the conversions were largely due to that man, that while the services were going on, he had been around in the crowd doing personal work. I found that it was so.

9. *Get a gospel wagon if you can.*

Of this we shall have more to say wher we speak of Gospel Wagon Work.

IV. Don't.

1. *Don't unnecessarily antagonize your audience.*

I heard of a man addressing a Roman Catholic audience in the open air and pitching into the Roman Catholic Church and the Pope. That man did not have good sense. Another man attempted a prohibition discourse immediately in front of a saloon. He got a brick instead of votes.

2. *Don't get scared.*

Let Psalm 27:1 be your motto: "The Lord is my light and my salvation; whom shall I fear? the Lord is the strength of my life; of whom shall I be afraid?" There is not a particle need of being scared. You may be surrounded by a crowd of howling hoodlums, but you may be absolutely certain that you will not be hurt unless the Lord wants you to be hurt; and if the Lord wants you to be hurt, that is the best thing for you. You may be killed if the Lord sees fit to allow you to be killed, but it is a wonderful privilege to be killed for the Lord Jesus Christ. One night I was holding a meeting in one of the worst parts of Chicago. Something happened to enrage a part of the crowd that gathered around me. Friends near at hand were in fear lest I be killed, but I kept on speaking and was not even struck.

3. *Don't lose your temper.*

Whatever happens, never lose your temper. You ought never to get angry under any circumstances, but it is especially foolish to do so when you are holding an open-air meeting. You will doubtless have many temptations to lose your temper, but never do it. It is very hard to hit a man when he is serene, and if you preserve your serenity, the chances are that you will escape unscathed. Even if a tough strikes you, he cannot do so a second time if you remain calm. Serenity is one of the best of safeguards.

4. *Don't let your meeting be broken up.*

No matter what happens, hold your ground if you can, and you generally can. One night I was holding a meeting in a square in one of the most desperate parts of a large city. The steps of an adjacent saloon were crowded with men, many of whom were half drunk. A man came along on a load of hay, went into the saloon and fired himself up with strong drink. Then he attempted to drive right down upon the crowd in the middle of the square, in which there were many women and children. Some man stopped his horses, and the infuriated man came down from the load of hay and the howling mob swept down from the steps of the saloon. Somehow or other the drunken driver got a rough handling in the mob, but not one of our number was struck. Two policemen in citizens clothes happened to be passing by and stopped the riot. I said a few words more, and then formed our little party into a procession, behind which the crowd fell in, and marched down to the mission singing.

5. *Don't fight.*

Never fight under any circumstances. Even if they almost pound the life out of you, refuse to fight back.

6. *Don't be dull.*

Dullness will kill an open-air meeting at once. Prosiness will drive the whole audience away. In order to avoid being dull, do not preach long sermons. Use a great many striking illustrations. Keep wide awake yourself, and you will keep the audience awake. Be energetic in your manner. Talk so people can hear you. Don't preach, but simply talk to people.

7. *Don't be soft.*

One of these nice, namby-pamby, sentimental sort of fellows in an open-air meeting, the crowd cannot and will not stand. The temptation to throw a brick or a rotten apple at him is perfectly irresistible, and one can hardly blame the crowd.

8. *Don't read a sermon.*

Whatever may be said in defence of reading essays in the pulpit, it will never do in the open air. It is possible to have no notes whatever. If you cannot talk long without notes, so much the better; you can talk as long as you ought to. If you read, you will talk longer than you ought to.

9. *Don't use cant.*

Use language that people are acquainted with, but do not

use vulgar language. Some people think it is necessary to use slang, but slang is never admissible. There is language that is popular and easily understood by the people that is purest Anglo-Saxon.

10. *Don't talk too long.*

You may have a number of talks in an open-air meeting, but do not have any of them over ten or fifteen minutes long. As a rule do not have them as long as that. Of course there are exceptions to this, when a great crowd is gathered to hear some person in the open air. Under such circumstances I have heard a sermon an hour long that held the interest of the people, but this is not true in the ordinary open-air meeting.

V. Things absolutely necessary to success.

1. *Consecrated men and women.*

None but consecrated men and women will ever succeed in open-air meetings. If you cannot get such, you might as well give up holding open-air meetings.

2. *Depend upon God.*

There is nothing that will teach one his dependence upon God more quickly and more thoroughly than holding open-air meetings. You never know what is going to happen. You cannot lay plans that you can always follow in an open-air meeting. You never know what moment some one will come along and ask some troublesome question. You do not know what unforeseen event is going to occur. All you can do is to depend upon God, but that is perfectly sufficient.

3. *Loyalty to the Word of God.*

It is the man who is absolutely loyal to God's Word, and who is familiar with it and constantly uses it, who succeeds in the open air. God often takes a text that is quoted, and uses it for the salvation of some hearer. Arguments and illustrations are forgotten, but the text sticks and converts.

4. *Be frequently filled anew with the Holy Spirit.*

If any man needs to take advantage of the privilege of fresh infillings of the Holy Spirit, it is the open-air worker. Spiritual power is the great secret of success in this, as in all other Christian work.

CHAPTER VII

TENT WORK

I. Its importance and advantages.

1. *You can reach people by the tent you can reach by no other method.*

People that you cannot get inside of a church or mission hall, people that will not even listen to preaching from a Gospel wagon, people that you could not step up to and talk with personally, will come into a tent. The tent itself awakens curiosity. It looks like a circus. Time and again I have preached in a tent where six-sevenths of the audience were Roman Catholics; and not only did we get them into the tent, but many of them were won to Christ. It is stated in the official report of a large and successful tent work that 95 per cent of the audience was composed of thieves, murderers, drunkards and abandoned women. The other 5 per cent were respectable people. A great many of the abandoned classes were converted. People who tried to pull the tent down, threw stones at the workers, cut ropes, and stood outside and tried to prevent people going in, before the meetings had been going on very long were on their knees calling on God for pardon. One of these had recently been released from prison where he had served fourteen years as a safe breaker. He became a very bright convert.

2. *They are portable.*

Wherever you put a church up, there it must stay; you cannot easily move it. But if you put a tent up in one neighborhood, if it proves to be a poor neighborhood you can move it to another, or when that neighborhood is worked out you can move it to a new one, at a small cost.

3. *It is inexpensive.*

A new tent can be purchased for anywhere from $150 to $350, or you can get them second hand, but this does not pay.

The life of a tent is about three years. You have to pay extra for the seats, but these can be made out of lumber that can afterwards be used for other purposes. For many reasons canvas benches are better.

4. *Tent work turns the season of the year which is regarded the poorest for evangelistic effort into the very best.*

Ask almost any pastor what he regards as the best season for evangelistic work, and he will tell you the second week in January, or Lent. If you ask him what is the worst season, he will tell you July and August, but with a tent July and August prove to be the best season in the year for evangelistic work. This has been demonstrated in Chicago, Philadelphia, New York, Boston and in many smaller cities, and in country towns. There can be little doubt that the number of conversions in tents in the summer far exceeds the number of conversions in evangelistic services in churches in the winter.

II. How to conduct tent meetings.

1. *Have the right sort of a man in charge of the tent.*

The most important thing in any tent work is the man who has the superintendency of the tent. If you have the right man the rest will take care of itself, and if you have the wrong man, nothing that you can do will make a success of the work. What sort of a man is needed? A man who is perfectly fearless, who can stand up when ruffians are stoning the tent, and not be the least bit ruffled if a stone comes through the tent and strikes him on the back of the head; a man who can stand the boys shooting at him with tacks, and sharp double-pointed tacks striking him in the face; a man who can stand perfectly unmoved with a lot of roughs moving about and seeking to disturb the meeting in every possible way; a man who trusts God, and believes that God is going to take care of him.

In the next place he should be a man who has handled men; a man who can go into a mixed crowd of Protestants and Catholics, and hold this disorderly crowd in the hollow of his hand so that they will behave; a man who has control of his own temper as well as control of the crowd; a man who is never ruffled, just stands there perfectly serene with sunshine in his face but with a grip like iron upon the audience; a man who can preach a plain direct Gospel sermon; a man who can hold the attention of people who are not in the habit of paying attention to ministers when they preach. To put it in a word, you want a man filled with the Holy Ghost, who preaches the Gospel in the power of the Spirit, who if he has time to prepare will prepare, and if he does not have time will stand up without a word to say, but just look to God to give him the message, and as soon as he gets it will give it to the people in the power of the Holy Ghost.

2. *Have the right sort of a tent.*

The larger the tent is, the better, other things being equal. It is a great mistake to get too small a tent; they are unserviceable. If enough people do not come at first to fill your tent, you can so arrange the seats in the middle of the tent that it is not noticed that there is a large vacant space on the outside. If the tent is small people will think it is a small thing, and your attendance will be small. A big tent makes a large impression upon the neighborhood.

3. *Get the right place to locate your tent.*

A good place is one where the crowds gather, upon some great thoroughfare where they are sweeping by by hundreds and by thousands. Tents should often be taken into rough neighborhoods. Some one may ask, "Is it safe there?" The safest place on earth is where the Lord takes you. The safest place for Moses was out in the river among the crocodiles, when God was taking care of him in the little ark. You can put a tent anywhere with safety if God leads you to put it there. We located a tent once where there were two murders during the first week within a block of the tent. One of the men was in the tent a half an hour before he was stabbed. He was urged to take the Lord Jesus Christ that night, but he said, "No, I cannot do it to-night, I will come Sunday night." Within half an hour he was found dying in a lot, where he had been stabbed.

Always select a dry spot. Be careful not to get into a place where you are going to be flooded out. If you are not on your guard at this point, you will oftentimes see what seems to be a beautiful place for a tent, but the first thunder storm that comes up the tent will be useless.

4. *Choose the right sort of a man to be janitor.*

The man who acts as janitor is next in importance to the man who superintends the tent. He must be fearless; he must be exceedingly wise and extremely patient. If your janitor loses his temper, you are going to get into trouble. If you have a Christian man who is wise and firm and gentle and loving and fearless, you are all right.

5. *Be determined that you are going to have your own way in your tent.*

Set about that in the very first meeting. If you let the crowd get the upper hand of you once, they will have it for all time; but if you show them the very first time that you are going to have your way, you will have it. Be very pleasant, but be as immovable as a rock. If it becomes necessary, take a man by the collar and help him out of the tent, but be sure you do it with a genial, winning, smile. This often proves a means of grace to this kind of people. Do not turn a man out if you can help it, but turn him out rather than have your meeting broken up or seriously disturbed. Drunken men may be allowed some liberties because they know no better, but have it distinctly understood that they cannot go beyond a certain point.

6. *Give a good deal of thought to the singing.*

Have the very best singing that you can get. Have as big a choir as you can possibly gather together, but allow no one in the choir who is not saved. It is well to have an orchestra if you can get it.

7. *Have the very best preaching that can be secured.*

But what is good preaching for a church is not always good preaching for a tent. A tent preacher should be a man who can hold the attention of plain people. Many a man who can preach to great audiences in a church is an utter failure in a tent.

8. *Always have an after meeting and do personal work.*

The purpose of tent meetings is not to keep men out of

the saloons; they do keep men out of the saloons, but the purpose of tent meetings is to bring men to Christ. A man once said to me, "This is magnificent. Here are almost a thousand people here who are not Christians. It is magnificent if not a soul of them was converted, for it keeps them out of the saloons." But if all we do for men is to keep them out of the saloon for an hour or two, not much is accomplished. What tent work is carried on for is to lead men to a personal acceptance of the Lord Jesus Christ. The best way to accomplish this is by definite, personal, hand-to-hand work in the after meeting.

9. *Have children's meetings in connection with your tent work.*

The neighborhoods where tents are ordinarily put up are thronging with children. It would be easy to fill the tent with children, but it is not best to allow them in the evening service unless they come with their parents. If they are allowed in the evening service, they will crowd out the grown people; but the children must not be neglected, therefore have special services for the children in the tent in the afternoon. Tell them they cannot be admitted to the evening service unless they bring their parents with them. In this way a great many parents will be induced to come to the evening meetings for the sake of the children. The results that are accomplished among children in tent meetings are astonishing. These children come largely from utterly unchristian homes, but many children even of Jewish parents and of drunken parents are won to Christ. A little boy came to one of our tents one afternoon. He heard the story of the Cross, accepted Christ, and went straight home. That night he brought with him his father and brother, and they were both converted, and then he brought two other brothers and two sisters, and these four were converted. His mother who was a backslider was brought back to the Lord. There were also two older daughters who led lives of sin. The whole family had been converted except these two abandoned girls. One of the workers started out with the determination to bring those two girls down to the meeting, and if possible get them to accept Christ. Some of the other workers stayed at home and prayed. This worker pled with the girls to come down to the meeting, and at last persuaded them to come. They got there very late, and just as they entered Major Whittle was talking about wayward girls, and before the meeting was over these girls were rejoicing in Christ. Three boys, four girls, father and mother, brought to Christ through the conversion of a little boy.

10. *Encourage the mothers to come and bring their babes.*

If they can't bring their babies they can't come at all. One very successful tent worker promised a rattle to every baby brought a certain night. The scheme took, and mothers and babies and baby carriages came pouring in that night. They had a wonderful meeting, and that man gained the love of the whole community. Another night he had a water melon meeting, and that was a great success.

III. Where to conduct tent work.

We have already spoken about putting up tents in crowded parts of our great cities, but that is not the only place.

1. *In the portion of a city where you wish to organize a church.*

You may not be quite sure whether it would be wise to start a church in that locality. Set up a tent and make a test of it. In one locality in Chicago where a tent was set up, a Methodist church and Baptist church were organized, a Congregational mission revived, and one other mission started.

2. *In country towns.*

One of the solutions of the summer problem in country churches is for the church to get a tent and hold its services in that during the summer months. Many will go to it who will not go to the church. Oftentimes it is well for all the churches of a country town to combine in a summer tent work.

3. *Religiously destitute sections of the country.*

There are many places in our country where there are many people but no church for miles. Tents can be set up in these remote parts of townships, and a splendid work done

It would be well for country pastors to take tents out on to the borders of their parishes and do Gospel work there.

4. *Summer resorts.*

We think that if people go out to spend the summer anywhere, we cannot reach them, but there is no place where you can reach them better, provided you go at it wisely. Set up a tent near where the great vacation throngs congregate. People at these resorts do not know how to Spend Sunday; they do not like to go to the country churches, but they will go to a tent.

CHAPTER VIII

THE USE OF AUTOS, TRAILERS, ETC.

The Christian worker should always watch for new methods and new means of presenting the gospel. The message is changeless, but we must not be blind to the changes in our civilization which offer the possibility of fresh approach with our message.

I. Means of reaching the people.

1. *Trailer Evangelism.*

Not many can afford to purchase and maintain a trailer, but through such a vehicle, trailer camps, work camps, migratory groups, and otherwise inaccessible places and persons can be reached. Much of the work by means of a trailer is of the colportage type.

2. *Auto Evangelism.*

You have seen political caravans. Why not a caravan of cars to a given town for a great open-air meeting?

3. *Truck Evangelism.*

The business man who owns a clean, open truck can make a contribution to the cause by loaning the truck for a chain of open-air meetings. The singers and speakers can use the truck as a platform. Such services should be bright and brief, and Gospels and good tracts should be left in the hands of the interested. Also, an invitation to attend services at some permanent meeting place should be extended.

II. Mechanical aids.

There are several mechanical aids to open-air meetings which should be used where it is possible to purchase them.

1. *Public Address System.*

Nearly everyone has some measure of acquaintance with this help to speech and hearing. It carries the speaker's voice to all within sight, without strain on ear or throat. This device can be tuned up or down, and should never be so loud as to be annoying. Music can be played on a phonograph and carried through the loud speaker. Such a system can be purchased at a reasonable price.

An auto equipped with such a device can tour a city and announce special meetings. Some cities have ordinances against sound trucks, etc. Always inform yourself as to the law.

2. *Sound Films.*

We all recognize the value of the visual in attracting and holding attention. Biblical pictures on inexpensive films can be effectively used for children and grownups, for, remember, no one is ever too old to be interested in pictures.

Machines which have films and sound synchronized are also most effective. While these are somewhat expensive to produce, they are not expensive to use. They always hold attention, if the material is good and is well presented.

III. Things to keep in mind.

In all of the things mentioned in this chapter there are a few things to be always kept in mind. The kind of evangelism presented here is what could be named rapid evangelism. In ordinary parlance it might be called "hit and run." It is an attempt to reach people who are on the move, and who rarely or never enter a church.

1. *This evangelism must be of a concentrated nature.*

The message should be short. Not more than two verses of a song should be used. The entire program should be planned. The technique used may be similar to that of radio broadcasting. Note how the broadcasters do it. They are trying to hold attention.

2. *This demands the best we have.*

It is always unfortunate when a Christian service in the open air has a cornetist who blows two sour notes a minute. In the days of the forty-niners the sign in the boom town saloon said, "Don't shoot the piano player. He's doing the best he can." But that isn't good enough; certainly not for the Lord's work. Because of the radio, nowadays people have an improved taste. As a Christian worker yours should always be an improved service. Let us give our Lord the best we have, and strive to make that better.

3. *All equipment should be kept in good condition.*

Cars and trucks should be clean and fresh. Public address systems should be smooth and clear. Pictures must be replaced when worn or faded.

Workers, too, should be neat. Women in particular should give careful thought to their dress and general appearance, that they may bear consistent testimony for their Lord. For the most part men are more effective in work of this type.

4. *All meetings of this kind should be thoughtfully planned and prayerfully carried through.*

Many people fail in services of this variety because they depend on their natural "gift of gab," rather than on the Holy Spirit and real preparation. A radio program may sound casual and spontaneous, but it is in reality carefully planned and rehearsed in every detail. You are not putting on a show, so you are not going to rehearse your message, but do not leave things to chance. As in all service for the Lord, work and prayer are essential to success.

CHAPTER IX

COLPORTAGE WORK

I. Colportage work defined.

What is Colportage work? By Colportage work we mean the distribution of religious literature from house to house. As a rule, the literature thus distributed is sold, sometimes for its full value, sometimes at less than cost.

II. Its importance and advantages.

1. *People who fail in other lines of Christian work can succeed in Colportage work.*

There are many who wish to work for the Lord, and feel they have a definite call to give their whole time to that work, who are unable to preach to edification, who are incompetent to run a mission, who would not even succeed as house to house visitors. What can they do? They can do Colportage work and oftentimes meet with great success in it. I have in mind one man who felt a call to Christian work, but it soon became evident that he had no gifts whatever that would warrant his preparation for the ministry. He was exceedingly slow and tiresome in speech, he lacked fire, and apparently lacked energy. He was induced to take up the Colportage work, and he became one of the most successful colporters I ever knew, not only making a very generous living by the work, but also reaching many homes and touching people who could be reached in no other way. Another man who could not even speak to edification in prayer meeting, who was exceedingly limited in all directions, sold during a single month 1,200 volumes and cleared about $54 over and above expenses; the same person cleared about $400 in ten months. Going from town to town, he was the means of doing untold good. Superannuated ministers who have reached the point where their services are no longer in demand for churches, do not need to give up the Lord's work. They can take up Colportage work, and perhaps be more useful than they were in their preaching days.

Ministers and other Christian workers who are broken down physically, and unable to bear the strain of regular work, can take up Colportage work with great advantage to their health, and accomplish very much for the Master.

2. *Colportage work reaches neglected districts.*

All over the land there are stretches of country so sparsely settled that it would be impossible to maintain religious services, yet in these thinly settled districts taken together, there are thousands upon thousands of souls that need to hear the Gospel. Oftentimes they can be reached by Colportage work better than in any other way. One solution of the religious problem in the country is to be found in Colportage work.

3. *Colportage work is self-supporting.*

The Colporter needs to have no missionary society back of him. He can go out and sell his books and support himself, and if he has any gift in this direction, make a comfortable living. Take for example the books of the Bible Institute Colportage Association. They contain some of the very best evangelical literature of the day, books adapted to the unsaved to lead them to Christ, books on the deeper Christian life, books on Christian work. They are written by some of the best known and most gifted authors, men like F. B. Meyer, Campbell Morgan, Andrew Murray, D. L. Moody, Major D. W. Whittle, Charles Spurgeon, and others. These books can be secured in quantities by the Colporter at seven cents each, while he sells them for fifteen cents each, thus making eight cents on each book sold. It is a comparatively easy thing to make from $1.50 to $5 a day at this work.

4. *Colportage work converts sinners and builds up Christians.*

All over our land to-day there are many people who have been led to Christ, and many Christians who have been led into a deeper knowledge of Christ, through the work of Colporters.

5. *Its results are permanent and ever-widening.*

A preacher goes away, but a book stays. One man reads a book and is blessed by it and hands it to another, and he still to another. A single book may be read by scores of persons.

6. *It opens doors to other work.*

Many a man begins Christian work as a humble Colporter, but as he goes from house to house and village to village with the little books that carry the knowledge of Jesus Christ, he soon begins to preach the Word, and is quite likely in time to receive a call to be a pastor or an assistant pastor.

7. *Colportage work is a splendid preparation for other Christian work*

The Colporter gets right into the home, gets acquainted with all kinds of men, has to learn through necessity the modes of convincing men. There is perhaps no better preparation for many phases of ministerial work than the work of a Colporter.

III. How to do colportage work.

1. *Get a few books to begin with, and then begin.*

A man once came to me out of money and out of employment. I bought for him four Colportage books for 28 cents, and sent him out. He came back in less than half an hour with 60 cents. He then took his share of the money and bought himself other books, and thus the work widened. The way to begin is to begin.

2. *Visit every house and store and saloon.*

When one undertakes to do Colportage work in any given district, as a rule it is well to visit every house and store and saloon in the district. Of course, if one continues to work the same district, he will soon learn what houses can be visited again and again, and what places to avoid. Experience shows that many even in saloons will buy the books, and sometimes the saloon-keepers themselves, and no one can measure the good thus done.

3. *Leave the books in envelopes for examination.*

Some have found it very useful to have envelopes that

will contain the books, and leave the books in every house on a street, giving notice that they will be called for afterward, and if the people wish to keep the books, they can leave the money in the envelope; if not, return the books. Opportunities for conversation are often thus opened. One prominent Christian worker, wishing to experiment on the work for himself, went down one of the leading streets of a western city, leaving a book in every house. As he came back, he found interesting opportunities for speaking with people whom the ordinary missionary could not reach. Even where the books are not purchased, they will often be read and so the truth will get a hearing.

4. *Churches can employ a church visitor without expense to themselves, by equipping the church visitor with Colportage books which they can sell, and thus meet their expenses.*

Of course the visitor must have the public endorsement of the pastor of the church, and in this way he gets an entrance for his work. This plan has been adopted with great success in some quarters.

5. *Get pastors to recommend the books.*

When the Colporter visits a new village, he should look up the pastors of the place and present to each of them a copy of one of his best books. In this way the interest of the pastors will be enlisted, and if they will speak a word of endorsement in the prayer meeting or some other place, it will be a great help. Many churches have the Colportage books on sale in the vestibule.

6. *Get pastors to preach on certain lines, and then go around and sell the books that bear upon the subject in which the pastor has awakened an interest.*

For example, if the pastor speaks upon the baptism with the Holy Spirit, go through the community with McNeil's "Spirit-Filled Life."

7. *Attending religious conventions.*

A great work can be done by Colporters attending religious conventions, and there disposing of books along the lines of the subjects treated in the conventions.

CHAPTER X

SERVICES IN THEATRES, CIRCUSES, ETC.

I. Importance and advantages.

1. *Many people are likely to be reached by services in theatres, circuses, and other places of entertainment, who are not likely to be reached elsewhere.*

Actors, actresses, and the other employés of theatres seldom attend services at churches; it is difficult also to find them in their homes, but they can be reached on their own ground. At the very first service in Forepaugh's circus tent in Chicago during the World's Fair, an actor was brought under deep conviction of sin and converted to Christ. In services held in the city of Minneapolis I had frequent opportunity of speaking personally with the actors and other employés of the places. But not only can the employés be reached, but also the frequenters. We held services one New Year's afternoon in the Theatre Comique in the city of Minneapolis. A few days afterward I received an anonymous letter from an Iowa city. The writer said that he had been present at the theatre service that day. It was the first time he had been in a religious service for years, although in the old country he had been a local preacher. In the two or three weeks preceding that service, he had squandered over $300 in that theatre, but the word spoken that afternoon had brought him back to Christ. The man afterwards returned to Minneapolis and made himself known, and subsequently became a deacon and one of the most faithful workers in our church.

2. *Another advantage of services in a theatre is their novelty and attractiveness.*

The interest especially of young men is awakened by seeing a service advertised in a theatre. They go out of curiosity, and an opportunity is thus offered of bringing them to Christ. Everything about the place attracts them; they like the surroundings; they are off their guard and the Gospel gets an entrance into their hearts.

3. *Many are converted.*

It has been the writer's privilege to conduct services every Sunday afternoon for several winters in the theatres of one of our American cities, and during the World's Fair to conduct theatrical services for many weeks, seven nights in the week In both places most encouraging results followed. In the services in Chicago many were converted every night. At a recent theatre service for men only in a southern city, about one hundred and fifty men professed conversion.

II. How to conduct.

1. *The first important matter in the conduct of theatre services is the choice of the theatre.*

What sort of a theatre to choose depends upon the purpose for which the meetings are held. If the aim is to get hold of those who have sunken into the deepest depth of sin, of course a theatre of the lower order is preferable. On the other hand, there are objections to such a theatre. It is not a good place to take people, but you are not likely to take anybody there except those who frequent it already, or those who go for a definitely Christian purpose. Nevertheless great care should be exercised in the choice of workers for such a place. Girls and boys should not be taken to such a place unless they already frequent it. A young man approached a prominent business man in the city of Minneapolis who was handing out dodgers on the street, inviting people to the Theatre Comique for a Gospel service. The young man said, "Do you know what kind of a place the Theatre Comique is?" The business man replied that he had not lived in Minneapolis twenty years not to know. The young man asked again, "Do you think that such a place is a proper place to hold a religious service?" The reply was made, "When you go fishing, where do you go?" The young man smiled and answered, "Oh, I see, I go where the fish are." A good many fish were caught in that pool, though it was a cesspool.

If the aim is to reach a better class of people, of course one must engage a theatre of the higher order. During the

World's Fair the Haymarket Theatre and Columbia Theatre in Chicago were packed to overflowing each Sunday morning, to hear the Gospel preached by leading preachers of this country and Europe, and there were a great many conversions.

Sometimes the size of the theatre will be a determining factor. Twenty thousand people could be crowded into the Forepaugh tent, and were crowded into it each morning that services were held there; this in spite of the fact that the heat was almost insufferable. The circus men were so astonished at the vast audiences that came out to religious services, that they approached Mr. Moody to see if he would not furnish a speaker to go around with their show and hold services every Sunday, they offering to pay all the expenses.

It is best to select, if possible, a theatre that is in use rather than one that is abandoned. If the theatre has been given up, the probability is that people did not go to it, and they will not be likely to go to a religious service in that place. I knew of a case of what appeared to be a very desirable theatre being purchased to hold religious services in. It seemed to be in a good locality and well adapted to the work. The theatre, however, had been abandoned by the theatrical people, and it was never possible to get the people to attend religious services there in any great numbers.

2. *The second point of importance is securing the theatre for the services.*

Oftentimes this is not a very difficult matter. Theatrical people are frequently very glad to have their building used for religious services. I once went to the proprieter of a very vile den to see if I could secure his place for Gospel meetings. To my surprise, he received me very cordially, and said certainly we could have the place, and he only charged a nominal rent. Going the next year to another theater in the same city, only a theatre of a much higher order—a very attractive and respectable place—I inquired of the manager if I could secure his theater for Sunday afternoon services. He replied, "Certainly." When I asked him what he would charge for it, he asked me if there was any money in it. I told him none at all, that we were going to spend money and not take it in,

"In that case," he said, "you can have the theatre for nothing." He stood to this agreement, furnished light and heat, ushers and everything, and would take absolutely nothing for it. Even the stage manager was in attendance every Sunday to see that everything was in perfect order. As a rule it is far better to rent a theatre than to buy it. If you buy it, it ceases to be a theater and becomes your church, and the very people you wish to get hold of are no longer attracted.

3. *Exercise great care about the music.*

Provide just as large a choir as possible. Secure the very best leader possible; the best leader is a man with a good large voice, a great deal of enthusiasm and ability to get people to sing, who is filled with the Holy Ghost, and knows how to sing to save. In addition to a good leader and a large choir, it is well to have male choruses, duets, quartettes and solos. A band is sometimes helpful, but not at all a necessity. A good cornetist is of great help, but the singing attracts as much as instrumental music, and does far greater execution.

4. *Secure the best possible speakers.*

No man is a good speaker for a theatrical service who does not preach the straight Gospel, and preach it in a way to attract and hold the public. If there is one person in the community who has a peculiar gift in this direction, it is best usually to have him do the major part of the speaking week after week. It will do to throw in another speaker occasionally, and good may be accomplished by it, but one speaker who knows the audience and the work, and follows one sermon up by another, will accomplish the most definite and most satisfactory results.

5. *Be sure that the services are thoroughly evangelical, and emphatically evangelistic.*

Very little good comes from holding meetings in theatres and similar places unless these meetings are emphatically Gospel meetings. Preaching along ethical and social and philanthropic lines accomplishes very little good. If, however, the meetings are thoroughly evangelical and evangelistic, the ethical and social results will necessarily follow.

Drunkards will be converted and give up their drinking, gamblers will give up their gambling, impure people will forsake their impurity, politicians will be brought to Christ and thus their politics will be reformed. I was talking to a converted politician last night. The night he came to the meeting where he was converted (during the World's Fair) he had been out with a number of his political friends. They had been planning for his election to an important office here in Chicago. At the service he heard nothing about political reform; he heard the simple Gospel, a Gospel that would save the slave of drink. He accepted Christ that night. The result has been that his whole life, personal, domestic, commercial and political, has been renovated. A sermon on political reform would not have touched him at all.

6. *Advertise the meetings largely and widely.*

Large billboards such as the theatrical people use for their own advertisements are perhaps the best of any, but the newspapers should also be used to the utmost. Newspapers are generally willing to do a great deal of free advertising for services of this character. Men, with invitations to the meetings, should be placed upon all the street corners for blocks around. Transparencies, carried through the streets by men, attract the attention and bring many to the services.

7. *Have a thoroughly drilled corps of ushers.*

Sometimes the theaters provide their own ushers, and for many reasons it is well to use them. They know the building, understand just how to seat people, and furthermore they need to hear the Gospel themselves and are likely to be converted.

8. *Have wise and well-trained personal workers scattered through the audience.*

This is of the very highest importance, even more important in a theater than it is in a church. No speaker can take note of what is happening in every part of a theater. Many men and women will be touched by the sermon, but only touched. If gotten hold of right then and there by a watchful and wise worker, and the effect of the sermon followed up, that person will be converted, whereas if they are allowed to go out, the impression will soon die away and the person may be lost forever. These workers should be carefully trained, as to exactly where to sit, and what to do during the service, and at the close of the service.

9. *Have after-meetings.*

This is of the highest importance. For details regarding aftermeetings, see chapter on "Aftermeetings."

10. *Invite the audience to the churches.*

There is a prevalent opinion among the masses of the unchurched that they are not welcome at the churches. We should do everything in our power to disabuse them of this false notion. The theatre service affords a splendid opportunity for doing it. It is well to have the ministers themselves extend the invitation. In this way a permanence is given to the work. The church is the only thing that goes on continually. Missions, theatre services, tent services, come and go, but the church was established by Christ and perpetually continues. A work that does not lead the people ultimately into the churches and get them connected therewith, seldom results in any permanent good. It is well to have printed invitations from the churches to distribute among the audience. These invitations should be gotten up in an attractive form so that the people will be glad to take them home and keep them.

CHAPTER XI

ORGANIZING AND CONDUCTING A GOSPEL MISSION

I. Importance of Gospel missions.

1. In every large city, and in many of our smaller cities, there are great masses of the people that the churches are not reaching. The reasons why they are not being reached by the church are various. First of all because of the location of the churches. The churches as a rule in our larger cities are inaccessible to the great majority of our poorer population. The churches follow the well-to-do people up-town, as a rule, and where the thickest population is, where the people are to whom the Lord Jesus especially ministered during His life, there the churches are not. The churches are not reaching them because they are not near enough to where these people are. In the second place, the services of the regularly organized church are of such a character that they do not reach them. Oftentimes when they pretend to preach the Gospel they do not preach it; and, when they do preach the Gospel, it is preached in such a manner that it does not take hold of the common people. A laboring man, a poor man, an ignorant man, a beggar or a drunkard, who wishes to be reformed, goes into many of our churches, and the minister stands up and preaches the Gospel of the Lord Jesus Christ, and yet he preaches the Gospel in such a manner that it does not leave any impression upon the man's mind. The preacher is before everything else a scholar and a literary gentleman, and he does not know how to get down to the hearts and lives of ordinary folks. In the third place, the whole atmosphere of the church is not such that these people feel at home. Sometimes the style of dress the social etiquette the music, the whole general conduct of the church is such as to repel them. Down in the mission, on the other hand, there is an entire absence of con-

ventionality, but there is a friendliness, a kindliness, a home-likeness that their hearts warm to. There is something that attracts them to the place, and they go again and again until the Spirit of God opens their hearts and they are saved.

It is the work of the mission to gospelize these large masses of men and women and children existing in all our larger cities, and in many of our smaller cities, who are not reached by the ordinary ministrations of the church. It is to *gospelize* the masses not simply to reach them. It is of no great importance to know merely how to reach the masses, any one can reach the masses, but the question is, how to gospelize them. The work of the mission is not to conduct innocent entertainments, nor to provide a nice, warm, pleasant place for the people to go into from the streets; it is not to clothe the poor and the naked: but the work of the mission is to bring the Gospel of the Lord Jesus Christ to bear upon the hearts and lives of lost men and lost women. What they find, or ought to find, in the mission, is the Gospel of the Lord Jesus Christ seven nights in the week. If they desire amusement, or weak imitations of dime museums, they can get them elsewhere. The true business of the mission, as well as the true business of the church of the Lord Jesus Christ, is to preach the Word of God, and to bring it to bear upon lost men. The Word of God is the one lever that will lift them, not only out of the ditch, but into the kingdom of God.

2. *The Gospel mission is important as a soul winner.*

The question of how to evangelize the masses is often discussed as if it were a problem that nobody had solved, but it has been solved. There is no experiment about it. There are many who know exactly how to reach the masses with the Gospel, and prove that they know how, by doing it. The Gospel missions are winning souls, and their chief importance lies in this fact. I have in mind a mission to which you can go any night in the fifty-two weeks in the year, and you will see anywhere from twelve to fifty men kneeling at the altar and seeking the Lord Jesus Christ. Go to many other missions and you will see practically the same thing. The Gospel missions of America are winning thousands upon thousands of poor lost men and women to Jesus Christ every year; winning them and saving them, transforming them, making them children of God, heirs of God and joint heirs with Jesus Christ, by the power of the Gospel of our Lord Jesus Christ. Here is where the prime importance of the mission lies, not because it is trying to do the work, but because it is doing it.

3. *Gospel missions are important as an inspiration to the churches.*

Some of the most satisfactory local revivals in the history of the country have come from some member of a church attending a mission, getting a new conception of the power of the Lord Jesus Christ, and going home and kindling his church. The fire has gone through the whole church, and the church has been awakened to a mighty work for God. Oftentimes when people who have not even attended a mission have read reports of the work, they have wakened up to the fact that Paul meant just what he said when he wrote that the Gospel was the power of God unto salvation to every one that believed, and they have gone to work with new faith and new energy, and the Gospel has proved a saving power in their own community.

4. *Gospel missions are important as a feeder to the churches.*

Many of the best working members, and sometimes the best paying members, in our churches to-day are converts of missions. Many rich people have gone from the regular churches down to the missions, and have been there converted, and have gone back to their churches to be a power and blessing. Some people get an idea that all men who are converted in missions are men of no gifts or promise. It is a great mistake. Many a man who has been converted in a mission is indeed from the deepest depths of poverty and ruin, but it is sin that has brought him to his present condition. When the mission has gotten hold of him and won him to Christ, oftentimes the man regains his old position in society and business. A man who had been mayor of a large Southern city, but who had gone down through drink until he was a penniless tramp, was converted in a New York mission. He afterwards became the manager of one of the largest publishing houses in America. The night of his conversion, discouraged, disheartened, despairing, he had started from his lodging house to go and commit suicide in the East River. He had gone to a saloon to get one more drink, was thrown out because he was penniless, was brought into a mission by one who saw him thrown out of the saloon, and was converted that night. Many a man who is to-day in the regular Gospel ministry was converted in a mission. One of the brightest and most promising congregational ministers that I know in our land, the beloved pastor of a well-to-do church, was converted in a New York mission.

5. *Missions are important as furnishing a place where members of our churches can work.*

A Christian cannot grow without work. One of the great troubles in many of our churches to-day is that there is nothing to do. The members go Sunday after Sunday and are fed and fed and fed until they are dying of spiritual dyspepsia, apoplexy, or both. A minister once said to me, "My greatest difficulty is that I haven't anything for my members to do." It was literally true. It was a college church, and a parish in which there were more workers than work. A mission gives Christians something to do, something exceedingly inspiring to do, something in which there is a tremendous uplift to their own spiritual energy. What a blessing would come to many of our wealthy churches, if the members of these churches who go Sunday after Sunday and hear the Gospel of the Lord Jesus, would go out from these churches down into the lowest parts of the city, and come right into living touch with lost men and women, and try to use the Gospel of the Lord Jesus Christ to lift them up where they ought to be. If they should do this, we would have new life in our prayer meeting, we would not have two or three long and labored prayers; we would have prayer after prayer, short, right to the point, appeals to God for His blessing upon this man or that woman. We would have a new conception of the power of the Gospel of the Lord Jesus Christ, we would have a new vision of the Lord Jesus Christ Himself. I never knew Jesus as I know Him to-day, until I knew what it was to go down among the poor and outcast, and kneel right beside a dirty drunkard, and put my arm about his neck, and whisper to him that Jesus died for him, and that Jesus came to save him and could save him, and then hear him with breaking heart lift his voice to God in prayer, and then see him rise a new man in Christ Jesus. I understood the Gospel then; I understood Jesus then; I saw Jesus then as I never saw Him before. If you wish to be a better Christian than you ever were in all your life, if you wish to understand the Lord Jesus as you never understood Him before in all your life, if you wish to have the spirit of prayer as you never had it before in all your life, go to work in a mission. If you are a pastor and wish to have a better membership than you ever had in your life, send your members out to work in a mission. If you have not a mission where they can do it, start one, have one anyhow. I pity from the bottom of my heart the man or woman who does not know the inspiration, the joy and uplift, that comes from going down into some mission where perhaps there are five, ten or one hundred lost men and women, and just pleading with them in the simplest language you can command, to take the Lord Jesus Christ who saved you.

II. How to start a mission.

The way to start a mission is to start it. A great many people talk about starting but they never start. In one city they had a great gathering and were going to build a $200,000 building. They had a wonderful meeting, and one man subscribed $30,000. Some one who was present was asked what he thought about it, and he replied, "I can tell you better after they have started." They never started. The whole thing went to pieces. Our country is full of people who are going to start missions and other Christian enterprises, but they never do it. The way to begin is by beginning.

1. *In the first place, be sure God wishes you to start a mission.*

It is not enough to be sure that you wish to start one. It is as a rule far better to go and help a mission already existing, than to go and begin a new one of your own. Many people hear of the wonderful work they are doing in some mission, and then go and start one without consulting the Lord. There have been hundreds of missions opened in this country that the Lord never wished opened, and if those who started them had gone to Him about it, they would never have been started.

2. *If you are sure that it is the Lord's desire that you start a mission, start with the determination to go through with it.*

People attend conventions or read articles about missions, and see only the bright side, they do not see that the work is also full of discouragements. If there is any work that is full of discouragements, it is mission work; so when you start, begin with the determination that you will go through every obstacle, and then you will get through.

3. *Be sure you get the right location.*

That is very important. Be sure and consult God about the place. There is a great deal in the place, and the place that you think best may not be the best place. Here are a few hints as to location:

(1) Go where there is the hardest work, not the most attractive work, to do.

(2) Go where there is the most need for work.

(3) Go where there are a great many passers-by.

(4) As a rule the first floor is best for many reasons, but there are some advantages in a second-floor mission.

(5) A vacant store, saloon or theater will answer the purpose for a mission excellently.

(6) Don't start on too large a scale. Everybody seems to wish a bigger mission than anybody else, and if they start on a large scale, as a rule in a few months they have enough of it. Sometimes the best place to start a mission is on a street corner. Go and hold an open air meeting, and if the Lord approves of your work, He will give you a more permanent place.

(7) The location of the mission must be largely determined by the purpose of the mission. If the purpose of the mission is to reach drunkards, the place for the mission is near the saloons; if the purpose of the mission is to reach fallen women, oftentimes it is desirable to have the mission right among the places that these women haunt, though if possible there should also be a home remote from the dens of iniquity

to which the converts can be sent. If the purpose of the mission is to reach the respectable poor, of course the location of the mission has to be determined by that fact.

4. *Furnish plainly.*

Fancy missions as a rule are failures. They are nice in theory, but plain ones do the work.

5. *When you have made up your mind where you are going to start, and have gotten everything ready, advertise your meetings everywhere; in the houses, in the stores, in the saloons and on the street.*

Send men and women out to bring people in, "compel them to come in." Get as many consecrated Christian workers as you can together. Expect fresh infillings of the Holy Spirit as you seek to win souls.

III. How to support the mission.

1. *Don't support it on credit.*

Many people get in debt and call it walking by faith. God says, "Owe no man anything." Running into debt is not faith, but disobedience. It is better to shut a mission up than to run it into debt. Debt dishonors God. If you run into debt you will be discredited, the church will be discredited, God will be discredited, sinners will stumble to perdition over the dishonor brought to the name of Christ.

2. *Do not support your mission by fairs, socials, imitation dime museums, or anything of that sort.*

The man who goes into the disgraceful methods of raising church finances that are so common in our day, lacks faith in God.

3. *Do not support your mission by indiscriminate solicitation.*

Never go to an ungodly man for money. God says that the sacrifice of the wicked is an abomination unto the Lord. He certainly does not wish us to use an abomination to support His work.

4. *If you are able to do it, it is oftentimes well to support a mission out of your own pocket.*

In almost every large city there are many Christian men who could support a mission. One of the most efficient missions in the world was for years supported by a business man out of his own pocket. He worked six days in the week the entire day, spent all the evenings at the mission, then went fourteen miles to his home, and before he could go to bed would have a long list of people to pray for. He was past fifty years old when he began this work; he kept it up for many years, and the work continues to this day. Another man of wealth in another city put $10,000 or more a year into a mission that he organized. He found that that work paid so much better than his business, that he finally turned his back upon his business and put himself into the work. He is still in the work, a young man at nearly three score years and ten. It does not require a very rich man to support a mission. Four young men in one city, each of them working on a meager salary, supported a very successful mission with scarcely any help from others. Of course it required self-denial, but they felt that the self-denial abundantly paid.

5. *One of the best ways to support a mission is to have an individual church back of it.*

The church will be a blessing to the mission, and the mission to the church. Every rich church ought to have one or more missions that it is supporting.

6. *The best way to support a mission in many cases, is to support it by the free will offerings of those who attend it.*

This is best even where the attendants are all poor people. Very few realize how much poor people can give and will give if they are interested in a work, and if the work really is of God. Far more missions as well as churches could be self-supporting if the people only believed it and undertook it. The people always appreciate the mission better, and think more of it, when they have money in it.

7. *Missions can be supported by faith.*

If you are SURE the Lord wishes you to carry on mission work, ask Him for means and He will supply them. You will not need to make personal solicitations from anybody but the Lord. I say this not from speculation, but from experience. Many others have had the same experience.

IV. How to conduct a Gospel mission.

1. *Let God conduct it.*

Missions often fail because there is too much of man's machinery and man's management. Cast-iron rules and cast-iron methods of conducting missions, red tape and other nonsense, shut God out. Give your mission over unreservedly to the control of God. Be sure you do it—seek His guidance and wait for it. The promise of the thirty-second Psalm applies as well to mission work as to other work: "I will instruct thee and teach thee in the way which thou shalt go, I will guide thee with mine eye." The trouble is, oftentimes we are not near enough to see the glance of the Father's eye.

2. *Conduct your mission along strictly Gospel lines.*

Refuse to be switched off on to side issues. Amusements and entertainments may be a good enough thing in their place, but the time is short and the Lord is at hand. We cannot afford to be reaching out in such indirect and indefinite ways. Thousands of souls are perishing, and the only thing that has God's power in it to save is the Gospel (Rom. 1:16). A fine text for the mission worker is, "I am not ashamed of the Gospel of Christ, for it is the power of God unto salvation to every one that believeth." The missions that have been successful are the missions that have held strictly to the Gospel, the missions that have given the Gospel clearly, simply and constantly. Experiments along other lines are nothing new. They have been tried for over a quarter of a century. I remember a church which in my early life seemed to me a model church. It had most cunningly devised machinery for reaching the people—lectures, entertainments, clubs, classes, etc., etc. It did reach the people, but it did not convert them. It grew marvelously, but it was made up of such heterogeneous and unconverted material that it went to pieces and ended in a free-for-all fight; yet every little while some new work is springing up, along these old and discredited lines, yet imagining that it is striking out in new and promising paths. The Gospel alone can do the work we aim to do. Run your mission along Gospel lines seven nights in the week.

3. *Tend strictly to business.*

Missions will not run themselves. People attend a few meetings of a successful mission, or read about them, and conclude that missions are a fine thing. Then they open one somewhere and expect it to go of itself, and it does go—to pieces. This has occurred again and again. There is no form of Christian work that demands more careful and prayerful watching and attention to business than mission work. A single ill-conducted service in a church may not do much harm, but a single ill-conducted service in a mission is likely to have far-reaching consequences of evil. One unfortunate meeting in a mission may mar the work for years.

4. *Put only tried men in the leadership of the mission.*

Use only men of irreproachable character, and who have a good understanding of God's Word, men of good common sense, and uncommon push. It is too much the custom if a notorious sinner is converted, to open a mission for him at once and put him in charge. He has not been tested, and nothing is known of his qualifications, but he has a remarkable story. The condition of many missions is simply horrible because of this sort of thing. Of course such a man ought to be set to work, and there is much that he can do, and do well, and without any risk. He can be used to hand out dodgers and to get people into the mission; he can testify humbly and effectively as to what God has done for him; very likely he can do most efficient personal work, but for his own sake and for Christ's sake, do not put him into any place of leadership until he is tried, and has proven the stability of his Christian character, his gifts and his Bible knowledge, to be such as fit him for the work: "Lay hands hastily on no man" (1 Tim. 5:22, R. V.); however good a man he may be, it will hurt him to put him forward at once.

5. *Make much of the Bible.*

People in a mission should be given a great deal of the Word of God. Stable and well-rounded Christian character is built upon a study of the Word of God. The Christian character that is built merely upon the foundation of experience is unreliable; it breaks down easily; but the Christian character that is built upon the Word of God never goes to pieces. The converts and attendants ought to be encouraged to study the Word for themselves. There should be classes also for thorough systematic instruction in Bible truth. There should be training classes where they are taught how to use the Bible in leading others to Christ. They should be encouraged to make much use of the Bible in giving their experience. In some successful missions, the men always begin their testimony by a quotation from Scripture, giving chapter and verse.

6. *Make much use of testimony.*

There can be no doubt of the great power of living testimony, especially in mission work. Men and women who regard themselves not only lost, but hopelessly lost, come into the mission and there hear some other man or woman who has been as deep down in sin as themselves, tell the story of the saving power of Christ. Hope is kindled in their hearts, and they turn to Christ and are saved. There are thousands of earnest Christians in our land to-day who were saved through the testimonies of redeemed men and women. Of course care has to be exercised as to the character of the testimonies thus given. We should be careful to see that it is genuine and not hypocritical; we should see to it that the men live out in their daily lives what they testify to in the evening meeting. If men give their testimony about their past sinful life in a boastful way, they should be instructed in private not to do this. Sometimes it is necessary to say a word about it publicly. But the fact that there are evils connected with the relation of our experience is not a sufficient reason for altogether giving up this mighty weapon of testimony.

7. *Make much use of music.*

Get the best music you can. Be sure it is converted music. Tolerate nothing but a converted chorister, a converted organist and a converted choir. Have an organist that you can depend upon. An organist of modest ability who is always there is much better than a much better organist who is sometimes late or absent. Get the best soloist you can, but be sure they sing hymns that contain the real Gospel, and sing them in the power of the Holy Spirit. Have duets, quartettes and choruses, but best of all, have lively congregational singing. Be careful in your selection of hymns. Choose hymns that are full of life and full of the Gospel. Sing them over and over again until you have sung them into the hearts of the hearers. Many a man will go out of the mission unconverted, but the hymn that he has heard will go on singing itself in his heart until it has sung him into the kingdom of God. It is wonderful how the gospel in song sticks in the minds of hearers.

8. *Make a great deal of personal work in the mission.*

It is not enough to get those who desire to be saved up to the altar, though that is a good thing to do; have workers deal with them individually. Be sure that the workers themselves know how to do personal work. One great cause of the instability of much of our mission work is that there has been no thorough hand-to-hand dealing with the converts.

9. *Look after your converts.*

Keep a list of them, and hunt them up in their homes if they have any. If they have no homes, hunt them up in their lodging houses or wherever they may be. Follow them up persistently, instruct them individually as to how to succeed in the Christian life. Be watchful to see that they follow the instructions given. Get them into some live church of Jesus Christ. We ought to be careful as to the church which mission converts join. Many churches would prove to be an ice-house to them, and would freeze them to death. It is oftentimes best to have the mission itself organized into a church, where there is regular church life, and where the sacraments of Baptism and the Lord's Supper are administered.

10. *Throw as much of the work as you can upon the converts of the mission.*

Send them out into the streets and saloons to invite people in; be careful, however, about sending reformed drunkards into saloons. Put the converts out on the street corners and in front of the mission with dodgers. Organize them into a choir and get them to sing. Train them to use their Bibles in dealing with inquirers. Work them into the Sunday School as officers and teachers as fast as it is wise. Organize them into lookout committees, sick committees, hospital committees, jail committees, etc. Set them to conducting cottage meetings. Use them in open-air work.

11. *Have plenty of good ushers.*

Let them meet people at the door and give them a warm handshake, and show them a seat. Ladies are oftentimes the best ushers for a mission. It has been a long time since some of those who enter the mission have come in contact with a pure woman, and her mere presence is a benediction; their hearts are touched, and memories of olden days come to mind.

12. *Let no one go out without a personal invitation to come to Christ.*

The best work in many a mission is that which is done with those who start to go out before the meeting is over. Some one stays near the door and follows out every one who leaves and preaches Christ to them. Many have been won to Christ this way, just outside the mission.

13. *Have no cast-iron form of service.*

It is well to begin one way one time and an entirely different way another. Let everything be unconventional. Avoid getting into ruts.

14. *Never be afraid of drunkards, thieves, thugs or cranks.*

You have God back of you, and if you look to Him, He will give you the victory every time. Many things may happen that would frighten an ordinary preacher out of his wits, but out of these very unforeseen incidents blessing oftentimes comes.

I was once conducting a meeting when a drunken man rose in the back part of the audience and wanted to speak. As he came forward I said, "Do you want us to pray for you?" The man faced the audience and broke out, "I am a damned fool!" then he apoligized for swearing. He said, "I did not mean to swear." I said, "My friend, you told the truth, you are a fool and you are damned, but Christ can save you. Do you wish us to pray for you?" And down the man went upon his knees. In a little while a tall, muscular, drunken lumberman rose to his feet and said he wished to ask a question. I replied, "All right, what is it?" He said, "I wish to ask about the blessed trinity." I said, "Never mind that now, Christ died for you; do you wish us to pray for you?" The man replied, "I am not such a fool but what I am willing to be prayed for," and down he dropped upon his knees. The power of God came upon the meeting, and there was great blessing that night.

15. *Depend upon the Holy Spirit.*

You may have the right machinery, you may have the building and the crowds, you may have even the Word of God itself, but unless you have the power of the Holy Spirit to accompany the divine seed as you sow it, your work will come to nothing. All this machinery, unless the power of the Holy Spirit is in it, is worse than useless, but if you have the fire from above, you will win souls.

CHAPTER XII

MEETINGS IN JAILS, HOSPITALS, POORHOUSES, ETC.

Jails, hospitals, poorhouses and other public institutions offer a very important and much-neglected field of operations for the devoted soul winner.

I. Importance and advantages.

1. *Many of the inmates of these institutions must be reached while there, or not at all.*

Many of them in fact spend pretty much all of their lives there, and many others still will die there.

2. *The inmates are oftentimes in a favorable mood for the reception of the Gospel.*

Things have gone against them. Life looks hopeless. The Gospel, which is full of hope, just appeals to their need. Take for example the men in jail. They have found out by bitter experience that "the way of the transgressor is hard"; they are humbled and sobered. They are very likely to be in a thoughtful mood; they have much time for thought, little opportunity in fact for anything else; furthermore the whisky is out of them, and with many of them the only time the whisky is out of them is when they are in jail or prison. There could not be a more favorable opportunity for preaching the Gospel. I have known many men who thanked God that they were ever sent to jail, for there they heard the Gospel, some of them for the first time, and others of them in a different mood from that in which they had ever heard it before.

3. *The converts can be followed up.*

A prisoner is reached with the Gospel one Sunday in jail, he is likely to be there the next Sunday as well, and perhaps for many Sundays to come, and there is an opportunity to get him thoroughly established before he is out in the world again. The same is true of an inmate of a hospital; he is reached one day, and is likely to be there where he can be dealt with for many days to come.

4. *The inmates have to attend.*

In some instances attendance is compulsory. When one is confined to a sick bed in the ward of a hospital where a religious service is being held, they are obliged to hear the Gospel preached and sung. Further than this, where the inmates of such institutions are not compelled to attend, there is so little to do that they are willing to go to anything for a novelty.

5. *The results of such services are very large.*

It has oftentimes been our privilege in the Cook County Jail to preach to fifty or more persons there, under charge of murder, besides great numbers of others. Very many of the most desperate and hardened characters have been converted in jail services. There is scarcely any other work that yields so important and so good results as jail work. Some of the leading ministers and other Christian workers of this country were converted while incarcerated. One of the leading ministers of one of our evangelical denominations, a man whose name is known not only in this country but in Europe, a man who has a remarkable power of preaching the Word of God, was first reached while in jail. At that time he was a brilliant but drunken lawyer. He was converted in jail, and has been for many years an honored preacher of the Gospel. In one of our cities a reckless young man was incarcerated under charge of arson. He had burned the property of his own father. His father was himself a Godless man. While in jail this young man was brought to Christ, and has been for years a most devoted Christian at the head of a very successful mission work. Jerry McAuley, perhaps the leader in rescue mission work in this country, was converted while in Sing Sing prison. Christian workers should see to it that every jail, poorhouse, and similar institution in the land has a regular evangelistic service. The formal services held under the city or state in such institutions frequently are purely formal, and of no real value. As a rule the best work is that which is done by volunteers. Services should also be held in every hospital in the land where it is possible to get an entrance.

II. How to conduct.

1. *First of all you must get permission.*

The way to get permission is to ask for it. The request should not be made in the way of a demand, it should be made with great tact and courtesy. If it is possible to get influence back of your request, get it.

2. *Keep the good will of the attendants.*

Here is a place where many zealous but unwise workers make a mistake; they unnecessarily antagonize jailers or keepers or nurses or other attendants. This is the height of folly. It does not cost much to keep the good will of people, and in a case like this it is of inestimable value.

3. *Be sure and violate none of the rules of the institution.*

Be careful at the outset to find what the rules of the institution are, and then observe them to the very letter. It makes no difference whether you think the rules of the institution are wise or not, keep them anyhow. It is not your business to make the rules, but to observe them.

4. *Attend strictly to your own business.*

Don't try to run the whole jail or hospital. Some men when they go to preach in an institution, seem to be seized with the idea that they own the whole institution. I have known workers to go to work among the inmates of a hospital, and then try to get them to give up the use of medicine and accept divine healing, or sometimes try to get them to go to some other hospital they thought was better. In such a case, the authorities are of course warranted in turning the workers into the street.

5. *Go regularly.*

Regular services, week after week, month after month, year after year, accomplish far more than spasmodic efforts. One great trouble in all this kind of work is, that there are so many people who get enthusiastic for some weeks, and then their enthusiasm cools. When institutions have a number of experiences with this kind of work, they become unwilling to permit a new band of workers to take up again a work that has so often failed in the past.

6. *Have good music, and plenty of it.*

These people get very little music, and they enjoy it. Frequently they enjoy the music more than they do the preaching, and it is easier to reach many of them by a solo sung in the power of the Spirit than it is by a sermon. Adapt your music to the circumstances; for example, in a hospital the music should not be loud or exciting; it should be bright and comforting. A doleful tune in a hospital may hasten the death of some of the patients, but a bright, cheerful, Gospel tune is likely to save the lives of some of the patients. The music that is adapted to a hospital is frequently not adapted to a jail, and vice versa.

7. *Preach the Word.*

Stick close to the Bible. Be simple, plain, vivacious, right to the point.

8. *Be wise in your prayer.*

An indiscreet prayer in a hospital may do much harm, so may an indiscreet prayer in a jail or workhouse.

9. *In a jail be careful to avoid all air of superiority.*

Many an inexperienced man begins to talk to the inmates in jail, as if he was an angel and they were demons. Such a man will get no hearing. Let the prisoners feel that you realize that you are their brother. Do not assume a patronizing air, avoid all unnecessary sentimentality and gush.

10. *Make use of testimony.*

Jerry McAuley was converted through the testimony of Orville Gardner. He had known Orville Gardner in the old days as a desperate character in New York, going by the nickname of "Awful Gardner." When he went to Sing Sing prison and saw Orville Gardner in the pulpit, he could hardly believe his own eyes; but when Orville Gardner rose and gave his testimony, it went home to Jerry McAuley's heart, and thoroughly roused him to a study of the Bible itself, with the result that he was converted in his cell. There are many men in this country to-day who in olden days have been inmates of jails and prisons—notorious criminals—but who are to-day living consistent Christian lives. The testimony of such a man has great weight with other convicts.

11. *Deal individually with the inmates.*

The public preaching does much good, but the personal work does more, it brings matters to a personal decision. The great majority of converts in jail work come through individual work. It may be difficult at first to get permission to deal individually with the inmates, but if you are wise, and win the confidence of the authorities, you will get the opportunity in time.

12. *Make a large use of tracts and other Gospel literature.*

Prisoners have so much time on their hands that they are ready to read anything. Select your literature very wisely. Goody-goody religious literature is not what is needed, but that which shows real ability and strength, and goes right to the heart of things. There is no better literature for use in jails and hospitals than that published by the Bible Institute Colportage Association. It is possible to get free grants from this society. While their prison fund is usually overdrawn, somehow or other they manage to honor drafts made upon them.

13. *Pray much in secret.*

Prayer is one of the great secrets of success in all forms of religious enterprise, but this is peculiarly true regarding work in jails, hospitals and similar institutions. If a record could be kept and published regarding God's answers to prayers for work under such circumstances, it would make a most interesting and inspiring book.

CHAPTER XIII

REVIVAL MEETINGS

By revival meetings we mean consecutive meetings, day after day and night after night, for the quickening of the life and activity of the church, and for the salvation of the lost. We speak of them as revival meetings because such meetings result from new life either in individuals or in the church as a whole, and if properly conducted always result in the impartation of new life to the church and the salvation of the lost.

I. Importance and advantages.

The importance of revival services can scarcely be overestimated. There are those who say that we ought not to have special revival meetings, but should have a revival in the church all the time. It is true that there should be a revival in the church all the time. There was a continuous revival in the apostolic church; there are churches which have a continuous revival in these days; but it is almost always the case that the churches which have a continuous revival are those which believe in and make use of special revival services, and what are known as revival methods.

1. *The first advantage of special revival services is that which comes from repeated and consecutive impression.*

An unsaved man hears a sermon on Sunday evening. An impression is made upon his mind by the truth he has heard, but the impression has not been profound enough to lead to his acceptance of Jesus Christ then and there. Before the next regular preaching service of the church comes, the impression has faded away, and an entirely new impression has to be made. If the Sunday evening sermon had been followed up by another on Monday evening, the impression of Sunday evening would have been deepened; if that had been followed by still another sermon on Tuesday evening, the impression would have been made deeper still, and very likely before the week was over, the man would have been converted. Only those who have made a careful and prolonged study of this matter can realize how important in the work of bringing men to Christ is the element of repeated and consecutive impression. Men who have attended church for years, and who have been only superficially impressed, are oftentimes readily brought to Christ in a series of consecutive services.

2. *The second advantage of revival services is that, if properly conducted, there will be an unusual amount of prayer, and unaccustomed earnestness in prayer.*

Some one may say that Christians ought always to pray, and so they should, but we have to take the people as they are. As a matter of fact, the average Christian does far more praying in a time of special revival services than he does at any other time. The professed Christians who spend as much time as they ought in regular prayer day by day, when there is no special effort being made for the salvation of the lost, are very rare indeed.

3. *The third advantage of revival services is that at such times Christians put forth special efforts for the salvation of the lost.*

Every Christian should do everything in his power every day of his life to lead men to Christ, but in point of fact very few Christians do this. How often those who are cold and indifferent and do almost nothing at all for the salvation of the lost under ordinary circumstances, will display a great activity at the time of special services, and not seldom those who have never been known as workers before not only take hold of the work during special meetings, but continue it after the meetings are over.

4. *Revival services awaken an unusual interest in the subject of religion in the community.*

The outside world is aroused to the fact that the church exists, and that there is such a thing as religion. They begin to think about God, Christ, the Bible, eternity, heaven and hell. People who are never seen in the house of God at any other time in the year will flock there during revival meetings. Many of them will be converted, and others will become attendants at the church. They find out what the church has to offer, and suddenly wake up to the fact that what the church has to offer is just what they need.

5. *As a matter of experience and history, revivals have been greatly honored of God.*

This is true in the history of the church as a whole and also in the history of local churches. The church of Christ has been saved, humanly speaking from utter ruin by the revivals which God has graciously sent from time to time in its history. As regards local churches, the churches which have grown and prospered are those that have believed in and made use of revivals. Study the yearbooks of the various denominations, and you will find that the ministers who have believed in revivals and have fostered them in their churches, are the ones who have been able to report from year to year accessions to their church, and gifts to the various branches of Christian activity. On the other hand, it will be found as a rule, an almost universal rule, that the ministers who have pooh-poohed revivals have had their churches run down on their hands. If there is anything that the history of the church of Jesus Christ absolutely demonstrates, it is the tremendous importance, if not the imperative necessity, of revivals.

II. Time to hold revival meetings.

When shall revival meetings be held in a church or community?

1. *When there are indications of special blessing.*

An alert pastor who keeps in touch with his people and the community will often be able to detect signs of special interest and blessing. He will notice a new interest in his preaching on the part of his congregation. He will have a new sense of liberty and power as he preaches. He will see tears in the eyes of his congregation as he speaks about sin and its consequences. People will come to him for spiritual counsel and to be shown the way of life. Perhaps members of his church who are more spiritually alert than himself will say to him that they think there are signs of blessing in the church or community. All these things are indications that God is ready to favor that church or community with an especial outpouring of His Spirit, and arrangements should be made at once to take advantage of these favorable conditions, and to gather a harvest of souls, by holding special revival services.

2. *When there is spiritual dearth in the community and church.*

When the Gospel seems to have lost its hold upon the people when the congregations are constantly declining and conversions are few; when iniquity and infidelity are rampant in the community; such a time is also an important one. Special effort should be put forth to arouse the church and to save the perishing. God has promised His special blessing at such a time. He has said, "When the enemy shall come in like a flood, the Spirit of the Lord shall lift up a standard against him" (Is. 59: 19). When everything goes hard in a church, and infidelity and irreligion and immorality seem to triumph, the minister whose trust is fixed upon God and in His Word need not become discouraged. Let him cry to God with a new earnestness and faith, and then go to work to bring about the conditions upon which God is always ready to bless His people.

3. *Revival meetings should be held in every church every year.*

This is entirely feasible. The writer of this book has been the pastor of four different churches, all quite different from one another; a village church with the usual village congregation and environment, a young suburban church in a large city, a church just organized for the masses in the heart of a large city, and an established metropolitan church with a large and varied membership. In each of these churches he found it quite possible to have special revival meetings every year. Largely as a result of these special revival meetings, each of these churches had what could probably justly be termed a continual revival, there being accessions to the church at every communion. Many other pastors ministering to churches of still different varieties from these here described, testify to the same experience.

As to the time in the year when these services can most wisely be held, this depends upon local conditions. It seems to be the experience of most pastors that the especially favorable time is the week of prayer, and the weeks immediately following. People expect something to be done at that time, and to a certain extent are ready for it. There is, however, a growing tendency to begin these meetings during Easter week or earlier in Lent. This is an especially favorable time in large cities on account of the Roman Catholic and Episcopalian element. In large cities the social life is at an ebb at that time. Even the theaters take this fact into consideration. While we may not personally believe in observing times and seasons and days, we ought not to loose sight of the fact that other people do believe in it, and we should take advantage of this fact as giving us an especially good opportunity of getting hold of people, and getting them out to hear the Word of God.

III. How to organize and conduct a revival meeting.

1. When it has been decided that the time has come to hold special services, *a letter should be addressed to every member of the church, stating the plans, and requesting their interest and prayer and co-operation in every way.*

It is sometimes well in connection with this letter, to give every member of the church some book to read that will stir them up to self-examination, to prayer and to effort. A book largely used by some evangelists and many pastors for this purpose, is the book, "How to Pray," by the author. It can be secured in paper cover for this purpose at a very low price. In the letter there should be a request that each member should answer it, pledging themselves not only to read the book that is sent, but also to prayer and co-operation in the work. The members of the church who have been absenting themselves from the church service or from the prayer meeting should be visited personally and dealt with gently but earnestly, and led to realize their responsibility to Christ and His church, and also their responsibility regarding the unsaved in the community.

2. *Meetings for united prayer should at once be begun.*

Sometimes it is wisest to hold these at the central church but oftentimes, especially when the membership of the church is very much scattered, it is better to have cottage meetings at first, in the various neighborhoods of the parish. These separate cottage meetings can afterwards be brought together for a united meeting at the church. If the revival services are to be of a union character, it is well for each church to begin prayer meetings by itself, and for them afterwards to come together for union prayer meetings. There short addresses should be given upon the importance of prayer and how to pray, but the major part of the meeting should be devoted directly to prayer. The people should be instructed as to what they should pray for; they should be drawn out in prayer for the membership of the church, then in prayer for the unsaved, and not merely for the unsaved in general, but for specific persons in whom they are interested; their duty to uphold the hands of the pastor in prayer should be emphasized; they should be instructed as to the lines along which they should seek God's help for the pastor—in his personal life, in his selection of topics to preach upon, in his preparation of his sermons, and especially that his preaching may be in demonstration of the Spirit and of power (1 Cor. 2:4; Eph. 6:19); they should be encouraged to pray for a special outpouring of the Holy Spirit in the community. Oftentimes it is important to get them to take a higher outlook than the needs of their own local community, and to pray for a general outpouring of the Spirit throughout the world.

3. *In the next place, a canvass of the entire community should be undertaken.*

The whole village or city or section of the city should be carefully mapped out, different districts assigned to different workers, and every house and store in the community visited. Those visited should be informed of the meetings that are to be held, but more important than this, as far as possible they should be dealt with and prayed with personally, in regard to their salvation. If the services are to be of a union character, the visitors should go out two and two, each one representing a different church in the community.

4. *After this preliminary work has been done, meetings should be announced at the church.*

The number of meetings to be held each day will depend very much upon the location and the interest. In many places it will be possible to hold only an evening meeting at first. In other places the meetings can be begun with as many as three or four meetings a day, for what may be best in this line in one place is utterly impossible in another. The ideal is a meeting for prayer, a meeting for the study of the Bible on the part of believers and an evening evangelistic service for the unsaved, with possibly a fourth meeting for children; but this ideal is not attainable in every community. Where it is not, there should at least be in addition to the evening meeting, a gathering for prayer. It may be held for prayer and prayer alone, or it may be wiser to have a meeting in the afternoon, part of the time being given to prayer and part to the study of the Word of God. One great reason why our modern evangelistic movements have lacked the old-time power is because the emphasis is not laid upon the prayer meeting that was in former days. In the great revival of 1857 more time and strength was put into prayer meetings than into anything else. In many places the meetings were entirely prayer meetings. We have swung to the other extreme, and in many cases evangelistic meetings are entirely meetings for preaching and singing. This is a great mistake. Wherever the church becomes lax in united prayer, the meetings will soon loose in power and come to a close as far as any real results are concerned.

The question often rises whether it is wiser to hold the meetings at a church or in a hall. This will depend somewhat upon circumstances. Each method has its advantages. Doubtless many people can be gotten out to a hall or to an opera house who will not enter a church; on the other hand, if people are gotten out to church and converted there, they will be more likely to remain in the church after the special meetings are over than if the meetings are held in a hall or opera house. The wisest plan in many instances is to begin the meetings in a church and then go to a hall or opera house, and then back to the church before they close, in order that those who have been interested in the opera house may be accustomed to and interested in the church before the special interest is over. As to whether the meetings are held in a church or hall oftentimes too is dependent upon whether they are meetings of an individual church or a union of several churches. Here again there are advantages in each plan. There is likely to be more harmony and united effort and less controversy and suspicion if the meetings are held by an individual church. On the other hand there can be no doubt that a community is moved by a union of all the churches in it, as it is not moved and cannot be moved by revival services held by an individual church. If revival services are held in the summer, oftentimes it is well to hold them in a tent.

5. *The children should never be forgotten in times of special interest.*

Special meetings for the children should be held. As a rule they should be held in the afternoon just at the time the school is closing, so that children can go directly from school to the meeting. They should be held at least five afternoons in the week. More about these children's meetings will be said in the chapter upon children's meetings.

6. *Of course the preaching is of very great importance in the conduct of revival services.*

(1) *Who should preach?*

The first question that arises is as to who should do the preaching. Wherever it is possible, it is well for the pastor of the church to do the preaching himself. It is said that some pastors do not have the evangelistic gift, and this is doubtless in a measure true, but most pastors can, to some extent, cultivate the evangelistic gift, if they only will. There is a great advantage in the pastor himself preaching. There is not such a likelihood that the interest shall suddenly die out when the special services are over. When it is not possible for the local pastor to do the preaching, he can often call in the help of some neighboring pastor who does possess the evangelistic gift. Even when the pastor himself is an evangelist, there is an advantage in calling in a fellow pastor for a special series of meetings. His is a new voice, and he is likely to preach the truth from another standpoint from that to which people have become accustomed. Many will go to hear him out of curiosity who might not attend special services conducted by the pastor, thinking they could hear him any Sunday. But we cannot depend altogether upon the local pastor or upon fellow pastors. It is by the ordination of God that there are evangelists in the church, and evangelists as a class have been greatly honored of God in the past history of the church. However clear it is that the pastor is possessed of the evangelistic gift, and however much he may have been used of God in leading the unsaved to Christ, if he is wise he will occasionally call to his help a man whom God has especially appointed to the work of an evangelist. Of course there are evangelists and evangelists. Some evangelists are mere adventurers, others are indiscreet and do much harm, but there are beyond question many men whom God has called to this specific work, and whom He wants in it, and there are indications that God is going to multiply the number of really reliable men who are in evangelistic work.

(2) *What to preach.*

What shall we preach in times of revival interest. (1) First of all, we should preach the Gospel, the Gospel that Christ died for our sins, according to the Scriptures, was buried and rose again. We should never get far from the Cross. We should preach the atonement over and over and over again. (2) We should also preach the utterly lost and ruined condition of man. (3) We should preach the bitter consequences of sin here and hereafter. We should declare the whole counsel of God regarding the judgment and regarding hell. (4) We should present the truth about conversion, regeneration and justification. (5) We should preach the Divinity of Christ. There is great correcting and converting and saving power in that doctrine. (Acts 2: 36, 37; 9: 20, 22; Jno. 20: 31.) (6) We should also preach to Christians about the Holy Spirit and His work, about prayer, about the power of the Word of God and the necessity of Bible study. One will find much instruction in regard to what to preach at such a time from the sermons of such men as Moody, Spurgeon and Finney. A study of the texts given in the first division of this volume in connection with the different classes of men with whom we have to deal in personal work will suggest many texts and topics for sermons.

7. *In revival services the music is of great importance.*

If possible there should be a large choir of converted men and women. They should have the leadership of a godly chorister. He should be a man who not only knows how to sing himself, but who can get others to sing. If there are in the community, or if there can be secured, men or women who can sing Gospel solos effectively in the power of the Holy Spirit, their services should be obtained. Impress upon the singers that they are to sing not merely to interest the people, but to convert them, and that they need a definite anointing of the Holy Spirit for their work.

8. *The testimony of saved people to the power and blessing of the Gospel is of great value in special revival services.*

Especially is the testimony of those recently converted effective. When men hear one who has recently come out from their ranks tell of what Jesus Christ has done for him, a longing is awakened in their hearts to find the same Saviour.

9. *When the meetings are held in a city of considerable size, it is well to have a noon meeting to which men in business and others are invited.*

Many can be gotten hold of in this way that can be reached in no other way.

It is well usually in a series of special services to hold meetings for men alone, in which sin is very plainly dealt with, and Christ as the remedy for sin presented. Meetings for women are also desirable. As a rule they should be conducted by women, though there are some men who seem to have a special gift in preaching to women. Generally, however, the men who are most inclined to take such meetings are least qualified to do it.

10. *Classes to train the workers in how to deal with inquirers are of the highest importance.*

Oftentimes it is well to hold these training classes before the general meetings begin, so that from the very first meeting you can have workers whom you may depend upon to do the work.

11. *Every general meeting should be followed by an after meeting.*

Definite instructions as to the conduct of after meetings will be given in a separate chapter.

12. *All the Christian people in the community should be set to work.*

They should be so aroused upon the subject of religion that all they will talk about everywhere is Christ and His claims upon men. They should be encouraged to go from house to house and store to store laboring with people and endeavoring to get them to accept Christ. Harm may be done in this way by indiscreet workers, but the harm that is done will be small indeed in comparison with the good that is accomplished.

13. *It is very important to make use of good religious literature in times of special interest.*

Tracts and books should be generously used. The Bible Institute Colportage Association has a very large selection of the most useful literature along these lines, that can be secured at a very low cost.

CHAPTER XIV

THE AFTER MEETING

I. Importance and advantages.

In successful soul-winning work the after meeting is of the highest importance. Every tent meeting, mission meeting and revival service should be followed by an after meeting. The wise and active pastor will also follow up every Sunday evening service with an after meeting. Many a mighty preacher fails to get the results he might from his preaching, because he does not know how to draw the net. He is successful at hooking fish, but does not know how to land them. A friend told me a short time ago that he heard a man one evening preach to a large congregation of men one of the best sermons he ever heard, and continued my friend, "I believe there would have been fifty decisions just then but just at the critical moment the evangelist did not know what to do, and let the meeting slip through his fingers." He asked them to stand up and sing some hymn and the men began to go out in crowds. He tried to get them together again, and there were some inquirers, but nothing like the results there should have been. Much good preaching comes to nothing because it is not driven home to the individual, and the individual brought then and there to an acceptance and confession of Jesus as Saviour and Lord.

1. *The first advantage of the after meeting is that it gets rid of that portion of the audience which is not in sympathy and is a hindrance to close work.*

It enables us to get near to the inquirer and meet his immediate need. Many things that it is impossible to do in the general meeting are very easily done in the smaller meeting which follows it. Some workers are very anxious to have every one stay to the after meeting, but frequently it is very fortunate that all do not stay. The smaller gathering is not only easier to handle, on account of its size, but it is also more sympathetic and more in keeping with the purpose of soul saving which is now in view.

2. *The second advantage of the after meeting is that men are brought to an immediate decision for Christ.*

This advantage rises partly out of the first. In almost every wisely conducted evangelistic service there will be some who have not really decided for Christ, but who are on the verge of a decision. Of course some of those, if allowed to go home, will decide for Christ in the home; but there will be many others, who, unless the impressions are followed up then and there, will loose their interest before another meeting is held. There is great need in all soul-winning work that we strike while the iron is hot. A wise worker and one of much experience, recently wrote substantially as follows about a meeting which she had attended in the East: "The sermon was grand, the Holy Spirit was manifestly present in power, and I could not help feeling if some experienced person was only present to conduct an after meeting then and there, we should have had great results, but the benediction was pronounced and the students allowed to go to their rooms. We have been trying to follow up the work since, and many have come out positively, but we could have had much larger results, with much less labor on our part if an after meeting had been held at once." It would be difficult to put too much emphasis upon the after meeting.

II. How to conduct an after meeting.

1. *The first point of importance in the conduct of an after meeting is the announcement of the meeting.*

The number who attend the after meeting and the character of those who attend, will depend very much upon the announcement. The announcement should be very clear and definite so there can be no mistaking what is meant. The anouncement should also be earnest. If the announcement is indifferent, people will think that the after meeting is of little consequence, and therefore will not stay to it. If the announcement is earnest, the people will think that the minis ter or evangelist thinks the meeting is of some importance, and will be likely to think so also. The announcement should be given in a winning and attractive way; it should also be urgent, but in our urgency we should avoid the impression that we think that any Christian who does not stay to the after meeting is necessarily committing some great sin. Many Christians have good reasons why they cannot stay to the aftermeeting, and if we are indiscreet in our urgency in giving the invitation to it, they will either stay to the after meeting when they ought not, or they will go away with the morbid sense that they have done something wrong, or worse yet, we shall bring them under the condemnation of the irreligious people who go away, and thus injure the cause of Christ. Sometimes an indiscreet urgency in the invitation to the after meeting keeps people away from the first meeting. The way we put the invitation, even in seemingly insignificant matters, is oftentimes of great consequence. For example, if we say, "Now, if there is any one here to-night who is interested, we should be glad to have them stay to the after meeting"; this will cause some person who may be interested to think that probably he is the only one in the whole audience who is, and as few people like to be considered singular, he will not be likely to stay. If on the other hand we say, "We hope that every one here to-night with whom the Spirit is working will stay to the after meeting"; this will cause those who are somewhat interested to think, 'Well, I am not alone, there are others interested beside myself," and so they will be likely to stay to the after meeting.

We do well to put our invitation in such a way that those who are not wanted in the after meeting will not feel at liberty to stay. For example, there are those who crowd after meetings out of mere curiosity, and are a great hindrance. If possible the invitation should be so worded as to shut this class out. There are others who go to oppose the work. The invitation should be so put as to shut this class out. It will not be possible to do it altogether in whatever way the invitation is put, and if the invitation does not succeed in doing it, other means will sometimes have to be taken. There are a third class who are very angry if you deal with them personally, but if the invitation has been wisely put, when any one gets angry when you approach them personally you can call their attention to what was said in the invitation, and show them courteously that, by coming to the after meeting, they expressed a willingness to be dealt with.

2. *The second matter of importance in the conduct of an after meeting is as to where it shall be held.*

As a rule it is better to hold it in another room from that in which the general meeting is held. If the after meeting is held in the same room as the general service, when the invitation is given for the general audience to withdraw, many that might have stayed to the after meeting are carried out with the tide, whereas if the meeting is held in another room, they see the tide setting in there, and are carried in with it. Of course oftentimes there is no other room that is available, and the after meeting has to be held in the same room as the general service; and there are times when it is better to hold it in the same room even when another room is available.

If the meeting is to be held in another room, it is very desirable that it should be a room that the people have to pass as they go out. Workers should be posted at every door of this room, to invite and urge the people to go in as they pass. It is exceedingly important that these workers be wise men and women. I have heard workers shouting out invitations to this second meeting as if it were a side show to a circus. Oftentimes the best way to give the invitation is to quietly slip up beside the one that you wish to get into the after meeting, hold out your hand and engage him in a few moments' conversation, and almost imperceptibly draw him into the meeting. Gentleness and courtesy and winsomeness in this matter are of great importance.

When the interest is very deep, you can have the second meeting in another building. Have the singing begin at once, just as soon as the people begin to pass the door.

3. *Make much of prayer in the after meeting.*

The meeting should be begun with prayer. Wait until every one is in and all is quiet. Insist upon absolute silence, then have all the Christians engage in silent prayer. It is well to suggest to them objects of prayer, as for example, that they pray for those who have gone to their homes undecided, then that they pray for the presence and power of the Holy Spirit in the meeting, then for the unsaved who are in the room. Two or three or more audible prayers by men and women whom you can trust should follow. Do not take any chances at this point, and let any crank spoil the meeting. Unless you know your people very well, it is usually best to name those who shall lead in prayer. Of course one can trust the Holy Spirit to take charge of the meeting, and should, but this does not mean that we should not exercise a wise control over the meeting. There will also be places for prayer later in the meeting, but there should certainly be prayer at the opening. If it should turn out in any meeting that there are no unsaved people there, it is oftentimes well to give the entire meeting up to prayer. A few months ago it turned out in an after meeting that there were only two or three unsaved people in the whole audience. These were taken to another room to be dealt with, and then I urged it upon the people that there must be something wrong with us or with the work because there were so few coming to Christ. The Holy Spirit carried the message home, and then we got down on our knees before God in prayer. The next night, largely as an outcome of that season of prayer, we had a meeting of great power.

4. *When the opening prayers are over, it is oftentimes wise to explain the way of life in as plain and simple a manner as possible.*

This is especially important if there are few workers present to deal with individuals. After explaining the way of life, and the steps one must take to be saved then and there, an invitation can be given to those who are willing to take these steps at once. They should be asked to rise, hold up their hands, come forward, or in some other definite way express their desire to begin the Christian life.

5. *Find out just as early as possible in the meeting, where all the people present stand.*

Then you will know what to do next. It is frequently

desirable to take some sort of an expression in the general meeting, though this should usually be done in such a way as not to put those who are not Christians in an awkward position. Indeed, as a rule, the moment the last word of the sermon is uttered there should be an opportunity for decision. This opportunity may be given in a variety of ways. You may ask the audience to bow a few moments in silent prayer, insisting courteously but firmly that no one go out for a few moments. If the interest is deep enough, you can then ask all those who wish to be saved, or all who have made up their minds "now and here" to accept Christ as their personal Saviour, to surrender to Him as their Lord and Master, and to begin to confess Him as such before the world, to rise, or to "come forward and give me your hand," or come and kneel at the altar. If the interest hardly warrants that, you can ask all in the audience who are burdened for unsaved friends, or all who are anxious for the salvation of some friend in the audience, to rise, and when they have risen, invite all who wish to be saved "right now" to rise. It is not well usually in the general meeting to ask all Christians to rise, as this makes it awkward for the unsaved, and they may not come back again.

Another good way is to say, "We are going to sing a hymn, and I do not wish any one to go out until it is finished. The Holy Spirit is evidently working in this meeting (don't say this unless it is true), and any one moving about may distract some one who is on the verge of a decision for Christ. Now, while we are singing the second verse, let all who will accept Christ (don't say if any *one* will accept Christ) arise." Stop when the second verse is sung and call for decisions, and then sing the third and fourth in a similar way. If there is an altar in the church where you are preaching, it is often better to have them come to the altar. If there is no altar, you can have the front seats emptied and use them for an altar. A solo may often be used in place of the congregational hymn, but be sure of your soloist and the solo which has been selected. It is safer as a rule to select the solo yourself.

Still another way is to say as you close your sermon, "We are going to have a second meeting, and all those who have been converted here to-night, and who desire to enter the joy of the Christian life, are invited to remain. We also want every one who is interested in his soul's salvation, and all Christians, to stay to that second meeting—you cannot afford to go away." Once in the second meeting, there are a variety of ways of finding out where the people stand. If the interest is very deep, call at once for those who wish to accept Christ to rise and come forward. On other occasions ask all who have accepted Christ and know that they are saved, and are walking in fellowship with Him, to rise. Now you and your workers can readily see who the persons are with whom you ought to deal. They are for the most part those who are still seated. Next ask those who wish to become Christians to arise. It may be well to sing one or several verses as this is done. One and then another and then many at once will often rise.

Whenever it is possible, it is well to have now still a third room into which those who have risen and desire to become Christians shall go. Have a wise man in charge of this room until you get there yourself. Have him put one worker, and one only, with each inquirer. These workers should be trained for the work. Every church and mission should have a training class for this purpose. When you have gotten all you can into the inside room, turn the outside meeting into a meeting for testimony and prayer, which either you or some wise worker manages. It is a great advantage to have a choir leader who can do that. The unconverted ones who have not gone into the inside room can be gotten hold of personally in this testimony meeting or afterward. Do not have any holes anywhere in your net if you can avoid it.

Sometimes it is well in the second meeting to ask all who were converted after they were fifty to rise, and then those who were converted after they were forty, thirty, twenty, ten, before they were ten; then ask all who will accept Jesus "to-night" to rise, and then all who really desire to know the way of life. In other meetings, all who have been Christians fifty years may be asked to stand, then those who have been Christians forty years, thirty, twenty, and so on down. A good method to use occasionally in the second meeting is to ask all who were converted after they were fifty to come forward and gather about the platform, and then those who were converted after they were forty, and so on. This will gradually thin out those who are seated, and the unconverted will begin to feel that they are left in the minority, and it may lead them to desire to be saved also. Especially will this be true if a man sees his wife leaving him, or a son his mother. Some may say there is too much method or maneuvering in all this, but it wins souls and this is worth maneuvering for. Jesus Himself told us to be as wise as serpents (Matt. 10: 16), and again we are told that the children of this world are wiser in their generation than the children of light. Evidently Jesus would have us exercise all honest ingenuity in accomplishing His work, especially the work of soul-winning. The methods suggested will suggest others. The great purpose of all these methods is to get many to commit themselves, and to bring them to a decision to accept Christ.

6. *The most important part of the after meeting is the hand to hand dealing with individuals.*

There has already been a suggestion as to how this should be done, but the hand-to-hand work should not be limited to those who go into the third room. Trained personal workers should be scattered all over the meeting, each worker having his own assigned place, and feeling his responsibility for that section of the room. He should be on the lookout for persons with whom he can deal either during the testimony meeting, or after the formal meeting is over. These workers, however, should be instructed to obey at once any suggestion of the leader of the meeting. I have been in meetings where the leader requested absolute silence, but indiscreet workers would go on talking to those with whom they were dealing. I have heard other workers talking with an inquirer when there has been a call for prayer. Such irreverence does much harm.

7. *There should always be workers near the door of the meeting to follow out any one who goes out before the meeting is over.*

They should approach such a one personally and deal

with him about his soul. Much of the best work that is done is done with people who have become so deeply interested that they try to run away from the meeting, but are followed out by some wise worker. It may be necessary for the worker to follow the fugitive down the street. I knew of one case where a very successful worker tried to engage a young man in conversation, and he started off on a run. The worker followed, and having better wind than the runaway, caught him after two or three blocks. The young man was so amazed, and so awakened by the worker's earnestness, and afterwards so instructed by his wisdom, that he accepted Christ then and there on the street. This would probably not be a wise method under ordinary circumstances.

8. *A good use may be made of the testimony of saved people in the after meeting.*

As a rule, however, there should not be a call for testimonies until those who are ripe for hand to hand work are taken into another room. Great caution needs to be exercised in the use of testimony. In almost every community there are men and women who are always willing to give their testimony at the first opportunity, but who kill any meeting where they are allowed to speak. It may be that they have no sense, or it may be that there is something crooked in their lives, and their testimony simply brings reproach on the cause which they pretend to represent. You must manage somehow to keep these people silent. You need to be on your guard too, that the testimonies are not stereotyped or unreal. They should be short, to the point, real, and above all, in the power of the Holy Ghost. There is a special power in the testimonies of those who have been recently saved. It is always a great help to the young converts themselves to be trained to give their testimony.

It is well oftentimes to have the Christians testify as to the Scripture which led them to Christ, or into a deeper experience of Christ's saving power. Dr. Dixon gives the following description of what was done and said in an after meeting which he attended:

"As soon as quiet was restored, there was an earnest prayer for guidance. The leader then arose and said: 'We will now hear from as many as can speak in five minutes the Scriptures which God used in showing them the way of life. We want simply the Word of God without comment. Rise and speak distinctly, with a prayer that God will bless others through the truth as He has blessed you.' The first one to respond was a young woman who quoted with a clear voice: 'Him that cometh unto Me I will in no wise cast out.' The leader said: 'That invitation is also a promise; it implies that all who come to Christ He will receive, but it says very much more. He will receive and never cast out. There is in it saving and keeping power. It is the Scripture for those of you who are afraid that you may not hold out.' The next witness was a man of middle age, who said: 'He is able to save to the uttermost all who come unto God by him.' The leader: 'God is all-powerful, but you make Him able by accepting the Lord Jesus Christ, and this ability is based upon the fact that He ever liveth to make intercession for us.' Third witness: 'Come unto me all ye that labor and are heavy laden, and I will give you rest.' Leader: 'Do you want rest of heart? Come to Jesus for it now.' Fourth witness: 'Look unto me and be ye saved all ye ends of the earth.' Leader: 'Looking is not a long process. You can look as quick as a lightning flash; look this moment and live.' Fifth witness: 'There is therefore now no condemnation to them who are in Christ Jesus.' Leader: 'We who have accepted Christ need not fear the judgment day. Our case has been settled in the court of mercy where Jesus Christ is the Advocate.' Sixth witness: 'To as many as received Him to them gave He power to become the sons of God.' Leader: 'And if sons, then heirs, heirs of God and joint heirs with Christ. Will you not accept this rich inheritance through Christ this evening?' Seventh witness: 'The blood of Jesus Christ His Son cleanseth us from all sin.' Leader: 'Then do not try to cleanse yourself, and do not divide your trust between the blood and ordinances. The Blood is all-sufficient; accept Jesus Christ and the Blood cleanses at once.

" 'There is a fountain filled with blood,
Drawn from Immanuel's veins,
And sinners plunged beneath that flood,
Lose all their guilty stains.'

"Eighth witness: 'Believe on the Lord Jesus Christ and thou shalt be saved.' Leader: 'It does not say believe on Jesus, nor believe on Christ, nor believe on the Lord. Jesus means Saviour, and a Saviour from sin we need. Christ means the anointed one, the high priest and an intercessor, an advocate we need. Lord means Master, and the Master we need to rule our lives. You cannot accept Him as Saviour while you reject Him as Lord, nor can you follow Him as Lord while you reject Him as Saviour. His intercession is for those who accept Him as both Saviour and Lord. So you see, Paul preached to the jailer the full Gospel when he said, "Believe on the Lord Jesus Christ and thou shalt be saved." The little word *on* is very important; it does not say believe *about* the Lord Jesus Christ; you may believe all *about* Him without believing *on* Him. I believe much about Washington, Lincoln, and Grant, but I am not conscious of believing on either of them in the sense that I am depending upon them for anything. When your faith *about* Christ has been translated into faith *on* Christ, you are saved.' The invitation was then given, and a number came forward and gave the leader their hands, confessing Christ as their Saviour and Lord, the leader remarking that it was well to begin the Christian life with a handshake and pass it on to others."

9. *When any one has clearly and fully accepted Christ, insist upon an open confession of Christ.*

If it can be done without disturbing other workers, have them stand right up then and there and confess Jesus as their Lord, and their acceptance of Him. If the inquirer has been taken into an inside room, ask him out into the room where the general after meeting is going on, and have him give his confession there. Many a young Christian does not come out into the clear light for many days, if ever, because he is not shown the necessity of a public confession of Christ with his mouth. There is nothing more important for a young Christian's life than a constant confession of the Lord.

10. *Do not hold the general after meeting too long.*

Oftentimes it is well to tell the people in the first meeting that the after meeting will only be fifteen or twenty minutes long, or whatever you have decided upon. Many will be encouraged to stay by this, who would not think it possible to stay if it were to be a long meeting. When you have made a promise of this kind, be sure you keep it.

CHAPTER XV

CHILDREN'S MEETINGS

I. Importance.

No form of special meetings are of more importance than those which are intended for the purpose of reaching the children, bringing them to Christ, and building them up in Christ. They are important for many reasons.

1. *Because the conversion of children is important.*

The conversion of the children to Christ is a matter of the very first importance.

(1) The conversion of a child is important in the first place because children oftentimes die. Most people in Chicago die in childhood. For every one who dies between twenty and forty there are many who die between birth and twenty. So with very many of the children at any time upon the earth, they must be converted in childhood or pass into eternity unconverted. In spite of the large number of children's caskets that pass us in hearses, it is hard to bring people to realize how likely children are to die. We look at the white-haired man and say he is likely to die soon, but we look at the little child and think that child has many years before it. That is not at all sure. We have very rude awakenings from this dream. Mothers and fathers, do you realize that your children may die? Up quick, then, and lead them to Christ before that day comes. If you do not it will be the darkest day you ever knew, but if you have led them to Christ it will not be a dark day Lonely it will be, but not dark. Nay, it will be glorious with the thought that the voyage is over and the glory land reached quickly by one you love. Sunday School teachers, do you realize that any one of the boys or girls in the class you teach may die any day? Up, then, and win them to Christ as speedily as you may.

(2) The conversion of children is important, in the second place, because it is much easier to win a child to Christ than an adult. Dr. E. N. Kirk once said: "If I could live my life over again, I would labor much more among children." Children have no old prejudices to overcome as many grown people have. With the help of the Holy Spirit they are easily led to feel the great love of Christ in giving Himself to die for them, and when the simple story of His suffering and death is read and explained from God's Word, they believe it, and exercise saving faith, and there and then the Holy Spirit effects a change of heart. Mr. Spurgeon once said: "I could spend days in giving details of young children whom I have known and personally conversed with, who have given evidence of a change of heart," and he added, "I have more confidence in the spiritual life of such children whom I have taken into my church, than I have in the spiritual condition of adults thus received. I will go further and say that I have usually found a clearer knowledge of the Gospel and a warmer love toward Christ in the child convert than in the man convert. I may astonish you by saying that I have sometimes met with a deeper spiritual experience in a child of ten or twelve than in some persons of fifty or sixty. I have known a child who would weep himself to sleep by the month together under a crushing sense of sin. If you would know deep and bitter and awful fear of the wrath of God, let me tell you what I felt as a boy. If you want to know what faith in Christ is, you must not look to those who have been bemuddled by the heretical jargon of the times, but to the dear children who have taken Jesus at His word, and believed on Him, and therefore know and are sure that they are saved."

Every year that passes over our heads unconverted our hearts are less open to holy impressions. Every year away from Christ our hearts become harder in sin. That needs no proof. The practice of sin increases the power of sin in our lives. God and heaven and Christ and holiness lie very near childhood, but if the child remains away from Christ, every year they become farther and farther away. When I see a child walk into the inquiry room of a Sunday evening, I feel quite certain that if a worker of any sense gets hold of that child it is going to be converted; but when I see a man or a woman walk in there I do not feel at all as sure. The adult has become so entangled in sin, the mind has become so darkened by the error and skepticism that arise out of sin, there are so many complications added by each year, that the case of an adult is very difficult as compared with that of a child. The fact is, that, with very many, if they are not converted in childhood, they will never be converted at all. Fathers and mothers, that is true of the children in our homes. Sunday School teachers, that is true of the children in your Sunday School classes. It is now or never.

(3) The conversion of the children is important, in the third place, because converted children are among the most useful workers for Christ. They can reach persons who are inaccessible to every one else. They can reach their schoolmates and playmates, the Jewish children, the Catholic children, the children of worldly parents and infidels. They can bring them to Sunday School or to children's meetings, and to Christ. You and I cannot get close enough to them to show them how beautiful Jesus is, and what joy and blessing He brings. They can. Then they can reach their parents oftentimes when we cannot. They will not listen to us, but they will to their children. There was a rough, drunken gambler in Minneapolis, Minn. He often went by the mission door, but when a worker invited him in he repelled him with rude insults. But his child, about ten years old, was gotten into the Sunday School, and won for Christ. Then she began to work and pray for her drunken papa, and a cottage meeting was at last held in his wretched home. The father took down his overcoat to go to the saloon. Little Annie asked him if he would not stay to the meeting. He roughly answered, "No." 'Won't you stay for my sake, papa?" The man hung up his coat. The meeting began, and the man was surly and wished he was out of it. They knelt in prayer while he sat on the end of the sofa. One after another prayed. Then all were silent Then Annie's little voice was heard in prayer something like this: "God, save my papa." It broke the wicked man's heart, and then and there he accepted Christ. He

afterwards became a deacon in my church. When New Year's day came and many had testified for Christ, Annie arose and said: "Papa used to drink and mamma used to drink, grandpa used to drink, and grandma used to drink. But papa is a Christian now, and mamma is a Christian now, and grandpa is a Christian now, and grandma is a Christian now, and Uncle Joe is a Christian now, and auntie is a Christian now I guess we are all Christians down to our house now." But the little girl herself led the way. Wasn't the conversion of that child important? Many a hardened sinner and many a skeptic has been led to Christ by a child.

(4) The conversion of children is important because persons converted in childhood make the best Christians. If one is converted when he is old he has learned many bad tricks of character and life that have to be unlearned, and it is generally a pretty slow process. But when one is converted in childhood character is yet to be formed, and it can be formed from the beginning on right lines. If you wish to train a tree into a thing of beauty and symmetry you had better begin when it is young. If you want to form a character of Christlike symmetry and beauty you would better begin in childhood. That Christlike man of the olden time, Polycarp, who ended his life as a martyr at ninety-five, was converted at nine. That fine young man of the New Testament, Timothy, was brought up on Scripture from a babe. I rejoice with all my heart when an old broken-down drunkard is brought to Christ. It means so much. But it means so much more when a child is brought to Christ.

(5) The conversion of children is important, once more, because there are so many years of possible service before them. If one is to live to eighty, say, if converted at seventy there is a soul saved plus ten years of service. When the boy Polycarp was converted there was a soul saved plus eighty-six years of service. I think enough has been said to show that the conversion of the children is tremendously important, in fact, the most important business the Church of Christ has on hand. Surely it was well that Jesus said, "Take heed that ye despise not one of these little ones."

2. *Because many children will be brought to Christ in special meetings held in their interest, who will not be reached in any other way.*

It is a well proven fact that no other kind of meetings bring such definite results in the way of conversions as meetings held for the specific purpose of bringing the children to Christ.

II. When to hold children's meetings.

1. *In seasons of special revival interest.*

No revival is what it ought to be if a great deal of attention is not given to the children, and much prayerful effort put forth for their conversion. Whatever other meetings are held or omitted in times of special revival interest, meetings for children should not be omitted under any circumstances. Every pastor and evangelist should lay to heart the warning of our Master, "Take heed that ye despise not one of these little ones" (Matt. 18: 10).

2. *At summer conferences.*

At many summer conferences a great deal of attention is given to the children, with the most encouraging results; at other summer conferences the children are almost altogether neglected.

3. *At summer resorts.*

Children are found in great numbers at summer resorts. Oftentimes they have but little to do. It is frequently a rare opportunity to win them to Christ if wisely conducted meetings are held for their benefit. In England the services which are held upon the beach in summer have yielded remarkably encouraging results. The children gather there in great numbers.

4. *Regularly every week.*

About all that the average church does for the children is to have the Sabbath School services, and perhaps the Junior Endeavor meeting. This is not enough. There should be regular evangelistic services held for the children every week, especially in our city churches. In Newman Hall's church in London a children's meeting was begun which was conducted for many years every week. It began in the special revival services for children held by E. P. Hammond in London years ago. At one of these regular weekly children's meetings, I was told that a large share of the best workers in the church at that time had been originally converted during the revival services for children, and I saw from personal observation deep interest among the children still, and many were being constantly led to Christ.

III. How to conduct children's meetings.

1. *The first matter of importance is the arrangement of the children when they reach the appointed place of meeting.*

They should not be allowed to huddle together at will, but as they come in the door should be met by competent ushers, and seated in classes of four or five, with experienced Christian workers at the end of each class. There should first be a class of boys, then a class of girls. This will do very much toward preventing disorder during the meeting. The object of having a teacher at the end of the class is not merely to keep order, but that the teacher may deal personally with the children at the close of the service.

2. *Great care should be bestowed upon the singing.*

There should be a great deal of singing, for children love it, and the hymns should be bright and cheerful, and of a character that the children can understand. They should be taught the hymns verse by verse, and the meaning of the words of the hymn should be explained. Hymns setting forth God's love and the atoning death of Christ should be especially used. Children enjoy singing the same verse over and over again more and more heartily, under the conduct of an enthusiastic leader. In this way the truth is deeply impressed upon the heart, and will probably never be forgotten. A priest once said to a lady manager of an orphan asylum in Brooklyn, that they did not object to the religious lessons which they gave the children, but they did object to the hymns they taught them. "For," said he, "when once they have learned one of those hymns, it is very difficult for us to get them to forget it."

3. *Prayer is very important in the children's meeting.*

The prayer should be of such a character that the children can understand exactly what is meant, and there should often be prayers in which the children follow the leader sentence by sentence as he prays. This of course should not be done formally, but the children should be taught the meaning of the prayer and to offer it from the heart. It is necessary to teach children the purpose of prayer and to insist upon absolute attention and reverence while it is being offered.

4. *There should be a Gospel sermon which the children can understand.*

This sermon may contain some of the profoundest truths of the Gospel, but these truths should be expressed in words of which the children know the meaning.

(1) The sermon should be short; children were not made to sit still. A wise woman worker once said, "A boy has five hundred muscles to wriggle with, and not one to sit still with." There are a few rare men and women who can hold the attention of children for half an hour, or even an hour, I have seen it done; but for the average speaker to attempt to hold the attention of children more than fifteen or twenty minutes is positive cruelty.

(2) The sermon should be simple. This does not mean that it should be foolish, but the statements should be of such a character that the child takes in their meaning at once. There should be no long nor involved sentences; there should be no complicated figures of speech. But one who would preach to children must be very careful about his illustrations. If some of our speakers to children should question their audiences afterwards, as to what they had said, they would be astonished at the remarkable idea which the children had gained. One should be very careful to find out that the children really understand what he has said.

(3) The sermon should be full of illustrations. We do not mean that it should be nothing but a collection of stories; it should be a definite presentation of important truth with clearly stated points, but each one of these points should be illustrated so as to hold the attention of the child and fix it in its mind.

(4) The sermon should emphasize the following great and fundamental truths:

(a) That all men and all children are sinners, real sinners. Some people think of children as if they were angels; they are not, but sinners in the presence of a Holy God, and in their inmost heart they know this themselves. I do not know that I have ever seen deeper conviction than that which the Holy Spirit has awakened in the heart of a child.

(b) That Jesus died in our place. The most successful preachers to children are those who ring the changes on the doctrine of substitution. This truth should be illustrated over and over again in a great variety of ways. It is wonderful how children, whose minds haven't been corrupted by the errors of the day, grasp the great saving doctrine of the atonement.

(c) The need of a new heart. Regeneration is a big word, and a child will not understand it, but a child can understand what is meant by a new heart. Of course this will need explanation. I once asked a boy if he was saved, and he replied that he was. I asked him if he knew that he was, and he said he did. I asked him how he knew it, and he said because he had had a change of heart. I asked him how he knew he had had a change of heart. He said, "The other night when I was praying I felt a pain here" (placing his hand over his stomach). The boy had heard about a change of heart, and really thought that it was the change of the location of the heart from one part of the body to another, and that the pain he felt while praying was occasioned by this change in the location of his heart. The boy really had received a new heart, as he showed by years of devoted and active Christian service, but he had not understood the language used by those who spoke to him.

(d) That a new heart is God's gift in Jesus Christ.

5. *At the close of the service the children should be given an opportunity to decide for Christ.*

This opportunity may be given by having them stand, or hold up their hands, or in any other way the evangelist thinks wise; but every experienced worker knows that children go in crowds, and that if one child stands up other children are likely to follow, and one cannot safely take it for granted that every child who stands up knows what he is doing. It is well that the call for an expression be preceded by a season of silent prayer, and a very careful explanation made to the children what you propose to do, and what you want them to do. After a time of silent prayer, and also an explanation of what you want them to do in the time of silent prayer (never forget that children have to be taught line upon line, precept upon precept), go over your instructions again and again in different ways, until you are satisfied that you are understood.

6. *After the expression of a desire to become a Christian, there should be prayer for the children, and prayer in which the children who have taken the stand are instructed to follow.*

7. *When you are through dealing with the children in a body, have each teacher deal with her own class individually, making as clear as possible the way of life, and finding out definitely whether each child has accepted Christ, or will accept Christ.*

Each child who professes to accept Christ should be prayed with individually.

8. *Use children's tracts.*

Tracts can be secured with attractive covers, that the children will like to get. Tell the children beforehand that you are going to give each one who comes to the meeting a tract. Children will come a good ways for a bright tract. Be sure that the tracts contain the Gospel. Oftentimes it is well to read the tract to the children and preach upon it before you give it out, and then have them take the tract home, to fix the sermon in their minds.

9. *Many find the blackboard very useful in children's meetings.*

Children are oftentimes more easily reached through the eye than through the ear, and words or sentences written upon the board are more deeply impressed upon their hearts than those that are merely uttered to them. A few people have the gift of drawing well, but one can use the blackboard to advantage who cannot draw at all. Children are gifted with imagination, and if you tell them what your pictures are, they will understand, and it will do the work.

10. *Objects which the children can touch or even handle, are very useful as illustrating the truth.*

A person of any ingenuity can draw many lessons from a few candles and a tumbler of water, a magnet, and other objects that are easily secured. There are suggestive books upon object teaching for children.

11. *The use of the stereopticon will always draw a crowd of children.*

Children never tire of stereopticon pictures. If you can get children without the stereopticon, there will oftentimes be better results; for sometimes the children will be too much taken up with the pictures, but if you cannot get the children without using it, get the stereopticon. A bright little girl whose father uses a stereopticon a great deal was taken to a meeting for children where it was used. After a time she exclaimed, "I wish papa would show us more pictures and talk less." Nevertheless stereopticon services are oftentimes followed with abundant results in the conversion of children as well as adults.

12. *Be sure and bear in mind the purposes for which children's meetings are held.*

They are not held simply for the sake of amusing children. It is a poor use of time simply to amuse people. They are held, first, to convert the children, to lead them to a personal acceptance of Jesus Christ as their Saviour, to surrender themselves to Him as their Lord and Master, and to confess Him as their Lord before the world. Second, they are held in order that the children may be instructed in true Christian living, and in the fundamental truths of the Gospel.

13. *If the work among the children is to be really successful and produce permanent results, our dependence must be upon Bible truth, preached, or sung, or personally taught, in the power of the Holy Spirit.*

CHAPTER XVI

ADVERTISING THE MEETINGS

I. Importance.

It is of the utmost importance that wherever meetings are held they be properly advertised. Judicious advertising is important for three reasons:

1. *Because it gets people out to hear the Gospel.*

There is no hope of saving people unless they hear the Gospel, and they will not come and hear it unless they are informed that it is being preached. A mere general notice will not arouse their attention, but wise advertising will. The advertisement that gets a man out to hear the Gospel is just as important in its place as the sermon through which he hears the Gospel. The contempt in which some people hold all advertising is utterly irrational. Experience demonstrates that wise advertising has very much to do with the number of people who are reached and converted by the Gospel. I could tell from personal experience of many remarkable conversions that have resulted from judicious advertising.

2. *Advertising is important because it sets people to thinking.*

It is of the very highest importance to get people to thinking upon the subject of religion. The very simple reason why many people are not converted is because they give the subject of the claims of Christ upon them no attention whatever. It never enters their thoughts from one day's end to another. But a wise advertisement will arrest their attention and set them to thinking. It may bring up memories of childhood. It reminds them that there is a God. It tells them that Jesus saves. Some sentence in the advertisement may follow them for days, and result in their conversion to Christ. Instances could be multiplied of those who have never gone near the meeting advertised, but have been set to thinking and thus have been brought to Christ.

3. *It is important because of its direct converting power.*

Enough Gospel can be put in a single advertisement to convert anybody who notices it and will believe it. On every invitation card that goes out from the church of which the author is pastor is placed some pointed passage of Scripture, and many are those who have been won to Christ by the power of the truth thus set forth.

II. How to advertise.

1. *In your advertisements aim to reach the non-church goers.*

The church to-day is ministering largely to those who are already in attendance. A church that is truly Christian has the missionary spirit, and its first aim is to get hold of those who do not go to hear the Gospel. The church-goers will hear the Gospel anyhow, and our chief responsibility in our advertising work is to get the ear of those who are never found in the house of God. Theaters and saloons make every effort to get the attention of those who are not already patrons. These institutions do it in order to get their money and destroy their souls. How much more should the church do it in order to save them. Stores, papers and magazines offer special inducements to those who are not already their patrons; the church of Christ should do the same for a far higher purpose.

2. *Aim to set people to thinking.*

A commonplace advertisement does very little good, but an advertisement so phrased as to awaken the attention of those who see it and set them to thinking, accomplishes great good. Of course one ought not to stoop to anything which is in a true sense undignified, or grossly sensational, to awaken attention; but an advertisement may at the same time have proper dignity, and yet set forth the truth in such a striking way that even the godless cannot help but notice it. For example, a sermon was announced upon, "A Converted Infidel's Preaching." This part of the advertisement was in large black letters on a white background. At least one infidel came to find out what this infidel preached about. The converted infidel was Saul of Tarsus. What he preached about is found in Acts 9:20. That verse was the text of the sermon. The infidel mentioned was deeply impressed and went to the inquiry room, and two weeks after looked me up and told me that both he and his wife had accepted Christ. Several years before that a sermon had been preached on "A Bitter and Brilliant Infidel Converted." One of the leading daily papers was deeply interested as to who this converted infidel was, and sent for an outline of the sermon. Of course it was Saul of Tarsus, and the sermon was printed Monday with great letters running clear across the top of the page, "A Bitter and Brilliant Infidel Converted." Another sermon was announced on the subject, "Five Things That No Man Can Do Without." Tickets were scattered all over the city with the announcement of the subject upon them. Even the schools took it up, and the teachers discussed with their scholars what were the five things that no man could do without. The sermon was really a Bible Reading upon such texts as "Without holiness no man can see the Lord," "Without faith it is impossible to please him."

3. *In your advertisements, make much use of the Scripture that will convert.*

There are many who will read your advertisements who will not go to the church. Put enough Scripture on the advertisement to convert them.

4. *Advertisements of religious services should be well printed.*

They should be printed so they can be readily seen, and so that they will make an impression upon the mind. It is well oftentimes to have them printed in such a way that people will like to keep them as souvenirs, and thus they will go on doing their work for a long time.

5. *Use bulletin boards.*

(1) Every church should have one or more large bulletins standing out in front of the church constantly. On these announcements should be made of the services of the church, regular or special, from time to time. Something should always be upon the bulletin. The notice should be constantly changed so that people will be looking for something new. If there is no special service to be announced, a striking text of

Scripture can be put upon the bulletin. It is usually desirable to have these bulletins on feet so that you can move them from place to place.

(2) There should also be large bulletins in conspicuous places throughout the city, places where many cars or carriages pass. The anouncements upon these bulletins should be in such large letters that they can be read by people in the carriages or cars as they go by. One bulletin in a good place is worth ten in poor places. Make a study of locations for your bulletins.

(3) Secure wherever possible the use of the bulletin boards of theaters. There are oftentimes seasons of the year when the theaters are closed, and many theatrical proprietors will be willing to allow you the use of their bulletins, if not free, for a small compensation. Just the class of people you wish to reach will notice advertisements on these bulletins.

6. *Use the public bill boards of the city.*

This is a very successful way of advertising. Have your notices larger and more striking than those of others. Do not have too many words upon them, but big letters that can be read a block or more away. A very small body of Christians once used all the bulletin boards of Chicago with enormous notices, stated in a very striking way, about the coming of Christ. There was no notice at first as to where their meetings were to be held. Thousands of people in the city wondered what it all meant, and who put these notices up. The whole city was talking about the meaning of it. Reporters were sent here and there to find out who was back of it. When the meetings were held they were attended by large audiences. Unfortunately they had but very little to give the people when they got there, but as an advertisement it was a notable success. Of course these things cost money, but they usually bring in more than they cost. But cost however much they may, if they win souls for Christ, it pays.

7. *A large van with advertisements on all sides, driven up and down the thickly traveled streets, is a very useful and comparatively inexpensive form of advertisement.*

In connection with evangelistic meetings recently held in

Chicago a van eighteen feet long and ten feet high was covered with black cloth, on which was printed in white letters the announcement of the meetings and speaker. This was driven up and down the main thoroughfares and read by thousands. Many may say that this is undignified, but it serves to fill the church and bring men to Christ. It is better to sacrifice your dignity and fill your pews and save souls, than to keep your dignity and have an empty church and allow men to go down to hell.

8. *Transparencies are very useful and inexpensive as a means of advertising meetings.*

A transparency consisting of a wooden frame, say eighteen to twenty-four inches in length, and twelve inches high, with white cloth around the four sides on which are printed in black letters announcements of the meetings, can be made by almost anybody for a little cost. To the wooden bottom of the transparency, tallow candles are secured. When the candles are lighted, and the transparencies carried up and down the street, they will attract more people than the most artistic printed matter. The novelty of the thing is one of the strongest points in its favor. As many as possible of these transparencies should be sent out every evening. Sometimes it is well to organize the whole crowd of transparency bearers into a procession and send them through the more thickly populated part of the city. They may be laughed at, or even stoned, but what matters that if people are brought out to hear the Gospel and saved? I know personally of three conversions in two days from the transparencies that were carried up and down the streets of Chicago.

9. *Cards twelve by eighteen inches printed so that they can be read from the street are very useful, not only for special meetings, but to announce the regular services of the church or mission, and all kinds of special services.*

These should be handed around among the members of the church, or mission workers and their friends, to hang up in their windows. A man who placed one of these cards in his window sat behind the curtain of another window and watched results. It seemed as though almost every one who went by, men, women and children of all classes, stopped to read the sign through. Good is often accomplished by placing a pointed text in the window where people will read it. Many have been blessed by these texts. People are very ready to co-operate in this kind of work. A single church found several hundred persons in its membership who were willing to put these cards in their windows. When a large number of cards are noticed on different streets, they at once awaken comment on the part of the passers-by. They wonder what is going on, and go to the church to find out. Still larger cards, or better still, bulletins that are inexpensive, can be furnished to such members of the church as have stores. These bulletins can be placed out in front of the stores. They can be even used to advantage in private houses, where the houses stand in conspicuous places.

10. *Banners across the street attract attention.*

These, however, are very expensive, and should not be used unless it is in a place where very many people pass.

11. *Elevated cars and surface cars can be used to advantage for advertising purposes.*

We all know how many people read the advertisements that are seen in the elevated and other cars. This form of advertising, however, is very expensive, and if the city has been well placarded is unnecessary. If the great billboards are used all over the city it is doubtful of any one will see the advertisement in the cars that does not see it on the billboards.

12. *Small invitation cards should be used without stint.*

These should be handed out on the street corners, should be carried into houses, saloons, hotels, stores. It is well for the pastor on prayer-meeting night to have a supply of these tickets present, and before the meeting closes have them handed out to each individual, urging them to take them and give them out. The same method can be employed in other meetings. Very frequently when Mr. Moody was not getting the attendance at his services that he desired, he would have a large supply of tickets at one service, and have them dis tributed among the people to give out, and at the very next service, there would be a large increase in attendance.

13. *It is well sometimes to ticket a meeting, and allow no one to enter before a certain time without a ticket.*

This puts a premium on admission to the services, and people believe that it is something worth going to. Of course these tickets should be free, but people should be obliged to take some trouble to get them, to send a stamped envelope or call at a certain place to get them. If you do ticket a meeting, be sure and keep faith with the people. Never say no one will be admitted up to a certain hour without a ticket, and then let people in whether they have a ticket or not. The people who have taken the trouble to get a ticket will justly feel that they have been outraged.

14. *No other form of advertising is as good as personal invitation.*

Whatever else is done to advertise the meetings, be sure and get individuals to talk about the meetings to individuals, and to urgently invite them to come. There should be a systematic canvass of the entire neighborhood where meetings are held. The names and addresses of all non-church goers should be secured. Notices should be sent again and again to these non-church goers. They should be followed up by letters and postals. These things cost money, but these are the methods that are used by successful business houses in building up their business, and the church of Christ can afford to be no less active and earnest than a business house.

15. *Never forget the papers in your advertising.*

(1) First of all *make as much use as possible of the news columns of the paper.* Most newspapers are willing to assist to the utmost of their ability in pushing the work of any church that shows it is alive and aggressive. If notices and descriptions of meetings, and outlines of sermons, and other interesting matter is sent to them, they will publish it. They will often send reporters to the meeting if there is anything worth reporting. It is not fair to leave it to the papers to find out what is going on when it is more our interest than theirs

that is in hand. If you are not satisfied with the reporting of the newspapers by their own people, usually you can report the meeting yourself and they will accept your report if it is readable. Of course, if the newspapers get the idea that a man is trying to advertise himself, they will despise and ignore him, as they ought to, but if it is a legitimate making public of the work that he is at, the papers appreciate it. Many ministers and churches complain of not getting satisfactory reports from the newspapers, but they are more to blame than the newspapers. They think that the newspapers ought to know that they are alive and important, but newspaper men are very busy men and cannot be expected to know everything. They abuse the newspapers and then wonder why the newspapers do not support them.

(2) *Make use of the advertising columns of the newspaper.* This should not be done too generously, as it is not necessary, but an attractive advertisement should now and then be put in the amusement column. I say in the amusement column, for that is the column read by people looking for some place to go, by travelers and commercial men, by the very class which the church wishes to reach, and oftentimes fails to reach. A very large church that we know, whose audience used to fill only one floor, advertised a special evening service with a special subject, in the amusement column of the paper. The following Sunday evening the church was filled upstairs and down. There were perhaps 800 or 1,000 extra people present. The church kept up this special advertising for only a week or two, but the church has kept full from that day to this, though more than five years have passed.

16. *In your advertising never forget God.*

All your advertising will come to absolutely nothing unless God blesses it. His guidance should be sought as to how to advertise, and His blessing upon the advertisements that are sent out. A minister of the Gospel who found it difficult to get men to go out with the transparencies finally decided to carry them himself. As he went down one of the leading streets of the neighborhood, he did not enjoy the work, but he prayed that God would bless the transparency to the conversion of some one. The next night a man came to another member of the church and told him how he had been brought out to church by seeing the transparency at a certain point, and how he had been converted. This other member called the minister who had carried the transparency, and introduced him. The minister questioned him, and found out that it was undoubtedly by his transparency this young man had been attracted, as he stood upon the steps of a hotel. Thus he found that his prayer was answered. A few evenings after another young man told his story, and he had evidently been converted by means of the same transparency as it was carried back up another street. God is willing to bless everything we do, our advertising as well as our preaching, if we do it to His honor and under His guidance, and we should look to Him to thus definitely bless it.

CHAPTER XVII

CONDUCT OF FUNERALS

I. Importance of funeral services as a means of reaching men with the Gospel.

Funerals offer an excellent opportunity for getting hold of people and winning them to Christ. Many will attend a funeral service out of regard for the deceased or his family, who will not go to any other religious service. Atheists, Roman Catholics, and utterly irreligious people, are often seen at funeral services. It is a time when peoples' hearts are made tender by sorrow, and when men are solemnized by the presence of death and the nearness of eternity. He is a poor minister of Jesus Christ who does not seize upon such an opportunity for preaching the Gospel and bringing men to Christ. It was once the writer's privilege to conduct the funeral services of a man who up to a short time before his death had been an out and out infidel. His wife was a Roman Catholic. A little while before his death I had pointed him to Christ, and he had found forgiveness of sins, and had died rejoicing in the Saviour. As I stood by his casket, many of his old infidel friends were gathered around him. The opportunity was seized to preach the Gospel. The hearers were reminded of the long-standing infidelity of their friend, and then of how his infidelity had failed in the trying hour, and how he had found hope in Christ. As the sermon closed, I made an appeal to any who would then and there accept Christ as a Saviour. One man stepped forward, and reaching his hand across the coffin said, "I have been an infidel just as my friend who lies here, but I will now take Christ as my Saviour," and he gave me his hand upon it then and there. The wife of the man was also converted and united with our church and became a very faithful member.

II. How to conduct a funeral service.

Very few directions are needed as to the proper conduct of a funeral service. It should be conducted very much as any other Gospel service, with a special reference of course to the circumstances.

1. *It is important to have wisely selected music, rendered in the power of the Holy Spirit.*

One needs to be careful in regard to hymns sung at a funeral service. Some hymns that are supposed to be especially choice for such an occasion are sentimental trash. Hymns that are suitable for the funeral of a Christian are oftentimes not suitable for the funeral of an unconverted person. A good soloist who can sing effectively in the power of the Holy Spirit is a great help. A song properly rendered at such a time is likely to prove the means of some one's salvation. There is no place where a godless singer is more utterly out of place than at a funeral, and there is no place where a consecrated singer is more likely to be used of God.

2. *Great dependence should be placed upon the reading of the Word of God.*

Passages should be selected full of comfort for the sorrowing, but also passages that drive home to the minds of the unsaved the lesson of the occasion, namely, the nearness of death and the certainty of judgment. The Scriptures should not be read carelessly, but with the purpose of impressing their truth upon the hearts of the hearers. The presence and power of the Holy Spirit is greatly needed to this end.

3. *The prayer is of great importance.*

It should not be, as funeral prayers so often are, a mere attempt to say nice things, a smooth-flowing current of really meaningless words: it should be a real prayer, and a prayer of faith. There should be petition to God for His comfort to those who are in affliction; there should also be prayer that the lesson of the hour should not be forgotten, and direct prayer for the conversion of the unsaved who are present.

4. *Great wisdom and skill are necessary in the sermon or address.*

All unwarranted eulogy of the deceased should be

renounced utterly. If there have really been things worthy of imitation in the life of the one who has departed, it is well oftentimes to mention these, but to do it not for the sake of glorifying the dead, but for the sake of instructing the living, and leading them to the imitation in these respects, of the one who has gone. If the one who lies in the casket has been beyond question a true child of God, it is well to call attention to the fact, and emphasize how it pays at such an hour to have been a Christian. It is well sometimes to drive home the thought, that if some of those who were present were in the casket instead of the one who is there, there would have been no hope. There should always be a direct appeal to the unconverted to accept Christ then and there.

If the deceased was an unsaved man, there need be no personal reference to him at all. Of course there should be no pronunciation of doom upon him, but there should be a plain declaration of the one way of salvation through Jesus Christ. This truth should not be applied to the deceased, but to those who are still living. They can draw their own inferences as to the application, but experience proves that in such an instance if the work has been wisely done, the hearers will apply the truth to themselves instead of to the departed.

If there have been any special circumstances in connection with the death, these should be laid hold of as a point of interest that can be made to lead up to the truth. For example, if the deceased was clearly a true child of God, and some of the friends are Roman Catholics, it is well to emphasize the truth, backing it up well by Scripture, that the deceased has not gone to purgatory, but has departed to be with Christ. It was once my privilege to conduct the funeral of an earnest Christian woman, almost all of whose relatives were Roman Catholics. The church was filled with Roman Catholics. I made no reference whatever directly to the Roman Catholic church, but dwelt at considerable length upon the truth that those who have been saved by a living faith in Jesus Christ pass into no purgatory of torment, but pass at once to be with Christ. I did not use the word "purgatory." The Roman Catholic audience listened with great attention, and I have reason to think that the sermon was blessed of God. Of course if direct reference had been made to the fact that the woman had come out of the Roman Catholic Church and become a Protestant, there would have been trouble at once and no good accomplished.

5. *Always follow up your funerals by visitation.*

When you have been invited to conduct the funeral services of any person in a home, you have a right of entree into that home. Use it to the utmost. Take advantage of the circumstances. Deal with the people while their hearts are still tender with their great grief, and if possible lead them to the Saviour. Many an irreligious home has become a Christian home because a wise minister has followed up the advantage that has been given him by his being invited to conduct a funeral service there.

BOOK III

PREACHING AND TEACHING THE WORD OF GOD

CHAPTER I

HOW TO PREPARE A SERMON

There is no intention in this chapter of presenting an elaborate treatise on homiletics. It simply aims to give practical suggestions for the preparation of sermons that will win souls for Christ and edify believers.

I. First get your text or subject.

A great many neglect to do that, and when they get through preaching they do not know what they have been talking about, neither does the audience. Never get up to speak without having something definite in your mind to speak about. There may be exceptions to that rule. There are times when one is called on suddenly to speak, and one has a right then to look to God for subject matter and manner of address. There are other times when one has made full preparation, but it becomes evident when he is about to speak that he must take up some other line of truth. In such a case also, one must depend upon God. But under ordinary circumstances, one should either have something definite in his mind that he is to speak about, or else keep silent. It is true God has said in His Word, "Open thy mouth wide and I will fill it" (Ps. 81:10), but this promise, as the context clearly shows, has nothing whatever to do with our opening our mouth in speaking. Most people who take this promise as applying to their preaching, and who make their boast that they never prepare beforehand what they are going to say, when they open their mouths have them filled with anything but the wisdom of God. Christ did say to His disciples, "Take no thought how or what ye shall speak; for it shall be given you in that same hour what ye shall speak. For it is not ye that speak, but the Spirit of your Father which speaketh in you" (Matt. 10:19, 20); but this promise did not have to do with preaching, but with witnessing for Christ in circumstances of emergency and peril. In all cases of similar emergency, we have a right to rest in the same promise, and we have a right also to take the spirit of it as applying to our preaching. But if one has an opportunity to prepare for the services before him, and neglects that opportunity, God will not set a premium upon his laziness and neglect, by giving him a sermon in his time of need.

How shall we select our text or subject?

1. *Ask God for it.*

The best texts and topics are those which a man gets on his knees. No one should ever prepare a sermon without first going alone with God, and there definitely seeking His wisdom in the choice of a text or topic.

2. *Keep a text book.*

I do not mean the kind that you buy, but the kind that you make for yourself. Have a small book that you can carry in your vest pocket, and as subjects or texts occur to you in your regular study of the Word, or in hearing others preach, or in conversation with people, jot them down in your book. Oftentimes texts will come to you when you are riding on the street cars or going about your regular work. If so, put them down at once. It is said that Ralph Waldo Emerson would sometimes be heard at night stumbling around his room in the dark. When his wife would ask him what he was doing he would reply that he had a thought and he wanted to pin it. Oftentimes when you are reading a book, a text will come to you that is not mentioned in the book at all. Indeed, one of the best ways to get to thinking is to take up some book that stimulates thought. It will set your own mental machinery in operation. Not that you are going to speak on anything in that particular book, but it sets you to thinking, and your thought goes out along the line on which you are going to speak. Very often while listening to a sermon, texts or subjects or sermon points will come to your mind. I do not mean that you will take the points of the preacher, though you may sometimes do that if you will thoroughly digest them and make them your own, but something that he says will awaken a train of thought in your own mind. I rarely hear a man preach but his sermon suggests many sermons to me.

Put but one text or subject on a page of your text book. Then when points or outlines come to you jot them down under the proper text or subject. In this way you will be accumulating material for future use. After a while texts and topics and outlines will multiply so rapidly that you will never be able to catch up with them, and will never be at a loss for something to preach about.

3. *Expound a book in order.*

Take a book of the Bible and expound it. You should be very careful about this however, or you will be insufferably dry. One of the best preachers in an eastern State undertook to expound one of the long books of the Bible. He made it so dry that some of his congregation said they were going to stay away from church until he got through that book, they were thoroughly tired of it. Study the masters in this line of work; men like Alexander Maclaren, William H. Taylor, and Horatius Bonar. F. B. Meyer's expositions on Abraham, Jacob, Elijah, Moses, etc., are very suggestive.

4. *Read the Bible in course, and read until you come to a text that you wish to use.*

This was George Muller's plan, and he is a safe man to follow. He was wonderfully used of God. When the time drew near to preach a sermon, he would take up the Bible and open it to the place where he was reading at that time, first going down upon his knees and asking God to give him a text, and then he would read on and on and on until he came to the desired text.

II. Find your points.

I do not say make your points,—find them, find them in your text, or if you are preaching on a topic, find them in the various texts in the Bible that bear upon that topic. It is desirable often to preach on a topic instead of on a single text. Never write a sermon and then hunt up a text for it. That is one of the most wretched and outrageous things that a man who believes that the Bible is the Word of God can do. It is simply using the Word of God as a label or endorsement for your idea. We are ambassadors for Christ, with a message. Our message is in the Word of God, and we have no right to prepare our own message, and then go to the Word of God merely to get a label for it.

How shall we find our points?

1. *By a careful analysis of the text.*

Write down one by one the points contained in the text. Suppose for example your text is Acts 13: 38, 39:

"Be it known unto you therefore, men and brethren, that through this man is preached unto you the forgiveness of sin, And by him all that believe are justified from all things, from which ye could not be justified by the law of Moses."

By an analysis of the text, you will find the following points taught in it:

(1) Forgiveness is preached unto us.

(2) This may be *known* (not merely surmised, or guessed, or hoped, or believed.

(3) It is known by the resurrection of Christ (this comes out in the "therefore" and the context). Forgiveness is not a mere hope, but a certainty resting upon a solid and uncontrovertible fact. The one who here speaks had seen the risen Christ.

(4) This forgiveness is through Jesus Christ. In developing this point, the question will arise and should be answered, How is forgiveness through Jesus Christ?

(5) Every one who believeth is forgiven. Under this point there will be four special points:

(a) He *is* forgiven (not *shall* be).

(b) *Every one* that believeth is forgiven (R. V).

(c) He is forgiven *all* things.

(d) The meaning of justified.

2. *Ask questions about the text.*

For example, suppose you take Matt. 11: 28 as a text:

"Come unto me, all ye that labour and are heavy laden, and I will give you rest.'

You might ask questions on that text as follows:

(1) Who are invited?

(2) What is the invitation?

(3) What will be the result of accepting the invitation?

(4) What will be the result of rejecting the invitation?

One of the easiest and simplest ways of preaching is to take a text and ask questions about it that you know will be in the minds of your hearers, and then answer these questions. If you are preaching upon a subject, you can ask and answer questions regarding the subject. Suppose, for example, that you are to preach upon the subject of the new birth; you could ask the following questions and give Bible answers to them, and thus prepare an excellent sermon:

(1) What is it to be born again?

(2) Is the new birth necessary?

(3) Why is it necessary?

(4) What are the results of being born again?

(5) How can one be born again?

If you answer the questions that suggest themselves to your own mind, you will probably answer the questions that suggest themselves to the minds of others. Imagine your congregation to be a lot of interrogation points. Take up their questions and answer them, and you will interest them.

3. *If you are going to preach upon a topic, go through the Bible on that topic and write down the various texts that bear upon it.*

As you look these texts over, they will naturally fall under different subdivisions. These subdivisions will be your principal points. For example, suppose you are going to preach on "Prayer." Some of the passages on prayer will come under the head of "The Power of Prayer"; that can be your first main point. Others will come under the head of "How to Pray"; that will be your second main point, with doubtless many subordinate points. Other passages will come under the head of "Hindrances to Prayer," and this will make your third main point.

III. Select your points.

After finding your points, the next thing is to select them. You will seldom be able to take up all the points that you find in a text, or upon a topic, unless you preach much longer than the average congregation will stand. Few ministers can wisely preach longer than thirty or forty minutes.

To a person just beginning to preach, twenty minutes is often long enough and sometimes too long. At a cottage meeting fifteen minutes is certainly long enough, and usually too long. The more you study a subject the more points you will get, and it is a great temptation to give the people all these points. They have all been helpful to you, and you wish to give them all out to them, but you must bear in mind that the great majority of your congregation will not be so interested in truth as you are. You must strenuously resist the temptation to tell people everything you know. You will have other opportunities to give the rest of the points if you give well the few that you now select; but if you attempt to tell all that you know in a single sermon, you will never have another chance. In selecting your points, the question is not which points are the best in the abstract, but which are best to give to your particular congregation, at this particular time. In preaching on a given text it will be wise to use certain points at one time and certain other points at another time. The question is, which are the points that will do the most good and be the most helpful to your congregation *on this special occasion.*

IV. Arrange your points.

There is a great deal in the arrangement of your points. There are many preachers who have good points in their sermons, but they do not make them in a good order. They begin where they ought to end, and end where they ought to begin. What may be the right order at one time may not be the right way at another time. There are, however, a few suggestions that may prove helpful:

1. *Make your points in logical order.*

Put those first that come first in thought. There are many exceptions to this rule. If our purpose in preaching is not to preach a good sermon but to win souls, a point will oftentimes be more startling and produce more effect out of its logical order than in it.

2. *Do not make your strongest points first and then taper down to the weakest.*

If some points are weaker than others, it is best to lead

along up to a climax. If a point is really weak, it is best to leave it out altogether.

3. *Put that point last that leads to the important decision that you have in view in your sermon.*

It may not in itself be the strongest point, but it is the one that leads to action; therefore put it last in order that it may not be forgotten before the congregation are called upon to take the action that you have in mind.

4. *Give your points in such a way that the first leads naturally to the second, and the second to the third, and the third to the fourth, etc*

This is of great importance in speaking without notes. It is quite possible to so construct a sermon that when one has once gotten well under way everything that follows comes so naturally out of what precedes it that one may deliver the whole sermon without any conscious effort of memory. When you have selected your points and written them down, look at them attentively and see which point would naturally come first, and then ask yourself which one of the remaining points this would naturally suggest. When you have chosen the two, in the same way select the third, and so on.

V. Plan your introduction.

One of the most important parts of the sermon is the introduction. The two most important parts are the introduction and conclusion. The middle is of course important; do not understand me that you should have a strong introduction and conclusion and disregard all that lies between, but it is of the very first importance that you begin well and end well. In the introduction you get the attention of the people; in the conclusion you get the decisive results; so you should be especially careful about these. You must catch the attention of people first of all. This you should do by your first few sentences, by the very first sentence you utter if possible. How shall we do this? Sometimes by a graphic description of the circumstances of the text. Mr. Moody was peculiarly gifted along this line. He would take a Bible story and make it live right before you. Sometimes it is well to introduce a sermon by speaking of some interesting thing which you have just heard or seen—some incident that you have read in the paper, some notable picture that you have seen in a gallery, some recent discovery of science. In one sermon that I often preach, and that has been used of God to the conversion of many, I usually begin by referring to a remarkable picture I once saw in Europe. I start out by saying, "I once saw a picture that made an impression upon my mind that I have never forgotten." Of course everybody wants to know about that picture. I do not care anything about the picture; I only use it to secure the attention of people and thus lead directly up to the subject. If you have several good stories in your sermon, it is wise to tell one of the very best at the start. Sometimes a terse and striking statement of the truth which you are going to preach will startle people and awaken their attention at the very outset. Sometimes it is well to jump right into the heart of your text or subject, making some crisp and striking statements, thus causing everybody to prick up their ears and think, "Well, I wonder what is coming next."

VI. Illustrate your points.

Illustrate every point in the sermon. It will clinch the matter, and fasten it in a person's mind. Think up good illustrations, but do not over-illustrate. One striking and impressive illustration will fasten the point. More will be said about illustrations in a future chapter.

VII. Arrange your conclusion.

How shall we conclude a sermon? The way to conclude a sermon is to sum up and apply what you have been saying. One can usually learn more as to how to close a sermon by listening to a lawyer in court than he can by listening to the average preacher in a pulpit. Preachers aim too much at delivering a perfect discourse, while a lawyer aims at carrying his case. The sermon should close with application and personal appeal. It is a good thing to close a Gospel sermon with some striking incident, an incident that touches men's hearts and makes them ready for action. I have often heard men preach a sermon, and right in the middle they would tell some striking story that melted and moved people, then they would go on to the close without any incident whatever. If they had only told the story at the close, the sermon would have been much more effective. It would have been better still if they had had that moving story in the middle, and another just as good or better at the close.

A true sermon does not exist for itself. This, as has already been hinted, is the great fault with many of our modern sermonizers. The sermon exists for itself as a work of art, but it is not worth anything in the line of doing good. As a work of rhetorical art it is perfect, but as a real sermon it is a total failure. What did it accomplish? A true sermon exists for the purpose of leading some one to Christ or building some one up in Christ. I have heard people criticise some preachers, and say that they broke nearly all the rules of rhetoric and of homiletics, and that the sermon was a failure, when the sermon had accomplished its purpose and brought many to the acceptance of Christ. Again, I have heard people say, "What a magnificent sermon we have just heard!" and I have asked, "What good did it do you?" and they would say, "I do not know as it did me any good." I have further asked, what good it did any one else, what there was in it that would particularly benefit any one. It was a beautiful sermon, but it was a beautiful fraud. A few years ago a well-known professor of homiletics went to hear Mr. Moody preach. He afterwards told his class that Mr. Moody violated every law of homiletics. Perhaps he did, but he won souls to Christ by the thousands and tens of thousands, more souls, probably, in one year than that professor of homiletics ever won to Christ in his whole lifetime. A scientific angler will get a fishing rod of remarkable lightness and elasticity, a reel of the latest pattern, a silk line of the finest texture, flies of the choicest assortment, and he will go to the brook and throw out his line with the most wonderful precision. The fly falls where he planned that it should, but he does not catch anything. A little boy comes along with a freshly-cut willow stick for a rod, a piece of tow string for a line, a bent pin for a hook, and angle worms for bait. He throws out his line without any theoretic knowledge of the art and pulls in a speckled trout. The boy is the better fisher. The man has a perfect outfit, and is wonderfully expert in throwing his line, but he does not catch anything. A good deal of our pretended fishing for men is of the same character. Let us never forget that we are fishers for men, and our business is to catch men alive for Christ. Let us not try to save our sermons, but to save men's souls.

VIII. Think your sermon out closely.

I would not advise you to write your sermons out, because what you have written might afterwards enslave you, but I would advise you to do a great deal of writing, not for the sake of preaching what you have written, but for the sake of improving your style. Most emphatically would I advise you never to read a sermon. The more preachers I listen to, the more firmly convinced do I become that a sermon ought never to be read. Of course, there are advantages in writing the sermon out and reading it, but they are counterbalanced many times over by the disadvantages. I once heard a man deliver an address, who said before beginning, that as he wished to say a great deal in a very short time, he had written his address. It was a magnificent address, but he had no freedom of delivery, and the audience did not get it at all. As far as practical results were concerned, it would have been a great deal better if he had said less and spoken without his manuscript. Furthermore, it is not true that a man can say more without a manuscript than he can with it. Any one who really has a call to preach can train himself to speak just as freely as he writes. He can be just as logical. He can pack his sermon as full of matter and argument. His style can be just as faultless. It will be necessary, however, that he should think out closely beforehand just what he is going to say. After thinking your sermon all out carefully, when you come to preach, your mind will naturally follow the lines along which you have been thinking. You set the mental machinery going, and it will go of itself. The mind is just as much a creature of habit as any part of our body, and after one has thought consecutively and thoroughly along a certain line, when he takes up that thought again his mind naturally runs in the grooves that have been cut out

CHAPTER II

PREPARATION AND DELIVERY OF BIBLE READINGS

I. Different kinds of Bible readings.

There are many different kinds of Bible readings, and it is well to bear in mind the distinctions between them.

1. *The Whole Bible Topical Bible Reading.*

By this we mean the Bible reading that takes up some topic and goes through the whole Bible to find its texts for the study of the topic. For example, if the Bible reading is on the subject, "The Power of Prayer," passages for the illustration and exposition of the subject are taken from any book in the Bible where they are found.

2. *The Book Topical Bible Reading.*

By this we mean the taking up of a topic as it is treated in a single book in the Bible; for example, the Holy Spirit in John's Gospel, or the Believer's Certainties in the First Epistle of John. These subjects are handled simply as they are treated in these individual books.

3. *The Chapter Topical Bible Reading.*

In this, the subject is handled simply as it is found in a single chapter in the Bible; for example, the Freedom of the Believer in Rom. viii; or, the Priceless Possessions of the Believer in Phil. iv; or, the Glory of the Believer in 1 John v; or, Christ as seen in 1 John ii.

4. *The General Survey of a Book Bible Reading.*

In this form of Bible reading there is a rapid survey of the salient facts or great truths of some book in the Bible.

5. *The General Survey of a Chapter Bible Reading.*

This varies from the preceding one, in that a single chapter is considered instead of an entire book.

6. *The Running Commentary Bible Reading.*

7. *The Mutual Help Bible Reading.*

II. The choice of subjects.

The first matter of importance in the construction of Bible readings is the choice of subjects. The following suggestions will help in this choice of subjects:

1. *There are some great subjects that every pastor and teacher and evangelist should take up, such as the following:*

(1) The Power of the Blood of Christ.
(2) The Power of the Word of God.
(3) The Power of the Holy Spirit.
(4) The Power of Prayer.
(5) How to Pray Effectually.
(6) Justification.
(7) The New Birth.
(8) Sanctification.
(9) God's Plan for Every Believer's Life.
(10) Assurance.
(11) Faith.
(12) Repentance.
(13) Love.
(14) Thanksgiving.
(15) Worship.
(16) Future Destiny of Believers.
(17) Future Destiny of Impenitent Sinners.
(18) The Second Coming of Christ.
(19) Fulfilled Prophecies.

2. *Go through Bible Text Books and Concordances noting subjects for Bible Readings.*

3. *Get suggestions from suggestive books of Bible Readings.* For example, Inglis' "Pegs for Preachers and Points for Christian Workers." Do not adopt these plans outright, but simply get suggestions.

4. *Keep a blank book and note down such subjects as occur to you from time to time.*

5. *Get your subject for the meeting immediately in hand, by prayer.*

III. The getting together of material for Bible readings.

Having chosen your subject, the next thing to do is to get your material. This can be done in the following way:

1. *Look up in the Concordance the passages having the word or synonymous words in it.*

Suppose, for example, that the subject is "The Power of Prayer"; look up passages in the concordance under the words pray, prayer, intercession, supplication, ask, cry, call, and synonymous words. Some of these passages you will reject at once; many will not relate to prayer at all; others will relate to prayer, but not to the power of prayer; other passages you will note, to be used or rejected later. It will save time, if, instead of writing the passages down on first going through the concordance, you mark them by some sign on the margin of the concordance.

2. *Look up the subject and related subjects in your topical text book.*

Suppose, for example, the subject in hand is "The Power of the Blood"; look up passages under the following subjects: Reconciliation, Atonement, Redemption, Death of Christ.

3. *Look up the subject and related subjects in the book, "What the Bible Teaches."*

4. *In your general Bible study be always on the watch for passages bearing on the subjects upon which you intend to teach.*

There are many passages which bear upon a subject which you will find neither in a concordance nor text book; but if you study your Bible with an alert mind, these passages will be noticed by you and can be jotted down as you come to them.

5. *Put on your thinking cap and see if you cannot call to mind passages on the subject in hand.*

Sometimes it is well to construct a Bible reading absolutely without reference to concordance or text book. Of course this will be impossible for one who has not a good general knowledge of the Bible, but a Christian worker should always be growing into a walking concordance and Bible text book.

IV. The selection and arrangement of material

1. *Having gotten your material together, see what you can dispense with, and strike it out at once.*

The following four points will be helpful in the exclusion of material:

(1) Substantially the same material in different forms.

(2) Comparatively unimportant material.

(3) Material not adapted to the needs of the congregation for which you are preparing.

(4) Material about which you are uncertain.

2. *Form your principal divisions and arrange your remaining material under them.*

When you have excluded all the material that you can dispense with, look carefully at the material remaining. As you look at it, it will begin to classify itself. Some of it will fall under one division and some under another. When you have obtained your main divisions, look at the material in each division, and this oftentimes will begin to arrange itself in subdivisions.

3. *Get your divisions in the best possible order, and the subdivisions under them also in the best order.*

The following suggestions will help in this:

(1) Bring together points that naturally go together.

(2) As far as possible have each point lead naturally up to the next point.

(3) When possible, have a climax of thought with the strongest point last.

(4) Put the points that lead naturally to decision and action last.

V. The delivery of the Bible reading.

1. *Sometimes give the passages out to others to read.*

(1) Write them out on slips of paper and hand them out. In such a case, be sure that those who take the passages will really find them and read them in a clear tone. Have them stand up to do it unless the audience is very small.

(2) Call the passages off, and have those who take them call them out after you. If two take the same passage, say which of the two shall have it.

2. *Oftentimes read the passages yourself.*

In order to do this you will have to acquire facility in the use of your Bible, but this comes readily with practice. Some find it helpful to write in red ink in their Bible at the close of the first passage where the next one is to be found, and at the close of the second where the third is to be found, etc. If this is done, an index should be made on the fly-leaf of the Bible of subjects, and of the first text under a subject. When the same text comes in a number of Bible readings, use various colored inks, or number the marginal text that follows it, so that you will know which applies to the particular subject in hand.

CHAPTER III

ILLUSTRATIONS AND THEIR USE

Nothing goes further toward making an interesting and effective speaker than the power of illustration. All preachers who have been successful in reaching men have been especially gifted in their power of illustration. Much of the power of Spurgeon, Moody and Guthrie lay in their power of apt and impressive illustration.

I. Their value.

1. *To make truth clear.*

No matter how clearly an abstract truth is stated, many minds fail to grasp it unless it is put in concrete form. Ministers are probably better able to grasp abstract truth than any other class of people, and yet I have noticed that even they, in order to understand truth, need to have it illustrated in concrete form. It was once said of a certain minister by one of his parishioners, "He is a remarkable man: he is so profound that I cannot understand him." This was said in honest admiration and not as a criticism, but obscurity is not a mark of profundity. It is possible to take the profoundest truth and make it so plain and simple that a child can understand it. Obscurity is rather a mark of intellectual weakness than of intellectual power, for it requires brains to make a profound truth clear and simple. But nothing will go further to make clear a truth which is of difficult statement and profound, than the skillful use of illustrations

2. *To impress the truth.*

It is necessary in a public speaker that he not only make the truth clear, but that he impress it upon his hearers. A truth may be so stated as to be clearly understood, and yet make but little impression upon the mind. There is perhaps nothing that will do more to impress the truth upon the mind, than the wise use of illustrations. Take for example Rom. 1:16:

> "For I am not ashamed of the Gospel of Christ; for it is the power of God unto salvation to every one that believeth; to the Jew first, and also to the Greek."

This verse may be clearly understood and yet make little impression upon the mind of the hearer, until you tell the story of some poor degraded wretch who has been wonderfully saved by the Gospel. Then the truth is not only understood but impressed upon the mind.

3. *To fasten the truth.*

How often you have heard a sermon, and the only thing that fastened itself in your memory was the illustration. You cannot forget an illustration, and with the illustration you remember the truth which it was used to illustrate.

4. *To attract and hold attention.*

There is little use in talking to people unless you have their attention. Nothing is more effective in accomplishing this object than the apt use of illustrations.

5. *To rest the mind.*

If you talk continually for twenty minutes without an illustration, people begin to get very tired. Most people are not used to thinking consecutively for twenty minutes, and when you require them to do so without giving an illustration to rest and refresh the mind, they become very weary; but if here and there you drop in a good illustration, it serves to rest the mind. A two hours' sermon by a man successful in illustration will tire you less than a ten minutes' sermon by others. I once heard a man talk two hours to children. He held their attention spell-bound from beginning to end, and they did not seem to be tired at the end, but would have liked to have had him gone on. The whole secret of it seemed to be that he had marvelous power of illustration. When you find that your audience is growing tired or listless, drop in an illustration. This was Mr. Moody's constant practice. When he found his audience was heavy or getting restless, he would bring in one of his best stories out of his inexhaustible fund of anecdotes.

II. Classes of illustrations.

1. *Biblical illustrations.*

That is, incidents from the Bible and pictures of Bible scenes. Christ made much use of this kind of illustration. There is reason to believe that it is the very best method of illustrating a sermon. One of Mr. Moody's greatest gifts was his power to make a Bible incident live before you; Zaccheus, the woman who was a sinner, the woman with an issue of blood, and many other Bible persons, became living, breathing beings in whom your deepest interest was aroused. In order to acquire this gift, study Bible incidents carefully, then write them out; study them over and over again and re-write them; tell these incidents to others, especially to children; endeavor to make them as living and interesting as you possibly can. The power to do this will grow rapidly. About the only genius there is in it is the genius of hard work. That is true of almost any form of genius. There is scarcely anything that a man cannot accomplish if he only puts his mind to it. Hard work will accomplish almost anything. If you are going to gain this power of Biblical illustration, you must try and try and try again. Never be discouraged. You can certainly cultivate this faculty if you only work hard enough.

2. *Incidents from your own experience.*

There is power in an incident that happened in your own experience, that there is not in an incident which you have taken from somebody else. There is also great danger in the use of this class of illustrations; the danger is that you will make yourself too prominent. One has to be on constant guard against that. Unless one is very careful, he will soon find himself parading himself, his excellences and wisdom and achievements. It is a very subtle snare. In using these incidents from your own experience, you must put yourself in the background just as far as possible. Cases are not rare where the imagination, in the use of incidents, has grown to such an extent that workers have been found borrowing incidents from the experiences and lives of others, and transferring them to their own experience. Within the past month I have received information of one who is going up and down the country telling of things which are known to have happened in the life of Mr. Moody, as though they had happened in his own life. There is danger too that as you repeat a story again and again it will grow in its proportions, and at last there will be little likeness between the incident as you tell it and the event as it really occurred. And yet you will yourself get to believe, unless you are scrupulously truthful, that it actually happened that way. It may not be that "all men are liars," but most story tellers get to be liars unless they are on their guard. When it is once found out that a man is given to exaggeration (lying), and it will always be found out sooner or later, his usefulness is at an end.

3. *Anecdotes.*

Almost every one is interested in a story. The great power of one of the best-known after-dinner speakers in our country lies in his power to tell a good story. Lawyers and politicians and platform speakers generally, make a large use of the anecdote in their speeches. Preachers of the Gospel do well to make use of the same form of illustration. Anecdotes may not be as dignified as illustrations from science and poetry, but they are more effective, and effectiveness is what the true preacher is aiming at. There is, however, great danger that the matter of story telling be much overdone. One hears sermons which are simply a string of anecdotes, and after a while this becomes disgusting to an intelligent hearer.

4. *History.*

Illustrations from history have the advantage of dignity as well as forcefulness. The question is often asked me by young men preparing for the ministry and evangelistic work, "What do you think a man ought to study outside the Bible?" and I always advise them, whatever else they study, to study history. It is a most useful branch of knowledge in itself, but is of special value to the public speaker. Very few people know much about history, and if you can bring forward from history well-chosen incidents, both the truth and the illustration will be interesting, instructive and effective. It serves furthermore to awaken the confidence of the people in the speaker. An argument from authentic history is one of the most unanswerable of arguments.

5. *Illustrations from science.*

The natural sciences afford many beautiful and suggestive illustrations. Striking and impressive illustrations of Bible truth can be found in astronomy, botany, chemistry, geology, physics, and other natural sciences. But this is a form of illustration in the use of which one needs to exercise great care. Be very careful that your illustration illustrates. I have heard scientific illustrations used when the illustration needed more explanation than the truth it was intended to illustrate. Be very careful that your science is correct. What is considered scientific knowledge to-day is likely to be found to be scientific error to-morrow. I have heard much scientific falsehood used in illustrating sermons. Do not use exploded science to illustrate Gospel truth. One great fault with the use of scientific illustrations is, that the average preacher is likely to accept a scientific doctrine just about the time the scientific world gives it up.

6. *Illustrations from the poets.*

An apt quotation from the poets often serves to illuminate and fix the truth. These are very easy to get, for there are excellent collections of classified quotations from the poets.

7. *Illustrations by visible objects.*

It is sometimes well to use objects, not only in talking to children, but to grown-up people as well. For example, Rev. E. P. Hammond makes a very successful use of the magnet and different kinds of nails; small nails, large nails, straight nails, and crooked nails, in illustrating the doctrine, "I if I be lifted up from the earth will draw all men unto me."

III. How to get illustrations.

1. *Be on the lookout for them.*

Cultivate the habit of watching for thoughts, watching for texts, watching for points, and watching for illustrations; in other words, go through the world with your eyes and ears open. One of the greatest faults in the training of children in the past has been that we have not trained the child's faculty of observation. Cultivate your own power of observation. Henry Ward Beecher was a striking example along this line. He was one of the most gifted men in the power of illustration. Wherever he went, he was always on the lookout for something with which to illustrate the truth. He would talk with all classes of men and try to get from them illustrations for his sermons. James A. Garfield was another example of the same thing. One day he was walking down a street in Cleveland, Ohio. He heard a strange noise coming out of the basement of a building he was passing. He said to the friend who was with him, "I believe that man is filing a saw. I never saw a saw filed, I am going down to see how he does it." Spurgeon was a most illustrious example. He not only went through the world with his own eyes open, but it is said that he kept three or four men in the British Museum all the time looking for illustrations for him. The one who would be a mighty preacher to men must associate much with men.

2. *Keep a book of illustrations.*

Take this book with you wherever you go. Whatever you see on your travels that seems to afford likely matter for an illustration, jot it down. Whenever you hear a good illustration in a sermon or address, jot it down. The book of illustrations that you make for yourelf is far better than the book of illustrations that you purchase; too many others have that book, and sometimes when you are telling some of the stories in it, you will see a smile pass over the faces of your congregation at the familiarity of the story. And some one may come up to you at the close of the sermon and say, "I always liked that story."

3. *Study the masters in illustration;*

Such men as Moody, Spurgeon, Guthrie. Do not adopt their illustrations too extensively, but see how they do it.

4. *Cultivate the habit of talking to children.*

I do not know of anything that will make a man more gifted in the power of illustration than talking to children. You are simply obliged to use illustrations when you talk to children, and thus you acquire the power to do it. By talking to children you will not only cultivate the gift of using illustrations, but also a pure Anglo-Saxon style.

IV. How to use illustrations.

1. *Be sure you have something to illustrate.*

Do not preach a sermon for the sake of the illustrations. One hears many sermons where it is hard to avoid the conclusion that the sermon was gotten up for the sake of the stories that are told in it, rather than for the sake of the truth it professes to teach. Indeed, it is sometimes hard to tell what the truth is that the man is trying to illustrate. A literary friend once came to me in great disgust after a service he had attended. I asked him how he enjoyed the service. "It was all bosh. The man preached his whole sermon to work up to the point of getting off a quotation from Scott's Marmion at the end. He did that well, but the whole performance was disgusting." Yet this preacher was considered by some a great pulpit orator.

2. *Be sure that your illustrations illustrate.*

3. *Avoid threadbare stories.*

But it is well to bear in mind that a story that is threadbare in one place may be perfectly new in another. It is well, however, to be over-cautious rather than under-cautious in the matter of threadbare stories.

4. *Do not make up stories.*

If you make up a story and tell it as if it were true, it is a lie. There are religious adventurers in our country, sometimes calling themselves by the noble name of evangelists, who go here and there making up the stories that they tell. It is time this sort of thing was stamped out. True evangelists are suffering much injury from this class of men.

5. *When you tell a true story, tell it exactly as it is, or do not tell it at all.*

There are some who exaggerate their stories because they think in this way they will be more impressive. Perhaps they call this a pious fraud, but pious frauds are the most impious and blasphemous on earth.

6. *Do not take a story that some one else told of his friend, and say, "A friend of mine" did so and so.*

7. *Often begin your sermon with an illustration.*

In this way you get the attention and gain the interest of your audience at the very outset.

8. *Often close your sermon with an illustration.*

This, if wisely done, will not only serve to fix the truth, but to touch the heart.

CHAPTER IV

TEACHING THE BIBLE

I. The importance of Bible teaching.

1. *The Bible is the Word of God.*

The man who is really teaching the Bible may be confident that he is doing a good work, for beyond a doubt he is teaching the truth of God.

2. *There is a great demand in our day for Bible teachers.*

The man who takes up the teaching of the Bible, and does it in an interesting way and in the power of the Spirit, is bound to get a hearing and to do great good. In the city of Chicago popular evening Bible classes have been in operation for four years. The first year there was one class, the second year four classes, the third year five classes, and the fourth year it was necessary to reduce the number of classes in order that the teacher might go two evenings in the week to Detroit and St. Louis. In the five classes there was a weekly average attendance of about six thousand. The great interest people have to-day in studying the Bible is illustrated by the Saturday evening class at the Chicago Avenue Church. People come out at five o'clock and remain until nine. From five until six there are about seven hundred in attendance, from seven until nine between twenty and twenty-five hundred. Similar interest in Bible study has been shown in other cities. In every city and village there should be systematic Bible teaching; nothing else will draw and hold such large and interested audiences.

II. Methods of Bible teaching.

1. Expounding the Scriptures.

This consists in the simple reading of a passage of Scripture with such comments as illuminate its meaning and enforce its teaching. Mr. Spurgeon had a great gift in this direction. Mr. Moody used to say, "I would rather hear Mr. Spurgeon expound the Scripture than preach, I get more out of it." The following suggestions are offered to aid in expounding the Scripture to edification:

(1) *Make thorough preparation.*

There are those who think that it takes no preparation to expound the Scripture, that all that is necessary is to go into the pulpit and read a chapter and make such desultory comments as come to mind. There may be some profit even in that slipshod way of expounding the Scripture, but it has done much to bring Bible exposition into disrepute.

(2) *Avoid rambling.*

There is a great temptation to the expositor, when he has started out upon one line of thought, to branch from that on to another and from that still on to another, until it is almost impossible to get back to the chapter.

(3) *Avoid tediousness.*

(4) *Seek for connected lines of thought.*

Suppose, for example, you are expounding the fourth chapter of Philippians; instead of reading through with disconnected comments, go through the chapter with this line of thought: Seven Present Privileges of the Believer:

(a) Constant joy (v. 4).

(b) Absolute freedom from care (v. 6).

(c) Abounding peace (v. 7).

(d) An ever-present friend (v. 9).

(e) Never-failing contentment (v. 11).

(f) All-prevailing strength (v. 13).

(g) Inexhaustible supplies for every need (v. 19).

Or take for example the 23d Psalm; it can be divided as follows:

(a) Every need met (vs. 1-3).

(b) Every fear banished (v. 4).

(c) Every longing satisfied (vs. 5-6).

Or take Ps. 1: 1-3. Entitle your exposition, God's Picture of a Happy Man. Three leading features of this picture will be, in the first verse, the happy man's separation from the world, the second verse, the happy man's occupation in the world, and the third verse, the happy man's fruitfulness before the world. A still different division would be, the first verse, the happy man's separation unto God; the second verse, the happy man's communion with God, and the third verse, the happy man's fruitfulness in God.

Or suppose you are expounding the second chapter of 1 John. Your exposition might begin with the introduction, "This chapter presents to us seven comforting views of Jesus":

(a) Jesus as an advocate with the Father (v. 1).
(b) Jesus as a propitiation for our sins (v. 2).
(c) Jesus as our light (v. 8).
(d) Jesus as the anointer with the Holy Ghost (vs. 20-27).
(e) Jesus as the Christ and Son of God (vs. 22-23).
(f) Jesus as the great promiser (v. 25).
(g) Jesus as the Coming One (v. 28).

If you are using 1 John 3, you could begin with an introduction like this, "This chapter brings to us seven great facts about believers":

(a) Believers in Jesus are now children of God (vs. 1, 2, R. V.).

(b) Believers shall be like Jesus when He comes (second part v. 2).

(c) The believer does not make a practice of sin (vs. 5, 6, 9, 10).

(d) The believer knows that he has passed out of death into life (v. 14).

(e) The believer has boldness before God (vs. 19-21).

(f) The believer may have power to obtain from God by prayer whatsoever he asks (v. 22).

(g) Believers in Jesus have the gift of the Holy Spirit (v. 24).

Of course these are only outlines, and the points made are the headings for different divisions of the exposition.

(5) *A Bible with a wide margin, or an interleaved Bible is very useful in expository work.*

(6) The *Synthetic Bible Study Course* (from Genesis to Revelation), by James M. Gray, D.D., LL.D., is replete with sermonic suggestion for one who would know how to expound the Scriptures interestingly and profitably. (Send for literature.)

(7) *The Book of Psalms is a good book with which to begin your expository work.*

Of course we do not intend by this that every Psalm should be expounded.

2. The conversational Bible class.

This is a very interesting method of teaching the Bible.

(1) *Have the class meet in a very informal way, if possible around a long table.*

(2) *Take some book in the Bible and assign a portion for careful study.*

(3) *Read verse by verse and give each one an opportunity to state what he has gotten out of the verse, or ask questions upon the verse.*

(4) *Hold your class to the passage and subject in hand.*

(5) *Avoid trifles.*

In almost every class there is likely to be some empty-headed member who will want to spend all the time in discussing some trifle.

(6) *It is often well to assign questions beforehand to be looked up by individual members of the class.*

3. The topical or doctrinal Bible class.

Such a class is of immense importance in a church. Very few people in our day are being carefully indoctrinated in the great fundamental truths of the Bible. In consequence of this they are likely to be led off by any errorist that comes along, provided he is a bright talker, or skillful in producing the impression that he has an unusual amount of Bible knowledge. The following are suggestions as to how to conduct these classes:

(1) *Make a careful list beforehand of the great doctrines that you wish to teach.*

Take these doctrines up in systematic order.

(2) *Arrange all the Scriptures that bear upon these doctrines in an orderly and logical way.*

(3) *In the class you can either read from the Bible and expouna what the Scripture says on these doctrines, or you can have the different passages of Scripture read by members of the*

class, and let the class put the contents of the Scripture into systematic form for themselves.

The latter is the better way provided your class is of sufficient intelligence to do the work well. Sometimes it is better yet to give out the Scripture beforehand, and have the class bring in the results of their own study and thought in systematic shape. Three important points must be borne in mind in all this work:

(1) Be systematic.

(2) Be thorough.

(3) Be exact.

The Book, "What the Bible Teaches" is the outcome of a topical doctrinal Bible class conducted through two years, and may be suggestive to others as to how to do this work.

4. Study of individual books.

This is the best and most important of all methods for continuous work. By this method of study a class can be continued from five to ten years, or indefinitely.

(1) *Introductory work.*

Assign the lessons to the class beforehand; have them find and bring in answers to the following questions:

(a) Who wrote the book?

(b) To whom was it written?

(c) Where written?

(d) When written?

(e) Occasion of writing?

(f) Purpose for which written?

(g) Circumstances of the author when he wrote?

(h) What were the circumstances of those to whom he wrote?

(i) What glimpses does the book give us of the life and character of the author?

(j) What are the leading ideas of the book?

(k) What is the central truth of the book?

(l) What are the characteristics of the book?

(2) *Have the class divide the book into its principal sections.*

(3) *Take it up verse by verse and study.*

At each lesson have the class bring in an analysis of a certain number of verses. Insist:

(a) That nothing shall be in the analysis that is not in the verse.

(b) That as far as possible everything that is in the verse shall be in the analysis.

To accomplish this, when any member of the class gives an inadequate analysis, ask him if that is all there is in the verse, and keep on asking him questions until he has brought out all that you see in the verse.

(c) Let what is found be stated as accurately and concisely as possible.

Do not be contented when a member of the class puts something into his analysis somewhat like to what is in the verse, but demand that it shall be a precise statement of what is in the verse.

(4) *Have the class bring together all the teachings on the various subjects scattered through the book.*

(a) To this end, have them first make a list of subjects treated in the book.

(b) Arrange these subjects in their principal subdivisions.

(c) Go through the analysis already made, and bring the points in the analysis under the proper headings in the classification of teaching.

5. Classes for the rapid survey of all the books in the Bible.

This is sometimes called "the Synthetic Method of Bible Study." Assign the class a certain number of chapters, wherever possible an entire book, to read over and over again, and then when they come together, go over the book rapidly, bringing out the salient points about it and its teaching. Dr. James M. Gray's book, "The Synthetic Study of the Bible," will be suggestive for this work.

6. Classes for the study of the Bible by chapters.

(1) These classes can be conducted in a variety of ways. Perhaps the simplest method is to give out four questions for the class to be prepared upon, writing answers to these ques-

tions for each chapter. The Bible can be covered in about two years in this way if two chapters are prepared each day. The questions are:

(a) The subject of the chapter. (State principal contents of the chapter in a single phrase or sentence.)

(b) The principal persons of the chapter.

(c) The truth most emphasized in the chapter.

(d) The best lesson in the chapter.

(e) The best verse of the chapter (memorized).

(2) A somewhat more elaborate, and much more valuable method, is to give out eight questions:

(a) The leading facts of the chapter and the lessons they teach. These facts with the corresponding lessons should be given one by one and written out.

(b) Wrong things done and mistakes made. That does not mean mistakes made by the author of the Bible, for there are none, but the mistakes which are recorded in the chapter as made by various persons.

(c) Things to be imitated. That is, things different persons have done as recorded in the chapter, that are worthy of our imitation.

(d) Most important lessons in the chapter. It is best to restrict the number of lessons to not more than five (or not more than ten) or such number as you deem best.

(e) The most important lesson in the chapter.

(f) The great texts in the chapter (written out in full).

(g) The truth most emphasized in the chapter.

(h) The personal blessing received from the study of the chapter.

This is an especially helpful way to study the Acts of the Apostles. The author has obtained one of the greatest blessings that he has ever received from Bible study in the study of the Acts of the Apostles in this way.

(3) A still more elaborate method for the study of the Bible by chapters is to give the class the following twenty questions and suggestions:

(a) Read chapter five times.

(b) Note any important changes in R. V. from A. V.

(c) Discover and study parallel passages and note variations.

(d) Date of events in chapter?

(e) Name of chapter?

(f) Outline of chapter?

(g) Best verse? Mark and commit to memory.

(h) Verses for meditation; note and mark.

(i) Verses for thorough study; note and mark.

(j) Texts for sermons; note, mark and outline the sermons.

(k) Characteristic, striking and suggestive words and phrases; mark and study.

(l) Leading incidents?

(m) Persons; what light upon their character and lessons from their lives?

(n) The most important lessons in chapter?

(o) The most important lesson in chapter?

(p) Central truth?

(q) Places; locate and look up their character and history.

(r) Subjects for further study suggested?

(s) Difficulties in chapter?

(t) Personal blessings received from the study of the chapter.

First. What new truth learned?

Second. What old truth brought home with new power?

Third. What new course of action decided upon?

Fourth. Any other blessing received from the study of the chapter?

Of course these suggestions and questions can be varied to suit the class and the judgment of the teacher.

7. Classes for the study of the Bible for use in personal work.

Such a class should exist in every church and mission. Book I of this volume will give hints for the conduct of such a class.

8. Teaching the International Sunday School Lesson.

Whatever other lines of Bible teaching we may take up, we cannot afford to exclude the International Lessons. Whatever imperfection there may be in the lessons as assigned by the international committee, they have one advantage which cannot be overlooked; they are studied by the great mass of evangelical church members throughout this country and Great Britain. The Minister or Christian worker who is not studying these lessons and teaching them will be out of line with the Bible thinking of the great mass of the church of Jesus Christ. Helps for the study and teaching of these lessons are so abundant and so excellent, that there is no need that anything be added in this book. The author's own method of teaching the lessons is sufficiently indicated in his book, "The Gist of the Lessons." It might be added, however, that he teaches the lessons, not by lecturing to his class, but by asking them questions. It is far better to get people to see the truth by asking them questions, than it is to tell them the truth. We give for illustration his questions as prepared beforehand on the lesson for March 10, 1901:

JESUS AND CAIAPHAS

(Matt. 26: 57-68)

I. Peter warming himself at the enemies' fire, 57, 58.

57. What did they do with Jesus when they had arrested Him? Did they lead him first to Caiaphas? To whom? Why not to Caiaphas first?

Who were assembled with Caiaphas? What was the name of this body? What was there illegal about their assembling?

58. What are we told about Peter that sounds well? What two words are added that make it sound badly?

If we follow Jesus, how should we follow Him? How are many professed Christians to-day following Jesus? Did Peter really follow Jesus at all? What followed Him? What did not follow Him? (cf. Matt. 16: 24). How far did Peter follow? What led Peter to follow Him? What foolish thing did Peter do? (cf. Ps. 1: 1; Ps. 26: 4-10; 2 Cor. 6: 14-17). Into what trouble did Peter's following Jesus get him? What will be the usual result of following Jesus without following Him with the whole heart? What ought to have kept Peter from following at this time? (John 13: 38; John 18: 8; John 13: 36).

What had Peter done with all the warnings of Christ? What question had he asked of Christ when He said, "Thou canst not follow me now"? (John 13: 37). What boast had Peter made? What is he now undertaking to do? Which knew Peter better, the Lord or Peter himself? Why did not Peter sit by himself instead of with the enemies of the Lord? What arguments are produced to-day for conformity to the world? How much value is there in them? How much of the peril that he feared did Peter escape? How alone did he escape finally? What is the only way that any one can escape who seeks to make friends with the world? (James 4: 4; 1 Cor. 15: 33, R. V.; Prov. 13: 20; Eph. 5: 11, 12). When, alone, should we associate with bad company? If we do not go with them for the definite purpose of leading them to Christ, how will our association with them result? Did Peter have such a purpose in associating with these servants? (John 18: 18). When a follower of the Lord Jesus seeks to warm himself by the enemies' fire, what will you soon hear about his doing?

II. The Son of God slandered and silent, 59-63a.

59. What was the one fixed purpose of Jesus' judges? In order to carry out this purpose, what did they not hesitate to do? Were these judges respectable men as the world goes? Were they religious men? Of what have we an example here? (Jer. 17: 8; Rom. 8: 7).

60. With what success did they meet in their attempt to find false witnesses against Jesus? Were there any who were willing to curry favor with the authorities by swearing falsely? What was the trouble with their testimony? (Mark 14: 56). What conclusive proof have we here of the spotlessness of Jesus' character and life? How did Jesus feel about these false testimonies against Himself? (Ps. 35: 11, 12, 15, R. V.). What is there to-day that parallels the utter unfairness of these judges? When all the other false witnesses failed, who came?

61. To what did they swear? Was there any truth in

that to which they took oath? (v. 61, cf. John 2: 19). What is the most dangerous of all lies?

62, 63a. What reply did Jesus make to these false charges? Why did not Jesus reply? What prophecy did He fulfill? (Is. 53: 7). To whom did He commit His case? (1 Pet. 2: 23). What example is there in all this for us? (1 Pet. 2: 21; Ps. 37: 5, 6). How was the high priest affected by Jesus' silence?

III. The Son of God revealed and rejected, 63b-68.

63b. What did the high priest finally say to Jesus? What was the intention of the question? Did it result in entrapping Jesus?

64. In what did it result? What was Jesus' answer? If Jesus is not divine, what is He?

How did Caiaphas feel when he heard Jesus' unequivocal assertion of His Deity? Why was Caiaphas glad? What did Jesus add that changed the gladness of Caiaphas into fear? In that coming judgment day, who will be the judge, Caiaphas or Jesus? What position will Caiaphas occupy? What should all who are now sitting in judgment on Christ remember? (Acts 17: 31; John 5: 22, 23). What is meant by saying that He is coming "on the clouds of Heaven"?

65. How did the High Priest treat this claim of Jesus? Upon what charge was Jesus sentenced to death? Who to-day practically assent to the justice of this charge?

66. What was the sentence pronounced?

67, 68. What did they do with Jesus after pronouncing this sentence? (cf. Luke 23: 11; Mark 15: 16-20). For whom was it He suffered so? (Is. 53: 6). What was fulfilled in all this? (Is. 50: 6; 53: 3). What is revealed about the human heart in its treatment of the Son of God?

General Questions.

What lessons do we learn from Peter's action? What proofs have we in the lesson, of the Deity of Christ? What proofs of the desperate wickedness of the human heart? In what points does Jesus set us an example in this lesson? In what points did the Jewish rulers do wrong? What is the most important lesson of the passage?

CHAPTER V

TEXTUAL SERMONS IN OUTLINE

We print in this chapter a number of outlines of textual sermons. It is not intended that these outlines shall be used exactly as here given; they are simply offered by way of illustration and suggestion. We first give outlines of sermons for Christians, and afterward outlines of sermons for the unsaved.

LOVE TO CHRIST

"I am ready not to be bound only, but also to die at Jerusalem for the name of the Lord Jesus." Acts 21: 13.

INTRODUCTION.—This text reveals the secret of the beauty and untiring activity and matchless success of the life of Paul. This secret can be put in three words, LOVE TO CHRIST. The Lord Jesus had Paul's whole heart. There have been many great men and great women in the history of the church of Jesus Christ. Some of their names we know. Some of their names we do not know now, but we shall some day. These great men and women are the men and women who have had a great love for Jesus. A man may have great gifts, but, if he has not great love for Christ, he is after all as sounding brass and a clanging cymbal. Men and women who have a great love for Jesus—that is what the church needs to-day. And a great love to Christ is what each one of us needs in our own heart.

I. What Love to Christ will Lead to.

1. To Obedience to Christ. John 14: 15.

   To the one who loves Jesus the words of Jesus will be his most precious treasure. John 14: 21, 23. The one who loves the Lord Jesus will not be contented with doing the will of Jesus when the knowledge of that will is forced upon his attention. It will be his constant study to discover more and more about the will of Jesus.

2. Purity.

Jesus is the Holy One of God. He is infinitely pure. He hates sin. He hates sin in the life. He hates sin in the heart. If I love Him I will wish to be all that pleases Him.

3. Study about Him.

We all wish to know all we can about those we love. If we love Jesus we will study about Him. We will study the four gospels and the prophecies and the epistles and the Revelation of Jesus. Not from a sense of duty but because we want to know about Jesus.

4. Communion with Jesus.

We always delight in communion with those we love.

5. Love to Christ will lead to likeness to Christ.

We grow like those we love.

6. Love to Christ will lead us to work for Christ.

7. Love to Jesus will lead to sacrifices for Jesus.

Listen to the catalogue of what Paul gladly bore for Christ. 2 Cor. 11: 24-27.

8. If we love Jesus we will proclaim Jesus.

II How Learn to Love Him.

Some of us have said in our hearts, "I wonder if I do love Christ?" Well the Bible tells how to have love.

1. We learn to love Christ by dwelling upon His love to us. 1 John 4: 19.
2. To learn to love Jesus we must study much of Him in the Scriptures. The way to learn to love Him is to learn to know Him.
3. It is the Holy Spirit who teaches us to love Jesus. He takes of the things of Jesus and shows them unto us. He bears witness of Jesus. He imparts to us His own love for Christ.
4. We learn to love Jesus at the Lord's table. There we see Jesus.

LOVE FOR SOULS

"Therefore watch, and remember, that by the space of three years I ceased not to warn every one night and day with tears." Acts 20: 31.

INTRODUCTION.—This text gives us a look into the life and into the heart of Paul that stirs one's soul to the very depths. It is one of the most wonderful pictures in the Bible. (Picture.) It opens to us one of the great secrets of Paul's power.

I. The Importance of Love for Souls.

1. Because love for souls is an essential element of Christ-like character. Not to have a love for souls is to be radically unlike Christ.
2. Because love for souls is necessary to successful efforts for their salvation.
3. Because lack of love for souls reveals either great hardness of heart or inexcusable ignorance.

II. How Manifested.

1. In a deep concern for their salvation.
2. In earnest efforts for their salvation.
3. In our being in a constant lookout for opportunities to have some one.
4. In our going out to seek for them.
5. In joy over lost souls saved.
6. In sacrifices made to save them.
7. In deep sorrow of soul for those who will not be saved. Too often we are provoked rather than sad.

III. How Obtain.

The great fact to bear in mind in seeking an answer to this question is that love for souls is the work of the Holy Spirit. This we all believe theoretically. I wish we might be made to see it vividly and feel it to the very depths of our soul. Feel it deeply that the Holy Spirit alone can impart to you this glorious grace.

But on which conditions does He impart it?

1. A deep and genuine desire on our part for a love for souls.

2. Prayer. Luke 11: 13. The prayer should be definite. Not merely for the work of the Holy Spirit in general, but for this specific and definite work of the Spirit. It seems to be a law of the Holy Spirit's operation that He only gives that which we definitely see to be His work and definitely seek. Prayer. Expectant. Personal.
3. The Spirit works through instrumentalities. The Truth. What Truth?
   (a) The value of the soul.
   (b) The peril of the soul.
   (c) Christ's love for souls. 2 Cor. 3: 18.
4. The Spirit works more largely as we put into operation what He has already wrought. Go to work.

SOUL WINNING

"The fruit of the righteous is a tree of life; but he that winneth souls is wise." Prov. 11: 20.

INTRODUCTION.—Men's answers to the question who is the wise man. God's answer, "He that winneth souls is wise." Every wise man will make soul-winning the business of life.

I. BECAUSE IT IS THE WORK CHRIST HAS APPOINTED US TO DO. Matt. 28: 19; Mark, 16: 15. This is Christ's commission to His disciples. Not to apostles only. The apostolic church undoubtedly understood that the commission was for the whole church and not merely to the officials. Acts 8: 4. The idea of the church so prevalent to-day that soul winning is the business of a few officials in the church is utterly foreign to the New Testament ideas of the church. There every believer is a soul winner.

II. BECAUSE IT WAS THE BUSINESS OF LIFE WITH JESUS CHRIST AND BY MAKING IT THE BUSINESS OF OUR LIVES WE ARE FOLLOWING HIM. Luke 19: 10. No one has a right to call himself a follower of Christ who is not a soul winner, who is not going out to seek and save the lost.

III. BECAUSE IT IS THE WORK IN WHICH WE SHALL ENJOY THE UNSPEAKABLE PRIVILEGE OF CHRIST'S PERSONAL PRESENCE Matt. 28: 20. It is a wonder that men pay so little attention to the very clearly stated condition of the promise. It is when we go His way, that He goes ours. It is when we go forth with Him that He goes forth with us.

IV. Because it is the work for which the gift of the Holy Spirit is bestowed and in which we enjoy the fullness of the Spirit's power. Acts 1:8. The gift of the Holy Spirit is bestowed for a special purpose and enjoyed in a special work. That we may be witnesses, that we may have power in soul winning, not merely for our own personal blessing and enjoyment.

V. Because it is the work that produces the most beneficent results. Jas. 5:20. It saves souls from death. Three things here to notice.

1. The value of that which is saved, a soul. Mark 8:36.
2. The second thing to notice is the awfulness of that from which the soul is saved, "from death." Not a mere cessation of existence but the degradation of existence, eternal shame and infamy, agony.
3. That to which the soul is saved.
   To happiness.
   To holiness.
   To glory.
   To fellowship, and likeness to God.

VI. Because it is the work that brings the largest and most enduring reward. John 4:36; Daniel 12:3. Many wish to shine here on earth. I would rather shine up there in eternal splendor. The brightest star in any galaxy of earthly glory soon fades. Earthly glory is not worth the seeking. But it pays to shine up there, to shine as the stars forever and ever.

Conclusion.—Will you make soul-winning the great business of your life? Oh, for a church of men and women who would say and say honestly, "From this time I live for one purpose. I live to seek and save the lost. As God gives me health by consecrated living, by earnest and unceasing praying, by unwearied working, I will do what lies in me to rescue the perishing."

SAVING SOULS FROM DEATH

"He which converteth a sinner from the error of his way shall save a soul from death." Jas. 5: 20.

I. The Glory of the Work.

Those are stirring words.—Startling words. Are there souls in danger of death? There are. Where? About us everywhere. Every soul that has erred from the truth is in the way of death and unless converted will perish forever. The darkness of eternal and eternal death will soon close in upon him. But if we arise and by the power that God gives us convert that soul from the error of his way we will have saved a soul from death. It is a great privilege to save a human life. But what is that from saving a soul from death? The life we save must soon be given up after all. But when I save a soul I save its eternity. One soul saved for eternity is worth a million lives saved for ten, fifteen, twenty or fifty years. And how much more fearful is that from which the soul is saved. When the soul finally dies there is no hope beyond.

II. Who Can Save Souls?

Everyone of us. It is God of course in the last analysis who converts sinners and saves souls. But the text makes it very plain that He does this glorious work through us. There are some who would sit down and wait until God saw fit to convert the sinner. The farmer might as well sit down and wait until God saw fit to give a harvest. God saves no souls without us. The number of unsaved men on the earth to-day who will be saved depends entirely upon the faithfulness of those who are already saved.

III How Can We Convert Sinners.

1. First of all by prayer. 1 John 5: 16. Prayer avails more than any other thing for the conversion of sinners.
2. In the next place we can convert others from the error

of their ways, and so save them, by taking them to the place where they will hear the Word of God preached in purity and in power.

3. We can convert sinners from the error of their ways and so save their souls from death, by ourselves giving them the Word of God in the power of the Spirit. You may not be able to preach but you can do personal work.
4. We can convert sinners and so save their souls by giving our testimony of what the Lord has done for us.
5. By the use of tracts and books. If you cannot talk much you can give others a good tract and get them to read it.

CONCLUSION.—These are some of the ways to save souls. There may be others but these are enough to begin with. Now begin. Begin to-day and then keep it up as long as you live.

WHY EVERY CHRISTIAN SHOULD WORK WITH ALL HIS MIGHT FOR THE SALVATION OF THE LOST

"He which converteth a sinner from the error of his way shall save a soul from death." Jas. 5: 20.

INTRODUCTION.—Every Christian should work with all his might for the salvation of the lost. There is something seriously wrong with any professed Christian who is not working constantly and working hard to get men to forsake sin and to accept Jesus. Such a person is fearfully backslidden. One of the most important marks of a true and satisfactory Christian experience is an earnest desire to see others saved, and constant efforts to that end. Luke 19: 10.

I. Why?

1. Because God is glorified by the salvation of the lost. Nothing glorifies God more than the conversion of a sinner. John 17: 4; John 3: 16.
2. Every Christian should work with all his might for the salvation of the lost, because God has commanded us to do this work

3. Every Christian should work, etc., because of love to them. It is an awful thing to think of what it means to be lost. It is an awful thing to think of what it means to be lost now, to say nothing of what it means to be lost hereafter. What can we do for others like saving them from sin and from its consequences? How our hearts are stirred when we hear of millions whose bodies are starving in India and elsewhere, but what is this to millions whose souls are starving, who are in sin away from God and without Christ. It is better far to save one perishing soul than to save ten million starving bodies.
4. Every Christian should, etc., for his own sake. Our eternal reward depends upon our earnestness and untiring activity in soul winning. Daniel 12: 3. Every new soul won is a new jewel in our Saviour's crown and a new jewel in our crown.

II. How?

1. By prayer. Praying for the lost is not only our duty toward the lost, but it is our first duty. We can accomplish more in that way than in any other single way.
2. By effort. Prayer is the first thing but not the only thing. Begin trying to lead men to Christ.
3. By training. We must train for the work in order to do the best work.
4. Seek and obtain God's power. Acts 1: 8. This power is for us all. Luke 11: 13; Acts 2: 39; Acts 5: 32. Every Christian man and woman here can have the power of the Holy Ghost. Give yourself wholly to God. Ask, believe, claim and go to work.

WITNESSING

"A true witness delivereth souls." Prov. 14: 25.

INTRODUCTION.—Our text to-day tells us one way and a most effective way of saving souls, that is, by witnessing "A true witness delivereth souls." By testifying to the truth especially to the truth concerning Jesus we bring men to accept Jesus and thus deliver them from guilt and sin and from eternal death. This was the work of John the Baptist. John 1:7. This was the work of the apostles. John 15:27. This is the work of the Holy Spirit. John 15:26. This was the work of Jesus Himself. Isa. 55:4; John 18:37.

I. Who Should Be a Witness?

To this question the answer is very plain, every one who knows Jesus. If you have found Jesus there rests upon you a solemn obligation to tell others about Him. What would you think if people were dying by the thousand of a plague and some man had knowledge of a sure cure and kept it to himself for fear some one might not listen to him or might laugh at him?

II. To What?

1. First of all and most of all to Jesus Christ. Acts 10:43; John 15:26. It is not so much of doctrines as of a person that we should speak, of Jesus, His death, His resurrection, and the power of His death and resurrection, as we know them in our own lives.

III. When and Where?

Testify wherever you get a chance and whenever you get a chance. Paul is a pretty good example. We find in giving his testimony in the synagogue, in the market places, from house to house, in the open air, by the riverside, in jail, on shipboard, in camp, at his work, at meals, to Jews, to Gentiles, to theological professors, to ecclesiastical courts, to governors, to kings and queens, to jailors, to soldiers, to sailors, everywhere and all times of the day and night, and to everybody. A few specific places:

1. In our homes. Mark 5:19.
2. In our places of business.
3. On the cars and on the streets.
4. The church meetings for testimony.

IV. What Are the Conditions of Effective Witnessing?

1. The first condition is a true life back of the testimony. If a man is not straight in his business, the more he

keeps his mouth shut about Christ the better it is for the Christ and His cause.

2. The second condition of effective testimony is personal knowledge of the facts. If we are to be effective witnesses for Christ and His truth we must seek the largest and clearest possible knowledge of Him and of the truth as it is in Him.
3. The third and crowning condition of effective witnessing is the enduement of the Holy Spirit. Acts 1: 8. There is great power in Holy Ghost testimony. There is little power in our testimony if the Holy Ghost be not upon us.

SPREADING THE GOSPEL

"Therefore they that were scattered abroad went everywhere preaching the word." Acts 8: 4.

INTRODUCTION.—Seven years after Pentecost the church and the gospel were still very largely confined to the city of Jerusalem. Then God stirred up the nest and sent them forth. The gospel was spread by preaching it. There are four things in the text to notice. Who preached, what they preached, why they preached, where they preached.

I. Who Preached?

"They that were scattered abroad," i. e. the rank and file of the church (cf. Acts 8: 1). They simply spoke the Word. Wherever they went they told the story of Jesus and salvation in Him and what He had done for them. This is the most effectual and the most needed kind of preaching. This is the only way the gospel will ever have that spread that Christ intended it should have, by everybody who knows it and believes it and has felt its power telling it out among those with whom they come in contact.

II. What They Preached.

Notice what they preached. "Preaching the Word," or if we were to translate literally, "telling the good news of the Word." They declared God's own Word.

III. Why They Preached.

1. First of all they preached the Word because they believed it. 2 Cor. 4: 13. How can any one believe this book and the wonderful promises it contains and not speak?
2. They preached in the next place because they believed men were perishing. That was what the Word told them. John 3: 36.
3. Because they had themselves been blessed by the Word. How can any one who has tasted the blessings of the gospel keep it to himself?
4. Because their Master had so commanded them. Matt. 28: 19.

IV. Where They Preached.

They preached "everywhere."

PENTECOSTAL POWER

"And when the day of Pentecost was fully come, they were all with one accord in one place. And suddenly there came a sound from heaven as of a rushing mighty wind, and it filled all the house where they were sitting. And there appeared unto them cloven tongues like as a fire, and it sat upon each of them. And they were all filled with the Holy Ghost, and began to speak with other tongues, as the Spirit gave them utterance." Acts 2: 1-4.

Introduction.—The second chapter of Acts forms one of the most inspiring, if not the most inspiring, page of Christian history. There is a hush. Then suddenly there comes straight from the throne of the ascended Christ a sound of a mighty rushing wind. They know what it means. Startled and yet filled with unutterable joy at the fulfillment of the promise for which they had so long waited they look up. A strange sight fastens their gaze. Describe. Summarize rest of chapter.

This Pentecostal power is the subject of our study.

I. The Character of the Power.

Acts 1: 8. It was power for testimony and service.

II. The Source of the Power.

Acts 1:8. The Holy Ghost. The Spirit of God Himself wielded the Sword of the Spirit.

III. The Human Conditions of the Power.

In other words, what had the 120 done that prepared the way for and made certain the coming of the Holy Spirit in this Pentecostal Display of Power.

1. The disciples were wholly surrendered to Christ.
2. The disciples were obedient. Ch. 1:4, comp. 2:1.
3. The disciples recognized their need. Ch. 1:14. There must be a clear recognition.
4. The disciples intensely desired. Ch. 1:14; ch. 2:1. For ten days they bent their thought and prayer largely to this one point.
5. The disciples prayed. Ch. 1:14. Luke 11:13.
6. The disciples believed. They expected. 1 John 5:14, 15.

IV. How Manifested.

1. Spoke in the Spirit's power. v. 4. Gave up their own strength and wisdom and used God's.
2. Testified to "the mighty works of God." No talk of self. Self was lost sight of.
3. Preached *Christ*. vs. 22-35.

V. Results.

1. Multitude, amazed, marveled, perplexed. vs. 6, 7, 12.
2. Some mocked. v. 13.
3. "Men pricked to their hearts." v. 37. Genuine conviction. The need of this day.
4. Genuine conversion. vs. 41, 42.

CONCLUSION.—Can we have this power and similar results? Yes, if we will meet the conditions. Heb. 13:8. Acts 2:39.

THE PRAYER OF A RIGHTEOUS MAN

"The supplication of a righteous man availeth much in its working. Jas. 5: 16, R. V.

Introduction.—The Revised Version is a decided improvement upon the Authorized Version. First because it brings out the character of the prayer, "supplication." Secondly, because the Authorized Version produces the impression that the petitions of a righteous man avail much when they are offered in fervency, while the Revised Version correctly gives the impression that all petitions of a righteous man are effective.

The central thought of our text is, that there is great force or power, great ability to effect results, in the prayer of a righteous man. The word translated "availeth" is precisely the same word translated "can do" in Phil. 4: 13. If it were translated the same here the verse would read, "The prayer of a righteous man can do much because (or while) it worketh." The prayer of a righteous man can do much.

I. For Whom can the Prayer of a Righteous Man Do Much?

1. First for himself.

   If we wish anything for ourselves the most effective way to get it is to ask for it. Prayer avails much in our own lives. It obtains what can be obtained in no other way, and things that can be obtained in other ways are oftentimes obtained in a less questionable way and in a way much more to God's glory by prayer.

   (a) Prayer can get victory over besetting sin.

   (b) Prayer obtains wisdom. Jas. 1: 5.

   (c) Prayer obtains an insight into and understanding of the Word of God. Ps. 119: 18.

   Prayer will remove more difficulties in the understanding of the Word than the Commentaries will.

   (d) Prayer brings Christ to dwell in our hearts by faith. Eph. 3: 14, 17.

   (e) Prayer avails to bring the Holy Spirit in all His fullness, with all His graces and bestowments of power into our hearts and lives. Luke 11: 13.

In every direction prayer avails for our spiritual welfare and strength and growth as almost nothing else does. Is. 40: 31.

(f) Prayer not only avails in spiritual lines but in temporal as well. Phil. 4: 6.

2. The prayer of a righteous man can do much not only for himself but for others.

(a) It can do much for the unsaved. 1 John 5: 16.

(b) Prayer can do much for your preacher. It will bring him wisdom, and the power of the Holy Ghost. Eph. 6: 19, 20.

There are other directions in which prayer can do much for the church, for missions, for civil government.

Conclusion.—In closing note whose prayer it is that so avails. "The prayer of a righteous man." That is the prayer of a man who orders his life according to God's will as revealed in His Word. John 3: 22.

A MIGHTY PRAYER

"Then the fire of God fell." 1 Kings 18: 38.

Introduction.—This world has been witness to many mighty prayers—prayers that have wrought marvelous results. But there have been few prayers recorded in the world's history that have produced more marked and astonishing results than the one whose answer is described in our text. Describe circumstances and scene. That prayer brought the fire of God down to this earth. A mighty prayer. He was a man with "like passions with us." Jas. 5: 17, R. V. So we can by prayer effect as great things as Elijah did.

How Elijah Prayed.

1. We notice first of all that Elijah's prayer was to the true and living God.
2. Elijah's prayer was the prayer of a man who was obeying God. (v. 36.) God demands reciprocity. If He is to do what we ask of Him, we must do what He asks of us.

3. Elijah's prayer was for God's glory ("Let it be known this day that thou art God in Israel").
4. Elijah's prayer was for something God had promised or had stirred him up to ask for. ("Let it be known," etc., "I have done all these things at thy word.")

   If you wish to pray as Elijah did wait upon God as he did to teach you by His Word or by His Spirit what to pray for.
5. Elijah's prayer was based upon shed blood.
6. Elijah's prayer was earnest.
7. It was a believing prayer. Elijah had no doubt that he would get what he asked.

WORSHIP

"The hour cometh and now is when the true worshippers shall worship the Father in Spirit and in truth: for the Father seeketh such to worship him." John 4: 23.

INTRODUCTION.—This text informs us that God is seeking worshippers. (R. V.) The one thing above all else that God desires of men is worship. It is sometimes said "we are saved that we may serve." This is true, but it is still more profoundly true that we are saved that we may worship.

I. What is Worship?

It is a definite act of the soul in relation to God. The term is used in our day in a very vague and general and unscriptural way. The worship of God is the soul bowing down before God in absorbed contemplation of Himself. "In our prayer we are occupied with our needs, in thanksgiving we are occupied with our blessings, in worship we are occupied with Himself."

II. The Duty and Blessedness of Worship.

1. We owe worship to God. It is our first duty toward Him. There is definite commandment in the N. T. as well as the Old that we worship Him. If we do not worship God we are robbing Him of that which is His due.

2. But worship is not only a duty, it is a privilege, a privilege full of blessing.
   (a) There is no deeper joy, no purer joy than that which springs from the adoring contemplation of God.
   (b) It also brings likeness to Him. It is by looking at Him we are made like Him. Our complete transformation into His likeness will come through the complete and undimmed vision of Himself.
   (c) Worship is a blessed privilege again because it brings power, power for life, power also for service.

III. How to Worship Acceptably

1. "In the Spirit." This means in the Holy Spirit. Comp. Phil. 3: 3, R. V. The only true worship, the worship which is acceptable to God, is the worship which the Holy Spirit inspires.
2. The only acceptable worship is worship offered through Christ. John. 14: 6.
3. "In truth." That is, in reality.

Conclusion.—Shall we not say that there shall be more of worship in our lives from this time, and that our worship shall be of that character that God seeks from us?

SEPARATION

"Wherefore come ye out from among them, and be ye separate, saith the Lord, and touch no unclean thing; and I will receive you, and will be to you a Father, and ye shall be to me sons and daughters, saith the Lord Almighty." 2 Cor. 6: 17, 18, R. V.

Introduction.—In this text we have a very precious promise but also a very plain and explicit commandment.

All of Israel's ills in the Old Testament arose from the fact that they did not heed Jehovah's call to separation. Ps. 116: 34-36, 39, 40-42. The believer's failure to heed God's call to separation is the cause of the powerlessness and lack of blessing in the individual and the church.

I. First of all it is clear that we must separate ourselves from every form of sin. Ch. 7: 1.

II. In the next place there should be separation from the methods and practices and fashions of the world. Rom. 12: 1, 2. A Christian is a citizen of another world, and has no right to take his pattern from this. (Phil. 3: 20, R. V.)

III. There should be separation from worldly affiliations.
This comes out clearly in the words which precede our text. Vs. 14-16. The child of God has no right to enter into any partnership with the unsaved. A woman who is a believer, i. e., who has a saving faith in Jesus Christ, has no right to enter into a matrimonial yoke with an unbeliever, i. e., one who has not a saving faith in Jesus Christ. Neh. 13: 26.
A Christian has no right to be yoked together in business partnership with an unsaved man.

IV. There should be separation from everything that entangleth. 2 Tim. 2: 4.

V. There should be separation from professed Christians who are living in known sin. 1 Cor. 5: 11.

VI. There should be separation from professed Christians who walk disorderly, i. e., who refuse to obey the teachings of the Word. 2 Tim. 3: 6, 14.
This does not mean that there should be separation from a brother who is merely in the faith.

VII. The Commandment is not "come out from the church." It was coming out from unbelievers and idolaters that Paul was talking about. Read vs. 14: 18. Nothing was further from Paul's thought than telling people to come out of the church. True separation is not merely separation from but separation to. Our separation is from all uncleanness *unto Christ.*

VIII. True separation will not only be a separation unto Christ but also a separation unto all those who belong to Christ.

A REMARKABLE ROBBERY

"Will a man rob God? Yet ye have robbed me." Mal. 3: 8.

INTRODUCTION.—When the strange question of the text is first put to us, we are disposed to answer at once, "No, certainly not, certainly no one will reach such a pitch of blind and desperate wickedness as to rob God." But God gives a different answer. He says, "Ye have robbed me."

I. How Can a Man Rob God?

A man can rob God by holding back from Him anything that is His due.

1. The gifts and offerings that are His due. All our money belongs to God.
2. The time that is His due.
3. The service that is due Him.
4. The surrender that is due Him.
5. The glory that is due Him. No glory is due to ourselves for any of our achievements, physical, mental or spiritual. No one of us has a right to boast of anything we accomplish. The Glory all belongs to God, and to Him we should render it. If we take to ourselves this glory that rightfully belongs to God we have robbed Him of His due.
6. The Confession that is due Him. We owe to God the Father and to His Son Jesus Christ to confess them as our God and Saviour before the world.
7. The Thanksgiving that is His due.
8. The Worship that is due. Worship is due to God from man. This is God's first great claim upon man. This is His supreme right. If you do not give it you rob Him.

II. The Monstrous Guilt of Robbing God.

"What of it?" "What of robbing God?" To rob God is infinitely more monstrous than to rob man.

1. God's rights are the supreme rights. All our modern moral philosophy is out of joint because it puts the rights of the finite above the rights of the infinite,—the rights of the creature above the rights of the creator.
2. The monstrousness of robbing God is seen if we think of the way in which God has dealt with us. God is love and all His ways with man are ways of love.

III. The Consequences of Robbing God.

Mal. 8:9. "Ye are cursed with a curse." The whole land of Israel was cursed because they robbed God. The fundamental cause of the want and misery and ruin that fill this land to-day is that the nation has robbed God. What is true of the nation is true of the individual. Our robbery of God is withholding from us the fullness of blessing God has for us.

Conclusion.—We have seen some of the ways in which man robs God, we have seen the enormity of this sin, we have seen the curse and blight that come into our own lives from it. The practical conclusion of the whole matter is self-evident. Let us repent of our sin to-day, let us confess it to God to-day, let us render to Him to-day and from this time on the full measure of that which is due Him, and He will open the windows of heaven and pour into our lives a blessing that there shall not be room enough to contain it, an overflowing blessing.

WALKING WITH GOD

"Enoch walked with God: and he was not; for God took him." Gen. 5:24.

Introduction.—This is one of the most fascinating and thrilling verses in the Bible. It sounds more like a song from a heavenly world than a plain statement of an historic fact regarding a humble inhabitant of this world of ours.

I. What is it to Walk with God?

To walk with God means to live one's life in the consciousness of God's presence and in conscious communion with Him, to have the thought constantly before us, "God is beside me," and to be every now and then speaking to Him and still more, listening for Him to speak to us. In a word, to walk with God is to live in the real, conscious companionship of God. Enoch walked with God not in a few rare occasions of spiritual exaltation, such perhaps as most of us have known, but for 300 consecutive years after the birth of Methuselah. Gen. 6:22. It is possible for us to have the consciousness of the nearness and fellowship of God in our daily life, to talk with Him as we talk to an earthly friend—yes, as we talk to no earthly friend—and to have Him talk to us, to commune with Him too in a silence that is far more meaningful than any words could be.

II. The Results of Walking with God.

1. Great joy, abounding joy. Ps. 6: 11.
   In one of the loneliest hours of His lonely life Jesus looked up and said, I am not alone because the Father is with me. John 16: 32.
2. Abiding peace. Ps. 16: 8, 11.
3. Spiritual enlightenment.
   Communion with God rather than scholarship opens to us the mind and thoughts of God.
4. Purity of heart and life. Nothing is so cleansing as the consciousness of God's presence.
5. Beauty of character. We become like those with whom we habitually associate.
6. Eminent usefulness.
   Enoch has wrought out immeasurably more good for man than Nebuchadnezzar, who built the marvelous structures of Babylon; than Augustus, who "found Rome brick and left it marble"; than the Egyptian monarchs who built the pyramids.
7. We please God. Heb. 11: 5, R. V. This is more than to be useful.
8. God's eternal companionship. "Enoch walked with God: and he was not; for God took him."

III. How to Enter into a Walk with God.

1. First of all we must trust in the atoning blood of Christ. Heb. 11: 5, cf. v. 4.
   God is holy and we are sinners. Sin separates as a deep and impassable chasm between us and Him. There can be no walking with Him until sin is put away, and it is the blood that puts away sin. Heb. 9: 22.
2. If we would walk with God we must obey God. John 14: 23, R. V.

3. If we would walk with God we must cultivate the thought of His presence. We must "practice the presence of God."

THE BELIEVER'S DEAREST TREASURE

"Yea verily, and I count all things to be loss for the excellency of the knowledge of Christ Jesus my Lord: for whom I suffered the loss of all things, and do count them but dung, that I may gain Christ." Phil. 3: 8, R. V.

INTRODUCTION.—It is evident from this text that the Believer's Greatest Treasure is Christ Himself. To the true believer Christ is infinitely dearer than all else. He counts all things but refuse in comparison with Christ. But why is Christ the Believer's Dearest Treasure?

I. Because of What He has Done for Us.

When we learn the meaning of Paul's words, "He loved me and gave Himself for me," then we cannot help but cry with Paul, "I count all things," etc.

II. Because of What He has Brought to Us.

1. First of all Christ has brought us pardon.
2. He has brought us peace.
3. He has brought us victory. He has brought us victory over sin.
4. He has brought us fruitfulness.
5. Eternal life. *Eternal Life.* ETERNAL LIFE.

III. Because of What He Himself is.

Jesus Christ is vastly more than anything He has done or brought. If we must lose all and everything and could have Jesus He would satisfy every longing, and fill every crevice and corner of the heart. Do you know the most precious promise of this Book? Listen! "We shall see him as he is."

CHRIST AND THE CHURCH

"Christ loved the church," etc. Eph. 5: 25-27.

I Christ's Relation to the Church.

Christ's relation to the church is summed up in one word. He *loved* it. That love has manifested itself in the past in one way. It is manifesting itself in the present in another way. It will manifest itself in the future in still another way.

1. Christ's love for the church in the past has manifested itself by His giving Himself for it.
2. The love of Christ is manifesting itself in the present in sanctifying it and cleansing it. In separating it from the world unto God, and in cleansing it from its sin. This He does by His Word. This sanctifying and cleansing by the Word is really effected by Christ Himself coming to dwell in us. So we may say that Christ manifested His love for us in the past in giving Himself *for* us, and He is manifesting His love to us in the present by giving Himself up *to* us.
3. Christ's love has not completely manifested itself even yet. It has a future manifestation. This same epistle tells us that the great manifestation of His love lies in the future. That it is "in the ages to come" that God is to "show the exceeding riches of His grace in kindness toward us in Christ Jesus." Eph. 2:7. What is to be the future manifestation of Christ's love for the church? Read v. 27, R. V. He is going to take the church by the hand and present it to Himself as His own bride—all glorious—not having one single spot—not having one smallest wrinkle—not anything of that sort—but holy, and without blemish. Oh, stand and contemplate the Bride of Christ as Christ Himself shall make her in the future manifestation of His love at His coming. "*A glorious church.*"

GRIEVING THE SPIRIT

"Grieve not the Holy Spirit of God, in whom ye were sealed unto the day of redemption." Eph. 4:30, R. V.

I. Meaning of the Text.

1. These words bring out very clearly the personality of the Holy Spirit.

2. The words again bring out the love of the Spirit. The Holy Spirit's deep personal love for the children of God.
3. The words of the text bring out very forcibly the absolute holiness of the Spirit.
   The Holy Spirit is grieved by our foolish and wicked words and deeds and thoughts, not merely because He loves us, but because He is holy, and abhors all that is unholy, and grieves when anything unholy touches those He loves.
4. The words of the text bring out again the extreme sensitiveness of the Spirit.
5. The words of the text bring out the fact that the Holy Spirit observes and understands all our acts and words and thoughts.

II. To Whom does Paul Write these Words?

To Christian people, to saved saints. In our text itself he speaks of those to whom he writes as being "sealed unto the day of redemption." It is the child of God who grieves the Holy Spirit of God. He does not leave us when we grieve Him. It is not the Bible, but modern perversion of the Bible that speaks of the "grieving the Spirit *away*." We are sealed by Him not for a day or a week or a year, but "unto the day of redemption."

GRIEVING THE HOLY SPIRIT OF GOD

"Grieve not the Holy Spirit of God." Eph. 4: 30.

INTRODUCTION.—The fact that our wrong acts, words and thoughts cause such deep grief to our great friend and constant companion, the Holy Spirit, is a mighty motive for a life pure in word, deed and thought.

By just what sort of acts is the Holy Spirit grieved? The Apostle mentions some of them very definitely in the passage of which our text is the keynote.

I. First of all lying is one of the things that grieves the Holy Spirit. Vs. 25.

The Holy Spirit is "the Spirit of truth," and He hates

with immeasurable hatred all falsehoods—all lies—black lies and white lies. It causes great grief to Him when a lie escapes the lips of a child of God.

II. We grieve the Holy Spirit by uncontrolled anger. V. 26.

III. The next thing that is mentioned as grieving the Holy Spirit is stealing. V. 28.
Some of you think, that surely doesn't mean me. Are you quite sure about it? What does it mean to steal? To take something from another without giving him a just equivalent.

IV. The Holy Spirit is grieved by corrupt conversation. V. 29. "Corrupt speech" literally translated would read "rotten speech." But you will note that it is not enough to abstain from corrupt speech, we must speak "such as is good for edifying, as the need may be, that it may give grace to them that hear." The Holy Spirit is grieved not only over our use of corrupt speech, but also over our neglect of good speech.

V There is a whole class of actions, words and feelings that grieve the Holy Spirit. You will find them in v. 31.

1. Bitterness.
2. Wrath, sudden anger.
3. Anger, settled anger.
4. Clamour. That means the noisy assertion of our own rights and wrongs.
5. Evil speaking.
6. All malice. That is the root of all the rest of the evils mentioned.
   In contrast with these actions that grieve the Holy Spirit cited in v. 31, verse 32 sets forth the attitude of heart and life toward one another that is well pleasing to Him. Unless we are thus "kind, tender hearted," the Spirit is grieved.

Conclusion.—Let me say in closing there is one way in which we may always be sure of pleasing Him, i. e., by surrendering to Him the absolute control of all our thoughts, words and acts, by being "filled with the Spirit" in every realm of our being and life.

GRIEVE NOT THE HOLY SPIRIT

"Grieve not the Holy Spirit of God." Eph. 4: 30.

INTRODUCTION.—These words should be so deeply engraved upon the heart of every child of God that they should never be forgotten. They are words that should ring in our ears day and night, in all our temptations to do unholy things; in our personal lives, in our home life, in our social life, in our business life, in our church life. Reflection upon these words will help us to solve many perplexing problems. Ought I to do this thing? many a Christian has often to ask. Always settle such questions in the light of the text, Will it grieve the Holy One of God, or will it delight the Holy Spirit of God if I do it?

I. Why not Grieve the Holy Spirit?

1. First of all we ought not to grieve the Holy Spirit out of consideration for Him.

   The claims of the Holy Spirit upon each of us are infinitely greater than those of a mother. We should have a more tender consideration for Him than for her. Not only is He a being of wondrous dignity and glory, a Divine being, whose rights are supreme, but He is a being of wondrous, matchless tenderness and love. A mother's love is nothing to the love of the Spirit.

2. We ought not to grieve the Holy Spirit out of consideration for ourselves.

   The results of grieving the Holy Spirit are very grievous to ourselves. What are they? The Holy Spirit cannot do His whole work when He is grieved. He is hindered from doing in us what He would do. For any measure of blessing and power in any direction we are absolutely dependent upon the Holy Spirit.

   (a) If the Holy Spirit is grieved our prayers will be hindered.

   (b) The great secret of profitable Bible study is studying the Bible under the Holy Spirit as our teacher. If then the Holy Spirit is grieved we lose something of our joy in Bible Study and almost all of our profit.

(c) Again true joy is the fruit of the Holy Spirit. Gal. 5:22. If, then, the Spirit is grieved our joy will be hindered. We may even lose altogether the joy of our salvation.

(d) Power in service is lost by grieving the Spirit. The warning of our text is a very important and very solemn one. How much depends upon our heeding it.

II. How We Grieve the Holy Spirit of God.

Anything that is unholy or wrong in deed or word or act grieves Him.

BE FILLED WITH THE SPIRIT

"Be filled with the Spirit." Eph. 5:18.

I. The Exact Meaning and Force of the Words.

1. Look at the word "filled." That is a big word, and it grows upon one as he looks at it. "Filled." "Be filled with the Spirit." How many of us can deliberately and honestly say, I am "*filled* with the Spirit"? "Filled." To be filled with the Spirit means to have the Spirit pervading with His holy and glorious presence every chamber and nook and corner of your being, controlling every purpose, every affection, every thought, every fancy, every action, every utterance.

2. The tense of the verb is the present, which indicates that the process of filling must be continuous and constant. It will give Paul's thought, to translate it, "Be continually getting filled." Yesterday's filling will not do for to-day. We must be like glasses that are kept full of water by being kept constantly under the ever-flowing fountain. And each new filling should be larger than the last.

3. Notice the word "with." Literally translated the passage would read, "be filled in the Spirit." The

thought is that the sphere of the believer's life is "in the Spirit," and he must let this Holy Spirit in which he is and lives get into him and fill him. If we are believers in Christ we are "in the Spirit." He surrounds us and rests upon us with His glorious and holy presence, but He may not be in us yet in any large measure. We may be half full still, or nearly full still with the muddy water of our own pleasures and notions and purposes and ambitions. Paul's thought is to let this water of life in which you float flow in and expel all else until the tumbler itself is full of that in which it floats.

II. The Obligation.

Having found the exact meaning of the words, let us look at the solemn obligation of obedience to them.

1. Paul's words are a command. They are in the imperative mood.
2. But there is a further obligation to be filled with the Spirit because if we are not filled we dishonor Jesus Christ. Every Christian who is not filled with the Spirit dishonors Jesus Christ.
3. Not being filled with the Holy Spirit is not merely a serious lack, it is a grievous sin.
   It is a sin out of which many other sins spring. The only way to prevent the flesh bringing forth its awful brood of vices and sins is by being filled with the Spirit.

III The Results of being Filled with the Spirit.

1. The first result would doubtless be new love. Gal. 5:22.
2. The second result will be great joy. The fruit of the Spirit is first love, then joy. The Holy Spirit is "the oil of gladness." Get filled with the Spirit and you will be filled with gladness.
3. Other graces of character will follow. "Peace, long suffering, gentleness, goodness, faith, meekness, temperance. Gal. 5:22, 23. A spirit-filled man will be

a lovely man and a spirit-filled woman will be a lovely woman.

4. Thanksgiving. V. 20.
5. Power in prayer. Eph. 6:18.
6. Power in service. Acts 1:8.

IV. How?

The truth is, the Holy Spirit is dwelling in each one of us and wants to fill us if we will only let Him. Our chief business in the matter is to let go the hindrances.

1. The first one is sin. The Spirit is Holy. The Holy Spirit.
2. The second hindrance is pride.
3. The third hindrance is everything that is of self or of the flesh.

Having done this, having let go every sin, having let go all pride, having let go everything that is of self and the flesh, just look to the Holy Spirit to come in and fill every part of your being, to take complete possession of everything, of every thought and purpose and affection and plan and act, and word. Ask Him to do it, expect Him to do it. Wait patiently, quietly upon Him. That is all; He does all the rest.

TRAVAIL FOR SOULS

"For as soon as Zion travailed, she brought forth her children." Isa. 66:8.

INTRODUCTION.—This text applies primarily and historically to Israel, but it states a great principle that has been illustrated over and over again in the history of the church and of individuals—that travail of soul is necessary if souls are to be born into the kingdom of God.

I. The Need of Travail for Souls.

Every great religious awakening has been born out of travail of soul on the part of some one. Martin Luther, Wesley, Whitfield, Jonathan Edwards, James Brainerd, Finney, the Irish Revival, Moody. It is doubtful if ever a single soul is born again without travail of soul on the part of some one.

II. Absence of This Travail of Soul To-day.

That this travail for souls does not exist widely to-day is evident from several things:

1. The comparatively small attendance of the membership of the church upon special meetings.
2. The small effort made to bring others out to the meetings.
3. The conduct of Christians who do attend the meetings.
4. The small amount of agonizing prayer that is going up to God.

III. How This Travail of Soul may be Brought about.

Two things are evident:

1. That travail of soul is necessary if there is to be a great work.
2. That this travail of soul does not exist to any great extent to-day.

The question then that confronts us is, How can we secure this all-needed travail for souls.

1. By confessing its absence—confessing it to God. God forgives our sins when we confess our sins. He supplies our lack when we confess our lack.
2. By being willing to endure agony of soul that others may be saved. Many want an easy, happy religion. Many a woman never has a child because she is not willing to pay the price of having a child. Many a Christian, etc., because, etc.
3. By giving ourselves up to do all in our power to save the lost.
4. By prayer. Rom. 8:26, 27; Luke 11:13.
5. By dwelling upon the truth that will bring us to realize the wretched condition and awful peril of those who are out of Christ.

HOW TO SECURE HEAVENLY TREASURE

"Lay not up for yourselves treasures upon earth where moth and rust doth corrupt and where thieves break through and steal: but lay up for yourselves treasures in heaven where neither moth nor rust doth corrupt, and where thieves do not break through and steal." Matt. 6: 19, 20.

Introduction.—It is one thing to be saved and another thing to gain a reward. It is one thing to get to heaven and quite another thing to lay up for ourselves treasures in the heaven we are to enter. Earthly treasures have little worth. How can we use these years, how can we use our lives so as to make eternity richer? How can we secure heavenly treasure? We go to the Word of God for our answer to this question, and we easily find it.

I. The first part of the answer we find in Matt. 19: 21. By using the means we have, not for ourselves but for others, we secure heavenly treasure. If you would secure heavenly treasures, give, give, give.

II. The second way of securing heavenly treasures is very closely akin to the first. Matt. 19: 29. By forsaking the things that are naturally dear to us for Christ's name's sake we secure heavenly treasures.

III. We can secure heavenly rewards or treasures by suffering persecution and reproach for Christ's sake. Matt. 5: 11, 12.

IV. We gather fruit unto life eternal. We secure heavenly treasure by reaping souls, i. e., by winning souls to Christ. John 4: 36; Dan. 12: 3.

V. We gain a heavenly crown, a crown of righteousness, a most desirable heavenly treasure, by loving His appearing. By looking forward with glad, joyous anticipation to His coming again.

Conclusion.—The way to secure heavenly treasures is simple enough. The Word of God makes it plain.

AN APPROVED WORKMAN

"Study to show thyself approved unto God, a workman that needeth not to be ashamed, rightly dividing the word of truth." 2 Tim. 2: 15.

Introduction.—These words were originally addressed to a minister of the gospel, but they properly apply to all Christians; for every Christian should be in some sense, and in some sphere, a preacher of the truth. So the exhortation of the text is an exhortation intended for us.

I. The first thought it contains for us is that we are to seek to present ourselves "approved *unto God.*"
The approval of men we are not to seek.
The approval of God we are to always bear in mind and to seek in all we do and all we are.

II. The second thought our text contains is that in order to present ourselves approved unto God we must "give diligence," or make it a matter of earnest study and effort. There is no possibility of drifting into a life or work well pleasing to God.

III. The third thought our text contains is that in order to be approved of God we must be *workmen.*
God is a worker, and He desires all His children to be workers. There is a kind of teaching nowadays that seems to say, "It is not so important that you work. The important thing is that you get right with God yourself." But our text says that you cannot get right with God unless you become what He Himself is—a worker.

IV. But our text teaches us that in order to be approved of God we must not only be workmen, we must be certain kind of workmen, "a workman that needeth not to be ashamed." It is not enough to work, you must do good work.

V. The fifth thing our text teaches is that in order to be workmen who need not to be ashamed we must "rightly divide," or "handle right," literally "cut straight" the word of truth. In other words, we must know our Bibles and know how to use them.
It is useless for a man to seek to be a workman that needeth not to be ashamed and neglect the constant, prayerful, thoughtful study of the Word of God.

THE TRIUMPHANT CRY FROM THE CROSS

"It is finished." John 19: 30.

INTRODUCTION.—What did this dying utterance of our Lord and Saviour mean? What was finished?

I. First of all, His own sufferings were finished. Luke 12: 50

The dread of horror of all these years, yes of the ages, was over.

II. The mission upon which God had sent Him into this world was finished. John 17:4.

III. The prophecies concerning the sufferings and death of the Messiah, which angels and the prophets themselves desired to look into (1 Peter 1:11-13) were finished. This is the immediate thought of the context where our text is found.

IV. The work of atonement was finished. There is absolutely nothing left for you or me to do to atone for sin. It is all done.

V. Another thing still was finished, and that is the Mosaic law—as far as its claims on the believer are concerned. Col. 2:14; Rom. 10:4; 7:4.

VI. There was one thing more that was "finished" at the cross, i. e., Satan's power. Heb. 2:14, R. V.; Col. 2:15, R. V.

CONCLUSION.—How full of meaning are the three words of Christ's triumphant cry from the cross.

JOINT HEIRS WITH CHRIST

"If children then heirs, heirs of God and joint heirs with Christ, if so be that we suffer with him, that we may be also glorified together." Rom. 8:17.

INTRODUCTION.—This text is one of the most remarkable in this book which is so full of remarkable statements. Few of those who read it and reread it take in its stupendous import.

I. What Does it Mean? JOINT HEIRS WITH CHRIST.

What can it mean? What does it mean? It means precisely what it says. It means that we are heirs of God in the precise sense and to the full extent that Jesus Christ is. It is true that Jesus Christ is the heir of God by His own eternal sonship, and that we are heirs of God only because of our relation to Him, because we are in Him; but being in Him, we are so identified with Him by the union of faith, that His entire inheritance becomes ours. All of God's that belongs to Christ, belongs also to me by virtue of my union with Christ. I am a joint heir with Christ. Let us come more to specific things in which Christ and we are heirs of God.

1. First of all Christ is an heir of God's infinite wisdom, and therefore so are we. Col. 2: 3; comp. 1 Cor. 13: 12.
2. Christ was an heir of God's infinite power, and therefore so are we. Matt. 28: 18; comp. 1 Cor. 15: 43.
3. But there is something better yet in God than His omniscient wisdom and His almighty strength to which Christ and we are heirs. Christ was heir to God's goodness, to His infinite holiness, and therefore so are we. 1 Peter 1: 16; Eph. 5: 27.
4. Christ was heir to God's glory and therefore so are we. Heb. 1: 3. In John 17: 22 Jesus distinctly declares "The glory which thou hast given me I have given unto them." R. V.
5. We are heirs of God's dominion. Rev. 3: 21.

II Who are Heirs of God and Joint Heirs with Christ?

1. "If children then heirs; heirs of God and joint heirs with Christ." But who are children of God? Turning back to John 1: 12 we get God's own answer.
2. The fourteenth verse of the chapter from which our text is taken puts it in a different way. The one "led by the Spirit" is the Son, and so the heir and the joint heir with Christ.
3. There is one more thought upon who are "joint heirs with Christ" in the very verse from which our text is taken. "*If so be that we suffer with him*, that we may also be glorified with him." R. V. The heirs with Christ hereafter are evidently those who suffer with Christ here. *With Christ.*

THANKSGIVING SERMON

"And Jesus said, Were there not ten cleansed? but where are the nine?" Luke 17: 17.

Introduction.—This is one of the saddest utterances that ever fell from the lips of Jesus. Jesus loved men, and like every one who truly loves, He desired love in return. When those He helped returned, as the poor Samaritan, with thanksgiving, it filled His heart with joy; when those He helped forgot to return thanks, it filled His heart with sorrow. The day should be pre-eminently what it professes to be, a day of thanksgiving to God

I. The Duty.

1. We are commanded again and again to give thanks. Ps. 100: 4; Eph. 5: 4; Col. 3: 15, 17.
2. The rendering of thanks unto God is more acceptable to Him than costly sacrifices. Ps. 69: 30, 31.
3. The early Christians gave themselves continually to praise and thanksgiving. Acts 2: 46, 47.
4. Thanksgiving was habitual with Jesus Christ, our example. John 11: 41; Matt. 11: 25.
5. Giving thanks unto the Father, is one of the inevitable results of being filled with the Spirit. Eph. 5: 18-20.
6. Thanksgiving is a necessary accompaniment for prevailing prayer. Phil. 4: 6.

II. How to Render Acceptable Thanksgiving. Eph. 5: 20.

1. It should be "in the name of our Lord Jesus Christ."
2. It should be "to the Father."
3. It should be constant.
4. It should be for all things.

III. For What to Return Thanks To-day.

We have to-day many causes for thanksgiving, national and individual. Specify some of them. Each of us should go alone with God some time to-day, and think over the general blessings that we have received with others, as a nation, and the specific causes that there are for thanksgiving in our national life and the individual blessings that we have received.

GOD IS LOVE

"God is Love." 1 John 4: 8.

INTRODUCTION.—That is the most wonderful sentence ever written or spoken. We owe this great truth wholly to the Bible. Not merely announced in the Bible, it runs through the Bible. Ask me to put into one sentence what the Bible teaches and this is the sentence, "God is Love."

I. How has God Shown that He is Love?

1. By creating us and the universe. Creation was an act of love. The story of creation in Genesis 1 is a love story.
2. By punishing sin as soon as it entered the world and ever since. God's unsparing and, if need be, endless punishment of sin is because God is love.
3. By forgiving sin when it is repented of. Is. 55: 7. With the first pronouncing of doom upon Adam and Eve there is also a message of mercy.
4. By giving His Son to die in our place. This was the supreme manifestation of God's love. 1 John 4: 10; John 3: 16. The measure of love is sacrifice and God made an immeasurable sacrifice.

II. What is Our Duty?

We see, then, God is love. What is our duty in view of that great and glorious fact?

1. To accept His love. There can be no greater sin than to despise and reject the love of God. There can be no clearer revelation of the utter badness and wickedness of our hearts than to despise and reject the love of God.
2. We should return God's love with love. 1 John 4: 19.
3. Surrender absolutely to Him.

GOD'S WONDERFUL LOVE

"God so loved the world that he gave his only begotten Son: that whosoever believeth on him should not perish but have everlasting life." John 3: 16.

INTRODUCTION.—No other verse in the Bible has been used to the salvation of so many sinners as this.

I. The Objects of God's Love.

The world. God's love is limited to no race, no class. There is not a man or woman in the world so vile that God doesn't love them. Therefore we ought to love them too.

II. The Greatness of God's Love.

The measure of love is sacrifice. What sacrifice has God made for us? Gave His only begotten Son.

For some reason it was necessary that God give His Son to suffer if you and I were to live eternally. And God gave His Son to die. No one can fathom the agony it cost the Father.

III. The Offer of God's Love.

The offer of God's love. What is it? Eternal life. Love of man to man has prompted great gifts but there is no gift like this. Any one who believes gets this gift. "Whosoever."

IV. Our Treatment of God's Love.

But what are we doing with this love of God? This too is wonderful.

1. Some deny it.
2. Some only mention the God who so loved them, etc., to take His name in vain.
3. Some are conscious rebels against God.
4. Some trample His love under feet and despise it.
5. Many neglect His love.
6. Some accept it. Will you to-night?

WANTED—FIGHTING CHRISTIANS

"Fight the good fight of faith." 1 Tim. 6: 12.

"Endure hardness as a good soldier of Jesus Christ." 2 Tim. 2: 3.

INTRODUCTION.—Christian life is a warfare, not a picnic. There are battles to be fought, enemies to be conquered, victories to be won. Of course, there are wonderful feasts to be enjoyed all along the way, but fighting and not feasting is our special business.

Three things to know if we are to obey our text.

First—Who our enemies are.

Second—How to fight them.

Third—The conditions of success in our warfare.

I. Our Enemies.

Who are our enemies? Who and what is it that we are to fight?

1. The Devil. Eph. 6: 11, 12.
2. The World. 1 John 5: 4. The world has its ideas, its ambitions, its usages, its disposition, its aims; and the ideas of the world, the ambitions of the world, the usages of the world, the aims of the world are contrary to the mind of God.

   The world seeks to bring us all under its sway, under the dominion of its ideas, etc. It is our business to fight the world, to resist its attempt to bring us into bondage to itself.
3. The Flesh. Our third enemy is the flesh, our own flesh.
4. Sin. Sin will attack us. We should fight it back. We need not yield to it or be overcome by it for one single moment. If we are knocked down by it we should jump up at once and renew the fight and conquer. But it is not enough to fight sin in your own life. Fight it in the lives of others.
5. False Doctrine. We must resist error of doctrine in ourselves; we must not ourselves argue it with others. Jude 2, R. V.

   Some think that false doctrine is not worth fighting against. It is more worth fighting against than political tyranny in its worst forms. True doctrine is salvation and life. False doctrine is damnation and death.

II. How to Fight.

1. First of all we must fight to win. No Christian has a right to expect defeat or to be defeated.
2. We must fight energetically.

3. We must fight wisely. The way to get wisdom for our holy war is by prayer. Jas. 1:5. Much of our fighting must be done upon our knees.
4. We must fight persistently. This warfare is never done until Jesus comes or God calls us home. The trouble with many a Christian warrior is that he fights intermittently

III. Conditions of Victory.

1. First, faith in Jesus Christ. 1 John 5:4, 5.
2. We must be strong. Eph. 6:10; Eph. 3:16; 1 John 2:14.
3. We must be ready to "endure hardness" or "suffer hardship." 2 Tim. 2:3.
4. A knowledge of weapons.
   (a) We must know what the best weapons are. The great weapon of our warfare is the Word of God.
   (b) But we must not only know what the best weapons are but we must actually have these weapons.
   (c) We must know how to use our weapons.

ETERNAL LIFE OR THE WRATH OF GOD—WHICH?

"He that believeth on the Son hath everlasting life: and he that believeth not the Son shall not see life, but the wrath of God abideth on him." John 3:36.

INTRODUCTION.—One of the most meaningful and glorious phrases that ever were uttered is that which was so often upon the lips of Jesus Christ—"Eternal Life." One of the most awful and apalling phrases ever uttered is this other that Jesus uses in our text, "the wrath of God." It cannot be put into words, it cannot be conceived even in fancy, all the wealth of glory there is wrapped up in those two words, "eternal life." Neither can it be put into words, nor conceived by human imagination, the depth of horror, shame and woe that are wrapped up in that other phrase,—"the wrath of God." It is between these two, that each of us to-night are called to take our choice.

. **The Things Contrasted.**

1. "Eternal life"—what is it?
   (a) First of all, it is really life. 1 Tim. 6: 19, R. V.
   (b) Eternal life is fullness of life. It is life abundant. Jno. 10: 10, R. V. It is full of beauty, full of peace, full of satisfaction, full of joy, full of glory.
   (c) Eternal life is a life of the highest knowledge. John 17: 3. Eternal life is knowledge of the Infinite.
   (d) Eternal life is the life of God. 1 John 1: 2. Eternal life is the life of the holy, blessed God, the infinite life imparted to us.
   (e) Eternal life is endless life. Endlessness is not the most essential characteristic of eternal life. Its quality is more than its duration but nevertheless it is endless.
2. "The wrath of God" what is that? It is just what the words express. It is the intense and settled displeasure of the infinitely holy Being Who created us and all things, and Who has the absolute control of all the powers of the universe.

   "The wrath of God," "the wrath of God,"—there is nothing more awful than that. To have yon Holy One, yon Holy Being before Whom the seraphim veil their faces and cry, Holy, holy, holy, to have yon omnipotent and infinite Ruler of this universe, yon mighty One Who holds the sun and moon and stars, all the stupendous worlds of light that stud the illimitable expanse of heaven, in the hollow of His hands, as well as shapes the whole history of this tiny ball that we call the earth, to have Him displeased with us, to incur His wrath, His intense, deep-seated, settled displeasure. "Eternal life"—"the wrath of God." Which will you choose?

3. **How Decide.**

By what act do we determine whether Eternal Life or the Wrath of God is to be our portion? Listen to God's own answer to this question. It is not the answer of all mod-

ern philosophers. It is not the answer of all modern theologians. It is not the answer of all modern preachers, but it is God's answer, and it is sure. (Quote text).
The act by which we bring upon ourselves "the wrath of God": "He that believeth not the Son shall not see life, but the wrath of God abideth upon Him." It makes no difference who or what you are.

HOW TO BECOME SONS OF GOD

"But as many as received him, to them gave he power to become the sons of God, even to them that believe on his name." John 1: 12.

Introduction.—If I could tell how to become a son of a monarch or a millionaire I would get many eager listeners. To be a child of God involves much more: much more in the life that now is—much more in the life which is to come.

I. What is Involved in being a Child of God?

1. Our absolute security in this present life.
2. The supply of every real need. Matt. 6: 8. Not every fancied need.
3. Joy. The child of God must be happy for this is God's world.
4. Peace.
5. Likeness to God. The one who becomes a child of God must ultimately become like God. 1 John 3: 1, 2.
6. Infinite joy hereafter. Rom. 8: 17.

II. How may We Become Sons of God?

But some one may say, "Are we not already sons of God? We are not. We are all God's offspring (Acts 17: 28), i. e., we are His creative work, and man was originally made in God's image, but we are not all sons of God in any such full sense as involves the things just mentioned. John 1: 12; Gal. 3: 26; John 8: 44.
Any hopes built upon the supposition that all men are God's sons, are built upon the sinking sand, and they will fall some day and crush you.

How, then? John 1:12. Simply receiving Jesus makes us sons of God. What is it to receive Jesus? We cannot afford to make any mistake here, too much depends upon it, too much in the life that now is—too much in the life to come.

What is it—etc.? What is it to receive any man? It is to take him as that for which he offers himself. If a man offers himself as a physician, to receive or take him, is to take him as your physician, and to put the care of your health into his hands. If any man offers himself as a husband, to receive him or take him is to accept him as your husband. Any young man or young woman knows when a young man says to a young woman, "I want to be your husband, will you take me?" just what he means. Now to receive Jesus is just to take Him as He offers Himself.

1. He offers Himself as our atoning Saviour, as the one who bore our sins in His own body on the cross. Matt. 20:28. Will you take Him as that?
2. He offers Himself as our deliverer from sin's power. John 8:36.
3. He offers Himself as our rest-giver. Matt. 11:28. Will you take Him as that?
4. He offers Himself as our teacher. John 13:13; Matt. 23:8. Will you take Him as that? Will you submit your mind to Him for Him to teach you what He will, accepting of His teaching as the truth of God?
5. He offers Himself as our way of access to God, and as the incarnation of the truth, and as our life. John 14:6. Will you take Him as this?
6. He offers Himself as our King. John 1:12. Will you take Him as your King?
7. He offers Himself as our Lord and God. John 5:22, 23. Will you accept Him for all that He has offered Himself, or may offer Himself, studying more and more to know all that He does offer Himself to be? Of course this is an act of faith, but it means that you will become sons of God.

III. Who may Become Sons of God in this Way?

Any one (read the text). How sweeping it is. It leaves no one out. You may be the ripest scholar, or you may be utterly without education, but if you receive Jesus, instantly you become a child of God.

You may be a person of amiable, attractive and lovely character, or you may be the vilest sinner. I know a man who was deep in sin, utterly enslaved; he was deep in unbelief also, but one day he received Jesus,—took Him for all He wished to be to him, and he became a child of God. God gave him evidence of sonship by setting him free from the bondage of sin, sending His Spirit into his heart bearing witness, etc.

Conclusion.—It is possible for any one in this house to become a child of God this moment. Do you wish to? You must accept Jesus, that is all. Will you do it? Ah, some of you hesitate! How foolish! Can this world offer anything so good, so glorious, for time and eternity as becoming a child of God?

I know a man who once had this same opportunity put before him. At first he thought he would accept it, but then he thought again and said, "No, I better not, I am a lawyer, and it may interfere with my practice." He rejected the opportunity. He went right down and became an infidel, as so many become who resist God's spirit and God's love. He sank lower yet. From a place of prominence he became despised for his low acts, and could get no clients. He became the laughing stock of the community. It was a life thrown away. Yes, and an eternity thrown away.

GOD-GIVEN CONVICTION

"They were pricked in their heart." Acts 2:37.

Introduction.—It is not a pleasant thing to be pricked in one's heart with a conviction of sin. Indeed it is a most distressing experience, but it is an experience which if rightly received leads to very great blessing. The very worst thing that can happen to you is to be able to sit here entirely unmoved by what you hear.

There are three things to consider about our text.

I. Why they were pricked in their heart.

II. How they were pricked in their heart.

III. The results of their being pricked in their heart.

I. Why these Men were Pricked in their Heart.

They were pricked in heart because their conscience long asleep was at last awake, and they saw the appalling enormity of the sin they had committed in crucifying Jesus Christ. They were at last awakened to the fact that God had raised Jesus from the dead and exalted Him to His own right hand. They understood that Jesus whom they rejected was both Lord and Christ.

Every one in this audience who is rejecting Jesus Christ will some day awake to the fact of who Jesus is, the dignity, majesty and glory of His person, and then you will be pricked in your heart. It may be too late then, but it will not be too late to-night.

II How they were Pricked in their Heart.

1. By the preaching of the Word of God. Peter's sermon did it and that sermon was pretty much all Bible.
2. By Peter's testimony to a risen and exalted Saviour.
3. By the power of the Holy Spirit (cf. John 16: 7, 9).

III. The Results of their being Pricked in their Heart.

There are many who do not wish to be pricked in their heart because it is not a pleasant experience, but we will see that though it is a bitter medicine, the results are glorious.

1. The first result of their being pricked in their heart was that they turned from their awful sin.
2. The second result of their being pricked in their heart was that they publicly confessed their sin and their acceptance of Christ.
3. The third result was that they were saved. v. 47. To be pricked in heart now and to yield to it means that you will be saved from having your heart gnawed through all eternity by the worm that dieth not.

Conclusion.—This is a great text, "they were pricked in their heart." Let us wait a few moments silently and prayerfully, and see if the Holy Spirit will not prick some here in their hearts. You have committed the same awful sin that those mentioned had committed. You have crucified the Son of God. Think of that. Say to yourself, "I am guilty of the awful sin of crucifying Christ." Ask God to make you feel it. Ask the Holy Spirit to open your eyes to see your appalling guilt. Is something pricking your heart now? Then yield. Repent. Turn from sin, accept Christ, begin to confess Him. Who will?

WHAT TO DO WITH JESUS

"What shall I do with Jesus, which is called Christ?" Matt. 27: 22.

Introduction.—No man ever asked a more important question than Pilate asked here. A question that confronts us all. Pilate made a great mistake. He asked man what he should do with Jesus instead of asking God. But Pilate not only went to man with his question, he went to enemies of Jesus Christ and they cried out, "Crucify Him!" And it is to the enemies of Christ that many of you are going.

I. This Question is a very Personal Question.

It is, "What shall *I* do with Christ?" No one else can decide this for you. You will accept Christ for yourself or reject Christ for yourself. And you will go to heaven for yourself or go to hell for yourself.

II. The Question is furthermore, "What Shall I Do with JESUS?"

Not what shall I do with some creed, not what shall I do with the church, but, "What shall I do with Jesus Christ?"

III. The Question again is, "What shall I DO with Jesus?"

Not what shall I think about Him. God tells us very plainly in His Word what we ought to do with Jesus.

1. First of all we should listen to Jesus.
2. But it is not enough to merely listen to Jesus Christ. We should also accept Him (John 1: 12) as our atoning Saviour Who gave His life in our place, as our

Deliverer from sin's power, as our Teacher to whom we shall surrender the control of our thoughts, and as our Lord to whom we shall surrender the control of our lives.

IV. The next thing which God bids us do with Jesus is to be baptized in His name. Acts 2: 8.

V. Obey Him. John 14: 21, 23.

VI. Serve Him. John 12: 26.

VII. Follow Jesus Christ. John 12: 26.

VIII. Worship Him. Heb. 1: 6.

FALSE CHRISTS AND FALSE PROPHETS

"False Christs and false prophets shall rise, and shall show signs and wonders, to seduce, if it were possible, even the elect. But take ye heed, behold I have foretold you all things." Mark 13: 22, 23.

Introduction.—These words of the real Christ are very solemn. In them He tells us that false prophets are coming and warns us to be on our guard against them. The false prophets and the false Christs are here. There are many who take it for granted that if any man or woman makes great claims, those claims must be true, especially if they support those claims by reports of sickness healed and other wonders wrought. But Christ not only told us that false Christs and false prophets would appear, but He has told us that signs and wonders so remarkable would be wrought that they would mislead, if possible, the very elect.

I. How escape?

How can we escape from the snare of these false Christs and false prophets if they show such signs and wonders. This all-important question is answered in the Bible. There are five simple rules which if followed will save one from the snare of any or every false Christ and false prophet.

1. You will find the first rule in John 7: 17. A will wholly surrendered to God gives clearness of vision to detect error.
2. The second rule is in 2 Tim. 3: 13-17. When one has surrendered his will wholly to God the safeguard

against deceivers and false prophets is the study of the Word of God. Act 20: 29, 30. Study the whole book.

3. The third rule is found in Jas. 1: 5-7. Prayer to God for wisdom will save us from many a snare.
4. The fourth rule is found in Matt. 23: 8-10. Call no man master, acknowledge no man as authority, accept the authority of no one and nothing but Christ and the Bible in matters of faith and religion.
5. The fifth rule is found in Prov. 29: 25. If you wish to escape the snare of all false prophets and false Christs put away all fear of man and fear of the devil and trust in God.

MAN'S RIGHT ATTITUDE BEFORE GOD

"Nay but, O man, who art thou that repliest against God? Shall the thing formed say to him that formed it, why hast thou made me thus?" Rom. 9: 20.

INTRODUCTION.—There can be no more important or fundamental question than that of our right attitude before God. If we are in right relations to God we are in the way to be in right relations to all God's creatures, to all men and all things. If we are in wrong relations to God we are bound to be in wrong relations to all men and all things, to the whole universe that God made and governs.

I. First of all we should have a sense of our comparative nothingness.

God is infinite, we are finite. Is. 40: 15, 17. This sense of our comparative nothingness should have three phases:

1. We should bear in mind God's infinite majesty and our utter insignificance.
2. We should bear in mind the infinite wisdom of God and our utter ignorance.
3. We should bear in mind the infinite holiness of God and our utter vileness in comparison with Him.

II. The second characteristic of our attitude toward God should be trust.

We should trust God perfectly, we should have absolute

unquestioning confidence in Him. "Blessed is the man who trusteth in Jehovah." Jehovah is Infinitely Great, an awful gulf yawns between us and Him, but Jehovah is infinitely good and is worthy of the absolute confidence of the smallest and the greatest of His creatures.

III. But there should be one more characteristic of our attitude toward God. Not only humility and trust, but boldness.

Heb. 10: 20. He is infinite in majesty, infinite in wisdom, infinite in holiness; but the atoning blood of Jesus has put away our sins and made us sons of God, so that we no longer receive a Spirit of bondage again unto fear, but a Spirit of adoption, and look right up into the face of that infinite majesty, that infinite wisdom, that infinite holiness and call Him Father.

INFAMOUS INGRATITUDE

"Even denying the Lord that bought them, and bring upon themselves swift destruction." 2 Pet. 2: 1.

Introduction.—There is no sin more heartily and universally despised among men than ingratitude. The basest of all ingratitude is the denial of Jesus Christ who bought us, bought us at the cost of immeasurable agony and pain, bought us at the cost of His own blood. There is no one to whom we owe so much as to Jesus Christ. No one has ever brought so much to us. He brings us pardon for all our sins, if we will have it. He brings us peace that passeth all understanding. He brings us joy such as the world never dreamed of, joy unspeakable and full of glory. He brings us an inheritance incorruptible and undefiled that fadeth not away, laid up in store for us in heaven. He makes us heirs of God and joint heirs with Himself. Not only has He brought to us infinitely more than any other ever brought, or all others put together ever brought, He has suffered more for us than any other ever suffered. Phil 2: 6-8.

I. Who are Denying the Lord?

1. First of all the infidels, agnostics, skeptics and unitarians are denying the Lord.

2. There are many who believe in Jesus Christ, who believe that He is the Son of God, who believe all the Bible says about His life and death, about His atonement and His salvation, but they have never confessed Him publicly before the world. You are denying the Lord that bought you.
3. Many church members deny the Lord that bought them. You deny Christ in your business, you deny Christ in your social life, you deny Christ in your politics, you deny Christ in many places. When religion is sneered at in the place where you work you haven't courage to stand up like a man and say quietly but firmly, "Men, I don't agree with you. I believe in this Bible and in this Christ you sneer at. I know Jesus Christ is a Divine Saviour. He has saved me, He fills my life with joy, and He is my Lord."
4. Men who profess to be ministers of Christ, who set the authority of those whom they regard as scholars above the authority of Jesus Christ, and who care more for a reputation, for originality and scholarship than they do for the honor of Jesus Christ their Lord. There are men in the pulpit who are itching for that applause and are denying their Lord to get it. They would rather be untrue to Jesus Christ than to be considered behind the times.

II. Why Men Deny Their Lord.

1. Many do it out of cowardice.
2. For gain.
3. From pride.
4. Love of man.

A STRANGE HATRED

"They hated me without a cause." John 15: 25.

INTRODUCTION.—No other man has lived on this earth who has been so unanimously and so bitterly hated as Jesus Christ.

I. Hated by Men of His Own Day.

1. When He was here on earth He was hated by all classes of society.
2. The hatred of Jesus Christ was as bitter as it was universal.
3. This hatred of Jesus Christ was without a cause; it was wholly gratuitous.

II. Hatred of Men To-day.

As we read this history of the past it seems incredible that the men of Christ's day should have so hated Him; but He is just as bitterly hated to-day. The hatred of Jesus Christ to-day is not usually so outspoken as when He was here on earth, but it is no less real. There are many ways in which men show this hatred of Jesus Christ.

1. One of the commonest ways in which men show their hatred of Jesus Christ is by the delight they take in the fall of any man who bears the name of Christ or professes to be His disciple.
2. Hatred of Jesus Christ also shows itself in talking about and magnifying the inconsistencies of Christians.
3. Hatred of Jesus Christ shows itself in the persecution of those who believe in and confess Him.
4. Hatred of Jesus Christ is shown by attempts to disprove the truth of the record of Christ's life found in the four Gospels.
5. Hatred of Jesus Christ is shown by attempts to rob Him of the glory that is rightfully His. To Jesus Christ belongs divine honor, glory and adoration.
6. Men sometimes show their hatred of Jesus Christ by a simple refusal to have Him rule over them. Luke 19: 14. This hatred of Christ is still without a cause. It is wholly gratuitous.
   (a) It is true that Jesus Christ does condemn sin and demand that men should forsake it, and that is the reason many hate Him.
   (b) It is true that Jesus Christ demands absolute surrender, and that is why many hate Him. There

is no just cause for hating Christ. There is abundant cause why we should love Him.

(1) What He brings.

(2) What He has sacrificed.

SALVATION FOR EVERYBODY

"The gospel of Christ is the power of God unto salvation to every one that believeth." Rom. 1:16.

INTRODUCTION.—There are some people who think that God has provided salvation for just a chosen few. That is a great mistake. God has provided salvation for everybody. There are three great truths in our text:

I. There is something that has power to save anybody and everybody.

II. That something that has power to save anybody and everybody is the Gospel.

1. Some of you may ask how I know the Gospel of Christ has power to save anybody. (1) Because this book says so. (2) Because I have seen it save men and women of all classes.
2. What is it to "save"?
   - (a) To save first of all is to save from guilt.
   - (b) To save is to save from the power of sin.
   - (c) To save is to save from the eternal consequences of sin.
3. But whom can the Gospel of Christ thus save? Anybody and everybody.
   - (a) First of all it can save outcasts.
   - (b) The Gospel can save infidels, the most determined and bitter infidels.
   - (c) The Gospel can save scholars.
   - (d) The Gospel can save deluded people.
   - (e) The Gospel can save moralists.
4. Nothing but the Gospel has this power to save. It takes the power of God to save, and the Gospel of Christ is the only thing that has the power of God in it.
5. What is the Gospel? Gospel means glad tidings or

good news. What is the good news that saves? Turn to 1 Cor. 15: 1-4.

(a) The good news is then, first, "That Christ died for our sins." Gal. 3: 13; 2 Cor. 5: 21.

(b) The good news is, second, that Christ was buried. He was buried and my sin was all buried with Him.

(c) Third, "He rose again."

He is a living Saviour and has all power in heaven and on earth, and however weak I am when I have to fight the world, the flesh and the devil, I can look up to this living Almighty Saviour and trust Him to give me victory.

III. **The Way to Experience this saving power of the Gospel in our own lives is by simply believing the Gospel**: "To every-one who believeth." Believes what? The Gospel.

WHAT MUST I DO TO BE DAMNED?

"He that believeth not shall be damned." Mark 16: 16.

INTRODUCTION.—The word damned has largely fallen into disuse partly because it is used so much by profane people, partly because we live in an easy-going way that recoils from a vigorous statement of unpleasant truths. Damned means condemned, condemned of God, but damned is a much more vigorous word than condemned; it carries much more meaning to the average mind. It summons at once before our imagination all the awful consequences of being condemned of God. We will let the text stand there as it reads in the A. V. "He that believeth not shall be damned." Any man who hears the Gospel and persistently refuses to believe it and receive it shall be damned. All any one needs to do to be saved, saved to the uttermost, is to believe on the Lord Jesus. All that any one needs to do to be damned, damned to the uttermost, is to refuse to believe on the Lord Jesus. It is not necessary in order to be damned that one be what the world calls a wicked person.

1. First of all the man who does not believe the Gospel and believe in Jesus Christ must be damned, because

every man is a sinner and God is holy, and if man does not find some way in which the sin that separates between him, a sinner, and the Holy God, can be put away, he must necessarily be separated from God forever, and separation from God is damnation; and the only way in which sin can be put away from between us and God is by the atoning death of Jesus Christ, and the one condition upon which that atoning death avails for you or me is that we believe on Him who died, therefore if we will not believe on Him we must be damned.

2. Refusing to believe on Jesus Christ is in itself a damnable sin, and reveals a damnable state of heart.

GOD IS LOVE

"God is Love." John 4:8.

Introduction.—The world would never have known that God is love had not God revealed it in His Word. We must go, then, to the Bible for the interpretation of it. How, according to the Bible, is the love of God manifested?

I. Is. 48:14, 20, 21. God's love manifests itself in His ministering to our needs and joy.

II. Heb. 12:6-11. God's love manifests itself in His chastening us, in His sending us trial and pain and sorrow and bereavement.

III. Is. 63:9. God's love is manifested by His sympathizing with us in our afflictions.

IV. God's love is manifested again in His never forgetting those He loves. Is. 49:15, 16.

V. God's love manifests itself in His forgiving our sins. Is. 38:17; Is. 55:7.

God will not pardon sin of we hold on to it. There is a fancy about God's love that because God is love He will pardon and save all men whether they repent and believe on Christ or not. It is wholly unscriptural. To believe it you must give up the Bible, but if you give up the Bible you must give up your belief that God is love, for it is from the Bible we learn it, and there is no other proof. One of the most illogical systems in the world is universalism.

VI. God's love is manifested in His giving His own Son to die in our place. John 3: 16; 1 John 4: 10. This manifestation of God's love is stupendous, it is almost past believing, but it is true.

CONCLUSION.—Such is the love of God. What are you going to do with that love?

THE MOST WONDERFUL THING IN THE WORLD

"God so loved the world that he gave his only begotten Son, that whosoever believeth on him should not perish, but have everlasting life." John 3: 16.

INTRODUCTION.—The most wonderful thing in the world is the love of God.

I. The Objects of God's Love. "The World."

1. Men of all races.
2. Men of all classes.

   That God should love the good we can understand, but that God should love the vile, the outcast, the worthless, the vicious, the criminal, that is the thing that is hard of comprehension, but that is what the Bible tells us. That is what the Bible emphasizes. Rom. 5: 7, 8.

II. The Character of God's Love.

1. It is a pardoning love. Is. 55: 7; Ps. 32: 3, 4.
2. It is a chastening love. Heb. 12: 6.
3. It is a sympathizing love. Is. 63: 9.
4. It is a long-suffering love. 2 Pet. 3: 9.
5. It is a self-sacrificing love. John 3: 16.

III. Our Treatment of God's Love.

1. Accepting His love. The result of yielding to God's love is eternal life. John 3: 16.
2. Rejecting His love. What is the result of rejecting His love?

   (a) First of all, awful guilt.

   (b) The loss of eternal life. John 5: 40.

   (c) Awful punishment. Heb. 10: 26-31.

GOD LOVES THE WHOLE WORLD

"For God so loved the world, that he gave his only begotten Son, that whosoever believeth in him should not perish, but have everlasting life." John 3: 16.

INTRODUCTION.—This is perhaps the most remarkable statement the world ever heard. There are volumes packed into that little sentence. The verse tells us God's attitude toward the world, God's attitude toward sin, God's attitude toward His Son, God's attitude toward all who believe in Jesus Christ, and God's attitude toward all who do not believe on Jesus Christ.

I. God's Attitude toward the World.

Love.

II. God's Attitude toward Sin.

Our text shows us that God's attitude toward sin is hate.

III God's Attitude toward His Son.

"*His only-begotten Son.*" God's attitude toward His Son is love. But God gave that Son He so infinitely loved, that Son who from all eternity has been the object of His delight. God gave that only begotten Son for the world, for you and for me.

IV God's Attitude toward Believers and Unbelievers.

1. God's attitude toward believers is to give them eternal life.
2. God's attitude toward those who will not believe. With great grief and reluctance God withdraws from them the infinite gift He has purchased at such cost and which they will not have. He leaves them to "perish."

A "GOOD MAN" LOST AND A BAD MAN SAVED

Luke 18: 9-14.

INTRODUCTION.—Some of you may think I have this subject twisted, and that it ought to read: A good man saved and a bad man lost. But it is right just as it is. Jesus Christ Himself has given us the picture of the good man and the bad man, and Jesus Himself is responsible for the statement that the good man was lost and the bad man saved.

I. The Good Man Who was Lost.

1. We notice first of all that he was a moral man in his personal habits.
2. Square in his business relations.
3. Highly-respected member of society.
4. The Pharisee saw no flaw in himself. He was the best man—in his own estimation—that he knew. (R V.)
5. This Pharisee was a religious man.
6. This Pharisee was a generous man. He could tell God that he gave a tenth of all he made. But he was lost. Why? For precisely the same reason that many here to-night are lost.
   (a) He trusted in himself, v. 9.
   (b) He despised others.
   (c) He did not acknowledge himself a sinner.
   (d) He did not cry to God for mercy.

II. The Bad Man Who was Saved.

1. First note he had been an immoral man.
2. He had been irreligious.
3. He was looked down upon by his fellow men
4. He saw many faults in himself.

III. Why was this Man Saved?

1. He saw himself a lost sinner.
2. He saw he could do nothing to save himself.
3. He saw that there was a God of mercy.
4. He just cried to this God to have mercy upon him.
5. He was in earnest.

FOUND OUT

"Be sure your sin will find you out." Num. 32: 23.

INTRODUCTION.—No man can escape his own sins. No man ever committed a single sin that he did not pay for it some way. No man ever committed a single sin by which he was not a loser. There never has been a sin committed in this earth that paid.

I. How Men's Sins Find Them Out.

1. Men's sins find them out by the execution of human laws.
2. Men's sins find them out in their own bodies.
3. Sin finds us out in our characters. For every sin you commit you will suffer its character. Every sin breeds a moral ulcer.
4. Again your sin will find you out in your own conscience.
5. In your feelings.
6. In your children. That is one of the most awful things about sin; its curse falls not only upon us but upon our children also.
7. Your sin will find you out in eternity. This present life is not all. There is a future life, and our acts and their consequences will follow us into it.

CONCLUSION.—Is there a man here to-night contemplating sin? Don't do it. But many of us have sinned already and our sins are finding us out already. What shall we do? Fly to Christ. Gal. 3:13.

NO PEACE

"There is no peace, saith my God, to the wicked." Is. 57:21.

INTRODUCTION.—It is better to have peace in one's heart and deep poverty than to have overflowing plenty and no peace. To have no peace means to be in hell.

I. Who are the Wicked?

All men and women who refuse to bow to the rightful authority of Almighty God and obey Him whatever He may command are wicked. God's first and fundamental demand on men is that they believe on His Son Jesus Christ and accept Him as Saviour and Lord. 1 John 3:23; John 6:29. Every one therefore who does not believe on the Lord Jesus Christ and accept Him as their Saviour and Lord is a rebel against God and belongs to that class whom God designated as "the wicked."

II. No Peace for the Wicked.

1. First of all there is no peace with God.
2. In the next place there is no peace in their own souls. There are several things that rob the wicked man of peace:
   (a) Conscience.
   (b) The fear of calamity.
   (c) The fear of man.
   (d) The fear of death.
   (e) The fear of eternity.
3. There is no peace for the wicked in the life to come.

NO HOPE

"Having no hope." Eph. 2: 12.

"Others which have no hope." 2 Thess. 4: 13.

INTRODUCTION.—There are no words in the language more dreadful than those two: "No hope."

I. Who have no Hope.

There are three classes who have no hope:

1. The man who denies or doubts the existence of a personal God, a wise, mighty, and loving ruler of this universe, has no hope. He may cherish fond wishes about the future, but wishes are not hope. Hope is a well-founded expectation.
2. The man who denies the truth of the Bible has no hope. He has no expectation for the future that has a solid and certain foundation underneath it.
3. The man who believes in the Bible but does not accept and confess the Christ it presents as his own personal Saviour and Master has no hope.
   The Bible holds out absolutely no hope to any except those who accept the Saviour whom it is man's purpose to reveal. John 3: 36; Heb. 10: 26-30.

II. In what Sense have these three Classes no Hope?

1. They have no hope, no well-founded and sure expectation of blessedness for the life that now is.
   (a) In the first place they have no guarantee of continued prosperity.

(b) They have no guarantee of continued capacity to enjoy prosperity even if it continues.

(c) They have no guarantee of continued life.

2. But infinitely worse than this is the fact that they have no hope for the life that is to come.

(a) The man out of Christ has no hope of blessedness after death.

(b) No hope of glad reunion with friends who have gone or may go.

(c) No hope of pardon.

(d) No hope of escape from the wrath of God against sin and unbelief. Rom. 6: 23.

III The Believer in Christ has Hope.

1. He has hope for the life that now is. Rom. 8: 28; Phil. 4: 6, 7, 19; Rom. 8: 32.

2. Hope for the life to come. Tit. 1: 2.

Conclusion.—Which do you prefer to-night, the no hope of men out of Christ, or the glorious hope of Christians? You have your choice. Which will you take?

FALSE HOPES

"Many will say unto me in that day, Lord, Lord, have we not prophesied in thy name? and in thy name have cast out devils? and in thy name have done many wonderful works? And then will I profess unto them, I never knew you: depart from me, ye that work iniquity." Matt. 7: 22, 23.

Introduction.—We see clearly from this text that there are many who expect to enter the kingdom of heaven who will not succeed, many who expect to spend eternity in heaven who will spend eternity in hell.

I. What are some of the False Hopes Men Entertain?

1. The hope that "God is too good to damn any one."

(a) A very sad confession for any man to make who is living a life of sin is that he believes in the goodness of God. What shall we say, then, of the man who is living in sin, who tramples God's holy will under foot, who breaks God's laws, and makes God's goodness an excuse for doing it?

(b) What proof is there in the Bible or history or experience that God is too good to punish the wicked? 2 Pet. 3:9.

(c) But not only is the hope that God is too good to punish men for sin and the rejection of Christ contrary to Scripture, it is also contrary to the teachings of history and experience.

2. The hope of being saved by our own goodness. Rom. 3:20; Gal. 3:10.
3. The hope that a man can be saved by a mere religious profession. This is the false hope of the text quoted.
4. The hope that a man can be saved by a faith that does not lead a man to quit sin. Jas. 2:14, R. V.; 1 John 5:4, 5.
5. The hope that a man can be saved without being born again. John 3:3.

SPEECHLESS BEFORE GOD

"And he was speechless." Matt. 22:14.

I. What is the wedding garment? Rev. 19:7, 8; Eph. 4:24; Rev. 13:14. The wedding garment is righteousness and true holiness of character. It is Christ Himself. If we are to appear at that supper and keep our places, then we must be clothed with righteousness of heart and life, we must be clothed with true holiness, we must put on Christ Himself so that the beauty of Christ is seen in our lives.

II. Why the one not having on a wedding garment is cast out.

1. First because he is not fit for heavenly society. Heaven is a prepared place for prepared people, a holy place for holy people.
2. Because it is his own fault that he has not on a wedding garment.

Conclusion.—Have you on the wedding garment? The time for the wedding supper is fast drawing nigh.

PATHS TO PERDITION

"Enter ye in at the strait gate: for wide is the gate, and broad is the way, that leadeth to destruction, and many there be which go in thereat." Matt. 7:13.

I. The shortest path to perdition, the straightest and quickest way there is, is suicide.

II. The second path to perdition is impurity.

1. First of all impurity breeds unbelief in God and Christ and the Bible.
2. Impurity entangles people in relations that it is hard to get out of, and that one cannot remain in and be saved. Hell will be crowded with adulterers and adulteresses.
3. The next path to perdition is the love of money. 1 Tim. 6:9.
   (a) It leads to dishonest methods of acquiring money.
   (b) The consuming love for money blinds many men to the fact that there is anything but money worth striving for, so they leave their souls and their eternal interests utterly neglected.
   (c) Many who love money, when they are awakened to the fact that they have a soul and that it is lost won't come to Christ for fear they will have to give this money up if they do.
4. Love of pleasure is another path to perdition.
5. Infidelity. 2 Thess. 1:7-9; Mark 16:15, 16, R. V.
6. Reliance upon a mere profession of religion. Matt. 7. 21-23.
7. Putting off your conversion. Prov. 27:1; Prov. 29:1.

THE FAILURE OF JESUS CHRIST

"O Jerusalem, Jerusalem, thou that killest the prophets, and stonest them which are sent unto thee, how often would I have gathered thy children together, even as a hen gathereth her chickens under her wings, and ye would not!" Matt. 23:37, 38.

Introduction.—These are among the most tender, pathetic, painful and passionate words that ever fell from the lips of Him who spake as never man spake. It is the utterance of a heart that was aching for a love and trust that were denied it, and well-nigh breaking with a sense of disappointment at the utter failure of cherished desires.

I. The First Lesson is that All Christ's Efforts sometimes Fail.

II. The Second Thought of the Text is Why Jesus Christ Fails.
It is put in the text in three words, "ye would not." "I would;" ye would not.

III. The Results of Failure.
"Behold your house is left unto you desolate." The result of the failure of Jesus Christ is utter desolation for the one in whom He fails.

AN IDIOTIC BARGAIN

"What shall it profit a man if he shall gain the whole world and lose his own soul?" Mark 8:36.

I. Note First the Things Which are Contrasted.

1. The things which are contrasted are not the present and the future.
   It is true that the man who loses his soul does lose the future—the eternal future—but he does not gain the present. The one whose soul is saved does not lose the present to gain the future. He does indeed gain the future, the eternal future. He does not lose the present to gain it.
2. The things which are contrasted are the world and the soul. The world, the seen, tangible world, the world of sense and all it can give, money, pleasure, honor, "the lust of the flesh and the lust of the eye and the pride of life" (1 John 2:16). That is the one thing. The other is the soul, or the life. The man himself, the unseen, inner, real man. To lose our soul or life, is to lose ourselves, to lose true manhood, to fail of what God created us and intended us to be, to have the image of God rubbed out and the image of the devil stamped in its place, to lose all that is divinest and grandest about us, and with it to lose true peace, true joy, true and abiding glory and renown, the esteem of God, co-heirship with Christ, the "inheritance incorruptible and undefiled and that fadeth not away which is laid up for us in heaven."

3. Many are trading their souls for far less than the whole world.

II. Is there any Danger of Losing our Souls.

Yes. How do men lose their souls?

1. By persistence in sin.
2. The rejection of Christ.

Conclusion.—Every one out of Christ is losing his soul. Every year the ruin becomes more complete. And it will go on until the last spark of true manhood is extinguished, until the last trace of the Divine image is obliterated, until the last breath of peace is vanished, until the last note of joy is silenced, until the last glimmer of glory is gone out, until the last whisper of approval has died away, until the last phantom of hope has disappeared, until this glorious and undying soul which God made in His own image and which Christ died to save, in hopeless discord with itself, contorted into the very image of Satanic evil, tempest tossed with vile and insatiable passions, scorned by its fellow victims and itself, agonizing over its fathomless woe, nursing to its bosom its inconsolable despair, passes out "into the outer darkness where there is the weeping and the gnashing of teeth." Is the whole world worth such a sacrifice?

A BRILLIANT AND BITTER INFIDEL CONVERTED

"And Saul, yet breathing out threatenings and slaughter against the disciples of the Lord." Acts 9: 1.

"What shall I do, Lord?" Acts 22: 10.

Introduction.—These texts set before us two scenes in the life of Saul of Tarsus. In the one we see Saul of Tarsus filled with hate of Jesus Christ breathing threatening and slaughter against His disciples, in the other we see the same Saul of Tarsus on his face before Jesus Christ, acknowledging Him as Lord and surrendering the whole control of his life into Jesus' hands. Saul of Tarsus was the most brilliant and most bitter disbeliever in Jesus Christ the world ever saw; he became the most devoted believer in and servant of Jesus Christ of whom history informs us. We are to study the thrilling conversion of this remarkable man.

I. Why He Was Converted.

1. First of all he was converted because he was sincere.
2. Saul of Tarsus was converted because he studied the Scriptures. Many a skeptic and infidel is not converted because he won't study the Scriptures.
3. Saul of Tarsus was converted in the third place because he yielded to the light when it came.

II. How the Bitter and Brilliant Infidel Was Converted.

1. First of all the life, character and testimony of Stephen led to his conversion.
2. The second thing that led to the conversion of Saul was prayer. Stephen prayed for him.
3. The third thing that led to Saul's conversion was that Jesus Christ met him. That was the decisive thing.
4. He cried and cried honestly, "What shall I do, Lord?"

III. The Results of the Conversion of the Brilliant and Bitter Infidel.

1. Saul of Tarsus became a completely transformed man, a gloriously transformed man.
2. Became a mighty power for good.
3. He obtained priceless possessions for himself.

Conclusion.—Such were the results of his conversion, such will also be the results of your conversion. Will you not then be converted to-night?

A HARD ROAD

"The way of transgressors is hard." Prov. 13:15.

I. In the Life that now is.

1. Makes an uneasy conscience.
2. Sin will inevitably be followed by exposure.
3. Wherever there is sin there will also be penalty.
   (a) One of the penalties of sin is the loss of the confidence of our fellow man, and the consequent loss of opportunity.
   (b) A second penalty of sin is the physical penalty. There is the most intimate connection between our bodies and our characters.

(c) A third penalty of sin is a loss of grip. It is a well-known fact that when sin gets into the lives of business men they oftentimes lose their grip on business, and hurry on to financial ruin, when it enters the lives of artists they often lose their genius and skill, when it enters into the lives of authors their minds become clouded.

(d) A fourth penalty of sin is bondage.

(e) Blindness. Sin robs the sinner of the vision that is most priceless,—moral and spiritual vision.

II. In the Life to Come.

The penalties of sin do not end with the life that now is. Sin and suffering forever go hand in hand. If we die sinners we shall go into the next world sinners, and being sinners we shall be sufferers. In this life we may get the first fruits of our sin, but there we get the full harvest.

CONCLUSION.—What, then, shall the sinner do? Is. 55: 7.

HOPELESS CASES

"Give not that which is holy unto the dogs, neither cast ye your pearls before swine, lest they trample them under their feet, and turn again and rend you." Matt. 7: 6.

INTRODUCTION.—It is evident from the text that there are men and women in the world whose case is hopeless. Men and women who are so wedded to sin and swill that it is a waste of time, and worse than a waste of time, to preach God's truth tothem; you might as well cast pearls before swine, you will only be torn for your trouble. As hogs want corn and swill, and not pearls, so these want animal gratification and sin, not truth.

Who are the swine that it is useless and worse than useless to cast pearls of God's precious truth before?

I. Those Who Are Not Hopeless Cases.

1. The men of no race upon earth are hopeless cases simply because they belong to that race.
2. Great sinners are not hopeless cases. 1 Tim. 1: 15.
3. Skeptics are not hopeless cases.

4. Men who are morally weak, or morally impotent, men who have no will power. 2 Cor. 12: 9.

II. Cases that Are Hopeless.

1. First of all, the cases of men and women who have died without Jesus Christ are hopeless. John 8: 21.
2. The case of any one who has committed the unpardonable sin is hopeless. Matt. 12: 31, 32.
   What is that sin? Many who think they have committed the unpardonable sin have not approached it.
3. The blindly conceited man. Prov. 26: 12.
4. The man who will not give up sin is a hopeless case.
5. Those who won't give up their unbelief are also hopeless cases.
6. The man whose conscience is seared by persistent resistance to the Holy Spirit.

Conclusion.—Some of you who have thought yourselves hopeless cases are not, so turn to Christ and He will save you to-night. But there are some here to-night who do not think their cases hopeless, who indeed are not much concerned about themselves, who are fast hurrying toward a position that is hopeless.

WHERE WILL YOU SPEND ETERNITY?

"Whither goest thou?" John 16: 5.

Introduction.—The most important question that can face any man when he comes to leave this present world is, "Whither goest thou?" or, "Where will you spend eternity?"

I. First of all remember there is an eternity.

II. In the next place remember you must spend that eternity somewhere.

III. Remember, in the third place, that the question where you will spend eternity is vastly more important than the question where you will spend your present life.

IV It is possible for us to know where we shall spend eternity.

V. Bear in mind that we will spend eternity in one of two places—in heaven or in hell.

VI. Where you will spend eternity will be settled in the life that now is. John 8: 24, 21; 2 Cor. 5: 10.

VII. Where you will spend eternity will be determined by what you do with Jesus Christ. John 3: 36; 2 Thess. 1: 7-9.

GOD'S LAST INVITATION

"Whosoever will let him take the water of life freely." Rev. 22: 17.

INTRODUCTION.—This is God's last invitation. With it this great book of invitations closes.

I. What is the Water of Life?

1. The water of life is the Holy Spirit. John 7: 37-39.
2. The Holy Spirit is a Divine Person who is ready to come into any man's being and take possession of it and rule it and fill it with joy and peace and beauty.

II. Why the Holy Spirit is called the Water of Life.

1. First of all because He satisfies thirst. John 4: 14.
2. Because He not only satisfies but brings life. John 4: 14. The moment you take the Holy Spirit you get everlasting life.

III. How to Get this Water of Life. "Whosoever Will let him Take."

Two words to emphasize then, "will" and "take."

THE NEW BIRTH

"Ye must be born again." John 3: 7.

INTRODUCTION.—Describe circumstances and ——

I. The Necessity of the New Birth.

1. The necessity of the new birth is absolute. "Ye must be born again." There is nothing that will take the place of the new birth.
   (a) A moral life will not take the place of the new birth.
   (b) Quitting your sins is not enough.
   (c) Joining the church is not enough.
   (d) Being very religious is not enough.

2. This necessity of the new birth is universal. Absolutely no man will enter the Kingdom of God without the new birth. John 3: 3, 7.

II. What is the New Birth.

1. Baptism is not the new birth. Acts 8: 13, 21-23.
2. Church membership is not the new birth. Acts 5: 1-11.
3. Reform is not the new birth.
4. What is the new birth? 2 Cor. 5: 17.

III. How to be Born Again.

John 1: 12; John 3: 14, 15.

CONCLUSION.—This doctrine of the new birth sweeps away *false* hopes, but it substitutes a *true* hope.

SAVED

"For by grace are ye saved through faith." Eph. 2: 8.

I. Who are Saved?

Every one who believes in Jesus Christ is saved. Every one who really believes in Jesus as the Son of God and shows that he really believes by taking Jesus to be his own personal Saviour and his Lord and Master. To every such an one God says, as He says in our text to the believers in Ephesus, "by grace ye *are* saved."

II. From What we are Saved.

1. From all guilt. 2 Cor. 5: 21; 1 John 1: 7.
2. From God's displeasure.
3. I am saved from the condemnation of my own conscience; from remorse.
4. From the power of sin. John 8: 36.
5. From future judgment. John 5: 24; Acts 17: 31.

III. To What we are Saved.

1. To peace and joy. Rom. 5: 1; 1 Pet. 1: 8.
2. To a true and pure and holy and useful life.
3. To God's favor.
4. To Sonship. John 1: 12.
5. To eternal life. John 3: 16.

IV. How we are Saved.

1. We are saved by grace.
2. Through faith.

NO SALVATION EXCEPT IN CHRIST

"And in none other is there salvation; for neither is there any other name under heaven given among men wherein we must be saved." Acts 4:12, R.V.

I. There is Salvation in Jesus Christ.

1. In the first place it is certain because the Bible says so.
2. It is certain because experience proves it.
   (a) Jesus Christ saves from the guilt of sin.
   (b) Jesus Christ also saves from the power of sin.
   (c) Jesus Christ not only saves from the guilt of sin and the power of sin, but from the future penalty of sin.
3. This salvation is for all who will accept it. Acts 10:43.

II. There is no Salvation out of Christ.

1. This is plain from Scripture. Text: 2 Thess. 1:7-9.
2. Experience proves the same thing. Where is the man who has found salvation out of Christ?
   (a) Where is the man out of Christ who has found salvation from the guilt of sin?
   (b) There is no salvation from the power of sin out of Jesus.
   (c) But as there is no salvation from the guilt of sin or the power of sin out of Christ, there can certainly be no salvation from the penalty of sin.
3. How great, then, is the folly of those who ask us to give up Christianity because of difficulties of one kind or another!

III. To be Lost, all that is Necessary is simply to Neglect this Salvation that Jesus Christ Brings.

1. In order to be lost it is not necessary to commit any grave offences against decency or morality.
2. No conscious or outspoken rebellion against God is necessary in order to be lost.
3. No speaking against, contempt or spitting upon the salvation God has so graciously provided is necessary in order to be lost.
4. It is not even necessary to make a decided refusal to Jesus Christ's invitation to come to Him and be saved.

FORGIVEN

"Thy sins are forgiven." Luke 7:48.

Introduction.—These are very simple words but they are very blessed words and very wonderful words. They are specially wonderful when we consider Who spoke them and to whom He spoke them. Picture scene Matt. 11:28; Luke 7:36-50. They teach us several very important lessons.

I. That Jesus Christ has power to Forgive Sins.

Many claim this power. Jesus has it.

II. There is Forgiveness for the Vilest Sinner.

III. This Forgiveness is to be had Now.

IV. All that one has to Do to Get this Forgiveness is just to Believe. v. 50.

WHY I AM GLAD I AM A CHRISTIAN

"Thanks be unto God for his unspeakable gift." 2 Cor. 9:5.

Introduction.—The unspeakable or indescribably great and glorious gift of this verse is Jesus Christ. Jesus is God's greatest gift and in Him all other good gifts are included. John 3:16; Rom. 8:32. My heart and all that is within me echoes the words of Paul. I do thank God for Jesus Christ and am so glad that I have taken Him for my Saviour and surrendered to Him as my Lord and Master.

I. Why I am Glad I am a Christian.

1. In the first place I am glad I am a Christian because I know that my sins are all forgiven. The Christian knows that every sin that he ever committed is blotted out. How does he know it?
   (a) First by God's own statement to that effect. Acts 10:43; 1 John 1:9; 1 John 1:7.
   (b) By the testimony of the Holy Spirit. Acts 10:43, 44.
2. Because Jesus Christ has set me free from sin's power.
3. Because I know that I am a child of God. John 1:12.
   (a) I know it, first, because His book says so.
   (b) I know it for the Spirit of God bears witness with my spirit that I am a child of God. Rom. 8:16.

4. I am glad I am a Christian because I have been delivered from all anxiety and fear. Phil. 4:6, 7.
5. Because I have found a deep and abiding and overflowing joy. 1 Pet. 1:8.
6. Because I know I shall live forever. 1 John 2:17.
7. I am glad that I am a Christian because I know that I have an "inheritance, incorruptible," etc. 1 Pet. 1:4, 5.

GOD'S TESTIMONY TO JESUS CHRIST

"And lo, a voice from heaven, saying, This is my beloved Son, in whom I am well pleased." Matt. 3:17.

INTRODUCTION.—The most fundamental and important question in religion is, Is Jesus Christ the Son of God? If He is, your duty and mine is clear. If He isn't, then while our duty on many great questions may not be clear, some things at least are settled. On many occasions and in many ways God has testified that Jesus Christ is His Son. It is not only in times lying in the past, of which we have a record in that unique book the Bible, but also in our own day, that God is bearing testimony, that He is His Son.

I. God Testifies that Jesus is His Son in the Passage before us.

With an audible voice from heaven. (Describe scene.) That settled it. There is no more room for controversy or debate or doubt. "But," some will say, "suppose this didn't happen? Suppose the record here in Matthew and the other Gospels is a fabrication?"

The testimony of such witnesses as those to whom we owe those records and who were present and who sealed their testimony with their blood, is to be received against the testimony of those who don't even claim to have been there, and who didn't live until centuries afterward, and who admit that they know nothing about it, and who spin their theories not out of any recorded facts but out of their inner consciousness. It is a question of observed fact against speculative guesses. Which will you believe?

Another place where God gave His testimony to Jesus by an audible voice: Transfiguration. Matt. 17:5.

II. God bore Testimony to Jesus Christ by the Miracles He gave Him to Do.

John 3: 2. For centuries the enemies of Christ have been trying to invent a theory to discredit these Gospel stories. Every effort has failed utterly. One theory is set up simply to give way to another. But if Jesus did these things, His claims are established by facts.

III. God has borne Witness to Jesus Christ by the Resurrection from the Dead.

The certainty of the resurrection. This settles the question. Jesus' claims. Put to death for making them. Claims that God would set His seal to this claim by raising Him. God did this. God's testimony by the resurrection absolutely unanswerable.

IV. God Himself bore Witness to Jesus Christ by His Ascension.

To this there were many witnesses. At least eleven. Luke 20: 50, 51; Acts 1: 6-9. This Ascension settles the question of Christ's Sonship.

V. God bore Witness to Jesus Christ by the Gift of the Holy Spirit.

The coming of the Holy Spirit was a conclusive proof of Jesus' claims that He was the Son of God and that He was going to the Father. When the Holy Spirit came upon them so unmistakably the disciples knew for a certainty that Jesus was with the Father and had received for them the Holy Spirit as He promised. Acts 2: 32, 33.

VI. Not only did God give the Holy Spirit at Pentecost in Testimony to Jesus' Divinity! God gives the Holy Spirit to-day to those who Accept Him as Divine and Surrender their Wills to Him.

Acts 5: 28-32. This is a very practical, present-day proof.

VII. God bears Testimony to-day that Jesus Christ is the Son of God in another way, and that is by the Transforming Power of Christ in the Soul.

Jesus Christ proves Himself Divine to those who accept Him as Divine. The question of whether or not Jesus is the Son of God may be settled by an appeal to God's testimony to Jesus Christ in the past, but it may be also settled by an appeal to God's testimony to Jesus Christ to-day.

CONCLUSION.—In seven ways, then, God has borne testimony to Jesus Christ that He is His Son. This, then, is the question that confronts every one here to-night who is out of Christ, "What shall I do with the Son of God?"

LOST—SAVED

"The Son of Man is come to seek and to save that which was lost." Luke 19: 10.

INTRODUCTION. — That verse contains two short words that have a world of meaning in them. One of the words has a whole world of light in it. The other word has a world of darkness in it.

I. Lost.

Our text suggests the great truth that every soul out of Christ, every soul that Christ has not definitely saved, is lost.

1. In that you are a sinner.
2. Slaves of sin. John 8: 34.
3. All out of Christ are lost in that if they do not turn to Christ they will be lost eternally. Every man out of Christ is lost now and he will be lost eternally unless Christ saves him.

II. Saved.

Here our text comes in with its message of hope and joy. You are lost, but the Son of Man came to seek and to save that which was lost.

1. He is seeking to save you.
   (a) by His providence.
      (1) That is why you are here to-night.
      (2) Death of child.
      (3) Sickness, etc.
   (b) By His Spirit.
   (c) By His Word.

2. He can save.
    (a) From guilt of sin.
    (b) From power of sin.
    (c) He came to seek the utterly lost.

Conclusion.—Every man or woman will go out of here to-night lost or saved.

A CONVERTED INFIDEL'S PREACHING

"And straightway he preached Christ in the synagogues, that he is the the Son of God." Acts 9: 20, R. V.

Introduction.—There was perhaps never a more amazed audience than that one that heard Saul's first sermon in Damascus. (Describe circumstances.) The first thing I want you to look at is the preacher in the text, the second thing to look at is the preacher's message.

I. The Preacher.

Three good reasons why this particular preacher's message should command attention and be accepted, taken together they prove that the message is undoubtedly true.

1. First of all, he had been an enemy of Jesus whom He now proclaimed to be the Son of God.
   The doctrine that Jesus was the Son of God was not something that Saul had taken up without any thorough thought. Saul had opposed this doctrine with all the vigor of an intense soul. When a man like that turns completely around and says, "I was wrong, utterly wrong; Jesus is the Son of God," we ought to give his change of opinion careful attention.
2. Saul's testimony ought to have great weight for another reason, because of what he sacrificed for his opinion. Saul's change of opinion cost him much, it cost him everything of a worldly character that he possessed. When a man of brains and education like Saul of Tarsus makes sacrifices like that for a change of opinion his new opinion must command great consideration.

3. But there is a third reason and a better one yet, why Saul's opinion must have weight, indeed, the reason is so absolutely conclusive that if we are thoroughly honest we must say Saul was certainly right in what he says, and Jesus, as Saul says, "the Son of God." That reason is the way in which Saul came to change his opinion.

Saul tells us why he changed his opinion. He says it was because as he came near to Damascus at the noon hour he saw Jesus Himself in such glory that it blinded him, and he heard Jesus say, etc. (Acts 9:5, 6; 22:16-18). Now if Saul really saw Jesus thus in the glory, and Jesus said this, and Saul was commissioned to be His authoritative representative, then Jesus certainly is the Son of God; there is no more room for debate.

Did Saul really see Jesus and hear Him say these things? He says He did. Then Saul either lied, or made the story up, or else he was mistaken, or had a sunstroke or something of that sort. Did he lie and make the story up? Men do not manufacture lies for the sake of sacrificing home, position, money, comfort, ease and everything dear in life for them. Was Saul the victim of delusion and fancy through sunstroke, or overwrought imagination or something of that kind? The recorded and well-attested facts in the case make this theory impossible.

Some one may say that the whole story in Acts is a fiction. Let him study it. I challenge any honest lawyer or historical critic to study these stories and say they do not bear the unmistakable marks of truth. We arrive, then, at this point: that Saul of Tarsus changed from a bitter infidel to a believer and preacher, that Jesus is the Son of God because Jesus Himself appeared to him in glory as the Son of God. Saul actually saw Him, and He appointed Saul His authoritative representative. It is then absolutely settled not as a theological speculation but as an established fact that Jesus Christ is the Son of God.

II. The Message.

1. It is not that Jesus is a good man or even the best man that ever walked the earth. "Jesus is the Son of God."
2. Not merely Jesus is a great teacher, but Jesus is the Son of God.
3. Not merely Jesus is a perfect man and our example, but Jesus is the Son of God.
4. Jesus is the Son of God. What does that involve?
   (a) Absolute and whole-hearted trust in Him.
   (b) Trusting Him for salvation.
   (c) Surrender of our life to Him.
   (d) Surrender of our thought to Him.
   (e) There is saving power in the doctrine that Jesus is the Son of God. It will save any man who believes it from the heart and acts upon it.
   (1) It will bring Him life eternal. John 20: 31.
   (2) It will bring victory over the world. 1 John 5: 5.

THE APPALLING SIN OF UNBELIEF IN JESUS CHRIST

"He that believeth not is condemned already, because he hath not believed in the name of the only begotten Son of God." John 3: 18.

INTRODUCTION.—The failure to put faith in Jesus Christ is not a misfortune, it is a sin, a grievous sin, an appalling sin, a damning sin.

I. Unbelief in Jesus Christ is an Appalling Sin Because of Whom Jesus Christ is. Because of the Dignity of His Person, Jesus Christ is the Son of God.

A dignity attaches to Jesus Christ that attaches to the person of no angel, or archangel, to none of the principalities or powers in the heavenly places. His is the name that is above every name that at the name of Jesus every knee should bow and every tongue confess that Jesus Christ is Lord. An injury done to Jesus Christ is, then, a sin of vastly greater magnitude than a sin done to man.

II. In the Second Place Unbelief in Jesus Christ is an Appalling Sin not only Because of the Dignity of Christ's Person but also Because Faith is the Supreme Thing Which is Due to Him.

Jesus is worthy many things. But first of all, underlying all else, Jesus Christ is worthy of faith, man's confidence is due Jesus Christ.

III. Because Jesus Christ is the Incarnation of all the Infinite Moral Perfections of God's Own Being.

"God is light and in Him is no darkness at all." This infinite absolute light which God is, this infinite holiness and love and truth, is incarnated in Jesus Christ; and the refusal to accept Him is the refusal of light and choice of darkness.

IV. Unbelief in Jesus Christ is an Appalling Sin, Because it is Trampling Under Foot the Infinite Love and Mercy of God.

Jesus Christ is the supreme expression of God's love and mercy to sinners. John 3: 16.

Conclusion.—It is as clear as day that unbelief in Jesus Christ is an appalling sin. Theft is a gross sin, adultery is worse, murder is shocking, but all these are as nothing to the violation of the dignity and majesty of the person of Jesus Christ, the only-begotten Son of God, by our unbelief. Give up your awful unbelief in Jesus Christ and accept Him to-night.

THE SECRET OF A HAPPY LIFE

"Rejoice in the Lord always and again I say rejoice." Phil. 4: 4.

Introduction.—Every one wants to be happy. Every one ought to be happy. Every one can be happy. God has provided a way in which we can have joy every moment of our lives.

The secret of a happy life is a wonderful secret. The prescription is simple.

I. The First Ingredient in the Prescription is, Obtain the Forgiveness of Your Sins by Repenting of Them, Confessing Them and Accepting Jesus Christ as Your Saviour.

Ps. 32: 1; Is. 55: 7; Acts 10: 43.

II. **The Second Ingredient in the Prescription is to Obtain the Holy Spirit by Absolute Surrender to God.**
Acts 5: 32.

III. **The Third Ingredient is Prayer. Frequent Prayer.**
John 16: 24.

IV. **The Fourth Ingredient is Bible Study.**
John 15: 11.

DAVID'S SIN

"The thing that David had done displeased the Lord." 2 Sam. 11: 27.

INTRODUCTION.—The story is too horrible for public recital, though if one will read it in private with earnest prayer he may find exceedingly precious lessons in it. It was one of the most horrible and dastardly crimes of history. The record of it and its consequences has held many back from contemplated sin, and has brought hope to many a despairing heart.

The history of David's sin teaches seven great lessons.

I. That a very good man, if he gets his eyes off from God and His Word, may easily fall into very gross sin.

II. That God never looks upon any man's sin with the least degree of allowance.

III. That whatsoever a man soweth that he shall also reap, and like the farmer he will reap much more than he sows.

IV. The fourth lesson of David's sin is that the sin of God's servants gives great occasions for the enemies of the Lord to blaspheme.

V. That the sin of God's people is base ingratitude toward God.

VI. That there is full and free and abundant pardon for the vilest sinner.

VII. Pardon is found by the confession of our sin. Cf. Ps. 32: 1-5; Luke 18: 10-14.

JOYS OF THE CHRISTIAN

"Rejoice always." 1 Thess. 6: 16.

INTRODUCTION.—There are three things that Christians should do constantly: rejoice, pray, and give thanks. 1 Thess. 5· 16-18. Constant rejoicing, unceasing prayer, continual thanksgiving—this is God's will in Christ Jesus regarding us. "Rejoice always." That is our duty, that is also our privilege. God has made it possible for us to constantly rejoice. How much more our lives and our testimony would count for Christ if only we did rejoice always.

I. Joy of Sins Forgiven.

Ps. 32:1.

II. The Joy of Communion With God.

1 John 1:3; Ps. 16:11. Not only in heaven is there fullness of joy in God's presence, but in the present life there is fullness of joy in God's presence, in communion with Him. There are three methods of communion with God:

1. The first of these is prayer, breathing out to God the desires of our hearts.
2. The second method of communion is the method of thanksgiving.
3. The third method of communion with God is the method of worship. Worship is different from either prayer or thanksgiving. In prayer we are asking for something; in thanksgiving we are returning thanks for something; in worship we are just bowing before God contemplating and adoring Himself and His Son Jesus Christ.

III. The Joy of Feasting on the Word.

Jer. 15:16.

IV. The Joy of Victorious Service.

There is great joy in serving one we love, and especially is there great joy if our service is effective. The Christian loves Christ; his service of Christ may always be successful and victorious.

V. The Joy of Winning Souls.

Few joys this side of heaven so great as the joy of bringing someone else to Christ.

VI. The Joy of Suffering for Christ.

Acts 5:40.

VII. The Joy of the Holy Spirit.

1 Thess. 1:6.

SINCERE BUT NOT SAVED

"Send men to Joppa and call for Peter who shall tell thee words, whereby thou shalt be saved." Acts 11: 13, 14.

INTRODUCTION.—A man may be a sincere and earnest seeker after truth and still not be a saved man as yet.

I. The Character of Cornelius.

1. He was "a devout man." It is evident that his devotion was genuine for it affected his whole household, the soldiers under him and his kinsman and his near friends.
2. But Cornelius was not only a devout man towards God, he was also righteous towards man. V. 22.
3. Cornelius was a generous man.
4. Cornelius was a man of prayer.
5. Cornelius was an eager seeker after more light.
6. Cornelius was ready to obey the truth when he found it, whatever it might require of him. Altogether this man Cornelius was a man of singularly lofty character, yet with all this the inspired record tells us that Cornelius was not yet saved, that he needed salvation.

II. How Cornelius was Saved.

1. First of all he prayed for light. 10: 31, 32; comp. 10 : 22 and 11: 13, 14. Cornelius felt that he had not the whole truth. He knew he had not peace. He knew that for all his excellencies he was a sinner and needed pardon, and he sought God to find where pardon could be found.
2. He obeyed the light that God gave him step by step. There are some who will not take a step until God shows them the whole way. Such people never find the way. But if we are ready to take a step at a time God will lead us into the perfect day.
3. The third step toward salvation was, that he heard the simple Gospel of Christ crucified and risen again, and of remission of sins through simple faith in Him. The sermon Cornelius heard was very short. Peter simply told him a few facts about Jesus. How God

"preached peace by Him." How "He was Lord of all." How He had wrought wonders delivering people from the power of Satan. How He had been crucified and raised again. How He had been appointed of God to be "the Judge of living and dead," and then wound up by saying, "To Him bear all the prophets witness, that through His name whosoever believeth in Him shall receive remission of sins." That was all he heard and you have all heard it.

4. Then Cornelius took the decisive step. He believed in Christ right there and was saved at once. As good and exemplary as Cornelius was he was saved in the same way that the coarse, brutal, prayerless, godless Philippian jailer was saved, by faith in Jesus Christ for the pardon of sin. When Peter spoke of the forgiveness of sins he knew he needed it. When Peter said, "Whosoever believeth in Him shall receive remission of sins," he said that means me, and he believed and received remission then and there.

One more thing, the Holy Ghost came upon Cornelius then and there in testimony that God had accepted him, and he began to magnify God in the power of the Holy Ghost.

AN OPEN DOOR

"I am the door by me if any man enter in he shall be saved, but shall go in and out, and shall find pasture." John 10: 9.

INTRODUCTION.—Wide-awake men are always on the alert for open doors. Some are seeking an open door to wealth, others an open door to fame, others still an open door to power and others an open door to wisdom and learning. One of the chief differences between the men who succeed and the men who fail in this world is, that the former are quick to see the doors which stand open and quick to enter them, and the latter are so slow to see, or so slow to enter, that the door slams in their face while they are standing wondering whether they would better go in or not. An open door which if entered leads to more that is good and glorious than any other door that men have ever entered. John 10: 9. Jesus Christ is the Door.

I. To What is He the Door?

1. He is the door to salvation. "By me if any man enter in he shall be saved."
2. He is the door to life. John 10: 10, R. V.
3. Christ is also the door to liberty and security. "By me if any man enter in he shall be saved, and shall go in and out, and shall find pasture."
4. Jesus Christ is also the door to pasture. "Shall find a pasture." Food, satisfaction. It is in Christ alone that the soul of man can find pasture, find food, find satisfaction.

II. To Whom is the Door Open?

"I am the door; by me *if any man* enter in, he shall find pasture." That door is open to any man, to every man.

CONCLUSION.—The door stands open to all here. The door will not always stand open. Luke 13: 25.

A PLAIN ANSWER TO A GREAT QUESTION

"And brought them out, and said, Sirs what must I do to be saved?

"And they said, Believe on the Lord Jesus Christ, and thou shalt be saved, and thy house." Acts 16: 30, 31.

INTRODUCTION.—The question and answer are found in the sixteenth chapter of Acts.

I. The Importance of the Question.

II. The Plain Answer.

1. Note first the confidence of this answer. Thou *shalt* be saved. What made Paul so confident?
   (a) God had revealed it to him. Gal. 1: 12.
   (b) Paul had tried it.
2. Note second the completeness of the answer, "Believe in the Lord Jesus Christ and thou shalt be *saved.*" Not helped, not made better, not patched up, but "saved."
3. Note third and lastly the simplicity of the answer. "Believe on the Lord Jesus Christ and thou shalt be

saved." Can not any one understand that? To believe on any one is to commit yourself to them. To believe in a doctor when you are sick is to put your case in his hands, to surrender yourself to his directions. To believe in a life-boat when you are on a sinking ship is to commit yourself to it, get into it, to surrender yourself to its keeping. 2 Tim. 1: 12. "Believe on the *Lord Jesus Christ.*" Paul said, Believe in Him as *Lord*, the Divine One to whom we cry as did Thomas, "My Lord and my God." Believe in Him as *Jesus*, *i. e. Saviour*, the One who bore our sins in His own body on the tree, the One who, as a risen One in the place of power at God's right hand, saves from the power of sin day by day. Believe in Him as Christ; God's anointed king, to whom we shall render our homage and obedience. The One to whom we shall render absolutely the control of our lives. "Believe in the Lord Jesus Christ and thou shalt be saved."

AN IMPERATIVE AND IMMEDIATE NEED

"We must be saved." Acts 4: 12.

INTRODUCTION.—Every one here who cannot say, "I have been saved" should say with that intensity of emphasis that comes from depth of conviction, "I must be saved." You need a Saviour more than you need anything else. That is your most imperative and most immediate need.

I. Why We Need a Saviour.

1. You need a Saviour because you are a sinner. Rom. 3: 22, 23.
2. You need a Saviour, in the second place, because you have not only sinned but because you have committed the greatest sin a man can commit. Cf. Matt. 22: 37, 38.
3. You need a Saviour, in the third place, because you are under a curse. Gal. 3: 10.
4. You need a Saviour, in the fourth place, because you are in bondage to sin. John 8: 34.

5. You need a Saviour because you cannot save yourself.
   (a) You cannot save yourself from the guilt of sin.
   (b) Can we save ourselves from the power of present sin?
6. You need a Saviour because if you are not saved you must spend eternity in hell. Rev. 20: 15.

A KING'S FOLLY AND WHAT IT COST: A TRAGEDY

"Thou art weighed in the balances and art found wanting." Dan. 5: 27.

INTRODUCTION.—The Bible is the most dramatic book that was ever written, etc. (Picture scene.)

I. Belshazzar was Weighed in the Balance of God.

He had been weighed in other balances and not found wanting. Balance of his own judgment? Balance of public opinion? Balance of worldly philosophy.

We, too, each one of us, are being weighed in God's scales. The great question is What do we weigh there?

II. Belshazzar was found Wanting, Why?

1. V. 22. "Thou hast not humbled thine heart."
2. Belshazzar had refused to humble his heart in face of God's known dealings with others. "*Though thou knewest all this.*"
3. V. 23. Belshazzar had lifted himself up against the Lord of heaven.
4. V. 23, last half. "The God in whose hand thy breath is, and whose are all thy ways, hast thou not glorified."

III. The Consequences of Belshazzar's Folly. What it Cost.

1. His kingdom. V. 26. You too have a kingdom. Jas. 2: 5.
2. His life. V. 30. So with us. Rom. 6: 23.

THE WONDERFUL JESUS

"For unto us a child is born, unto us a Son is given; and the government shall be upon his shoulder: and his name shall be called Wonderful," etc. Is. 9: 6.

INTRODUCTION.—The prophet Isaiah with a mind illumined by the Holy Spirit looked down 710 years and saw the coming of Jesus of Nazareth and uttered the sublime words of our text. In them is wrapped up a world of meaning concerning the Divine Glory, the Matchless Character, and Wonderful Offices of our Lord. In the Bible names have meaning, especially when applied to God the Father, the Son, or the Holy Ghost. The name is a revelation of what one is. Jesus is called wonderful because He is wonderful.

I. Jesus is Wonderful in His Nature.

1. He is a Divine Being. He is Divine in a sense in which no other man is divine. The Bible is full of that great truth.
2. While He is Divine He is at the same time a Real Man. 1 Tim. 2:5.

II. Jesus is Wonderful in His Character.

His character was absolutely perfect. He was alsolutely without blemish and without spot. He was not only blameless but every possible perfection of character rested upon Him. There is not a perfection of character of which we can think that is not to be found in Him, and found in its fullness. His character is indeed wonderful. He is the wonder of the ages. He stands out absolutely peerless and alone. When any man ventures to put any one else alongside of Jesus Christ he at once loses the confidence of all candid and fair-minded men.

1. Jesus was perfect in holiness.
2. He was also perfect in love.

There are many other perfections in the character of Jesus; e. g., the perfection of His meekness and gentleness and humility and patience and courage and manliness.

III. Jesus is Wonderful in His Work.

1. In the first place He makes a perfect atonement for sin. Is. 53:6.
2. He also saves from sin's power. Indeed Jesus completely transforms men. 2 Cor. 5:17.
3. Jesus will do more wonderful things still in the future

CONCLUSION.—Jesus is indeed wonderful in the infinite glory of His Divine nature. He is wonderful in the matchless, absolute perfection of His character. He is wonderful in His work, blotting out all sin by His death, delivering from all sin by His resurrection life, transforming us from all remaining imperfection into the full glory of Sons of God by His living again. Jesus is the Wonderful. Now, what will you do with Him? What will you do with this wonderful Jesus? Will you accept Him or reject Him?

THE GREAT QUESTION OF THE DAY

"What shall I do with Jesus?" Matt. 27: 22.

INTRODUCTION.—If I should put it to this audience what is the great question of the day, I presume I would get a great variety of answers. Some would say, etc.

But there is a question of vastly more importance. A question upon the right decision of which immeasurably more depends. The question is this, "What shall I do with Jesus, which is called Christ?" It is not a new question. Pontius Pilate asked it more than 1800 years ago. Thousands upon thousands have asked it since. Upon a right decision of that question everything that is really worth having for time and for eternity depends. If you do the right thing with Jesus you will get everything that is worth having for time as well as for eternity. If you do the wrong thing with Jesus Christ you will lose everything that is really worth having for time as well as for eternity.

I. What we will Get if we Do the Right Thing with Jesus Christ.

1. If you do the right thing with Jesus Christ you will get forgiveness of sins. Acts 10: 43.
   What an unspeakable blessing the forgiveness of sins is. Ps. 32: 1.
2. You will get peace of conscience by doing the right thing with Jesus Christ.
3. You will get deliverance from the power of sin by doing the right thing with Jesus Christ.

4. You will get great joy by doing the right thing with Jesus Christ. 1 Pet. 1: 8.
5. If you do the right thing with Jesus Christ you get eternal life. John 3: 36; 1 John 5: 12.
   Eternal life. What has the world to put in comparison with that? Do the right thing with Jesus and you get eternal life, do the wrong thing with Jesus and you lose it.
6. There is something even better than eternal life that you get by doing the right thing with Jesus Christ. By doing the right thing with Jesus Christ you become a son of God and heir of God and joint heir with Jesus Christ. John 1: 12; Rom. 8: 17.

II. What is the Right Thing to Do with Jesus?

1. First of all to receive Him as your Saviour. John 1: 12.
2. Let Him into your heart. Rev. 3: 20.
3. Enthrone Him in your heart. He is the Christ, God's anointed King. Acts 2: 36.
4. Confess Him before the world as your Lord and Master. Matt. 10: 32, 33; Rom. 10: 9, R. V.

HOW TO BE SAVED

"And [he] brought them out, and said, Sirs, what must I do to be saved? And they said, Believe on the Lord Jesus Christ, and thou shalt be saved, and thy house." Acts 16: 30, 31.

INTRODUCTION.—God has not left us to guess how to be saved. The question has been asked and answered. The way of salvation is here made as plain as day. Notice the positiveness of the statement. All any one then has to do to be saved is to believe on the Lord Jesus Christ. (Cf. John 3: 16.)

What is to believe on the Lord Jesus Christ? What is involved in believing on the Lord Jesus?

I. Trust in Him for the Pardon of all my Sins.

"Believe on the Lord *Jesus.*" (Cf. Acts 13: 38, 39.)

II. The Surrender to Him of the Control of my Entire Life.

"Believe on the *Lord* Jesus."

III. Confession of Him as my Lord.

"Lord Jesus." Rom. 10: 9, R. V.

IV. The Surrender to Him of the Control of my Thoughts.

"Lord."

V. Looking to Him for Guidance.

VI. Study of His Words in order to Know His Will.

John 14: 23.

VII. Dependence upon Him for Strength to Do His Will.

John 15: 5.

CONCLUSION.—The first step of faith is possible right now, and it is absolutely sure that the moment you take it you will be saved.

THE ONLY FOUNDATION

"For other foundation can no man lay, than that is laid, which is Jesus Christ." 1 Cor. 3: 11.

INTRODUCTION.—Pholosophers and wise men have tried hard to lay some other foundation than Jesus Christ, but have failed utterly. Still they keep at it. They are bound in their foolish wisdom to find some other foundation than God's and in this way they are dooming themselves and their followers to wretchedness, failure, disappointment and sorrow here, and to shame, degradation and anguish hereafter.

I. Jesus Christ is the only Foundation for Obtaining the Forgiveness of Sin.

II. Jesus Christ is the only Foundation for Peace of Conscience

III. Jesus Christ is the only Foundation of Peace of Heart.

By peace of heart as distinguished from peace of conscience, we mean freedom from anxiety and worry.

IV. Jesus Christ is the only Foundation upon which to Build a Successful Attempt to Get the Victory over Sin.

John 8: 36.

V. Jesus Christ is the only Foundation for Comfort in Sorrow.

Matt. 11: 28.

VI. Jesus Christ is the only Foundation for Deep, Abiding, Overflowing Joy.

VII. Jesus Christ is the only Foundation for Hope.

VIII. The only Foundation for Eternal Life.

IX. The only Foundation for Social Regeneration.

WHEN IT PAYS TO BELIEVE IN JESUS CHRIST

"My God shall supply all your need according to his riches in glory, by Christ Jesus." Phil. 4: 19.

INTRODUCTION.—If there is anything in this world that pays it is to have a living faith in Jesus Christ. Just listen to that text. There is a guarantee to the believer on Christ to have every need supplied and that guarantee is good.

When it pays to be a believer in Jesus:

I. In Health and Strength.

It pays to be a Christian when one is well and strong. What has a strong man who is not a Christian to do that is worth doing? Without Christ there is nothing worthy for a well and strong man to do.

II. In Sickness.

It pays in many ways:

1. In the first place faith in Jesus Christ promotes restoration to health. It does this in an indirect way. Nothing is more conducive to health than a peaceful, contented, joyful, hopeful frame of mind. It is a certain fact that many people are well to-day who would be sick or dead if it had not been for direct answers to prayers for their healing.
2. It brings joy and blessing in the midst of sickness.

III. In Sorrow.

Happy is the man or woman who in the time of deep sorrow, the time when loved ones are taken away and the heart is lonely and aching, believes in Jesus Christ.

IV. In Adversity.

It makes one to rejoice and praise God in the midst of the loss of all one's property, and the complete overturning of our plans. Rom. 5: 3, 4; Rom. 8: 28.

V. In Prosperity.

No one needs faith in Jesus Christ more than a prosperous man.

1. Prosperity will eternally ruin any man who is not stayed and guided by a living faith in Jesus Christ.
2. In order to really enjoy their prosperity.

VI. In Death.

How dark is the hour of death if one has not a living faith on Jesus Christ. How bright is the hour of death if one has, etc. Phil. 1: 23; 2 Tim. 4: 6-8.

VII. In the Judgment.

It will pay to be a believer in Jesus Christ in the Judgment. Rom. 14: 12.

VIII. In Eternity.

In eternity to have believed in Jesus Christ will mean eternal life, eternal joy, eternal glory. In eternity not to have believed in Jesus Christ will mean eternal death, eternal darkness, eternal shame, eternal agony, eternal despair. John 3: 36.

ETERNAL LIFE, WHAT IT IS AND HOW TO GET IT

"The gift of God is eternal life." Rom. 6: 23.

I. What Eternal Life is.

1. Eternal life is real life. 1 Tim. 6: 12, 19, R. V.
2. "Eternal Life" is abundant life. John 10: 10, R. V.
3. Eternal life is joyous life. 1 Pet. 1: 8.
4. Eternal life is a life of true knowledge. John 17: 3.
5. Eternal life is endless life. John 10: 28.

II. Who can Have it?

Anybody. Rev. 22: 17.

III. How to Get it.

1. First it is a "gift."
2. It is "in Jesus Christ."
3. In order to get eternal life you have simply to take Him in whom it is. 1 John 5: 12.

REFUGES OF LIES

"Judgment also will I lay to the line, and righteousness to the plummet: and the hail shall sweep away the refuge of lies, and the waters shall overflow the hiding place." Is. 28: 17.

Introduction.—In the preceding verses of the chapter God has announced to Israel that there is a day of judgment coming for them. But the rulers of Israel regarded this warning with scorn. They spoke just as stout-hearted fools to-day talk. The Assyrian army came and destroyed the stout-hearted princes of Israel. Now God has declared there is to be another judgment, another hail, another day of dealing with ungodly and Christ-rejecting men. What these princes of Israel did: Strengthened their proud and wicked hearts and sought comfort in refuges of lies, in false hopes. Many are doing so to-day.

I. How to Tell a Refuge of Lies.

Five common sense tests by which you can tell a true refuge, one that will stand fast in the Day of Judgment from a false one, a Refuge of Lies, one that the tempest of hail shall sweep away and leave you exposed to the pitiless fury of the storm of eternal judgment.

1. The first test is this: Does the refuge in which you are trusting satisfy the highest demands of your own conscience. If not it will of course not satisfy God. 1 John 3: 20.
2. Is the refuge in which you are trusting delivering you from the power of sin? The refuge that cannot save us from the power of sin here cannot save us from the consequences of sin hereafter.
3. Will the refuge in which you are trusting stand the test of the dying hour?
4. Will the refuge in which you are trusting stand the test of the all-seeing eye of God in the judgment?
5. Will it stand the test of the Scripture? A refuge that will not stand the test of Scripture is utterly unreliable. The Bible is the book that the ages have tried and tested. Through these ages one philosopher after another has set up his opinions against the Bible.

But the philosophers each have had their day and gone down, but the Bible has withstood the wreck of the centuries.

II. Refuges Tested and Proven Refuges of Lies.

1. Universalism. Apply tests.
2. Infidelity. Apply tests.
3. Spiritualism. Apply tests.
4. Refusal to consider.
5. Morality.
6. Religious ceremonies.
7. Orthodoxy of belief.

CONCLUSION.—Is there a sure refuge? Yes. Is. 32. 2. Jesus Christ. Apply tests.

HARDENED

"But exhort one another daily, while it is called to-day; lest any of you be hardened through the deceitfulness of sin." Heb. 3: 13.

INTRODUCTION.—There is not a more solemn warning in the Bible than this. There is not a more timely warning in the Bible than this. All around us we see men and women who are being "hardened through the deceitfulness of sin." Three times in this one chapter God pleads with men, "Harden not your hearts."

I. Indications that one is Hardened.

1. The truth does not move us as it once did.
2. Jest about sacred things or listen approvingly to others when they jest about them.
3. Not deeply moved by thoughts of God's love.

II. Results of being Hardened.

1. The first evil that results from a hardened heart is a corrupt life. The hardening of the heart against the truth and against Christ leads inevitably to sin.
2. Spiritual blindness.
3. Loss of joy.
4. Utter despair.
5. Eternal death. Rom. 2: 5. There is no hope in the life that now is, there is no hope in the life that is to come for the man whose heart is finally hardened against Christ.

THE JUDGMENT DAY.

"He hath appointed a day in which he will judge the world in righteousness, by that man whom he hath ordained, whereof he hath given assurance unto all men, in that he hath raised him from the dead." Acts 17: 31.

INTRODUCTION.—Two events in the future are absolutely certain, the coming of Christ for His people, the coming of a judgment day for the world.

Note five things about this judgment day:

I. The Certainty of it.

The resurrection of Christ from the dead is a certain, incontrovertible fact, and it is a guarantee that there is a day of judgment coming. When Jesus was here upon earth He said that in coming days He would judge the world. (John 5: 22, 23.) Men scoffed at this claim. They put Him to death for making it, and the other claim involved in it, that He was the Son of God. But God set His seal to the claim by raising Him from the dead. The resurrection of Christ from the dead makes it absolutely certain that there is a Judgment Day coming.

II. The Universality of it.

"He will judge the *world.*"

III. The Basis of it, or About What the Judgment will be.

1. It will be about the deeds done in the body. 2 Cor. 5: 10, R. V.
2. The secret things will be judged. Rom. 2: 16.
3. The great basis of that judgment will be what men have done with Christ. John 3: 18, 19.

IV. Who will Sit as Judge.

That same Jesus whom you are rejecting to-day will be the judge in that day.

V. The Issues.

They will be eternal.

ETERNITY

"For our light affliction, which is but for a moment, worketh for us a far more exceeding and eternal weight of glory; while we look not at the things which are seen, but at the things which are not seen; for the things which are seen are temporal, but the things which are not seen are eternal." 2 Cor. 4: 17, 18.

INTRODUCTION.—The apostle Paul had to endure some things that to most men would seem very hard to bear, and some of these afflictions continued through years. But in speaking of these afflictions in our text Paul speaks of "our *light* affliction" and our affliction "which is *for the moment.*" Is thirty years but "a moment"? Yes, when compared with eternity. And is the loss of friends, the loss of ease, the loss of admiration and applause of man, the loss of home and native land, the loss of all men ordinarily hold dear, and imprisonment and shipwreck and scourging and wandering and hunger and stoning, is all this "light affliction"? Yes, when compared with the joy and honor and glory which is to be revealed to us. And when all the wealth, and pleasures and honors, that one can possibly get in this world are put in comparison with the eternal agony and ruin and despair and shame that it costs to live for the world, they too are nothing.

I. There is an Eternity and we Must Go there.

II. When and How we shall spend Eternity is Settled in the Life that now is.

III. How to Secure a Blessed and Glorious Eternity.

1. Believe on Jesus Christ. John 3: 16.
2. We must serve Jesus Christ.
3. The sufferings we endure, the sacrifices we make for Christ, make eternity richer. Matt. 5: 11, 12; Rom. 8: 18; 2 Tim. 2: 12.
4. We must use our money for Christ.

CONCLUSION.—The greatest practical question that confronts you and me to-night is, where shall we spend eternity, and how shall we spend eternity?

HELL

"If thy right eye causeth thee to stumble pluck it out, and cast it from thee: for it is profitable for thee that one of thy members should perish, and not that thy whole body should be cast into hell." Matt. 5: 29, R.V.

INTRODUCTION.—Text is from the Sermon on the Mount. Many persons who say they do not believe the whole Bible but they do believe the Sermon on the Mount.

I have also taken my text from the Revised Version for

some so-called liberal preachers are proclaiming to-day that the R. V. has done away with hell. There seems to be a good deal of it left in our text.

I. The Certainty of Hell.

Hell is a certainty.

1. Hell is certain because God's Word declares it. Matt. 25:41; 2 Thess. 1:7, 9; 2 Pet. 2:4, 9; Jude 14:15. Listen. Jesus spoke after He Himself had gone down into the grave and risen again and ascended to the right hand of God. He certainly knew now what He was talking about when He spoke of the future life. Rev. 21:8.
2. Experience, observation, common sense also point to the existence of hell.

II. The Character of Hell.

1. Hell is a place of physical anguish. This is plain from the Bible description of the future destiny of the impenitent. "Death" and "Destruction" are the terms most frequently used of the future punishment of sin. Both of these terms are defined in the Bible. Rev. 17:8; cf. Rev. 20:10; Rev. 21:8.
   In the next world we are not disembodied spirits. We have bodies. Not these same bodies, it is true, but bodies. The bodies of the damned will be the fit partner of the degraded spirits that inhabit them and partakers in all their shame and agony.
2. Hell is a place of remorse of conscience. Hell is a place of memory and remorse, remorse without a moment's rest, endless remorse.
3. Hell is a place of unsatisfied and consuming desires. Hell is a place where passion and desires exist in their highest potency, but where there is absolutely no gratification for them.
4. Hell is a place of ever-increasing moral degradation It is a "bottomless pit."
5. Hell is a place of shame.
6. Hell is a place of vile associations. Rev. 21:8.
7. Finally, hell is a place without hope.

A CHEERING PROMISE ABOUT HELL

"All liars shall have their part in the lake which burneth with fire and brimstone." Rev. 21: 8.

INTRODUCTION.—The subject of hell is one of the most awful subjects that any man can contemplate. There is but one subject that is more awful and that is sin. Sin is worse than hell. The suffering and misery that sin causes are not so awful as the sin which causes them. Hell with its vast ages of agony and shame is a frightful subject to contemplate, but even hell has its pleasant side. It is found in the text.

It is a comforting thought that there will not be one liar in heaven. There will be men in heaven who have been liars and have repented, but there will not be one man or woman there who persisted in their lying. I am sorry that there are any liars in the world, but there are, and as long as there are I am comforted to think that there is a hell for them to go to. A liar is a son of Satan, for the devil is a liar and the father of it. A liar is the most hopeless case on earth. He can only be saved by faith, and it is hard for a liar to have faith in God. He is such a liar himself that it is hard for him to put confidence in any one else. Men, you, that is the reason why so many liars are infidels. The case of the liar is very dark indeed, and we need not wonder that it is written that "all liars," etc.

I. Classes of Liars.

1. The slanderous liar, the liar who slanders his fellow men.
2. The atheistic liar. The slanderous liar slanders man, the atheistic liar slanders God.
3. The infidel liar. The slanderous liar slanders his fellow man, the atheistical liar slanders God, the infidel liar slanders the Bible, God's Word, infinitely the best book the world ever had; and in slandering God's Word he slanders the God who is the author of it.
4. The fourth class of liars are the Unitarian liars. The slanderous liar slanders his fellow man, the atheistical liar slanders God, the infidel liar slanders the Word of God and the God who is the author of it, and the

Unitarian liar slanders the Son of God. The apostle John tells us that the Unitarian liar is the liar of liars. 1 John 2: 22.

5. The universalist liars, they who say that there is no hell and no future punishment for sin. Any man who says this is a great enemy of his fellow man. He holds out false hopes to his fellow man, and lures him on to eternal ruin.
6. The sixth class of liars are those who make false excuses for not coming to Christ.

II. How to Escape Hell.

There is but one way in which you can escape hell. That is by the personal acceptance of Jesus Christ as your Saviour and Lord and the open confession of Him before the world. Acts 4: 12; John 3: 36; Matt. 10: 32, 33; 2 Thess. 1: 7-9.

"GOD'S BLOCKADE OF THE ROAD TO HELL"

"The Lord is . . . not willing that any should perish, but that all should come to repentance." 2 Pet. 3: 9.

Introduction.—If any man perish it is not God's fault. God has done and is doing everything in His power to bring men to repentance. If men will not repent they must perish. Sin and destruction must ever go hand in hand. Men must choose between sin and life. They cannot have both.

Any scheme of salvation that proposes to save a man while he continues in his sin is an absurdity on its very face. God will not and cannot save a man unless he repents. But God is doing all in His power to bring men to repentance. God has blockaded the road to hell, and if any man goes there it is of his own choice in spite of God's blockade. How has God blockaded the road to hell?

I. The Bible.

The first great obstruction that God has put in the road to hell is the Bible. The Bible with its warnings and its invitations and its promises is constantly calling every one of us to a holy life. The Bible is a constant protest against our sins and our unbelief and our impenitence.

II. Mother's Instructions.

A second obstacle that God has put in the road that leads to ruin is a mother's instructions.

III. Mother's Prayers.

A third obstacle that God has put in the road to hell is a mother's prayers.

IV. Sunday School Teacher's Instructions.

V. The Sermons that We Hear.

VI. Providential Occurrences.

Another obstruction that God places in the road to hell are various providential occurrences.

VII. The Holy Spirit.

One of the mightiest obstacles that God places in the road to hell is the striving of the Holy Spirit.

VIII. The Cross of Christ.

But the greatest obstacle of all that God has placed in the road to hell, the one without which all others would count for naught, is the cross of Christ.

CHAPTER VI

TOPICAL SERMONS IN OUTLINE

THE BIBLE: WHEREIN IT DIFFERS FROM ALL OTHER BOOKS

INTRODUCTION.—The Bible stands absolutely alone. It is an entirely unique book. It is not a book, it is *the* book. Wherein the Bible differs from all other books:

I. In its Depth.

The Bible is the unfathomable and inexhaustible book. It is unfathomable not because of the obscurity of its style, but because of the profundity of its teaching. The style is so simple and clear that a child can understand it, but its truth is so profound that we explore it from childhood to old age, and can never say that we have reached the bottom.

1. There are whole volumes of meaning in a single and apparently simple verse.
2. The Bible is always ahead of man. What other book ought to command the attention, the time and the study that this book does which is deeper than all other books, ahead of all other books and ahead of every age?

II. In the Absolute Accuracy of its Statements.

The Bible is the only book that always says all it means to say, and never says any more than it means to say.

III. In its Power

There is perhaps no place in which the supremacy and solitariness of the Bible shines out as in its power.

In what direction does the Bible show a power that no other books possess?

1. Saving power.
   (a) The Bible has unique saving power in individual lives.
   (b) It has saving power in national life.

2. The Bible has a comforting power no other book possesses.
3. The Bible has a joy-giving power no other book possesses.
4. The Bible has a wisdom-giving power that no other book possesses. Ps. 119:130.
5. The Bible has a courage-giving power no other book possesses. No other book has made so many and such peerless heroes.
6. The Bible has a power to inspire activity that no other book possesses.

IV. In its Universal Adaptability.

Other books fit certain classes, or certain types, or certain races of men, but the Bible fits man universally.

1. It fits all nations.
2. It fits all ages.
3. The Bible fits all classes.
4. The Bible fits all experiences. It is the book for the hour of gladness, and the book for the hour of sadness, the book for the day of victory and the book for the day of defeat. The book for the day of clearest faith, and the book for the day of darkest doubt.

V. In its History.

1. The Bible has been hated as no other book.
2. Loved as no other book.
3. Studied as no other book.
4. It has been victorious as no other book.

VI. In its Authorship.

Finally, the Bible differs from every other book in its authorship. Other books are men's books, this is God's book.

IS THE BIBLE IN DANGER?

Introduction.—Many consider that the Bible is in grave danger. Many think so because they are glad to think so; it gives their conscience some little consolation in a life of sin. Others fear so with great reluctance. They love the Bible, would be glad to believe, they are afraid that the old book must go. So let us honestly face the question, "Is the Bible in danger?"

We will not deny that the Bible has enemies and most gifted ones. Six reasons why the Bible is not in danger:

I. Because the Bible has already Survived the Attacks of 1,800 Years.

II. The Bible is not in Danger because it Meets and Satisfies the Deepest Needs of Man.

1. First of all the need of pardon and peace.
2. The need of man is deliverance from sin's power.
3. The need of comfort in sorrow.
4. Need of hope in the face of death

III. The Bible is not in Danger because there is Nothing Else to Take the Place of the Bible.

The Bible contains all the truth of moral and spiritual subjects that other books contain, it contains more than all other books put together, and it contains all this in portable compass.

IV. The Bible is not in Danger because it has a Hold that Cannot be Shaken on the Confidence and Affection of the Wisest and Best Men and Women.

The Bible has the distrust and hatred of some, but it has the confidence and affection of the wisest and especially the best and holiest of men and women. The men who know the Bible best are the men who trust it most and love it best. The Bible is distrusted and hated by those whose influence dies with them, the Bible is loved and trusted by those whose influence lives after them.

V. The Bible is not in Danger because it is the Word of God.

Many things prove that this book is the Word of God. Its fulfilled prophecies, its unity, its Divine Power, its inexhaustible depth, the fact that as we grow in knowledge and holiness—grow Godward—we grow toward the Bible.

VI. The Bible is not in Danger because any Honest and Earnest Seeker after Truth can find out for Himself that the Bible is God's Word.

CONCLUSION.—The Bible is in no danger. But while the Bible itself is in no danger those who vent their spleen upon it are in danger. It is no small sin to ridicule the Word of all-holy and all-mighty God. There are others who are in danger. Those who listen to the fascinating eloquence of an Ingersoll and allow it to lull them to repose in a life of sin.

INFIDELITY: ITS CAUSES, CONSEQUENCES AND CURE

I. Causes.

1. The misrepresentation of Christianity by its professed disciples. Two kinds of misrepresentation:
   (a) In doctrine.
   (b) In life.
2. Ignorance. Ignorance of what the Bible contains and teaches. Ignorance of history.
3. Conceit. Men become infidels because they find things in the Bible they cannot understand, because there are apparent contradictions which they cannot reconcile. To think that our finite minds could take in in a day or a month all the truth revealed by an infinite mind; to think that because I can't take a statement in it can't be true; to think because I can't find a solution to a difficulty, none can be found; is to think that my mind is infinite, that I know all things, is to think I am God.
4. Sin. This is the commonest and most fundamental cause of infidelity. In two ways:
   (a) Men sin and betake themselves to infidelity to find comfort in their sins.
   (b) Sin blinds their eyes to the truth of the Bible and makes it appear foolishness.

II. Consequences.

1. Sin. Infidelity breeds sin; there is no doubt of that

It is caused by sin and in turn begets a progeny like its ancestry.

2. Anarchy. Anarchists are always infidels.
3. Wretchedness and despair.
4. Suicide.
5. Hopeless graves.
6. Eternal ruin.

III. The Cure.

1. Christ-like living on the part of professed Christians.
2. A surrendered will on the part of the infidel.
3. The study of the Word of God.

WHY I BELIEVE IN JESUS CHRIST

INTRODUCTION.—There is nothing more important for a man for the life that now is and for the life that is to come, than a faith in Jesus Christ that is intelligent, clear and firm.

I. I Believe in Jesus Christ first of all because of the remarkable Fulfillment of His Prophecies.

Jesus Christ was a prophet. He made some astounding predictions regarding the future. Predictions that seemed incredible and in some cases absurd, but which history has fulfilled to the letter. Take for example His prediction of a world-wide conquest by His disciples. (In Matt. 28: 18-20.); Matt. 24: 1, 2, 5, 7, 10, 16, 26, 28; Luke 19: 41-44; 21: 20-24.

II. I believe in Jesus Christ, in the second place, because of His Fulfilled Promises.

Jesus Christ was not only a prophet but a promiser. He made promises of a most extraordinary character, but promises the truth of which any man could test for himself, and all who have tested the promises have found them true. E. g., Matt. 11: 28; Acts 1: 8; John 7: 17.

III. I believe in Jesus Christ, in the third place, because of the Wholesome Character of His Laws.

IV. I believe in Christ again because of the Way He Fits into and Fulfills all O. T. Types and Prophecies.

V. I believe in Jesus Christ because of the Fact of His Resurrection.

VI. I believe in Jesus Christ because of the Uniqueness of His Claims and the Way in which He Substantiates Them.

VII. I believe in Jesus Christ because of His Demonstrated Power to Save.

I believe that Jesus can save because He does save. I believe that Jesus can save because I have seen Him do it.

SOME ABSOLUTE CERTAINTIES

INTRODUCTION.—We live at a time when the religions and philosophies of all ages and all lands are being brought together for comparison. What an inextricable tangle there seems to be—Christianity, Mohammedanism, Buddhism and Zoroasterianism; all the various forms of materialistic and spiritualistic philosophy. Within Christianity itself what a conflict of rival theologies! Where is truth to be found? What is truth? It is a great relief and joy to find some certainties among this endless maze of uncertainties, to find something to stand upon and be able to say here at least I have solid rock underneath my feet.

A few of the fundamental truths about which there can be no honest question:

I. The first absolute certainty is that there is an absolute difference between right and wrong.

II. The second certainty is that a man ought to make an honest and diligent search for the truth and to follow every possible clue that promises to lead to it.

1. Here prayer comes in. It is a possible clue.
2. The Bible is at least another possible clue. Many very credible witnesses claim they have come to this book, not all prejudiced in its favor but honestly seeking truth, and have in this book found what they sought. These two clues should be followed together.

III. The third certainty is, a man ought to obey so much of the truth as he finds and as fast as he finds it.

IV. The fourth certainty is that every man is a sinner and needs a Saviour.

V. The fifth absolute certainty is that Jesus does save those who put their trust in Him.

VI. The sixth absolute certainty is that there is no other Saviour from the guilt and power of sin but Jesus Christ.

VII. The seventh absolute certainty is that the life of the one who accepts Jesus Christ as Saviour and who surrenders to Him as Lord, believes the promises and obeys the precepts of the Bible, is the noblest, fairest, happiest and in every way the most satisfactory life.

WHY I BELIEVE THAT JESUS CHRIST IS THE SON OF GOD

INTRODUCTION.—There is no subject more important than that of the Divinity of Jesus Christ. If Jesus Christ is not Divine, then Christians are idolaters. If Jesus Christ is Divine then all who do not acknowledge Him as such and accept Him as their Divine Saviour and Lord are guilty of the awful sin of rejecting the Son of God and denying Him the honor due to His name.

I. I believe Jesus Christ is the Son of God because of His own Claim to be the Son of God, and the Way in which He Substantiates that Claim.

Christ's claim to be divine is substantiated:

1. First, by His character.
2. His claim to be divine is substantiated by the miracles which He performed.
3. Christ's claim to be divine is substantiated, in the third place, by His influence on the history of the world.
4. Christs claim is substantiated, in the fourth place, by His resurrection from the dead.

II. Because of the other Teachings of the Bible besides His own.

III. Because of the Divine Power He Possesses To-day.

It is not necessary to go back to the miracles of Christ when upon earth to prove this. He has divine power, He exercises this power to-day and any one can test it.

1. He has power to forgive sins.
2. He has power to-day to set Satan's victims free.

IV. I believe Jesus Christ is Divine because of the Character of those who Accept Him as Divine.

V. I believe in the Divinity of Jesus Christ because of the Result of Accepting His Divinity.

The religion that accepts God the Father but rejects Jesus Christ His Son has no such deep and lasting moral power as the religion that accepts Jesus Christ as divine. Unitarianism does not save the fallen. Unitarianism does not beget a missionary spirit. Faith in Jesus as divine makes missionaries and martyrs, it produces men of prayer and faith. It produces consecrated living. The denial of the divinity of Christ tends to prayerlessness, religious carelessness, unbelief, worldliness, selfishness and easy-going living.

UNTO PRAYER

INTRODUCTION.—The great need of our day in our church life is more prayer. Passages that put this call in an especially impressive and instructive way: 1 Pet. 4: 7, R. V. The closing words, "*be sober unto prayer.*" The word translated "be sober" means to be "calm and collected in spirit." To be clear-headed. The thought is that prayer is a matter of greatest importance as the days go fast flying toward the end, and that it demands a man's best thought, and that a man needs a clear head before all else, in order that he may approach the great God acceptably in prayer. Prayer demands our best moments and our best thought.

I. 1 Cor. 7: 5, R. V. "**That ye may Give Yourselves unto Prayer.**" Here Paul says that there are certain duties incumbent upon married people that they may by mutual consent give up for a season that they may give themselves to prayer. That is, prayer is a matter of such vast importance, and for its proper prosecution demands such concentration of thought and disentanglement from other concerns, that matters of very great weight may properly be laid aside to attend to this weightier matter of prayer. The words translated "that ye may give yourselves unto prayer" mean literally "that ye may have leisure unto prayer." That is, prayer cannot be properly prosecuted by a preoccupied mind. It demands leisure. It demands the putting of all other things aside and attending absolutely and wholly to this.

II. The third passage is Col. 4: 2, R. V. "Continuing steadfastly in prayer, watching therein with supplication."

The words translated "Continue steadfastly in prayer" mean give constant attention to prayer, make a business of prayer. It is the same word used in Acts 6: 4, where the apostles wanted some one to be appointed to look after the poor in order that they might *give themselves continually* to prayer and the ministry of the Word; and in Acts 10: 7, where it is said of certain soldiers that they *waited on* Cornelius *continually;* and in Rom. 13: 6, where it is said of officials that "they are God's ministers, *attending continually* upon this very thing." It evidently means to make a business of a thing. We should make a business of prayer. It is Jesus Christ's business. That is what He lives for. Heb. 2: 25. When the Church of Christ does make prayer its business our eyes shall behold such great things in conversions and progress in life at home and missionary conquests abroad as we have never dreamed of. Our verse says something else about prayer than making it a business. "Continue steadfastly in prayer, *watching therein.*" It must be wide awake business.

III. Rom. 15: 30. **"That ye strive together."**

We should strive in prayer. The word translated "strive" means to "contend" or "fight" or "struggle" against opposition. To put forth intense and determined effort. The noun from which it is derived is translated "conflict" or "fight," as for example in 2 Tim. 4: 7. God demands the same earnestness in prayer that He does in work. We get the best things in work only by hard working, and we get the best things in prayer by hard praying. There are obstacles to be overcome by prayer, real obstacles, there are enemies to be conquered by prayer, live enemies, strong enemies, and the prayers that win take a vast outlay of soul energy.

Conclusion.—Four practical suggestions.

1. Set apart time from everything else for praying. A certain portion of every day and frequent special seasons.
2. Prepare for prayer.
   (a) Examine your heart and life to see if you are in praying trim, and if not, get into it.
   (b) Think carefully over the things that you are to pray for. Find the best, the most needy, most urgent causes.
3. When you undertake to pray summon all your spirit and energy and pray it through.
4. Look to the Holy Spirit to guide every step of the way, "praying in the Holy Spirit."

THREE FIRES

I. The Fire of the Holy Ghost.

Matt. 3:11; Acts 2:2-4.

1. First of all fire reveals. 1 Cor. 3:13. What does it mean to be baptized with fire? The answer to this is found in considering what fire does.
2. Fire refines and purifies. Is. 44; Zech. 1:3, 9; Mal. 3:1-3.
3. Fire consumes. It refines by consuming. Ez. 24:9-11. There is much in all of us that needs to be consumed, pride, vanity, love of money, love of pleasures, fear of man.
4. Fire illuminates. When one is baptized with fire, truth we did not see at all before becomes as clear as day, the Bible becomes a new book, glory shines from every page.
5. Fire, also, warms, it makes to glow.
6. Fire imparts energy. All forms of energy can be transformed into heat and by heat we can generate the different forms of force and motion.
7. Fire spreads.

II. The Fire that Tries Our Works.

1 Cor. 3: 13-15. Not a judgment regarding salvation. The persons whose works are here burned up are saved. It is a judgment regarding the works we do as Christians and the reward we shall receive for them. All the works we do for Christ, or professedly for Him, are to be tested. They are to be put to the severe test, the fire test. All that will not stand the fire test will be burned up.

III. The Fire of Eternal Doom.

2 Thess. 1: 7-9. Every one of shall know fire from God. Some of us, I hope, will know the fire of the Holy Ghost. Many of us, I know, will know the fire that tries and consumes our work which is not of the right sort in God's sight. Some shall know the fire of eternal doom. There is a fire of eternal doom. For whom is it?

1. To them that know not God.
2. To them that obey not the Gospel of our Lord Jesus.

Conclusion.—There are these three fires, one of which we all must know. Which shall it be?

THE BAPTISM WITH FIRE

(Matt. 3: 11.)

I. What Is the Baptism with Fire?

The interpretation that makes the fire of future judgment untenable.

1. In that case it should read "or fire."
2. The way coupled with Holy Ghost, not two "withs," as in A. V. and R. V.
3. Literal translation. "With Holy wind and fire."
4. Fulfilled at Pentecost. Acts 2: 2-4.

What is it to be baptized with fire? The answer found in considering what fire is said to do in Scripture and what came to the disciples at Pentecost.

1. 1 Cor. 3: 13. Refines.

2. Is. 4:4; Zech. 13:9; Mal. 3:1-3. Refines and purifies. The apostles after Pentecost compared with before.
3. Ez. 24:9-11. Consumes. John 5:35.
4. Illuminates. Jas. 16:13; 1 Cor. 2:14.
5. Fire warms, it makes to glow.
6. Fire imparts energy, generates power and motion.
7. Fire spreads.

The great need of ministers and Christian work, of individual Christians and the Church is a baptism with fire.

II. How Received.

How did the apostles receive it?

1. They recognized their need.
2. They believed it was for them.
3. They really desired it.
4. They continued steadfastly in prayer.
5. They were wholly surrendered to God's will.
6. They expected it.

One gets the baptism with fire in pretty much the same way as one gets water baptism. You wish to be baptized with water you go to one qualified to baptize with water, tell him what you want and put yourself in his hands for him to baptize you, you being willing to take upon yourself all the consequences of that baptism. Do just the same in this. There is but One qualified to baptize with fire. Jesus Christ, the risen Christ, is the sole and only baptizer with the Holy Ghost.

III. Stirring up the Fire.

2 Tim. 1:6.

1. This clearly implies that after one has received the baptism with fire it may burn low and must be stirred into a flame. Experience abundantly proves this.
2. How kindle into a flame?
   (a) Study of the Word. Eph. 5:18, 19; comp. Col. 3:16. Just as soon as any one neglects his Bible study the Holy fire burns low. Jer. 23:29.
   (b) Prayer. Acts 4:31.
   (c) Work. 1 Tim. 4:13, 14.

Conclusion.—Have you been baptized with the Holy Spirit and fire? Will you be to-day? Have you been and is the fire burning low? Will you kindle it into a flame?

POWER: ITS SOURCE AND HOW TO OBTAIN IT

Text. "God has spoken once . . . power belongeth unto God." Ps. 62: 11.

Introduction.—The great need in Christian work is power. The father and mother in the home. The Sunday-school teacher. The personal worker. We preachers of the Gospel. We must have power. We can have power. How can we get it?

I. The Source of Power.

Power belongeth unto God. All real power is from Him. We get power by getting in contact with Him, in union with Him. How often you see a man whom you supposed to be a comparative ignoramus doing a mighty work for God. Why is it? Somehow he has gotten into contact with God. He has got hold of God's power. If you have not the power nobody is to blame but yourself. God is not to blame for He longs to give; the devil is not to blame, for he can't hinder. You are to blame.

II. How Power Is to be Obtained.

What are the conditions upon which God bestows upon us the power that belongs to Him?

1. Is. 59: 1, 2. We must put away sin.
2. Judges 16: 15-17; cf. Num. 6: 1, 2, 5. We must be separated and stay separated unto God.
3. 1 Pet. 5: 5, 6. We must get down low before God. When we give up our own wisdom we get God's. When we give up our own power then and only then we get the power of God. Is. 40: 29.
4. Heb. 11: 32-34. We must have faith. How to get faith. Rom. 10: 17.
5. Luke 11: 5-10. If we are to get God's power we must ask for it. The place of prayer is the place where power is obtained. Is. 40: 31; Jas. 4: 2.

6. Acts 1:8; 4:31, 33. If we are to have power we must have the Holy Ghost. Luke 11:13; Acts 2:39.

THE CHRISTIAN WORKER AND THE HOLY SPIRIT

INTRODUCTION.—There are three passages in the Bible regarding the Holy Spirit that every one who wishes to be used of God in winning souls should ponder very deeply.

I. Luke 24:49.

1. *What is this enduement of power?*
   (a) A definite experience.
   (b) Separate and distinct from regeneration.
   (c) A clothing of the believer in Christ with the power of God.
2. How received. Can be variously stated.
   (a) Must believe there is such an enduement. Acts 19:1-6.
   (b) Must desire it. Is. 44:3.
   (c) Put away hindrances. The great hindrances, sin and self-sufficiency.
   (d) Absolute surrender. Acts 5:32.
   (e) Prayer. Luke 11:13; Acts 4:31.
   (f) Faith-claim. Mark 11:24, R. V.

II. 1 Thess. 5:19. **These words are addressed to believers. The Holy Spirit is here set forth as a fire. Significance: There is danger that this fire be quenched. Not enough to receive this fire. Must see to it that it is not quenched.**

1. How the Holy Spirit is quenched.
   (a) Through not yielding to the Spirit's suggestions. See context.
   (b) Through incoming of sin.
   (c) Through going back on our consecration.
   (d) Through self-indulgence.
   (e) Through pride.

If one has quenched the Spirit what shall he do? Go alone with God and find the cause. Then have done with it. Can power be renewed? Yes.

III. 2 Tim. 1:6. **Here again the Holy Spirit is compared to fire. The verse tells us it is not enough not to quench the fire. We must feed the fire and stir it into a flame. Here is where many fail.**

1. How?

   (a) The study of the Word. Eph. 5:18, 19; compare Col. 3:16.

   (b) Prayer. Acts 4:31.

   (c) Work. The exercise of the gift increases the power of the gift. 1 Tim. 4:14 (see context, vs. 13).

THE HOLY SPIRIT AND THE WORD

Introduction.—The one who would be an efficient worker for Christ must know the power of two things. The power of the Spirit of God and the power of the Word of God. These two are most intimately related to each other.

I. 2 Pet. 1:21; 1 Pet. 1:11; Heb. 3:7; John 4:26; 1 Cor. 2:12, 13. **The Holy Spirit is the author of the Word.**

II. Luke 1:67 (and which follows Scripture), 2:25, compare 2:32; Acts 2:4, 14-17, etc. (25-28); 6:5, compare ch. 7. (Whenever a man was filled with the Holy Spirit he was full of Scripture.) **The Holy Spirit leads men to the Word.**

III. 1 Cor. 2:14. **The Holy Spirit is the interpreter of the Word.**

IV. Acts 4:31, 34; 1 Cor. 2:1-5. **The Holy Spirit enables the preacher to communicate with power to others the truth he himself has been taught.**

V. The Word is the instrument the Holy Spirit uses in all His blessed work.

1. John 15:26, compare 5:39.
2. John 16:8, compare Acts 2:37.
3. John 3:5, compare 1 Pet. 1:23; John 1:18.
4. 1 Pet. 1:2, compare John 17:17.
5. 1 Cor. 12:9, f. cl., Rom. 10:17.
6. Rom. 8:16, compare 1 John 5:13.
7. Gal. 5:22, compare Jer. 15:16; John 15:11.
8. Rom. 15:13, compare v. 4 (hope).
9. Acts 9:31, compare Rom. 15:4 (comfort).

The Spirit of God works through the Word. If we wish the Spirit to do His work in our hearts we must study the Word. If we wish Him to do His work in hearts of others we must give them the Word. Eph. 6:17. But the Word alone will not do it. It is the Word and the Spirit. We must look to the Spirit to make His Word effectual. 2 Cor. 3:6.

SOME REASONS WHY EVERY SENSIBLE MAN SHOULD BE A CHRISTIAN

I. Every sensible man should be a Christian because the teachings of Jesus Christ are true and right and ought therefore to be obeyed.

A learned man is a man who knows a great deal, a sensible man is a man who acts upon what he knows. A man may have much learning and very little sense. The man who knows and believes the teachings of Christ to be true and doesn't act upon them has the least sense of all.

II. Every sensible person should be a Christian because the acceptance of Christ brings salvation.

Two things are perfectly clear to every candid person who considers the facts in the case. 1st. That men need salvation. 2d. That Christ does save those who accept Him. The first of these certainties every man knows from experience. The second of these certainties, that Jesus Christ does save those who put their trust in Him, any one can know not only from the sure Word of God that asserts, Rom. 1:16, but from observation as well. It is a simple incontrovertible fact that Jesus Christ has saved men.

III. Every sensible man should be a Christian because Christ brings a deeper, purer, more lasting joy to those who accept Him than can be found in any other way.

1 Pet. 1:8. Ask any one who has ever been a real Christian if he finds in Christ a deeper, purer, more lasting joy than he ever found elsewhere and he will tell you yes, far deeper, immeasurably deeper.

IV. Every sensible man should be a Christian because real faith in Christ prepares one for every emergency of life that can possibly arise.

Phil. 4: 11, 12; Heb. 11:6; Rom. 8: 28.

IMPORTANCE OF BIBLE STUDY

INTRODUCTION.—There is nothing more important for the Christian than Bible study. There is nothing as important except prayer, holy living and work. And the one who rightly studies his Bible will pray powerfully, live holy, and work earnestly and efficiently. Bible study is also important for the one who is not a Christian.

I. Bible Study is Important as a Means of Intellectual Development.

No other study offers the material for such an all-round development of the mental powers as the study of the Bible.

1. The Bible is the profoundest book that was ever written.
2. The Bible gives a wider scope for the legitimate use of the imagination and fancy than any other book, or all other books. It goes back into the eternal past, it looks forward into the eternal future. The greatest masters of literature have allowed their fancy to drink in its highest inspiration at the Bible fountain.
3. The Bible is the world's great masterpiece of style.
   (a) It is the world's marvel of condensed thought. Volumes are packed into a single verse.
   (b) It is the peerless model of simple, chaste, strong, Anglo-Saxon.
   (c) It is absolutely unrivaled in its power of terse and incisive statement.
   (d) It has a power that no other book possesses of saying things in a way that so penetrates the mind and fastens itself in the memory that they cannot be forgotten.

   Any man or woman who desires to write well or speak well should study the Bible above all other books.

4. Bible study affords such opportunity as is found nowhere else for the cultivation of the powers of observation, analysis, synthesis, inference, memory and recollection.

II. Bible Study is of the Highest Importance for the Promotion of Growth in Christian Character.

1 Pet. 2: 2.

III. Bible Study is Important for the Production and Development of Faith.

Rom. 10: 17.

1. Faith as opposed to unbelief.
2. Faith that prevails in prayer.
3. Saving faith.
4. Faith that expects and receives great things from God in work.

IV. Bible Study is Important as a Safeguard against Sin.

Ps. 119: 11.

V. Bible Study is Important as Filling the Heart with Joy.

Jer. 15: 16.

VI. Bible Study is Important as a Safeguard against Error.

Acts 20: 29, 30, 32; 2 Tim. 3: 13-15, R. V.

VII. Bible Study is Important to Make one Wise.

Ps. 119: 130.

VIII. Bible Study is Important as an Equipment for Christian Service. The Bible is the one Instrument God Honors in Christian Work.

2 Tim. 3: 16, 17.

Conclusion.—You will miss every richest blessing in life if you neglect your Bible.

HOW TO STUDY THE BIBLE

I. Study the BIBLE.

1. Not about the Bible, but the *Bible itself.* Satan kept men for years from any Bible study, now there is an interest, etc., he keeps them from real Bible study. Questions of authorship, date, etc., are quite impor-

tant, but studying these things is not studying the Bible.

2. Not helps and commentaries on the Bible, but the *Bible.*
3. Not devotional books. They are good in their place, but learn to go right to the fountain for yourself. The Bible itself the richest gold mine in the world.

II. STUDY the Bible.

Not merely carry it. Not merely praise it. Not merely glance over it. Not merely read. Study means close mental application. The Bible is profitable only by the truth in it and that you must digest. Take its books, its chapters, its verses, its individual words and study them. Ponder them. Look closely at them. Turn them over and over. Weigh them. Ps. 1: 2; Josh. 1: 8.

One great hindrance to real study is having so many chapters you must read in a day. Leads to skimming, thoughtless reading. Have a definite amount of time for study, but not a definite number of chapters or verses. Go fast or slow, according to what you are studying. Sometimes one verse, sometimes many chapters.

III. Study the Bible Daily.

IV. Have a Definite Amount of Time Set Apart for Bible Study and a Definite Time in the Day for it.

Don't trust to chance. Give the Bible the first place. Let all other books and all magazines and papers have a secondary place. One of the greatest enemies of profitable study is hurry. One of the greatest secrets of profitable Bible study is undisturbed concentration of thought. The best time, other things being equal, is the early morning.

V. Study Prayerfully.

Ps. 119: 18.

VI As the Word of God.

1 Thess. 2: 13.

1. Humbly and meekly. Cf. Jas. 1: 21.
2. Unquestioning acceptance of its teaching when definitely and clearly ascertained.

3. Absolute reliance upon its promises.
4. Prompt, exact, unquestioning obedience to every commandment.
5. As in God's presence. "God says this to me."

VII. Have some Intelligent and Definite and Systematic Method of Bible Study.

1. Study of the Bible in course.
   (a) Five points on each chapter.
      (1) Subject of the chapter. State principal contents of a chapter in a sentence.
      (2) Principal persons.
      (3) Leading lesson. Truth most emphasized.
      (4) Best lesson.
      (5) Best verse. Ponder it and mark it.
   (b) Synthetic.
      (1) Read continuously.
      (2) Read repeatedly.
      (3) Read independently.
      (4) Read prayerfully.
2. Thorough study of individual books.
3. Topical.
   (a) Be systematic.
   (b) Be thorough.
   (c) Be exact.
   (d) Write down your results.
4. Study for personal work.

FIVE PLAIN RULES FOR HOLY LIVING

INTRODUCTION.—The Bible is a plain book for plain people. It is true that the Bible sometimes takes us up to heights where our heads swim at the prospect that stretches before us. It is true also that there are places in this book so deep that no scholar's plummet has ever yet struck bottom. But the book abounds in plain, simple directions for every-day living. I come to you to-day with four simple rules for holy and healthy and happy living. It may seem to some of you like milk for babes, but it is well to remember that there are babes in most families, and even those who are sure they are full grown need plain victuals occasionally lest they get the dyspepsia. The fact is there are many spiritual dyspeptics in our day, and they are always grumbling at the food unless it is prepared by their own spiritual cook.

I. "Whatsoever He Saith unto you, Do it."

John. 2: 5.

These words were spoken on a certain occasion concerning Jesus by His mother. They gave directions as to the way out of an emergency then at hand. But they point the shortest and best way out of all emergencies that ever arise. There is no better rule for holy, healthy, and happy living than this, "Whatsoever Jesus says unto you, do it." Whenever in a quandary what to do, just find out what Jesus says and do it. Never mind what it is that He says, do it. The thing that He says to do may seem very insignificant, a matter of no great importance. Never mind that, do it. Something else may seem very like it, or "quite as good," but don't you do that something else. Do the thing, the exact thing that Jesus says. How many people are robbed of blessing by doing something "just as good" as what Jesus said, instead of doing the very thing Jesus says. "Do it." "Whatsoever." "Whatsoever." How are we to tell what Jesus says? He is here in the written Word, the words which He Himself spoke directly and the words which He spoke by His Spirit through apostles and prophets. Besides that He is present personally. Matt. 28: 20. If we are fully surrendered to His will He is always at hand to make known that will to us. Don't ask Him to make clear by His Spirit what He has already made clear by His Word.

II. "Do as Jesus Did," or to put it another way, "Do as Jesus would Do if He were in Your Place."

1 John 2: 6.

III. "Whatsoever is not of Faith is Sin." The Rule is this: "Do Nothing that you have Doubts about."

Rom. 14: 23.

IV. "Whatsoever ye Do, do All to the Glory of God." There are really two Rules in that one. The First is, Do Nothing that you can't do to God's Glory; that Settles a good many Questions. Second, When you Do the thing that you could Do to His Glory, actually Do it to His Glorv

1 Cor. 10:31.

V. Throw your Soul into Everything you Do; as unto the Lord, heartily.

Col. 3:23.

GREAT THINGS, AND HOW ANY ONE CAN GET THEM

INTRODUCTION.—There are many who think that only a few men can ever attain unto great things, that the great mass of men must rest content with small things. This is not so. The very greatest things, the things of infinite and eternal value, are open to all men. There is not a man or woman here to-night who cannot have great things, the very greatest, those of most priceless worth.

I. First of all any one here can have Great Joy.

1 Pet. 1:8.

II. Great Peace.

Phil. 4:6, 7.

III. Great Position.

John. 1:12. This position is open to any one who wishes to fill it. "As many as received Him to them," etc.

IV. A Great Hope.

Tit. 1:12.

V. A Great Inheritance.

1 Pet. 1:4, 5; Rom. 8:17.

D. L. MOODY: THE UNITY OF HIS LIFE

"This one thing I do, forgetting those things which are behind, and reaching forth unto those things which are before, I press toward the mark for the prize of the high calling of God in Christ Jesus." Phil. 3: 13, 14.

INTRODUCTION.—Mr. Moody loved to urge men to concentration of purpose and effort. He practiced it even better than he preached it. His life was a constant and unanswerable argument for the power of concentration of purpose and action. His life was one of marvelous unity. There was in it a seven-fold unity.

I. First of all, he was a man of one passion, love for Jesus Christ.

II. A man of but one aim, that aim was to please God.

III. He was a man of one book, the Bible.

IV. A man of one work, soul-saving. Mr. Moody did many things, but he always had one definite end in view, the salvation of the lost.

V. A man of one idea, "God is love."

VI. A man of one source of power, the Holy Ghost.

VII. A man of one endeavor, "to do what he could."

MESSIANIC PROPHECIES

INTRODUCTION.—Importance of subject. Peter's argument on the Day of Pentecost. Acts 2. Paul's argument. Acts 9: 22; 1: 3. Christ's argument. Luke 24: 27, 44. There are said to be 333 prophecies and references to Christ in the Old Testament which are expressly cited in the New Testament.

I. Classes of Messianic Prophecies.

1. Explicit prophecies that refer directly and wholly to the coming Messiah.
2. Explicit prophecies that have an immediate reference to contemporaneous or nearly contemporaneous persons and events, but which have their final and complete fulfillment in the Messiah.
3. Passages the Messianic application of which is not explicitly noted but which are fulfilled and marvelously fulfilled in Christ.
4. Types.

To the first class of prophecies—those that refer directly and wholly to the Messiah belong; e. g., Is. 53; Gen. 49: 10; Mic. 5: 2. A very strong attempt has been and is being made to show that Is. 53 is not

Messianic. It is said to refer to suffering Israel. This chapter cannot refer to Israel.

(a) The sufferer is represented as perfectly innocent and suffering for the sins of others. Vs. 9, 5, 6, 8.

(b) He is a voluntary and unresisting sufferer. V. 7.

(c) The sufferer is stricken for the transgression of another than himself, viz., God's people. V. 8. But Israel is God's people, so the sufferer cannot be. This 53d chapter has been accepted by the Jews themselves as Messianic in the Targruns, the Talmud, the Zohar. In the Jewish prayers on the Day of Atonement and by the Jews at the present time.

To the second class of prophecies those, etc., belong; e. g., Is. 7: 14; Ps. 72: 45.

To the third class of prophecies belongs Ps. 22 (vs. 1, 6, 8, 14, 18).

To the types belong all the sacrifices and institutions and personages; e. g., the Passover, Ex. 12, the goats on Day of Atonement, Lev. 16. The typical personages, Joseph, Gen. 37, David, Solomon; e. g., 1 Kings 4: 24-34; 10: 1-9.

II The Development of Messianic Prophecy.

Messianic prophecy in the Bible like everything else in God's world and Word grows. First we have only the seed of the woman shall bruise the serpent's head. Gen. 3: 15.

Next it is Shem's descendants. Gen. 9: 26, 27.

Then it is the seed of Abraham.

Then it is the tribe of Judah. Gen. 49: 10.

Then the Son of David.

Other particulars also are being constantly added.

III. What is Prophesied of the Messiah in the Old Testament.

1. His family. Jer. 23: 5, 6; 33: 15, 16. Of the family of David. He was to be born at a time when that family had been cut down and lost its glory.
2. State of family at His birth. Is. 53: 2; 11: 1. R. V.

3 The time of His appearing. Gen. 49: 10; Hag. 27: 9 Dan. 9: 25.

4. The place. Mic. 5: 2. Bethlehem.

5. His nature.
   (a) Mic. 5: 2; Ps. 45: 6; Ps. 110: 1; Ps. 2: 7; Is. 9: 6. Divine.
   (b) Is. 53: 3. Human.

6. His character.
   (a) Is. 53: 7. Meek.
   (b) Is. 42: 3. Gentle.
   (c) Is. 42: 2. Retiring. Avoiding notoriety.
   (d) Is. 42: 1; 11: 2. Full of the Spirit.
   (e) Is. 42: 4. Persevering.
   (f) Is. 11: 5. Righteous and faithful.
   (g) Is. 53: 10, 9, 4. Absolutely sinless. (Implied also in vs. 5, 6, 8, 12.)

7. Manner of birth.
   Is. 7: 14. Born of a virgin (see also Ps. 69: 8; 86: 16; 116: 16.

8. How treated by men.
   (a) Is. 53: 3; Ps. 118: 22. Despised and rejected.
   (b) Ps. 22: 3. Kings of earth, etc.
   (c) Is. 50: 6. Scourged, insulted, spit upon.
   (d) Zech. 11: 13. Sold for thirty pieces of silver.
   (e) Is. 53: 7, 8. Killed. Zech. 13: 7. Details of His death.
      (1) Is. 53: 5. Pierced. (Heb.) Zech. 12: 10.
      (2) Ps 22: 14, 17.
      (3) Ps. 22: 7, 8. Mocked while dying.
      (4) Ps. 22: 18. Garments parted while dying.
      (5) Ps. 69: 21. Given gall vinegar.
      (6) Isa. 53: 12. Made intercession for transgressors when He bore their sins.
      (7) Heart breaks. Ps. 69: 20; 22: 14.
      (8) Is. 53: 12, 9. Numbered with transgressors, made His grave with wicked and with the rich.
   (f) Ps. 110: 1, 3, R. V. His people will offer, etc.
   (g) His Resurrection. Is. 53: 10, 11; Ps. 16: 10.

(h) Ascension and seating at the right hand of God. Ps. 68: 18 (24: 7); Ps. 110: 1.

(i) Two advents.

(1) Once born as a man to be cut off. Mic. 5: 1, 2; Dan. 9: 26.

(2) Once coming in clouds. Dan. 7: 9, 10, 13, 14; Ps. 2: 8, 9.

(j) His work.

(1) Is. 53: 6, 8, 12. He should die in the place of others. Is. 53: 10, R. V., margin.

(2) He should be made a guilt offering for sin.

(3) Is. 61: 1-3.

a. Preach good tidings, etc.

b. Bind up broken-hearted.

c. Proclaim liberty to captives, the opening of prisons, etc.

d. To proclaim the acceptable year of the Lord and the day of vengeance of our God.

e. To comfort all that mourn.

f. To give unto those that mourn in Zion a garland for ashes, the oil of joy for mourning, the garment of praise for the Spirit of heaviness.

(4) Jer. 23: 5, 6. To reign as king and to execute judgment and justice in the earth.

Character of His reign. Zech. 9: 9.

a. Ps. 45: 6; 72: 5, 17. Eternally.

b. Ps. 72: 2.

c. Ps. 72: 4.

d. Ps. 72: 7.

e. Ps. 72: 8. Universal.

f. Ps. 72: 9-11. Absolute.

g. Ps. 72: 12, 13, 14.

(5) Ps. 110: 4. A priest.

(6) Deut. 18: 15-18. A prophet.

(7) Is. 42: 5, 6; 49: 6; 60: 1-3. A light of the Gentiles.

IV. Is Jesus of the New Testament this Prophesied Christ of the Old Testament?

THE SECOND COMING OF CHRIST (1)

I. The Certainty of His Coming Again.

John 14: 3; Heb. 9: 28; Phil. 3: 20, 21; 1 Thess. 4: 16, 17; Acts 3: 20. The coming again referred to in these passages is not an event that has already occurred.

1. Christ's coming at death, not the coming referred to.
   (a) Whatever coming of the Lord to meet us there may be at death—and there may be in a sense such a coming—He does not descend from heaven with the voice of the archangel and the trump of God, and all those who sleep in Christ are certainly not raised from their graves at the death of the individual believer. To refer this language to what occurs at death is to transform an inspired apostle into a crazy rhetorician.
   (b) Jesus clearly and definitely distinguished between death and His coming again in John 21: 22.
2. Not the coming of Holy Spirit at Pentecost. The coming of the Holy Spirit is in a very real sense a coming of Christ. John 14: 15-18, 21-23. But it certainly is not the coming referred to in the passages under consideration.
   (a) This is clear from the fact that all of these promises but one (John 14: 3) were made after the coming of the Holy Spirit and referred to something still in the future.
   (b) It is clear again from the fact that Jesus does not receive us to be with Him at the coming of the Holy Ghost.
   (c) The various things mentioned as occurring at His coming are all wanting at the coming of the Spirit.
3. Not the destruction of Jerusalem. The destruction of Jerusalem was in some sense the precursor, prophecy and type of the Day of the Lord that is to come. But

God's judgment on Jerusalem in its destruction is manifestly not the event predicted in the passages given.

Years after Jerusalem had been destroyed we find John still looking forward to the Lord's second coming as an event lying still in the future. Not any of these three events, death, the coming of the Spirit, the destruction of Jerusalem, nor all of them together, nor any other event of history that has as yet occurred, fulfills the very plain, explicit and definite predictions of Christ and the apostles regarding Christ's coming again.

II. The Manner of His Coming.

1. His coming will be personal. It is Jesus Himself. John 14:3; 1 Thess. 4:16. "I myself." "Himself." Acts 1:11, R. V. The Lord Jesus Christ. Phil. 3:20, R. V.
2. Bodily and visible. Heb. 9:28; Rev. 1:7; Acts 1:11. So beheld, beheld.
3. With great publicity. Rev. 1:7; Matt. 24:26, 27.
4. With great power and glory. Matt. 24:30; Matt. 16:27.
5. Sudden and unexpected. Matt. 24:42, R. V.; Matt. 24:44; Rev. 16:15; Luke 21:34-36.

THE SECOND COMING OF CHRIST (2)

I. The Purpose and Results of Christ's Coming Again.

1. John 14:3. Jesus Christ is coming again to receive His own unto Himself, that where He is, there they may be also.
2. Phil. 3:20, 21. Jesus Christ is coming again to fashion anew the body of our humiliation that it may be conformed to the body of His glory.
3. 1 John 3:1, 2. Jesus Christ is coming again to bring us unto perfect conformity with Himself.
4. Matt. 25:19 and 16:27. Jesus Christ is coming again to reckon with His servants and to reward them according to their works. 1 Cor. 3:13-15.

5. 2 Thess. 1: 10. Jesus Christ is coming "to be glorified in His saints, and to be marveled at in all them that believed."
6. Rom. 11: 26. Jesus Christ is coming again to deliver Israel and to turn away ungodliness from Jacob. Zech. 12-13: 6; Ez. 37: 23; 36: 25-27, 29; Zech. 8: 3, 7, 8; Ez. 36: 37, 38; Jer. 31: 3-7; Ez. 36: 33-37; Zech, 8: 3-5, R. V.; Zech. 8: 23; Isa. 49: 22, 23.
7. Jude 14, 15, R. V. Jesus Christ is coming again to "execute judgment upon all, and to convict all the ungodly of all their works of ungodliness which they have ungodly wrought, and of all the hard things which ungodly sinners have spoken against Him.' He is coming to render vengeance to them that know not God, and to them that obey not the Gospel of our Lord Jesus. 2 Thess. 1: 7, 8.
8. Luke 19: 12, 15; Matt. 25: 31; Zech. 14: 9. Jesus Christ is coming to reign as a King. Jer. 23: 5, 6; Ps. 2: 6; Rev. 19: 12, 15, 16; 20: 4; 11: 12; Is. 11: 1, 2, 4, 5.

   The coming again of Jesus Christ is the solution and only solution of all social problems.

   Oppression, poverty, crime, greed, injustice, will be at an end. "The earth shall be full of the knowledge of the Lord, as the waters cover the sea." Is. 11: 9.

THE SECOND COMING OF CHRIST (3)

When is Christ Coming Again?

1. Mark. 13: 32. The exact time of Christ's coming again no man knows, the angels do not know, and even Jesus Christ in the days of His humiliation and self-limitation of knowledge did not know. Jesus Christ wished to so emphasize the utter folly of all attempts to fix the date that as a man He put away the knowledge of it Himself. Deut. 29: 29; Acts 1: 7.
2. **While we cannot set the date of our Lord's return, the Bible does describe the character of the times.**

(a) It will be at such a time as when His disciples think not. Matt. 24:44.

(b) The world will not be looking for some great catastrophe, but will be absorbed in their usual pursuits. Luke 17:26-30.

(c) The last days and the time of the coming again of the Son of Man will be a time of apostasy, grievous times, and faith will be hard to find. 1 Tim. 4:1; 2 Tim. 3:1-5, R. V.; Luke 18:8.

3. The Lord may, for anything we know, come any time, any day, any hour. Mark 13:34-36; Luke 12:36; Matt. 25:13; Matt. 24:42, 44.

"Is not the world to be converted before He comes?" Rev. 1:7; Matt. 25:31, 32; 2 Thess. 2:2-4, 8; Luke 18:8; 21:35; 2 Tim. 3:1-5; Matt. 24:14.

Preaching for a witness is not the conversion of the world. Furthermore, this is before "the end" comes; but the coming of Christ in the air is not the end but the beginning of the end. Further still, the Gospel has in a sense, a biblical sense, too, been already preached to all nations. Rom. 10:18; Col. 1:23, R. V.

2 Thess. 2:1-4. The day of the Lord is not the coming of Christ in the air for His church, but His coming with His church to the earth in judgment. There may be, probably will be, an interval of several years between these two. It is doubtful if the Man of Sin can be revealed until the church is taken out of the way. V. 7. There is nothing whatever revealed in the Bible that must take place before Christ comes.

II. Our Attitude Toward the Coming of Christ.

1. We should be ready for our Lord's coming. Matt. 24:44. This is the great Bible argument for a pure, unselfish, devoted, unworldly, active life.

What constitutes readiness for the coming of Christ? Luke 21:34-36. The two parables in Matt. 25. 1 John 2:28.

2. Luke 12: 36, R. V. We should be watching and looking for the coming of our Lord.
3. 2 Pet. 3: 12, R. V. We should earnestly desire the coming of our Lord. 2 Tim. 4: 8.

THE RESURRECTION OF THE BODY

I. The Certainty of the Resurrection.

The resurrection of those asleep in Jesus is certain because it is certain that Jesus Christ Himself arose. 1 Thess. 4: 14, R. V.; 2 Cor. 4: 14. The resurrection of Jesus Christ is the sure guarantee of our own.

There are a good many things about the future that are uncertain. There is one thing that is absolutely certain, i. e., that these bodies of our dear ones who have fallen asleep in Jesus shall some day rise again.

II. The Character of the Ressurrection, or How are the Dead Raised?

1. 1 Cor. 15: 35-38. The resurrection body will not be precisely the same body that is laid in the grave. It may be like it in many respects, but in others it will be very unlike it, infinitely superior. We shall recognize our loved ones in the world to come. 1 Thess. 5: 13-15. "Together with them."
2. The resurrection body will be incorruptible. 1 Cor. 15: 42.
3. The resurrection body will be glorious and mighty. 1 Cor. 15: 43; Phil. 3: 20, 21; Dan. 12: 3. Shine forth as the sun. Matt. 22: 30; Luke 20: 35, 36.
4. Will be a heavenly body. 1 Cor. 15: 47-49. Earth has nothing like it. Rom. 8: 23; Phil. 2: 6; John. 17: 5.
5. Will be like the body of Christ's glory. Phil. 3: 20, 21, R. V.

HEAVEN: WHAT SORT OF A PLACE IT IS AND HOW TO GET THERE

INTRODUCTION.—There are many who think we know nothing about heaven, that it is all guess work. This is not so. God has revealed to us very much about it, and what He has revealed about it is very cheering and eminently calculated to awaken in every wise and true heart a desire to go there. If we reflected more about heaven it would help us to bear our burdens here more bravely, it would incite us to holier living, it would do much to deliver us from the power of the greed and the lust that is blighting so many lives, it would make us cheerier and more sunshiny. Those are very shallow philosophers who tell us that our present business is to live this present life and let the future take care of itself. You might as well tell the school boy that his present business is to live to-day and take no outlook into the future life of manhood, that he might wisely prepare for it on the one hand and feel its stimulus on the other. True thoughts of the life that is to come clothe the life that now is with new beauty and strength.

I. Heaven is a Place.

John 14: 3.

II. What Sort of a Place is Heaven?

1. It is a place of incomparable external as well as internal beauty. This appears from such descriptions as we have in the 21st and 22d chapters of Revelation. The God of the Bible is a God of beauty.
2. Heaven will be a place of holy and ennobling companionships. On the other hand there will be no unpleasant and degrading companionships. The devil will not be there. The lewd and the vulgar and the obscene will not be there. The avaricious and the scheming and the selfish will not be there. The liar and the slanderer and the backbiter and the meddler and the gossip will not be there.
3. Heaven will be a place that is free from everything that curses or mars our life here. There will be no sin. There will be no servile grinding toil. There will be no sickness or pain. Rev. 21: 4.
4. Heaven will be a place of universal and perfect knowledge. 1 Cor. 13: 12.
5. Heaven will be a place of universal and perfect love. 1 John 3: 2; 1 John 4: 8; Prov. 15: 17.

6. Heaven will be a place of praise. Rev. 7: 9-12.
7. Heaven will be a city which hath foundations, a continuing city. Heb. 11: 10; Heb. 13: 14.

Conclusion.—Is no heart stirred with a longing for that "better country"? Heb. 11: 16. We may all gain an entrance there. There is but one way, but that is very simple and open to all. John 14: 6; 10: 9. Accept Christ at once, and gain a right to enter and live forever in heaven.

CHAPTER VII

EXPOSITORY SERMONS AND BIBLE READINGS IN OUTLINE

GOD'S PICTURE OF A HAPPY MAN

(Ps. 1: 1-3.)

Introduction.—God is a great artist. There is no one that draws such perfect pictures as He. Some of God's pictures He Himself labels, others He leaves us to put the titles to. In the first Psalm, the first three verses, God has drawn a picture and labeled it, "The Picture of a Happy Man." "Blessed is the man," or rather, "O the happinesses of the man," etc. There are three leading features to this picture. In the first verse we see, the Happy Man's separation from the world. In the second verse we see, the Happy Man's occupation in the world. In the third verse we see, the Happy Man's fruitfulness before the world. Or, to put it in another way, in the first verse we see the Happy Man's separation unto God, in the second verse his communion with God, and the third verse his fruitfulness in God.

I. The Happy Man's separation from the world or separation unto God.

There are three points mentioned in which the happy man walks alone or separate from the world.

1. He walks not in the counsel of the wicked.
2. He standeth not in the way of sinners. If he finds that by some mistake he has got into the sinner's way, he gets out of it at once.
3. He sitteth not in the seat of scorners. He has no fellowship with irreverence, with jesting upon serious subjects, with murmuring against God, or frivolous and light and critical treatment of God's Word.

II. The Happy Man's occupation in the world, or communion with God.

1 He delights in the law of the Lord. He must find great pleasure in God's Word. Jer. 15: 16; Job 23: 12.

2. He meditates in God's Word day and night. Note the word "meditate." It means deep, intense reflection upon what God says. And then note "day and night."

III. The Happy Man's occupation in the world or his fruitfulness in God.

The man who maintains the separation from the world described in verse one and the communion with God described in verse two will be like:

1. A tree, i. e., he will have life, foliage and fruit, or life, beauty and utility.
2. He will be like a tree *planted*, not like one grown wild; i. e., he will be an object of care and culture, and the caretaker will be God Himself.
3. He will be like a tree planted by streams of water; i. e., there will be flowing around his roots a constant source of life, freshness, beauty, and fruitfulness. No fear of times of drought and barrenness for him.
4. He will bring forth fruit in its season.
5. His leaf shall not wither. There will be unfailing life and unfading beauty.
6. He shall never fail in prosperity. "Whatsoever he doeth shall prosper."

THE TWENTY-THIRD PSALM

PART I

INTRODUCTION.—The twenty-third Psalm is a great deep. It is an unfathomable ocean of truth. It is the first Scripture that most of us ever learned, but no one in the course of a lifetime has ever exhausted it, or gotten to the bottom of it. There are two methods of dividing the Psalm. According to the first, we divide it into two parts. The first part, verses 1-4, Jehovah, my mighty and tender Shepherd; the second part, verses 5, 6, Jehovah, my bountiful Host. According to the second method of dividing the Psalm, we divide it into three parts. Part one, verses 1-3, every want met; part two, verse 4, every fear banished; part three, verses 5, 6, every longing satisfied.

I. Every want met. 1-3.

1. The foundation thought of this part as well as the next is found in the opening words, Jehovah is my Shepherd. The figure of the Shepherd. It stands for love and care and protection and provision on God's part, and trust and obedience and following on man's part. Luke 15:4-6; John 10:11, and John 10:3, 4. The conditions of being Jehovah's sheep are: first, that we hear His voice; and second, that we follow Him; third, that we heed not the voice of strangers but flee from them. *My* Shepherd.
2. I shall not want. Ps. 84:11; Ps. 34:9, 10; Phil. 4:19; Matt. 6:33; Rom. 8:32; Heb. 13:5, 6.
3. The Psalm leads us on from the general statement, we shall not want, to specific wants supplied. In verse 2 we have four wants supplied. Rest and food and drink and leading provided. Literally translated, "He maketh me to lie down in pastures of tender grass, He leadeth me beside the waters of rest."
   (a) There is a two-fold rest in this verse, the passive rest of the sheep lying down on the soft, young, spring grass; the active rest walking beside the waters of rest. There is a two-fold rest in the Christian life; passive rest just lying on Jesus' bosom, active rest in serving the Lord "without fear in holiness and righteousness before Him all the days of our life." Luke 1:74, 75; Matt. 11:28, 29.
   (b) There is food as well as rest. "Tender grass."
   (c) Drink as well as food. Jehovah leads His sheep right beside "the waters of rest." What are these waters of rest which our Shepherd gives us to drink? Jesus Himself has interpreted it. John 4:14 and John 7:37, 38, 39. The Holy

Spirit is the water we drink. "Waters of rest." Gal. 5:22, 23.

(d) Guidance too. "He leadeth me." Jehovah leads, not drives, His sheep. In this and the following verses there are four places into which He leads: (1) By waters of rest; (2) paths of righteousness; (3) into and through darkness and sorrow and testing; (4) into His own house forever. A fifth want supplied is healing or reviving. "He restoreth" (or reviveth) "my soul." A sixth want supplied, "guidance." We have already had guidance in verse 2, but this is different guidance. There it was guidance by the waters of rest, here it is guidance in a holy walk. Notice the order of God's supply of our wants in this Psalm. Rest and food and life-giving water and the invigorating of our lives, precede the holy walk. All this "for His name's sake."

THE TWENTY-THIRD PSALM

PART II

II. Every Fear Banished. 4.

1. The Lord's sheep is now taken into new experiences. Having been made "to lie down in pastures of tender grass," and been led "in paths of righteousness," he is now led into the "valley of the shadow of death." The word translated "shadow of death" is of frequent occurrence in the Old Testament to express the deepest darkness. The Psalmist has not merely the experience of literal death in mind, but all experiences when the darkness is thick and profound.
2. In this dark valley Jehovah's sheep have no fears. "I will fear no evil." A true trust in God banishes all fear, under all circumstances, for all time. Is. 12:2; 26:3; Ps. 3:5, 6; Ps. 27:1-3; Ps. 46:1-3; 118:6; Is. 41:10, 13; Phil. 4:6, 7; Rom. 8:28, 31, 32, 34, etc.
3. The reason the Psalmist gives why he will not fear, "for thou art with me." Not because there is no

danger there, but because there is One mightier with us than any possible enemy. Is. 43: 2; Rom. 8: 31; Heb. 13: 5.

4. "Thou art with me." What difference does it make whether it is the pastures of tender grass or the valley of the shadow of death, if He is there.

5. "Thy rod and thy staff they comfort me." The rod and staff are the Shepherd's implements for quieting and guarding the sheep. The word translated rod means most frequently in the Bible usage, "a rod of correction." Our Shepherd's correction is most comforting to us. Then it means "a sceptre," and nothing is more comforting to a Christian than Christ's sceptre, and every true Christian is longing for the day when it shall sway throughout the earth. Then it means a shepherd's crook, which is doubtless the meaning here. Both the crook and staff with which Christ guides His sheep and wards off the enemy, the Word of God. Nothing comforts the Lord's sheep like the Word. Rom. 15: 4.

III. Every Longing Satisfied. 5, 6.

Jehovah Jesus appears no more as a Shepherd, but as a bountiful Host.

1. "Thou preparest a table before me." As to the general character of the feast, read Ps. 63: 5; 81: 16. The best things on the table. First, His Word. Jer. 15: 16; Ps. 19: 10. But there is something better than the Word to feed upon, and that is Jesus Himself. John 6: 55, 56.

2. Notice where we are feasted. "In the presence of mine enemies." John 15: 19; 2 Tim. 3: 12.

3. "Thou anointest my head with oil." Acts 10: 38; Heb. 1: 9. The anointing with which our Host anoints our heads is the anointing of "the oil of gladness," the Holy Spirit. 1 John 2: 20, R. V.

4. "My cup runneth over." John 7: 37-39.

5. Now we leave the feast for our earthly pilgrimage, but we are not unguarded. "Surely goodness and mercy

shall follow me." Notice how long this will continue. "All the days of my life."

6. Now me come to the end of our pilgrimage and pass out of time into eternity. "I will dwell in the house of the Lord forever."

THE SHEPHERD AND HIS SHEEP

INTRODUCTION.—The tenth chapter of John is one of the most beautiful, comforting and cheering and instructive chapters in this wonderful book.

I. The Sheep.

There are seven things told us about **Christ's sheep.**

1. Vs. 4. "They know His voice."
2. The 27th verse. "My sheep hear my **voice.**"
3. "They follow me."
4. V. 5. "They know not the voice of strangers."
5. "A stranger they will not follow."
6. "They will flee from" a stranger.
7. Christ's sheep know Him. They not only know **His** voice, they know Him; know Himself.

II. The Shepherd.

This chapter tells us seven things the Shepherd does for the sheep.

1. He knows His sheep.
2. V. 3. "He calleth His own sheep by name."
3. "He leadeth them out." Ps. 23: 2; Rev. 7: 17.
4. He "puts forth all His own." Sometimes the sheep hesitate to follow the Shepherd. In that case He does not leave them behind, but thrusts them forth. Christ has many ways of thrusting forth from the fold into the pastures, from the resting place into the feeding place, His laggard sheep.
5. "He goeth before them."
6. He "giveth His life for the sheep."
7. V. 28. "I give unto them eternal life." He gives life to the sheep. He gives absolute and eternal safety. They shall NEVER PERISH.

THE DRAMA OF LIFE, IN THREE ACTS

INTRODUCTION.—Jesus Christ is the author of this drama. It surpasses anything ever put on the stage in conciseness, in point, in graphic delineation, strength of characterization, in pathos and in fullness, height, depth and beauty of meaning. Its dramatis personæ are God, two men and Satan. There are three Acts, which may be described as: 1st Act, Wandering; 2d Act, Desolation; 3d Act, Return. There is a fourth act which we will not enter into to-night.

I. First Act. Wandering.

Scene 1. A beautiful home. An elderly white-haired father. The boy has become tired of restraints of home life. He longs for a life of untrammeled independence and freedom.

Scene 2. Home leaving.

In these two scenes we have a picture of the beginning and growth of sin. The Father of the drama represents God. The Son, man wandering from God.

1. In the first scene we have the picture of the beginning of sin. The young man desired to be independent of his father. Desired to do as he pleased. There is where sin begins; in a desire to be independent of God.
2. The Father granted his son's request, and this is precisely the way in which God deals with men.
3. In the second scene we have a picture of the growth of sin. The boy did not go away from Father and home at once. So it is with men when they wander from God into the far country of sin.

II. Second Act. In the Far Country, or Desolation.

The scene shifts. Hard times have struck the gay capital. Famine stalks the streets. The scene shifts again. A desolate field, a lonely carob tree with its long brown pods covered with dust from the arid land, hungry hogs. Our friend in ragged clothes, with hungry face, emaciated from famine, looking up into the carob tree, for "he would have fain have filled his belly with the husks that the swine did eat." In these three scenes of this act we have a vivid and suggestive picture of the fruits of sin.

1. The first fruit of sin is pleasure. Heb. 11: 25.
2. The second fruit of sin is want. "He began to be in want." The pleasures of sin have been followed by the want of sin, high times have been followed by hungry times. There is other hunger than physical hunger. There is soul want and soul hunger.
3. The third fruit of sin is degradation and abject slavery. "He went and joined himself to a citizen of that country; and he sent him into his fields to feed swine." This young man got rid of, it is true, his father's guidance and control, but he became the bondsman of a stranger. So it is with every one who throws off God's paternal control. He becomes Satan's swineherd. Hog tender for the devil. Each man here to-night has the choice to be a son of God in filial, joyous, ennobling and abundantly rewarded obedience, or Satan's slave in degrading and unrequited drudgery. Cf. Deut. 28: 47, 48. Which will you choose?

III. Last Act. The Wanderer's Return.

There are two scenes. The first is still the barren field. In this scene we have a picture of the remedy for sin and its bitter consequences. Note the steps.

1. He began to think. Note what he thought about, the better lot of his Father's servants.
2. The second step was, he resolved "I will arise." All our thinking will do no good unless it ripens into resolution. His resolution was threefold. "To go to his Father." To confess his sin.
3. "He arose and came to his father." That is the final step. Just come.

The final scene of the third act. The boy had forgotten the Father, but the Father had never forgotten the boy. We forget God, God never forgets us. He is waiting for your return to-night. Of what have we a picture here? Of God and God's attitude toward the wanderer that returns to Him. Have you wandered from God? Come back to God to-night. There only can joy be found. There is famine, degradation, want away from Him. Come home. Come just as you are. There is a welcome, a robe, a kiss, a ring, a feast awaiting you.

ABIDING IN CHRIST

(John 15:1-16.)

INTRODUCTION.—These are wonderful words. There is marvelous music in them. There is also inexhaustible meaning in them.

I. What is it to Abide in Jesus?

To abide in Jesus is to be in the same relation to Jesus as a living fruit-bearing branch to the vine.

No one is abiding in Christ that is not drawing his life constantly from Him. When a branch abides in a vine, its buds, blossoms and fruit are all the product of the vine, the life of the vine in the branch. So when we abide in Christ, all our thoughts, feelings and choices are the result of the life of Christ in us. They are His thoughts, His feelings, His choices, not ours. Jesus is willing to thus live His life out in us, and this is abiding in Jesus. Gal. 2:20.

II. How to Abide in Jesus.

How do we go about it practically, to thus abide in Jesus?

1. Renounce our own self life. We cannot live our own life and abide in Jesus at the same time. It is either our own life in us or His in us.
2. We must also look to Him and expect Him and trust Him to actually impart His life to us.
3. To abide in Christ, we must feed upon His words. V. 7.
4. To abide in Christ we must obey His words. John 15:9, 10.
5. To abide in Christ we must spend much time in prayer. John 14:12, 13, 14.

III. Results of Abiding in Jesus.

1. Much fruit. John 15:5. Our fruitfulness does not

depend upon what we are naturally. It depends upon the life of Christ in us. There will be fruit in our own lives. Gal. 5:22. There will be fruit in others. V. 16.

2. Power in prayer. V. 7. Abiding is the great secret of power in prayer. Our prayers will be the outcome of the life in us. It will be Christ praying in us and the Father heareth Him always. John 11:42.
3. Fullness of joy. V. 11.
4. Love. V. 12.
5. We become Jesus' friends. V. 14.
6. God is glorified. V. 8. Nothing so glorifies God as a Christian who is really abiding in Christ.

Shall we not to-day enter into this blessed and glorious life of abiding in Christ? If we know something of it, shall we not know it in its fullness?

FOUR SKEPTICS

Introduction.—Many people have an idea that all skeptics are pretty much alike, and that they are all a pretty hard crowd. But if every one will study his Bible carefully he will find that this is not so. He will find that skeptics differ every widely from one another, and that many of them so far from being a very hard crowd are a very respectable company. Now, there are pictured in the Bible four typical skeptics:

I. Nathaniel. John 1:45-51.

1. Note the kind of man Nathaniel was. He was a thoroughly good man. He was a sincere man, a pure man, an especially honest man, a religious man, but he was a skeptic.
2. He was a skeptic because he did not know the facts in the case. His skepticism did not come from badness of heart, but from ignorance. He was not ignorant about other things.
3. Note what Nathaniel did. See the honesty and humility and sincerity of the man. Philip said,

"Come and see. Just let me introduce you to Jesus." And Nathaniel accepted the offer at once.

4. Note the outcome. Nathaniel becomes a thoroughgoing believer. He met Jesus. Jesus spoke to him. His eyes were opened, and Nathaniel cried out, "Rabbi, thou art the Son of God, thou art the King of Israel." That is always the final outcome with the Nathaniel type of skeptics.

II. Thomas. John 20: 24-29.

1. Thomas was a good fellow in many ways. Kind-hearted, generous, noble impulses. John 11: 16.
2. Thomas had some grand faults, and his skepticism came from those faults.
   (a) He absented himself too much from the society of people of stronger faith than his own. John 20: 24.
   (b) Thomas was a man who was inclined to take a dark view of things. John 11: 16. It is a bad disposition, this of always looking on the dark side.
   (c) Then Thomas was governed by his senses. John 20: 25. He lived in the basement of his being. He only believed what he could see with his eyes, and feel with his hands.
   (d) The next failing of Thomas was that he was unwilling to take anything on any one's else testimony. John 10: 25. When a man thinks all the world are liars but himself, he is probably the greatest liar extant himself.
   (e) He was stubborn. He said, "Except," etc., "*I will not* believe."
3. But for all of Thomas' stubbornness he was honest at heart. The next Lord's Day he was not away moping by himself, he was with the disciples when the Lord came. Poor, slow, dull, melancholy, stubborn Thomas was convinced at last. Saw more than any of them had seen, and he cried, "My Lord and my God."

III. Pilate. John 18: 38.

1. The causes of Pilate's skepticism.
   - (a) The first cause of Pilate's skepticism was Pilate's wicked heart.
   - (b) Second cause of Pilate's skepticism was the entanglements of his life.
   - (c) The third cause of Pilate's skepticism was a lack of moral earnestness. Pilate was a trifler.
2. The result of his skepticism. The result was ruin for time and eternity.

IV. The King's Courtier.

Seventh chapter of 2 Kings.

1. The cause.
   - (a) The principal cause of this captain's skepticism is not at all hard to discover. It was simply self-conceit, scornful self-conceit. He could not see how God could do what He promised to do, and he had an idea that if he could not see how it could be done then it couldn't be done at all, for didn't he know everything? Could God possibly know anything he didn't?
   - (b) He had a lack of due consideration and respect for others and their opinions.
2. How the skeptic was treated.

   Elisha made no attempt to deliver him from his doubts. He simply answered: "Behold thou shalt see it with thine eyes, but shalt not eat thereof." That was wise treatment. There is no use wasting time upon a skeptic of this class.
3. The outcome.

   Everything came to pass just as God said it would. So shall it be to every skeptic of this class who does not speedily repent. The promises of God will all come true. Those for this life come true in this life, those for the life to come shall come true in the life to come; but he will have no part in them. They shall see, but not enjoy.

STEPHEN

Introduction.—There is no fairer life recorded in history than that of Stephen, excepting, of course, the life of Him of whom Stephen learned and after whom he patterned. The character of Stephen presents a rare combination of strength and beauty, robustness and grace. Stephen occupies but small space in the Bible, two chapters, and two verses. Yet in this short space a remarkably complete analysis of his character and the outcome of it is given.

I. Stephen's Character.

He was a remarkably full man.

1. He was "full of faith." Acts 6:5.
2. Was "full of grace." Acts 6:8, R. V. This is the reason why he was so much like Christ Himself. Christ was just living His own life over again in Stephen.
3. "Full of power."
4. Full of the Word of God. There is but one sermon of Stephen's reported. You will find it in the seventh chapter of Acts. What a sermon it is! Bible from beginning to end. He was full of the Word. This goes far toward explaining why he was also full of faith and grace and power.
5. He was "full of the Holy Ghost." 6:5; 6:10.
6. Stephen was also full of love. Acts 7:57-60.
7. Stephen was full of courage. Acts 7:51, 52.
8. He was a man of prayer.

II. The Outcome.

1. His face shone like an angel's.
2. He preached with unanswerable wisdom and power.
3. He wrought great wonders and signs, and the Word of God increased, and the number of the disciples multiplied in Jerusalem exceedingly.
4. Men were "cut to the heart" by his preaching.
5. But this conviction in this case did not result in conversion. They gnashed upon him with their teeth.
6. The heavens were opened and he saw Jesus and the glory of God.

I CORINTHIANS 13

Introduction.—The chapter naturally divides itself into three parts.

First part, verses 1-3, Love Contrasted, or the Absolute Indispensability of Love.

Second part, verses 4-7, Love Described, or the Everyday Manifestations of Love.

Third part, verses 8-13, Love Exalted, or the Peerless Preeminence of Love.

I. Love Contrasted, or the Absolute Indispensability of Love.

1. The first thing that Paul contrasts with love is the gift of tongues and the gift of tongues in its highest conceivable form. "Though I speak with the tongues of men and of angels."
2. The second thing Paul contrasts with love is the gift of prophecy.
3. Faith, miracle-working faith, miracle-working faith in the highest conceivable form, faith so as to remove mountains.
4. Magnificent giving. "Though I bestow all my goods to feed the poor."
5. Martyrdom. "If I give my body to be burned," but have not love, it profiteth me *nothing*.

II. Love Described, or the Every-day Manifestations of Love.

Love has fifteen marks which are never wanting where love exists.

1. The first mark of love is that it "suffereth long."
2. It "is kind."
3. "Love envieth not."
4. "Vaunteth not itself."
5. "Is not puffed up."
6. "Doth not behave itself unseemly;" i. e., does not do rude, ill-mannered, boorish things.
7. Love seeketh not its own."
8. Love is not provoked."
9. Love "taketh not account of evil."
10. Love "rejoiceth not in unrighteousness."
11. Love "rejoiceth with the truth."

12. "Love beareth all things."
13. Love "believeth all things."
14. "Love hopeth all things."
15. "Love endureth all things."

III. Love Exalted, or the Peerless Pre-eminence of Love.

To sum it all up in a few words, prophecies, tongues, knowledge have their day. Love has eternity. God is Love, and love partakes of His eternal nature. "Love never faileth." All other things are partial. Love is complete, perfect. There are three abiding things, faith, hope, love; but of even these three the greatest is love.

THE HOLY SPIRIT IN GALATIANS

INTRODUCTION.—The Epistle to the Galatians is a short book but a wonderfully instructive one. Its principal teaching is concerning God's way of justification. But it is very rich along other lines. One of the principal lines of thought is the contrast between living in the flesh and living in the Spirit, i. e., living in our own natural strength and living in the power of the Spirit of God. According to this book the great secret to a holy, happy, noble Christian life is living in the Spirit, crucifying the flesh with the passions and lusts thereof and walking by the Spirit of God. Let us look at some of our blessed relations to the Holy Spirit that are set forth in the book.

I. Gal. 3:2. Here we have the believer **Receiving the Holy Spirit.**

This receiving the Holy Spirit is a definite, conscious experience. Also Acts 19:2; 8:15-17. How received? "Hearing of faith."

II. Gal. 3:5. Here we have **the Spirit Ministered to or Continually Supplied to** the believer.

This is quite different from v. 2. There the Holy Spirit is given once for all, a definite experience in some definite moment of past time. The tense of the verb plainly and unmistakably shows that. But here we have a continuous supply of the Spirit's power.

III. Gal. 4:6. Here we have the **Holy Spirit Witnessing in our Hearts** to our sonship, crying out in our hearts Abba Father.

IV. Gal. 5:16. Here we have the believer **Walking by the Spirit.**

V. Gal. 5:22, 23. Here we have **Bearing of Fruit in the Spirit,** or rather **the Spirit Bearing Fruit in us.**

What beautiful fruit it is! Love, joy, etc.

VI. Gal. 6:7, 8. Here we have **Sowing to the Spirit.**

How can we make it sure that we shall sow to the Spirit? By surrendering the whole life to His absolute control. Yield to Him the control of your will, of your affections, of your thoughts, of your imagination, of your actions and your words. Yield your whole being up to be filled with His presence and His power.

SEVEN PRIVILEGES OF THE BELIEVER

(Phil. 4.)

I. It is the Privilege of the Believer in Jesus Christ to have CONSTANT JOY, to REJOICE ALWAYS.

V. 4.

II. Undisturbed Freedom from Care.

V. 6. How to realize this: "But in everything by prayer and supplication with thanksgiving let your requests be made known unto God." "In everything."

III. Abiding and Abounding Peace.

V. 7. "The peace of God which passeth **all understanding.'**

IV. An Ever-present Friend.

V. 9.

V. Never-failing Contentment.

V. 11.

VI. All-prevailing Strength.

V. 13.

VII. Inexhaustible Supplies for Every Need.

V. 19.

"*Every need* of yours"—"*supply.*" The R. V. reads "fulfill," i. e., fill full.

"Riches" is a great word anyhow, but when you put "HIS" before it, "His riches," who can measure it? But Paul does not stop there—"His riches *in glory.*" Perhaps some one wishes me to define that. Define that! I would as soon think of measuring the heavens with a foot rule. Notice one thing more, this filling full of every need is in Christ Jesus (R. V.). There is no filling full outside of Christ. There is nothing but emptiness outside of Christ.

It must be admitted that many Christians do not actually have every need "filled full." Why is it? Two reasons: First, they do not claim it. They are afraid to ask large things. They seem to be afraid of impoverishing God, that the great ocean of love and grace will run dry.

There is another reason. God's pouring in is conditioned upon our giving out. It was to believers who were giving out, constantly giving out, generously giving out, that Paul wrote, "My God shall," etc. V. 15.

The one thing that prevents many of you from having "every need of yours" filled full by Paul's God, "according to His riches in glory," is downright stinginess. Claim a full cup to-day and make it possible for God to fill it by filling the cup of some one else.

GOD'S PATTERN FOR A CHRISTIAN WORKER (1)

(2 Timothy 2.)

INTRODUCTION.—The text is a whole chapter,—the second chapter of 2 Timothy. In this chapter we have a marvelous picture, drawn by the hand of God, of the Christian worker. What he is. What he should be. What he should avoid. What he should do. And his reward.

I. What the True Christian Worker is.

1. He is a soldier. V. 3.
2. The Christian worker is also a "husbandman." V. 6.
3. The Christian worker is also a workman. V. 15.
4. The Christian worker is "a vessel." V. 21. He is some sort of a household utensil, as a dish, or pitcher,

or a cup, or a vase, something for the adornment and use of the Master's house. Many professing Christians are mere bric-a-brac in the church.

5. The Christian worker is a "servant of the Lord." The word servant here used means "bond servant or slave," and the thought is that we belong to another, we are not our own, Christ is our owner.

II. What the Christian Worker Should be.

1. He should be "dead"—dead with Christ. V. 11.
2. The Christian worker in the next place should be "strong." V. 1.
3. Should be taught of the Lord. V. 7.
4. There are three more things we should be. You will find them all in one verse. V. 24.
   (a) We should be "gentle."
   (b) We should also be "apt to teach."
   (3) Should be "patient," or, as the R. V. has it, "forbearing." "Patient of ills and wrongs."

GOD'S PATTERN FOR A CHRISTIAN WORKER (2)

I. What he Should Not Do.

1. V. 4. He should not entangle himself with the affairs of this life.
   Some of the things that entangle: Marriage to unconverted person, or even to a worldly professor. Business partnership with an unconverted man. The entrance upon speculative business enterprises. Running in debt. Rom. 13:8. The accumulation of wealth is to most men entanglement. 1 Tim. 6:9, 11. Secret societies and questionable pleasure are entanglements that hinder our testimony and impede our warfare.
2. The Christian should not "strive about words." V. 14.
3. V. 24. The servant of the Lord should not strive at all. Contend vigorously he may for the great vital truths, but always in a spirit of meekness, gentleness, patience and persuasiveness.

II. What he Should Do.

1. V. 4, R. V. Aim to please God.
2. V. 15. We should "study," or exert ourselves, "be diligent," to present ourselves approved unto God.
3. "Endure hardness."
4. V. 19, R. V. The one who names the name of Christ should depart from unrighteousness. All sin.
5. V. 22. Flee youthful lusts.
6. While there are some things for the Christian worker to run from, there are others for him to run after. Righteousness, faith, love, peace. How these four are to be pursued the last part of the verse indicates, "with them that call on the name of the Lord out of a pure heart." By prayer.

HEBREWS XI

INTRODUCTION.—The subject of the chapter is faith. What the chapter teaches about faith can be summarized under five general heads:

1. What faith is.
2. How faith acts, or how faith shows itself.
3. What faith gets.
4. What faith accomplishes.
5. How to get faith.

I. What Faith is.

It is clearly and simply defined in the first verse. The Revised Version rendering of this verse is easier to understand than the Authorized Version. Faith is the assurance and unshaken confidence that what God says is so even though at present there is no other evidence that it is so than that God says so.

II. How Faith Shows Itself.

1. Faith shows itself by standing unwaveringly on what God says. V. 3.
2. Faith shows itself in another way, i. e., by doing just what God bids. V. 4.

3. Faith shows itself again by cheerfully suffering affliction with the children of God. V. 23.
4. Faith shows itself by stopping at no sacrifice that God demands. Abraham. V. 17.

III. What Faith Gets.

1. Faith gets testimony right from God that the believer is righteous in His sight. V. 4.
2. Faith gets salvation. V. 7.
3. Faith gets life. V. 31.
4. Faith gets power to bring forth children for God. V. 11.
5. Faith obtains a heavenly and eternal home. V. 16.

IV. What Faith Accomplishes.

1. Faith overcomes difficulties that seem insuperable. Vs. 2, 9.
2. Faith wins victories over enemies that seem fortified behind impregnable walls. V. 30.
3. Faith accomplishes a host of things that the inspired author of our chapter was forced to bunch together and that we must bunch together. Vs. 32-34. Faith is the great conqueror, the great achiever. The man of faith is the man who moves the world and leaves his permanent impress upon it.

   Faith is the mightiest thing within the reach of man. It links man to the omnipotence of God.

V. How to Get Faith.

The chapter gives a short and simple answer to that question. The way to get faith is to listen to what God has to say and then just stand upon it, risk everything upon it. Read your Bible a great deal. Pay very careful attention to what it says. Ask God to make it very clear what it means. Then when you find a promise, no matter how big it is, believe it in all its height and depth and length and breadth, and stand upon it. When you find a commandment meant for you, no matter how hard it seems, just obey it. Do exactly what it says, and do it at once.

A FOURFOLD VIEW OF CHRIST IN HIS RELATIONS TO US

I. The first view of Christ and His Relations to us.

2 Cor. 5: 21; Gal. 3: 13. Here we see CHRIST **FOR US.** The Bible is full of this thought of Christ. **Is. 53: 6;** 2 Cor. 5: 21; 1 Pet. 2: 24; Matt. 20: 28.

II. Second view of Christ in Gal. 2: 20.

(Am. Ap. R. V.) **The view of Christ we have here is** CHRIST **IN US.**

III. Rom. 13: 14. **Christ on us.**

Christ clothing us with His own **likeness, so that we are** outwardly like unto Himself.

IV. John 14: 1-3. **Christ, the Living, Personal, Visible Christ with us.**

WHAT ONE GAINS BY FAITH IN CHRIST

(1 Pet. 1: 3-8.)

I. A New Birth.

V. 3.

II. A Living Hope.

"Unto a living hope."

III. A Substantial, Glorious and Eternal Inheritance.

The character of this inheritance:

1. It is "incorruptible."
2. "Undefiled," unsoiled.
3. "It fadeth not away."
4. Sure, it is kept, "reserved **in heaven.**"

IV. Absolute Security.

"Kept by the power of God through faith."

"Kept by *the power of God.*" "*Kept* by the power of God."

V. "Power and Honor and Glory at the Appearing of Jesus Christ."

V. 7.

VI. "Joy Unspeakable and full of Glory."

V. 8.

I JOHN I

INTRODUCTION.—This chapter sets forth seven present and priceless privileges and possessions of the believer in Jesus Christ.

I. Precious and Certain Knowledge.

1. What the believer knows. The believer knows eternal life. "I declare unto you the life, the eternal life, which was with the Father and was manifested unto us.
2. The certainty of what he knows. The knowledge of the life is certain. That which we *have heard;* that which we *have seen with our own eyes;* that which we *have beheld*, i. e., not merely seen but gazed at intently and studied; *our hands handled.*

II. Glorious Fellowship.

Fellowship with the Father and with His Son Jesus Christ.

III. Fullness of Joy.

"That your joy may be fulfilled" (filled full). V. 4, R. V.

IV. A Wonderful Message.

The message is this, "God is light, and in Him is no darkness at all." V. 5.

V. A Holy Walk.

It is our privilege to walk in the light, to walk in the knowledge of and obedience to the truth, to walk in holiness. V. 7.

VI. Cleansing from all Sin.

V. 7. The cleansing spoken of in this verse is cleansing from the guilt of sin. Wherever in the Bible cleansing is spoken of in connection with the blood, it always has reference to the removal of guilt, i. e., to pardon and not removal of the actual presence of sin that comes in v. 9.

VII. Cleansing from all Unrighteousness.

V. 9. Not only is it our privilege to be cleansed from all guilt by the blood, it is also our privilege to be cleansed from all unrighteousness in our life.

I JOHN II

INTRODUCTION.—This chapter presents to us seven comforting views of Jesus.

I. Jesus as an Advocate with the Father.

The first view of Jesus that the chapter gives us is found in the first verse. Here we see Jesus as our Advocate with the Father. Jesus always represents the believer before the throne of God.

II. Jesus as a Propitiation.

The second comforting view that the chapter gives us of Jesus is in the second verse. Here we see Jesus Christ as a "propitiation." A propitiation means "a means of appeasing." Jesus is a propitiation because by His atoning death on the cross God's wrath at sinners is appeased.

III. Jesus as an Abiding Place, or as our Life.

V. 6. Here we see Jesus as an Abiding Place, or as our life. It is our privilege to live in Christ, to abide in Him, to live and move and have our being in Him, to draw our very life from Him.

IV. Jesus as the Anointer.

Vs. 20 and 27. Here we see Jesus as the Anointer. The Holy One of verse 20 from whom we receive the anointing is Jesus, and the anointing that we receive from Him is tho Holy Spirit. Jesus pours out the oil of the Holy Spirit upon our heads. Acts 2:23.

V. Jesus as the Christ and Son of God.

Vs. 22 and 23. Here we see Jesus as the Christ and the Son of God. This is also a comforting view of Jesus. Indeed, it is a view that gives comfort to all the other views.

VI. Jesus as the Great Promiser.

V. 25. Here we see Jesus as the Great Promiser. He promises us eternal life.

VII. Jesus as the Coming One.

There is one more comforting view of Jesus given us in this chapter, verse 28. Here we see Jesus as the Coming One. Jesus came once. He is also coming again.

I JOHN III

INTRODUCTION.—This chapter declares to us seven great facts about believers.

I. Believers in Jesus are now Children of God.

Vs. 1 and 2. The great fact set forth is that we are now children of God.

II. Believers shall be like Jesus when He Comes.

The second great fact, etc., in verse 2. The great fact he declares is that when Jesus comes again we shall be like Him.

III. The Believer does not make a Practice of Sin.

Vs. 5, 6, 9 and 10. Here we see this great fact about believers in Christ: Those who have been born again, and abide in Christ, do not make a practice of sin.

IV. The Believer knows that he has Passed out of Death into Life.

V. 14. How he knows. V. 14-18.

V. The Believer has Boldness before God.

Vs. 19-21. The believer can come into God's presence and look up into His face and pour out his whole heart before Him. When is it that we have this boldness before God? When our own heart does not condemn us.

VI. The Believer has Power to Obtain from God by Prayer whatsoever he Asks.

V. 22. When has he that power?

VII. The Believer has the Gift of the Holy Spirit.

V. 24. The great fact about believers here set forth is that believers in Jesus Christ have the Spirit given to them. i. e., they have the gift of the Holy Spirit.

I JOHN IV

INTRODUCTION.—This chapter teaches us seven great lessons about love.

I. Love is of God.

V. 7. "Out of God."

II. God is Love.

Vs. 8 and 16. The great lesson about love taught here is

that God is love. Not only is love of God but "God is Love." Love is the very essence of God's character. God is Love. That is the great central truth around which the whole system of Bible truth revolves. That is the great foundation truth upon which the whole superstructure of Christian doctrine is built. We owe our knowledge of this truth to the Bible. Take away the Bible and the facts therein recorded and made known and we have no sure proof left that God is Love.

III. Jesus Christ is the Supreme Manifestation of the Love of God.

Vs. 9 and 10. God manifested His love, showed it in a visible way.

1. By sending His Son into the world. V. 9.
2. God manifested His love in Christ in a still further and more wonderful way. V. 10. He not only sent His begotten Son, but He sent Him to be a propitiation for our sins. We had sinned. God was holy. God's holy wrath must fall upon us and destroy us unless a propitiation is provided. God provided it Himself.

IV. If God so Loved us we ought also to Love one another.
V. 11.

V. He that Loveth others Dwelleth in God and God in him.
Vs. 12-16.

VI. There is no Fear in Love.

V. 18. The sixth great lesson about Christ taught here is that "there is no fear in love, but perfect love casteth out fear." Learn to love God and you will be delivered from all dread of God.

VII. "We Love because He first Loved us."

V. 19. The great lesson about love taught us here is that "we love because God first loved us." Love does not begin with our loving, but with God's loving. Not with our loving God, but with God's loving us.

I JOHN V

Introduction.—This chapter sets forth the seven-fold glory of the believer in Jesus Christ.

I. The Believer's noble Parentage.

"Whosoever believeth that Jesus is the Christ is born of God." V. 1. Every true believer in Jesus Christ can boast of the eternal, all-wise, all-holy, almighty God as His father.

II. The Believer's splendid Victory.

Vs. 4 and 5. Victory over the world.

III. The Believer's priceless Possession.

Vs. 11 and 12. The believer has eternal life. Not only has the believer eternal life, it is his privilege to know that he has eternal life. V. 13.

IV. The Believer's sure Confidence.

Vs. 14 and 15. The Believer's sure confidence is that if he asks anything that is according to the will of God he will obtain it.

V. The Believer's wonderful Power.

V. 16. The believer has the power to save by his prayer his erring brother's life. The death spoken of in this verse is eternal death, and the life spoken of is eternal life.

VI. The Believer's perfect Security.

V. 18, R. V. He that was begotten of God (i. e., Jesus Christ) keepeth him that is begotten of God from the practice of sin and from the clutch of Satan.

VII. The Believer's glorious Knowledge.

V. 20. The Son of God gives to every believer an understanding to know God. The knowledge of God, the supreme knowledge.

7 *Printed in the United States of America*